THE STILL SMALL VOICE

THE STILL SMALL VOICE

Reflections on Being
a Jewish Man

Edited by Michael G. Holzman

With foreword by Doug Barden,
Executive Director, MRJ

URJ PRESS   •   New York

Permissions

Every attempt has been made to obtain permission to reprint previously published material. The authors gratefully acknowledge the following for permission to reprint previously published material:

ACHIM MAGAZINE: "Judaism, Masculinity, and Feminism" by Michael S. Kimmel, Winter 1999; "Ready for Redemption: A Mikveh Experience of Personal Healing" by Steven Z. Leder, Winter 2004; "It Began with a Simple Invitation" by James Prosnit, Winter 2004. Used by permission of the authors and Men of Reform Judaism.

HARRY BROD: "Growing Up Jewish and Male" by Max Rivers. Published in *A Mensch Among Men: Explorations in Jewish Masculinity*, edited by Harry Brod (Freedom, CA: The Crossing Press, 1988). Used by permission of Harry Brod.

GARY GREENEBAUM: "Learning Talmud from Dad, Though Dad Knew No Talmud" by Gary Greenebaum. Published in *A Mensch Among Men: Explorations in Jewish Masculinity*, edited by Harry Brod (Freedom, CA: The Crossing Press, 1988). Used by permission of Gary Greenebaum and Harry Brod.

KTAV PUBLISHING: "My Father's Spirituality and Mine" by Eugene B. Borowitz and "Etz Chayyim Hi: It is a Tree of Life" by Norman J. Cohen, from *Paths of Faithfulness*, edited by Carol Ochs, Kerry M. Olitzky, and Joshua Saltzman. Copyright © 1997. Used by permission of Ktav Publishing.

REFORM JUDAISM MAGAZINE: "Teen Brotherhood" by Jason Freedman and Bobby Harris, "A Letter To My Sons" by Dana Jennings, "The Real Man" by Rabbi Joel Soffin, "Yearning for Father" by Paul Shoenfeld, and "Rabbi Bulman's Kiss & Other Lessons of a Newport News Childhood" by David Ellenson from Fall 2006. "Closing a Father's Eyes" by Simeon J. Maslin from Fall 1993. Used by permission of the authors and Reform Judaism Magazine.

JEFFREY SALKIN: "The Eternal Jew and His Paper Route" published in *Searching for My Brothers: Jewish Men in a Gentile World* (New York: G. P. Putnam's Sons, 1999). Copyright © 1999 by Jeffrey K. Salkin. Used by permission of the author.

Library of Congress Cataloging-in-Publication Data

The still small voice : reflections on being a Jewish man / edited [by] Michael Holzman ; with foreword by Doug Barden.
   p. cm.
  ISBN-13: 978-0-8074-1057-8 (alk. paper)
  ISBN-10: 0-8074-1057-8 (alk. paper)
  1. Jewish men—Religious life—United States 2. Masculinity—Religious aspects—Judaism. 3. Masculinity—United States. I. Holzman, Michael.
  BM725.S75 2008
  296.7081—dc22   2007034269

CONTENTS

PART 1. Top of the Mountain: Embracing Masculine Images

PART 2. Fleeing Ahab and Jezebel: Refusing Traditional Masculinity

PART 3. Going to the Wilderness: Searching for Identity

PART 4. Hearing the Voice: Finding the Self

PART 5. Finding Elisha: The Role Model

FOREWORD

In late 2005, based upon a decade of experience as the executive director for the North American Federation of Temple Brotherhoods (NFTB; newly renamed the Men of Reform Judaism [MRJ]), the men's arm of the Reform Movement, I wrote and distributed a monograph entitled *Wrestling with Jacob and Esau: Fighting the Flight of Men, A Modern Day Crisis for the Reform Movement.* The monograph comprehensively outlined the dimensions of an issue that I felt had long gone unnoticed: the diminished participation of men of all ages as religious preofessionals, lay leaders, volunteers, youth group leaders, and active temple members. The intent was to demonstrate that a confluence of various macro- and microeconomic, cultural, and sociological elements, some unique to liberal Judaism, but most impacting all liberal American religious institutions, had combined to seriously undermine men's active participation in the life of our religious community. Ignoring the phenomenon was no longer an option; the failure to address the issue, the failure to ameliorate the issue, would have a serious negative impact on the qualitative fabric and viability of the Reform Movement and the Jewish community as a whole. While there was little statistical, quantitative information to back up what I called a "crisis," especially with regard to adult males, there was an abundance of anecdotal information supporting my contention. With regard to the increasing absence of *young male teens* from the Movement's summer camps and temple youth groups, there was, in fact, a newly released body of hard evidence supporting my observations.

My goal was to place the issue of the disengagement of men on the front burner of the cultural gatekeepers of our Movement—rabbinic and lay congregational leaders, youth group leaders, camp directors, regional and national staff of the Union for Reform Judaism—the men and women, lay and professional, who have the influence to effect change. I provided a number of reasons why I felt our Movement had failed to grapple with the issue to date. As I spent the subsequent year accepting invitations to speak at numerous congregations and conducting regional and national sponsored workshops on the topic, one explanation in particular resonated with many audience members. I suggested that a major reason for our failure to acknowledge and then resolve this crisis has been the Movement's misinterpretation and subsequently faulty implementation of the goals of genuine feminism. Specifically, there had been a failure to distinguish gender *stratification* from gender *differentiation*. Rather than focusing, appropriately, on eliminating the uneven distribution of leadership positions, power, and related rewards of prestige, a considerable amount of Movement effort had been misspent on eliminating any and all signs of gender *differentiation*. This, in a sense, made all activities, be it prayer, study, or ritual activity, *gender neutral*. There had been a refusal to acknowledge that there may be a significant difference between male and female spirituality. Such a refusal was actually at odds with, if not outright anathema to, the ideals of genuine feminism.

Finding innovative and creative ways to make the synagogue more receptive to the needs and interests of women—exemplified by the introduction of monthly Rosh Chodesh services, women's study sessions, women's Passover seders, and adult *b'not mitzvah* experiences—have appropriately permeated our Movement. And if in fact this meant creating and maintaining "women's-only spaces" and activities within our congregations, either explicitly or by dint of subject matter, the Movement's leadership not only lent its wholehearted approval, but eagerly sought to develop and implement these programs to meet the well-articulated and vocal demands of women. Meeting the specific needs of men, however, whether young or old, including creating and maintaining men's-only spaces and activities, was sadly placed on the back burner. Such efforts were, in fact, too often viewed as politically incorrect, as a step backward in the Movement's advances in creating an egalitarian environment, as a misconceived attempt to revert to the patriarchic-dominated shul environment of forty years ago; in short, such efforts were considered to be wrong! *Then we wonder why men are disappearing!*

Our Reform synagogues have become a place where women appropriately feel welcome, a place where their opinions, values, and perspectives are sought after. In effect, the synagogue provides them with numerous venues where their personal life stories, as women, as Jewish women, can be told and retold. But what about men and their personal stories? What about synagogue venues providing opportunities for their storytelling, their recounting of key moments in their journey as Jews, as Jewish men? Is there room in the *beit t'filah*, *beit midrash*, and *beit k'neset* settings of our temples for a *beit achim*, a house of brothers? Not to replace, not to usurp, women's gains, but to find a way to balance the spiritual needs of both men and women. That is the exciting, and difficult, challenge before us.

To begin to rectify this situation, NFTB in the spring of 2006 introduced the NFTB "Jewish Men's Storytelling Project" as an ongoing feature in its magazine, *ACHIM*. The NFTB storytelling project's goals were simple, as I stated in the introductory essay:

> We want to give our members, the men of Reform Judaism, the opportunity to tell their tales, to share their tales, in their own words, with other men, with their brothers, with their sons and daughters, and with other family and community members. Each of us is on a unique Jewish men's journey, yet we often share mileposts with other men who have come before us, who journey alongside us, and who will come after us. Where in your life's journey did you come to see yourself as an adult, a male, a Jewish male? Where has your spiritual journey taken you—perhaps from Orthodoxy to Conservative to Reform, or from classical to "modern" Reform, or possibly even from non-Jew to Jew-by-choice? What males of an earlier generation had the most influence upon your life? How would you describe the relationship you had with your father? How do your memories of your own bar mitzvah and of growing up (or not growing up) in an extended Jewish home impact on how you live your life today as a Jewish adult? How does Reform Judaism speak to you?

In short, we wanted to give our brothers the opportunity to think about the memorable transformative events in their own lives, both positive and negative, and share their tales.

The book you are holding in your hands, *The Still Small Voice: Reflections on Being a Jewish Man*, takes this storytelling project a giant leap forward. And so I ask you to listen, please listen, to the voices of my brothers. They are your brothers, your husbands, your partners, your sons, and your grandsons. They are straight; they are gay. They have grown up Orthodox; they have grown up classical Reform. They are highly Jewish literate; they are functionally illiterate as Jews. They play sports (even hunt occasionally); they are, well, nerds and geeks. Some of the contributors are barely out of school (okay, some are still *in* school); some have been *zaydes* for years. Most have faced a variety of life's crises and, for the most part, overcome them; for others, critical relationships remain unresolved. Some of my brothers are angry and alone; some are happy and in wonderful relationships.

Their journeys as Jewish men have taken them from small towns in rural Maine or Texas to the overflowing-with-Jews suburbs of Long Island. They grew up in a town that could count the number of Jewish families on one hand; they were raised in the Bronx. Many have spent much of their adulthood out of harm's way; some have seen action in the battlefields of World War II, Korea, Vietnam, and the Persian Gulf. They are Americans, who also happen to be Jews; they are Jews, who also happen to be Americans. Some are to be found faithfully on Saturday morning in Torah study, while others are more likely to be found in shul on Sunday morning at the Brotherhood lox and bagel breakfast. Some even feel comfortable multitasking in numerous synagogue venues! Some are in touch with how their gender impacts their identity, what they do, and how others see and respond to them; while others had great difficulty even formulating an answer to our questions, as they believe their gender has been of little importance.

Some of my bothers are in touch with their *ruach*, their *nefesh*; they are truly blessed and are in touch with their spirituality; their inner voices speak to them loud and clear. For others, the disconnect is painful, the silence deafening.

Listen, please listen, to my brothers as this book of men's life stories seeks to raise the volume of men's voices. Listen to the nearly fifty brothers who have shared a piece of their personal Jewish life stories. Each story is unique, and collectively there is an extraordinary amount of diversity. That is not unexpected. At the same time, though this book is not meant to be a scientific, sociological analysis, there are themes that reemerge again and again. There are signposts that may guide others as we seek to find new directions, new paths to bring more men back to our community. Listen to David, Owen, and Jeff as they talk about the power of ritual to transform and reconnect. Listen to Dana, Bobby, Matthew, and Dan as they recount their work with teenage males and discover the need for adult male role models. The next generation desires to experience, to relate to, to learn from Jewish men in touch with their feelings—men prepared to expose their whole being, their struggles, both their strengths and weaknesses with others. And listen to Stephen and Joel as they relate the importance of *zaydes* in their lives.

Listen, and try to keep up, because there is a lot of men-in-motion going on! Men talk, they truly do, in the company of others, both men and women, but often they talk while *doing*. The power of dancing, singing, playing sports, camping, praying, mentoring, and yes, even of drumming, as effective vehicles to engage and reengage men in what Judaism has to offer comes through in these stories, again and again. And for me, most importantly, many of the contributors talk about the importance of creating in our synagogues, summer camps, and youth groups safe, warm, nonthreatening men's-only space for young male teenagers and for older male adults to have the opportunity to explore and celebrate what it means to be a contemporary, twenty-first-century liberal Jewish man.

Finally, listen to the words of my brother Rabbi Michael Holzman. Michael has provided us with a fascinating gateway to these articles by grouping them in sequences that parallel the trials and tribulations of the prophet Elijah. Most importantly, his introductory essay is nothing short of brilliant as he comprehensively analyzes and reviews the larger American societal issues of gender, masculinity, and religious identity that generations of Jewish men have sought to navigate—to decide for themselves where and when their own journeys would remain within the values and ideals of "mainstream America" and where they would diverge off and become "new Jewish men," adopting an alternative "countercultural" tradition, more in synch with both the best of traditional Judaism and the emerging contemporary images and ideals of authentic, liberal Jewish men.

Men need to share their stories with each other. It is a way of connecting with one another, with other men. Rabbi Harold Schulweis has said:

> My zeyde came to the synagogue because he *was* a Jew. His grandchildren, if they come at all, come *to become* Jews. But the synagogue will fail them if it thinks that it can be a surrogate for family and home. The rabbi is not father or mother, the lectern is not the table, the temple is not preparation for Jewish living at home. Adult education offers knowledge by description, which is far different than knowledge by acquaintance. . . . The synagogue must focus its energies upon the family . . . help *parents* recover their roles as singers of songs and tellers of tales, reclaim their generative power to create memories and to answer questions.

The organization I have the honor and privilege of directing is determined to be in the forefront of combating the disengagement of men from our community. Therefore, I would modify Rabbi Schulweis's comment and give it a deliberate gender slant, rephrasing it to read: "The synagogue must focus its energies upon the family . . . help *men* recover their roles as singers of songs and tellers of tales, help *men* reclaim their generative power to create memories and to answer questions. . . ." Of course we must have *both* men and women recover their roles as singers of songs and tellers of tales, but it is time to recognize that men and women have different songs to sing, different stories to tell. Men's voices are not better than women's; women's voices are not better than men's. Men's stories are not better than women's; women's stories are not better than men's. But, *they are different*. A vibrant Jewish community will benefit when we discover a loud chorus of both men and women singers and storytellers.

Sh'ma!

Doug Barden
Executive Director
Men of Reform Judaism
(formerly the North American Federation of Temple Brotherhoods)

ACKNOWLEDGMENTS

The process of writing any book requires encouragement, support, and guidance, and this is even more true when the subject has been rather far off of the popular radar. While all of the mistakes, errors, overstatements, and plain old bad ideas in this book are mine, I am humbled by all the people who helped me along the way (and who helped me find writers to contribute to this work).

My path to editing this collection begins with the encouragement of Danny Zemel, who has always challenged me to apply myself completely to the rabbinate. Danny continually inspires me to imagine that I can somehow contribute to the ever-renewing story of the Jewish people, and then he urges me to do so. His guidance led me to rabbinical school and sustains me so much in the rabbinate. He was the first person to read my contributions to this text and his responses were like manna.

Once in rabbinical school, I met Debbie Zecher who placed me firmly on the road to studying Jewish men, and who encouraged that study on every step of the way. After observing with Debbie the significant number of women who attended shul without their husbands, I began an internship, with NFTB (the North American Federation of Temple Brotherhoods—now Men of Reform Judaism) to study the issue, and little did I know how much that internship would affect my career.

The reason is that I met Doug Barden, the executive director of MRJ, and a great friend. Doug asked me to think seriously and then gave me the freedom to find my own path through the largely unmarked territory of Jewish men's study. Doug has the quality of every great supervisor and mentor of working hard to make sure that others succeed. Doug is a pioneer in the field of Jewish men's study, whose tireless energy on behalf MRJ will translate into affects so far beyond his professional duties. I am indebted to him for his ideas and his trust throughout my journey, including this project.

When this project came to my attention, a great number of people (in addition to Danny, Debbie and Doug) served as sounding boards and resources to the thought process of developing this work. In particular I want to thank Harry Brod, Steven Cohen, Aaron Panken, Stephen Pearce, Riv-Ellen Prell, Larry Schachner, and Shawn Zevit. As I experimented with different ideas for the book, Wendy Zierler was a tremendous fount of information, and a beacon of analysis as I navigated the intellectual seas of feminism. I thank Wendy especially for her honesty, trust, and intellectual rigor. Stuart Debowsky has been a fellow traveler for years and his support and help with finding writers was a tremendous help.

I am thankful for a group of my dearest classmates and colleagues who have been so supportive to all of my rabbinate. I especially want to thank those classmates who contributed to this book either directly or through your support, ideas and referrals: Craig Axler, Meir Feldman, Debbie Kassoff, John Linder, Sharon Litwin, and Jodi Smith. And although he is not a rabbinical school classmate, David Bergman has been my Talmud study partner for many years and continues to provide that friendship through the pages of this book as well.

As soon as I moved beyond ideas, Rabbi Hara Person, at the URJ Press, became an incredible guide, resource, and really a partner throughout the research, solicitation, editing, and writing process. Not only did Hara's support exceed my expectations, but her ideas and feedback were tremendously impressive. She is an incredible resource to the Reform movement. In addition I would like to thank the other members of the URJ Press who all contributed to this book, including Victor Ney, Ron Ghatan, Debra Hirsch Corman, Zack Kolstein, Elizabeth Gutterman, Rebecca Baer, Mike Silber, and Chris Aguero.

I also want to thank Congregation Rodeph Shalom and President Susan Klehr for supporting me throughout this process. I thank my colleague Jill Maderer for her ideas, and her insights into feminism. I especially want to thank William Kuhn for his encouragement, confidence, and trust as I accepted this endeavor. Bill has that quality of great senior rabbis who push each member of the synagogue team to pursue his or her strengths. In so many ways I count him as one of my mentors.

The story of this book begins with my education as a man, and that story begins with my first teachers, my parents. Through their values and examples I saw the myriad ways that a man can express himself. Because of their passion for life and dedication to Jewish pride and ethics I am the man that I am and the rabbi that I am.

Although I had been thinking about this topic for many years, when actual work of a project arrived, the time had to come from somewhere. As always, my wife, friend, and partner, Nicole Saffell Holzman, was constantly giving even though most of the time came from what was due to her. Without any sort of demand, Nicole has always forced me to create my own masculinity and to be the kind of man that operates in true partnership. As we raise our children, I hope this work helps Avi and Talia to grow into a Jewish world full of spiritually healthy men and women.

INTRODUCTION

Jewish men have it good. Take any reasonable standard of success, and we have achieved it. We win Nobels, Tonys, Pulitzers, and Oscars. We fill corner offices, and we run for the Oval Office. We publish our way into the ivory tower, and stacks of our books tower over the front tables at Barnes and Noble. We even play professional sports—surprise!—in numbers large enough, in fact, that my favorite football team had not one but *two Jewish quarterbacks at the same time*. And while this garnered a couple of small human-interest stories during the off-season, it was hardly a stop-the-presses Sandy Koufax item. (Alas—for me, the fan—they weren't exactly Sandy Koufax caliber players either.) If discrimination and lack of access once kept Jewish men down, today all the doors seem to be open, and we are walking through them.

Not only have we succeeded beyond imagination in every aspect of secular life, but we also have seemingly limitless possibilities in our Jewish lives. Never has the Jewish world been more accommodating, more open, and more inviting than now. Whereas in generations past strict rabbinic codes or social codes governed Jewish communities, today flexibility is the rule. No longer need a man fulfill the requirements of daily, weekly, or even monthly prayer, wearing his *t'fillin* dutifully. No longer need he master years of arcane Hebrew (or Aramaic) texts. No longer must he marry, and if he does, the bride need not be Jewish, and she need not even be a she, all of which—marriage, Jewish marriage, and straight marriage—were once the least common denominator(s) of communal life. These barriers too have (almost entirely) fallen.

So Jewish men have limitless opportunity simultaneously in both their secular and religious worlds. Then why do so many choose to apply their talents in only one dimension? Why do so many Jewish men put such mountainous amounts of energy into finance and forensics, physics and photography, law and literature, and every other area of the world, but those same men seem to barely develop their Jewish lives? Put another way, why can just about every rabbi, cantor, or synagogue professional name a dozen "great Jewish men" in their congregations—articulate, energetic, creative, insightful, powerful, charismatic, quiet, and/or brilliant—who have hardly dabbled in Judaism itself?

And even more troubling is the state of the souls themselves. Because when we look at these men, with all of these options available, we still find many of them struggling, even if they are unaware of the struggle. They have seen the world change around them, erasing some of the very paths etched onto their boyhood psychological maps.[1] They are a part of an economy that offers more and more opportunities for success, but on an ever steeper competitive slope. So things like pensions, vacations, job security, advancement, and simply wages all become less and less reliable to men who were trained to depend upon their reliability. Therefore, most broadly, Jewish men are a part of an American male community that has seen rising levels of loneliness,[2] depression, addiction, and suicide.[3] Men die earlier, when they get sick they stay in hospitals longer, they recover less readily, and they need more help when they age.[4] Even if they do not see these statistical discrepancies, Jewish men are a part of this trend.

In the midst of his success, too many a Jewish man remains alienated from his selfhood. Even though we have been accepted in virtually every way possible, many Jewish men still cling to the awkwardness and neuroses of a Woody Allen character in an ironic nostalgic way. When Neil Simon created his nebbishy, uncomfortable, and struggling characters, the quirky, self-deprecating Eastern European humor fit the times. Most Jews then still experienced closed doors and were not so far removed from actual Eastern European (or American) oppression. But why should an off-Broadway play like *Jewtopia* (also a book and soon a movie), written by two Jewish men born in the early 1970s, succeed so well based on the same brand of humor?[5] We are accepted today. We go to the gym. We date tall blondes. We play quarterback in the NFL! Then why should a coughing, bumbling, socially awkward Jew still be funny?

And those are just the social problems. What about the spiritual ones? What about the state of men's souls? I am not talking about esoteric Jewish philosophy, or picayune issues of Jewish law, or even a rudimentary familiarity with the prayer service. The discomfort I describe extends to the more basic questions and moments, the ones accessible without prerequisite. I am speaking of the expressive, garrulous litigator who sits speechless during premarital counseling when I ask him what it will mean to declare his bride "holy to me" under the chuppah. Or the father who continually answers his phone and responds to e-mail on his Black-Berry while his son and wife work with me for four sessions on a bar mitzvah *d'var Torah*. Or perhaps, most disturbingly, the Jewish husband who pretty much avoids the synagogue—services, classes, even religious school drop-off—while his converted, or even non-Jewish, wife becomes a regular without him. This last case is so common it became a joke on HBO's *Sex in the City* when one of the main characters converts and then prepares a major Shabbat dinner—brisket, matzah balls, the works—for her husband, who will not turn off the baseball game. Her response: "I gave up Christ for you, and you can't give up the Mets?"

Jewish men have scaled every mountain (some literally go to Everest—Jews on Everest, imagine that!) in the secular world, and they have (almost) every opportunity imaginable in the religious world. Yet many remain anxious, squeamish, and awkward when the time comes to actually consider their selves. And if we ask them to consider their souls, that might send them into conniptions.

While this generation has seen more material success, professional opportunity, educational access, and communal flexibility than most in Jewish history, we are certainly not the first to struggle with issues of the spirit. One paradigm for this struggle is a very familiar character.

Each year at Passover we speak and sing of the prophet Elijah, because the Bible predicts that he will be the harbinger of the ultimate redemption, the coming of the Messiah. But long before Elijah earned his quasi-messianic status, he was a prophet in ancient Israel. In the biblical stories toward the end of the ancient Jewish monarchy, generations after Kings Saul, David, and Solomon, after the kingdom has split into Israel in the north and Judah in the south, after a king named Ahab marries a Phoenician named Jezebel, the prophets of our God are under siege. Jezebel murders hundreds of them and promotes the worship of the god of her homeland, Baal. Elijah eludes her rampage and arranges with King Ahab what was, in its day, the Super Bowl of prophetic competition.

In the middle of a severe drought, Elijah challenges 450 prophets of Baal to a duel (I Kings 18). They will each prepare an altar and a sacrificial bull, address their deities, and then wait to see which sacrifice will be engulfed in fire, a sure sign of that god's power to end the drought. The prophets of Baal go first, wait, shout, pray, and then begin a "hopping dance." Elijah taunts them, giving us some of the oldest trash talk in Western civilization: "Shout louder! After all, he is a god. But he may be in conversation, he may be detained, or he may be on a journey, or perhaps he is asleep and will wake up" (I Kings 18:27). Elijah finally steps forward, sets up one stone for each of the twelve tribes, digs a trench around his altar, and then pours huge jugs of water over his sacrifice three times (and this in the middle of a drought), until the trenches are filled up like a moat. When he addresses God, the soaking-wet sacrifice is engulfed immediately. Elijah, victorious, then orders the execution of the idolatrous prophets.

He is at the top of his game.

But then something strange happens. Elijah hears that Queen Jezebel is angry and wants his head. So he runs. Far. He runs all the way from an area near present-day Haifa to Beersheva, and then deep into the desert, to the mountain of God at Horeb (Sinai). He is hiding from the queen. He is afraid. Does this make sense? After all that he has done with God's help? After invoking God in the way that he has, why should he fear? Why should such a powerful man, with such confidence in his beliefs, fear a tyrannous civil administration? Does he not believe in God's power of protection?

So God asks him, "What are you doing here, Elijah?" (I Kings 19:9).

Elijah explains his fear: "The people of Israel have broken their covenant with You, torn down Your altars, and killed Your prophets. I am the only one left—and now they are trying to kill me!" (I Kings 19:10).

In response, God then stations him on the rock, just like Moses many generations prior. And Elijah sees first a great and mighty wind splitting rocks. Then a tremendous earthquake. Then a consuming fire. In all three cases the text says that God was not present in any of those awesome displays (I Kings 19:11). Finally, Elijah hears what the text calls a *kol d'mamah dakah* (I Kings 19:12). A commonly used (and poetic) translation of this phrase is "a still, small voice." After hearing the sound, Elijah appears transformed. He is still afraid, and he uses the exact same language to describe his fear, but this time he is ready to return to the world of Jezebels and idolatrous prophets. The difference is his new knowledge that even when he is not performing grand displays, God's presence, and God's power, is always with him, in that still, small voice.

Elijah recognizes his power and his limitations. He carries the confidence of one who trusts his instincts, believes in his purpose, and relies upon his convictions even without grandiose displays of power. With his newfound relationship with God, his next step is, perhaps, the archetypical Jewish behavior. He seeks a student. Judaism does not really have a riding off into the sunset motif. Each of our heroes struggles with his or her fears and faults until the end. The classic example is Moses, who, despite his close relationship with God (Numbers 12 teaches that he was the only prophet to speak with God face to face), dies outside the Promised Land. The Jewish motif is the obligation of continuity, that each one should teach one. Moses's ultimate action is not a victory dance in the end zone west of the Jordan. Elijah, too, never takes a moment to celebrate either his triumph on Mount Carmel or his discovery on Mount Sinai. For both of them, achievement leads immediately to education. They both seek a student. For Moses it is Joshua, and Elijah finds the next great prophet, Elisha.

The challenge for Elijah, Elisha, Moses, Joshua, and for us is to hear the voice. Too often it is drowned out by stress, money, confusion, technology, fear, relationships, social expectations, ambition, and so many other noises. But more often we ignore it, or we do not even know how to hear it. More often, we men do not want to hear the voice. Like the injured athlete who does not want to come out of the game, or the traumatized soldier who cannot entirely return home, or the secret addict who drowns his pain in drink, or the workaholic professional who has forgotten how to relax, or the nervous teen who hides his insecurity behind machismo, in all of these ways we block out the still, small voice. We keep it small. We keep it miniscule. For some reason we do not want to hear it. Maybe, like Elijah running from Ahab and Jezebel, maybe we are afraid.

There is a reason why the central declaration of Jewish faith begins with the word Sh'ma, "Hear!" As if to say, Hey, listen up, the voice is right there if you can just notice it!

The purpose of this book is to explore the volume of that voice in a Jewish man's life, why some men seem to have the spirit on "mute" and others seem to hear just fine. I also seek to understand the *how* of Jewish men's spirituality, to check the connections between the radio receiver, the amplifier, and the speakers, to find the frayed wires of the soul and the working circuits of the spirit. And finally, I have enough chutzpah to listen in, to eavesdrop on the intimate, personal, vibrations of Jewish men's souls as they try to speak. Not only do I explore the why and how of spiritual hearing, but I also seek the content. I want to hear what the voices are saying.

My curiosity stems from a belief that the spiritual realm represents the most personal, most central, and perhaps the most important aspect of the human self. Deeper than the intellect, which we can control to filter and process information, and deeper than the emotions, which fluctuate and react to the world around us, I believe the spiritual is the core of who we are and what we believe. We find our experience of God in that spiritual core, deep within the soul. That is my way of the story of Creation, when God says, "Let us make human beings in our image" (Genesis 1:26). To be made in God's image is to have that piece of the divine implanted within the soul.

With this belief, my curiosity in the spiritual lives of Jewish men begins with a desire to visit the core of their identities, two concepts so central that most of them hardly notice: being a man and being a Jew. Without understanding how these aspects of identity function in Jewish men today, I will not be able to find their souls. Nor will they.

Is this a Crisis?

The kind of spiritual resistance, blockage, and deafness I describe manifests itself in ways both communal and personal. I am far more concerned with the latter, but it is in the former that we find context. Recently, communal settings have seen a widening disparity between male and female participation. Some have called this a crisis, especially Doug Barden, executive director for the Men of Reform Judaism (formerly North American Federation of Temple Brotherhoods).[6] Barden, in his monograph *Wrestling with Jacob and Esau: Fighting the Flight of Men: A Modern Day Crisis for the Reform Movement*, documents the growing gap between male and female involvement in Reform Jewish life and its implications. But this crisis is less a tsunami than a gradual rising of the sea level. Even if the numbers have become striking as of late,[7] they reflect a longer-term problem. This is not a sudden event.

The disparity between male and female participation in Jewish activities has been noticed both anecdotally and statistically. This disparity stems from an American cultural context that stretches back over two centuries. E. Anthony Rotundo, in his book *American Manhood*,[8] describes spheres of gender responsibility beginning in eighteenth-century America. Using the diaries and letters of middle-class white men, Rotundo claims that the Puritan model of manhood included men in a highly structured community. Values of individualism and aggression were suppressed so that men could fit into the hierarchal structure around them. Rotundo then continues to describe how nineteenth-century American values shifted from the community to the individual and with that shift came a shift in gender roles. As the influence of industry grew in the nineteenth century, men's focus moved to occupations sometimes at a distance from the family farm. In addition, while agriculture relies upon cooperation, communalism, and a connection to the earth, industry and urbanization rely upon competition, individualism, and dominance over the earth. This system promoted the very aggressive traits that the eighteenth-century Puritan community suppressed. Out of economic necessity, men made the transition to the newer, more competitive system, while women remained in the home (and church) to safeguard the older, more cooperative and nurturing communal structure. Eventually, values that began as occupational prerequisites became character definitions. Rotundo reports that as urban families moved farther and farther from occupational centers in the twentieth century, the distance between masculine, competitive, industrial values and feminine, cooperative, agrarian values widened as well. As this occurred, the church became even more associated with the feminine.

While most of the history described by Rotundo occurred when very few Jews lived in America, Jewish immigrants arrived in this culture and adopted many of its mores. However, one particularly Jewish factor that prevented the feminization of the synagogue was the traditional Jewish legal responsibilities of men. The synagogue could not be a feminized center as long as women were not technically counted as a part of the community. But as the twentieth century progressed, liberal Judaism grew, moved to the suburbs, and became a center for family activity. By the 1950s the Jewish community had embraced the Americanization of our faith. Pediatric religion reigned supreme, egalitarianism had begun to make its way into most communities, and the non-Orthodox Jewish community was primed to accept an American model of religion as a woman's activity. I mention the historical perspective because we must not think that current gender trends represent a sudden shift in the community. While they may signal subtle changes, gender disparity in the Jewish community is built upon generations of American religious culture.

When we look to current studies of American Judaism, the evidence of gender disparity rises beyond the anecdotal to be mentioned in serious research on the community. In their landmark 1998 study of the Jewish community, *The Jew Within*, Steven Cohen and Arnold Eisen determined that one of the major factors determining Jewish involvement is gender. In fact, they acknowledge that this factor carries more weight than even they anticipated at the outset of their study. "To a remarkable degree," they write, "the 'action' where Jewish activity among the moderately affiliated is concerned now rests with women, who undertake such activity either with or without the assistance of male partners."[9] At the conclusion of their book, they offer three reasons for such disparities.

First, they suggest that, despite the women's liberation movement, women are still predominantly responsible for the life of the home and that women are generally more concerned with spirituality. These two factors seem to have developed straight out of the American culture described by Rotundo. If this is true, I wonder if the reverse holds true. As women shift to more competitive, aggressive, occupational lifestyles, will men absorb more responsibility for the home and become more concerned with the spiritual? Some essays in this collection confirm this hypothesis and describe the mechanics of how domestic life reinforces religious activity and commitment.

Cohen and Eisen also theorize that the presence of female Jewish professionals attracts more women than men. A note about terminology is necessary. Undoubtedly the number of female professionals has increased in the Jewish community over the last generation. I would also like to introduce the idea that both female *and male* professionals are functioning in a more feminine leadership style. Cohen and Eisen seem to be talking particularly about actual females, but the more feminine style I propose includes more group-oriented decision making, less hierarchical structures, fewer competitive situations like elections, and more emphasis on sharing of personal experience and emotion. Either a female or a male can embody such a style, but the style is feminine, regardless of the sex of the leader. A move towards more feminine style in our communities is a natural—and intentional—outgrowth of the feminist movement. But we should not disregard its impact on male participation. While Cohen and Eisen seem to be talking only about actual female professionals increasing, I suggest that a more feminine style of leadership and programming by both females and males may attract more women than men.

Finally, Cohen and Eisen hypothesize that men are less likely to be satisfied by an environment focusing on search and struggle rather than goal and outcome. This last point requires further discussion. Cohen and Eisen theorize that the culture of synagogue life places more emphasis on the process of search and less on tangible objectives and that this emphasis attracts women but fails to attract men. In many ways this is true, but it is not the synagogue that has changed. Judaism has been emphasizing process going back to the convoluted debates of the Talmud. Even though a legal resolution was the goal of those debates, the gyrations and deviations of the text reflect a desire to capture a process of conversation. And while contemporary Orthodox men may have the tangible goal of finding halachic solutions to everyday problems, they too engage in *Torah lishmah*, learning for the sake of learning. The Jewish fascination with process is not new.

What has changed is the immersion of modern Jewish men in an American form of masculinity. With its emphasis on individualism, accomplishment, competition, and success (too often defined materially), American culture pushes men to achieve their goals and earn the rewards of capitalism. Many Jewish men swim happily in these waters. And since liberal Judaism does not even offer the goal of halachic resolution, in contrast to our Orthodox brethren, it becomes even more process oriented. My focus groups with Reform Jewish youth demonstrated the dissatisfaction with this orientation. Adolescent boys loudly complained about youth group programs that were all-discussion, group-process, open-ended programs with a lack of resolution.

Scholars at Brandeis University's Cohen Center for Modern Jewish Study confirm Cohen and Eisen's as well as my field research. In 2000, Charles Kadushin et al. published what has become known as the "Jewish Adolescent Study" and reported that boys viewed Judaism and Jewish activities in a significantly more negative light than did girls. These trends carried through all levels of Jewish involvement, whether formal or informal, school year or summer. Not only did boys opt out of Jewish activity, but they also were less affected by such activity and less interested in a spiritual search.[10] The findings showed that girls were more interested in future involvement, more willing to continue Jewish activity post–*b'nei mitzvah*, and more affected by Jewish experiences.

One important finding countered the disparity trend. When asked about finding meaning in life, boys and girls both responded that they were extremely interested (73 percent responded that such meaning is either very or extremely important), but far fewer showed interest in finding such meaning in a Jewish context (31 percent). Even for those Jews interested in spirituality, an interest that grew throughout high school, they did not see the synagogue as a place to turn for such a search; their involvement fell throughout high school. Interestingly, these trends in the search for meaning and spirituality did not differ across gender. From this we should not conclude that boys are less interested in meaning or in religion, but instead that when boys look for meaning, they choose the synagogue and Jewish activities even less often than girls. And when they do choose such activities, boys are less influenced by the experience. These findings seem to confirm Cohen and Eisen's theories about the reasons for gender's predominance and are in keeping with Rotundo's analysis of American history.

Let me be clear, this is not a book about numbers. In these pages we find the examination of the varied paths Jewish men take. Some of these paths cross the kinds of community programs, events, groups, and institutions that lend themselves to head counts and gender ratios. And where they do, they often substantiate many of the theories described above. When the included writers talk about communal programs, Jewish institutions come across as inarticulate in the spiritual language of men. That may help explain whatever numbers exist out there. Nevertheless, this problem is larger than numeric symptoms imply.

The problem of how we speak, or fail to speak, to men is a crisis. The use of the word "crisis" rankles some, because it elevates the concerns of a population that has enjoyed so many centuries at the top of the public Jewish agenda. In an op-ed piece in the *Forward*, Rabbi Rona Shapiro writes, "Thirty-five years ago—when women were not ordained as rabbis, when girls in the Conservative movement celebrated a bat mitzvah on Friday night, when Orthodox girls did not receive an education remotely comparable to that of their brothers, when women were not called to the Torah for aliyot or allowed on the bimah at all—where were the headlines proclaiming a girl crisis?" This either/or binary thinking is counterproductive for a healthy response to the needs of both sexes. Shapiro also fears that the talk of a crisis in relation to boys will "degenerate into sexist talk about girls and women." Again the thinking implies a zero-sum approach to Jewish life where shifting focus to the issues of disengaged men and boys implies a necessary disinterest—or worse, a disdain—for girls and women. Nothing could be farther from the truth. As Shapiro herself later asserts in her article, "Boys and girls alike suffer under the constructs of a patriarchal society. . . ."[11] The absence of men and boys implies a deeper problem that affects us all. A vacuum in any segment of the community raises alarms (or should) for the stewards of that community. Such an absence implies an exclusion, whether explicit—as in the near exclusion of women from the public sphere for most of Jewish history—or implicit. Even if we do not deliberately erect barriers against male participation, the absence of men may imply inadvertent obstacles. We may exclude men through the way we plan, promote, or execute our program. The deliberate obstacle is far easier to identify, even if it is more difficult to remove.

Any crisis in this book is the crisis of people in pain. Even though as I said at the outset, "Jewish men have it good," and most Jewish men enjoy relatively successful material lives, a life without spirit can easily become a life in pain, maybe an unrealized pain. While Jewish men do not generally represent the kind of tragic statistics of, say, African American youths in the inner city, when I hear of a nineteen-year-old Jewish boy who died of a heroin overdose, I cannot help but wonder about the crisis of his spirit.

The Jewish man "issue" in this book is less a question of whether or not men function within the Jewish system today, and more one of why and how. The crisis might be that the same Judaism that Abraham Joshua Heschel called, "irrelevant, dull, oppressive, insipid"[12] in 1955 may have become all the more so, especially for men, but also for women. If we are going to respond to the evident male disinterest, then we need to understand the men themselves. The communal problem is a reflection of the personal, and it is in the realm of the personal that we know so little.

What Does It Mean to Be a Man?

What does it mean to be a man? Fifty years ago, this was a ridiculous question. The expectations of manhood were assumed and understood. Men did not need to think about being men because most had little incentive to imagine any other form of existence. Because men have historically benefited from the privileges of their gender, they can ignore its existence. As Michael Kimmel, professor of Men's Studies at SUNY Stonybrook, explains in the introduction to his book, *Men's Lives*, "The mechanisms that afford us privilege are very often invisible to us. What makes us marginal (unempowered, oppressed) are the mechanisms that we understand, because those are the ones that are most painful in daily life."[13] Groups in power generally do not recognize the factor that grants them power. So, for example, in surveys about racism, white people have much more positive attitudes about race relations than do African Americans. Because the white folk enjoy the advantage of race, they fail to see differences in race.[14] The same is true for men; we fail to see differences in gender.

Therefore most men have never seriously thought about how being a man affects their lives, their perspectives, their relationships, and their spirituality. They may never have considered how their experience of religion may differ because they are men. They just assume that their experience is the generic experience, the norm. It always has been, right?

Why bother thinking about something like gender that hardly exists in the minds of most men? I once heard Kimmel, in public remarks, illustrate the point: "If I offer a class in Gender Studies, one hundred women will show up, and if I offer a class in Men's Studies, ninety women will show up with ten male friends they dragged along."

This question—what does it mean to be a man—only became intelligible in the last forty years, and then only because our understanding of the norm changed. In the last generation, women have moved from the margins of Jewish and general American life to the center. They have successfully introduced a new way of thinking about men and women and about masculinity and femininity. These ideas changed the way that we do just about everything, from sell soap to chat over the watercooler. No longer can a boss refer to the employees as "the guys," or a job applicant begin a letter with "Gentlemen," or a male Jew assume the rabbi on the bimah will look like him. Well, actually, the boss, applicant, or Jew *can* do any of those things, but will likely alienate employees, be turned down for the job, and be surprised (and uncomfortable) on *Kol Nidrei*. Men had to start thinking differently about the people around them because all of the sudden a whole lot of those people were women.

Not only did the faces change, but these new faces brought new ways of doing things with them. We started hearing more about collaboration, about sensitivity, about communication, and about nonhierarchical structures. New topics became common conversation as things like family leave, breast-feeding, girl power, the U.S. Women's Soccer Team, and glass ceilings started populating our speech.

With all of this change, many men became bits of flotsam bobbing in a swirl of new expectations. Maybe their office offered diversity training, or at least a liability-inspired course in sexual harassment, but for the most part, men had to figure out for themselves how to adjust to the new world order. Many men enjoy the new options afforded by the feminist movement, which is why television programs like *Queer Eye for the Straight Guy* can broadcast images of five gay men giving style advice to even the most macho types, like a former marine. When feminism opened the door to women, it also allowed men to explore a world of style, fashion, and expression beyond the thin noose of cloth allotted for expression in the uniforms of the past generations of suited warriors. This has spawned terms like "metrosexual," the sleek urban man who no longer relies on a wife or girlfriend to pick out his clothes. In a Jewish concept, it has spawned the industry of fancy new tallitot. Once upon a time, before women taught us better, our only choice was between black or navy blue stripes. Now we have choices in material, weave, weight, design, color, shine, pattern, and so forth. Other men take a decidedly more retrosexual approach, asserting a more public and manly masculinity. In the 1970s this approach led to Playboy Clubs, medallion necklaces, and the public display of hairy chests. The testosterone-rich successors of this form of "men's movement" still roam the streets today.

But other, more ideological movements and ideologies evolved in response as well. Rabbi Shawn Israel Zevit describes five different men's movements of the last generation: men's rights, which advocated on behalf of men on issues of employment, divorce, property, and other rights; men's liberation, which took on a self-consciously pro-feminist stance toward sexism, homophobia, and other vestiges of patriarchy; the men's recovery groups, which focused on healing from addiction and its effects; the conservative men's responsibility movement (my term, not Zevit's), which spawned the Promise Keepers and the Million Man March; and the mythopoetic, which sought a universal system of male values, looking to poetry, folklore, and mythology for common themes.[15]

This last example deserves further attention. Epitomized by the book *Iron John*, published in 1992 by Robert Bly,[16] the mythopoetic movement gained notoriety by holding retreats involving a return to nature, drumming, traditional male practices like sweat lodges, and other non-mainstream approaches to exploring masculinity. While this movement is colorful and offers a fascinating example of how to analyze a text for its deeper meanings, a process that in Judaism we call midrash, the intentionally unconventional approach turned off many. Ronald Levant, in his book *Masculinity Reconstructed*, explains why an Iron John style masculinity movement will not work:

> To propose, first of all, that men can restore their lost sense of masculine purpose and pride by engaging in modern-day versions of rites and rituals practiced in early native-American and other premodern societies is a romantic pipe dream at best. . . . Much as we bemoan

the ills of our postmodern society and enjoy escaping in fantasy to what we imagine to have been the nobler way of life of these pre-modern cultures, the truth is that, given a choice between living in their world or living in ours, most of us would choose the comforts and conveniences of modern life—even with all its problems.[17]

But this movement might be the most instructive in a Jewish context because of its dependence on text, interpretation, community, and ritual. After all, while Bly might rely upon folklore like the story of Iron John, we Jews have dibs on the most popular mythologies of all of Western civilization, the Bible.

These examples are interesting, and they show how the men who care have responded to change in so many ways, but the vast majority of men did what they always did, what they were socialized and trained to do. When faced with a problem, they looked for a solution: they looked to adapt to their new surroundings and to continue to work for the same goals as before: education, job, paycheck, house, family security, retirement in Florida. Most men did not really think about how all this change affected the meaning of manhood.

For these men something has been gnawing in the background. An idea is there, a strange vibe. We do not always realize it, but we can feel it, intuit it. These new beings that populate our world, these strange aliens that just popped up at work, at the gym, at the club about thirty years ago, the ones that keep popping up, they have this strange solidarity, this strange knowledge. Sure, they are the same women we've been dating, loving, living with, and admiring, with all of the allure, wit, creativity, insecurity, confidence, fickleness, stubbornness, and every other characteristic they have always had. But now they know something that we do not. They know what it means to be who they are; they have taken the time to define the terms. They are women, hear them roar.

The F Word

The source of this knowledge is feminism.

The term "feminism" inspires a great deal of anxiety among some men. The first anxiety comes from misreading feminism as nothing more than a corrective lesson to teach men how much they have subdued, subjugated, and subordinated women throughout the generations. This leads to a great deal of resentment, because (a) even though the ill-treatment may be true, nobody likes to hear it, and (b) "that was back then, and I am not like that now." Very few men think of themselves as proudly misogynistic, and most will resent feeling branded with that term for no reason other than our membership in the male sex. The feminism-as-solely-corrective misreading also leaves men with guilt. Especially Jewish men. This is because we care. We care because we come from a tradition that began in slavery, one that consistently reminds us to remember the orphan and the widow, because we were strangers in the land of Egypt. Judaism hammers home the idea of social justice, so when a Jewish man hears of thousands of years of male oppression, his bags are already packed and waiting for the major guilt trip. Finally, this misreading leads to despair. Because if feminism ends with the corrective, then it leaves most of Jewish tradition smoldering and laid waste. If we love the Torah, but feminism torches it due to the blatant sexism within, we are left with nothing.

The second anxiety comes from a fear that feminism means a loss of power. This is the old saw about limited resources and the divvying up of the pie. Every immigrant group has used it to fight against the next immigrant group. Whites used it to keep out African Americans. WASPS used it to keep out Jews. And many men today think it as they watch women enter spheres that were formerly safely reserved for men. But as we see the Asian, Indian, Hispanic, African American, female, gay, disabled, and Jewish leaders inventing new technologies, new fields, new areas of inquiry, new firms, new financial tools, new political lobbies, and so forth, we notice that the pie has gotten a lot bigger. Even though each new group adds more in the long run than it takes away, the initial fear remains.

And the final anxiety about feminism is political correctness. The term "politically correct" actually dates to the women's movement in 1975, which proudly claimed that it was a movement for more than "white, middle-class, straight women" and was moving in a more inclusive, "politically correct direction." Ironically this term became an epithet in the 1980s, used by political conservatives to criticize what they saw as enforced conformity of liberal ideologies.[18] The term implies rules that dictate certain "correct" behavior and speech for reasons that are valuable only for "political" reasons. If the reasons had intrinsic worth, then the speech would be simply "correct."

When men complain that feminism enforces political correctness, they either do not understand what it is really about, or they reject the belief that the ideas have their own worth. So when men complain about the words they can no longer use, the jokes they can no longer make, and the places where they can no longer put their hands, we must ask if they truly reject the worth of these communal standards. Do they really want to refer to women as "broads," a reference from the cattle industry referring to a side of beef? Are women no more than meat to be consumed? Do they really want to tell jokes that, while the speaker may see them as humorous, the audience will not? Do they really want to touch someone in a way that causes discomfort, reinforces unfair power differentials, and may even inspire physical fear? Probably not.

To be sure, some advocates on the left attempt to enforce a strict code of conduct, speech, and even thought that stifles free exploration and discussion. For men emerging from lifetimes of prefeminist socialization or men who are unfamiliar with the lessons of egalitarianism, this exploration is a necessary step on the path to embracing a new ethic. Men who sense a strict code will raise their guard and resist any positive change as a part of the unfair restrictions. The champions of a politically correct code, while well intentioned, actually obstruct the very social change they seek to enforce.

Nevertheless, the fear of political correctness may have gotten out of hand. When political conservatives have successfully painted their movement as the underdog of today's American politics (how they succeeded in this depiction through six years of control of all three branches of American government remains one of the great mysteries of contemporary society), they painted all of liberal thought as some sort of politically correct extremism. Use of terms like "Feminazis" by commentators like Rush Limbaugh vitiated any merit men may have discovered in the feminist argument. When a man invokes the fear of "political correctness," he covers confusion with a fear of social restriction. He has probably never had the opportunity to safely and respectfully wrestle with serious questions of egalitarianism. He is right, he is restricted in new ways, but if he really thinks about the value of those restrictions, he may eventually agree. The political correctness argument often blocks that agreement.

These anxieties—feminism as corrective, as a power grab, and as the enforcement of political correctness—have major ramifications. The first is that they reinforce the very social dynamics that necessitated feminism in the first place. If feminism really were a project of knocking men down a bit, that implies the same higher/lower, binary order that led to the subjugation of women. Second, when we conceptualize feminism as being only a pro-woman movement, we create the illusion that women alone can force change between the genders. If we truly seek to change society, both the disempowered Other, the women in this case, and the hegemonic Power, the men, will have to change. Envisioning feminism as a woman-only movement also implies that any attention paid to men is somehow counter to feminism.

That is the danger in the question I heard (from women and men) in the preparation for this book: "Do we really need another book about men? Was the last three thousand years of Jewish history not enough about men?" This question is very common, and not just among a reactionary or bitter wing of the feminist movement. It is the reaction I described in Rabbi Rona Shapiro's complaints about the use of the word "crisis." We find it in an interview with Rebecca Walker about her new book about men, *Reimagining Boyhood*, when Deborah Solomon, the highly respected interviewer for the *New York Times Magazine*, states, "But feminism began because women were at a social disadvantage. Men, as a group, are not socially disadvantaged, so they don't need special pleading."[19] Even though women still do experience real sexism (more on that later), allowing a knee-jerk rejection of men's issues reinforces gender inequality and fortifies a hierarchy of legitimacy. The question assumes an either/or thinking that only one gender at a time can fruitfully participate in the struggle we call Judaism. It implies that attention on men by definition will be harmful to women (as it has been in the past). And it reinforces the notion that women are still marginal, alternative, outside the male mainstream. These are the consequences that grow from the simple question above, which itself blossoms in the soil of misunderstanding feminism as a women-only movement.

The third and final ramification of our anxieties, misreadings and ignorance about feminism, is the stimulation of backlash. When we see feminism as a slap, a power grab, or a McCarthyist censorship regime, the natural instinct (especially for men) is to fight back. Backlash is an attack on feminists themselves and the idea of feminism. Such a backlash closes the door on voices who speak because they care about the ethical value of our community. The backlash only underscores the initial critique of unfair treatment. And the backlash also blinds the man to whatever value feminism may have for him.

Feminism for Men

Perhaps the biggest misunderstanding about feminism is that it is a women-only ideology. This is understandable because the word itself does contain the "fem" root. But think of how many words in English contain the roots, "he," "his," or "man" and apply equally to both genders. Women are included in **his**tory; they can be **he**roines, and we consider them hu**man**, hu**man**e, and part of **man**kind. So why should a little etymology issue exclude men?

I do not suggest that men hijack or appropriate feminism for themselves and embark on a project of correctives, power grabs, or the enforcement of political correctness. If we do, then we have missed the point. And male feminism[20] also does not mean advocating for equal rights for men or equal access to certain jobs (although equal-employment law certainly should and does apply to men). To understand how feminism applies to men, and thus how feminism induces us to ask the question, "What does it mean to be a man?" we need to understand feminism beyond our anxieties, stereotypes, and misreadings.

Many people (women included—even some feminists included) misunderstand feminism as nothing more than the movement for equal access, opportunity, rights, and remuneration as men. That is part of the concept, and it epitomizes the first wave of feminism championed by Susan B. Anthony, Elizabeth Cady Stanton, and others. That wave of feminism echoed the lessons of abolition, a movement that saw in the system of slavery the hypocrisy of the U.S. Constitution. The first wave of feminism sought to rectify the same hypocrisies through the enfranchisement of the vote.

But just as abolition freed the slaves into a still-racist world of Jim Crow laws, suffrage allowed women to vote in a system that still saw women as inferior, domestic, weak, and second-class. The sexism remained. And as racism led to the civil rights movement, sexism led to the second wave of feminism, the women's movement of the 1960s and '70s. At this moment, the parallel between the two becomes increasingly important, because women began to understand and discuss something that had been best articulated by the foremost thinker of African American culture in the early twentieth century, W. E. B. DuBois. In his classic text *The Souls of Black Folk*, DuBois describes how an African American sees himself as a disempowered class in American culture:

> After the Egyptian and Indian, the Greek and Roman, the Teuton and Mongolian, the Negro is a sort of seventh son, born with a veil, and gifted with second-sight in this American world,—a world which yields him no true self-consciousness, but only lets him see himself through the revelation of the other world. It is a peculiar sensation, this double-consciousness, this sense of always looking at one's self through the eyes of others, of measuring one's soul by the tape of a world that looks on in amused contempt and pity. One ever feels his two-ness,—an American, a Negro; two souls, two thoughts, two unreconciled strivings; two warring ideals in one dark body, whose dogged strength alone keeps it from being torn asunder.[21]

In this short paragraph, DuBois articulated the classic emotion of any disempowered class in a larger culture not their own. So we should not be surprised when that same idea of double consciousness became a pillar of second-wave feminist thinking.

To see the self through the eyes of those in power is an especially illuminating way to understand the quality that defines your status. For African Americans, that quality is skin color. For women, that quality is their gender. For gays and lesbians, that quality is not only sexual orientation (sex is usually a private matter), but also the public permission to be in love.

Through the consciousness-raising groups of second-wave feminism, women began to understand how they had been defined by the outside group, using solely that one quality, gender. In her book, *Standing Again at Sinai,* Judith Plaskow explains:

> But also, insofar as women are projected as Other, women's experience is doubled in a peculiar way. Knowing she is just herself, a woman must nonetheless deal with the imposition of Otherness. She must forever measure herself against a standard that comes from the outside. If she would act against prevailing stereotypes, she must do so being aware of their existence, and this adds an extra burden to whatever she undertakes.[22]

Feminists decided to look at gender, to embrace it, and to redefine how it applied to them. They decided that not only did they want equal access to the vote, schools, sports, jobs, and salaries, but they also wanted to bring their perspectives, their methods, their preferences, and their style. Mere access was not enough. They wanted to change the environment once they entered.

They taught us all that gender matters. It matters for all of us. Women and men. If today we see feminism as solely a movement for equal access, we will not understand the greater ramifications of the double consciousness. Feminism teaches that this consciousness affects a woman's entire life experience. I go further to say that it affects a man's experience as well. Once upon a time, men were so dominant that they may not have had to "measure [him]self against a standard that comes from the outside," but today that is no longer the case. The norm has moved so much (if it exists at all), and we all must be aware of the impositions and opportunities our gender puts before us.

This point is crucial. Whereas the female sphere was once so devalued and limited that men did not have such a double consciousness, today the values have shifted and the spheres are open, so both genders experience a doubled self-perception. For example, consider the man who steps into the female sphere, the man attending the "Mommy Group," or that same man out for a beer with the guys while they all want to talk about "work." Or less radically, the male professional—doctor, lawyer, rabbi, you name it—who finds himself a minority, or alone, in a staff of women.

I argue that feminism expands DuBois's work to touch all people, because what Dubois applies only to people who have color, feminism applies to all people who have gender, and that is everyone. Radical feminism applies that lesson to all people across a variety of dimensions (e.g., race, class, gender, nationality). Feminism teaches us all to be aware of how this part of our being affects our perceptions, processing, expression, reactions, language, expectations, psychology, and relationships. Fortunately, most of us do not live in a world that sees our gender "with amused contempt and pity," as DuBois put it. Nevertheless, we all live in a world with gender expectations—our own expectations and the expectations of those around us, expectations based largely on anatomy.

The double consciousness that DuBois described and that Plaskow applied to feminism assumes the perspective of a disempowered Other constantly aware of being observed by what I call Power. From this perspective, Power is a monolithic oppressor. But men operate as diverse individuals within the sphere of Power, and we too experience a different kind of double consciousness. Although we enjoy the benefits of male Power, we also must conform to the expectations of that Power. Those expectations have two negative consequences for men, even as they enjoy its positive rewards. First, male Power expectations contain some extremely unhealthy aspects. Hegemonic, stereotypical, traditional masculinity assumes a toughness and individualism that rejects a need for help even when such help is critical (as in the need to see a doctor). This masculinity suppresses emotion in favor of thought, forcing men to ignore real issues of emotional concern, which, of course, affects decisions, relationships, experience, generally all of life. Hegemonic masculinity also creates hierarchies within Power, leading to incredible loyalty to other men at or above one's level, but mistrust and abuse to those at lower levels. For example, the very male rituals of hazing enforce this loyalty but can hardly be considered healthy behavior. All of these result from the expectations of male Power, and each, along with many more, could command entire books of further study.

In addition, a man experiences double consciousness when he attempts to go outside male expectations. While almost all men function within the world of Power, most of us also find times in life when we desire a behavior or experience outside of that world. Contemporary men who decide to be stay-at-home fathers are not the first men to desire more time with children and less time (or no time) at work. Once, male domesticity placed a man outside the mainstream, but this has become increasingly more mainstream. Other non-stereotypical male behavior remains outside the norm. Artistic expression, homosexuality, dance, and certain professions continue to be considered stunted or impotent forms of manhood. That is why men in these roles often intentionally or unintentionally place themselves in the counterculture. The most obvious example of this rejection of mainstream masculinity is the embrace by the gay community of the term "queer." Even though these men enjoy some benefit of male Power, they too experience the double consciousness of an outsider. Even as men, they are not considered "real men."

For Jews and Jewish men, this outsider perspective becomes even more important, because we also have the consciousness of being seen as a Jew. In addition to the way we see ourselves (our first consciousness), the way that other men and women see us as either mainstream or irregular men (our second consciousness), we also feel the world seeing us as a Jew (our third consciousness). So consciousness becomes tripled. Then we can multiply consciousness by the number of dimensions—Asian, African American, Hispanic, disabled, gay, lesbian, transgendered—that may apply in the contemporary, heterogeneous Jewish community, and we see just how broadly DuBois's concept can be applied.

Feminism can be helpful for men because the tools of feminism can be applied to categories beyond the female. Fifty years ago the question "What does it mean to be a Jewish man?" would have sounded ridiculous. We did not think about it. We just were. In light of feminism and the changes it has wrought, the question makes sense. We can see ourselves both as an internally defined self and as a member of multiple groups. In the case of this book, the relevant groups are men and Jews.

In addition, by applying feminism to men, and thus transforming double consciousness from a negative burden to a normative cultural experience for all people, we deconstruct the notion that one Power—in this case straight, white, Ashkenazi, middle- to upper-class men—occupies the center, the norm, the mainstream, and that everyone else is alternative, marginal, or Other. By teaching men to see themselves as one among a cultural mix, we create multiple alternatives, each equal to the next. By focusing on men as men, we teach ourselves that we alone do not define humanity.

The End of Gender?

All of this talk of equal alternatives raises the possibility that we are too late. What if the pace of change has passed us by and the assumptions of women's equality with men have made the entire notion of gender irrelevant? More than one author in this collection ponders that possibility. (An additional author actually chose not to contribute an essay based on this exact notion—he had nothing special about men to write.) Gender is a category system used to explain differing behavior in society. For some, these categories—masculine and feminine—are too restricting, too fixed, and plainly inaccurate. The man who fixes cars but likes ballet or the woman who stays home with the kids but teaches her sons how to pitch a fastball is an example of how the gender category system may no longer make sense. In the past, we expected gender norms to align with sexual anatomy. Masculine women—tomboys—and feminine men—sissies— were generally ostracized, and no matter how far we think society has progressed, many people continue to feel isolated when the behaviors they embrace do not match the gender stereotypes for their sex. Nevertheless, today we accept and even encourage the adoption of behavior that crosses gender-sex expectations. We like to think that we can escape gender-specific boundaries and simply embody a complex mix of personhood regardless of gender.

Susan Fendrick, in her article, "Jewish Feminist Ritual and Brit Milah," illustrates how such gender neutrality has influenced the most gender-specific of male rituals, circumcision, or *b'rit milah*. She posits that feminism has made *milah* more inclusive in three ways. First, by creating a parallel ceremony for girls, the naming ceremony, or *simchat bat*, and infusing that with more creativity, parents have created a demand for a different kind of *b'rit milah* for boys. In addition, she notes that now, with the emergence of *mohalot* in the Reform Movement, women take part in every segment of the circumcision ceremony and that the use of female God-language makes the ritual even more inclusive of women. Finally, she notes that *milah* has moved from the synagogue to the home and become more of a private ceremony, followed by a more public baby naming—a ceremony initially created for girls—in the synagogue, "decentering circumcision itself."[23]

All of these observations reflect the move to erase gender lines and to follow the path begun with the 1817 constitution of the Hamburg Temple, which declared, "[A] religious ceremony shall be introduced in which the children of both sexes, after having received adequate schooling in the teachings of the faith, shall be accepted as confirmants of the Mosaic religion."[24] The founders of the Hamburg Temple desired a ritual that applied equally, and they saw a perfect opportunity in the ritual of their Lutheran neighbors. Confirmation made sense as a replacement for the single-gender bar mitzvah. Most synagogues continue to have this confirmation service, primarily as a way of keeping our students engaged beyond the seventh grade. Today that service is usually in addition to the bar mitzvah, a ritual so prominent that we could hardly imagine its disappearance. But ask around some of the older, more classical Reform synagogues and the members will tell of the days when almost no students had a bar mitzvah and the confirmation classes were larger than one hundred. So the desire to eliminate gender lines goes back almost two centuries.

In these examples, the most gendered rituals—*b'rit milah* and bar mitzvah—have been neutered. Since ritual represents the most public expression of Judaism, it has the greatest influence on the future. While text represents memory, ritual represents aspiration. So, if we can create and transform rituals such as *b'rit milah* and bar mitzvah so that they apply equally to boys and girls, then does gender really matter?

The answer is as obvious as the individual before us. As much as we may want to transform male rituals into neutral ones, the individual usually remains male.[25] I am all for inclusion of the mother, sisters, grandmothers, and anyone else in the birth ceremony for a little boy, but the fact remains that he is a boy. This fact is especially relevant, since that boy will be undergoing a ritual involving his genitals. To pretend that this ritual can somehow become neutral is to ignore the anatomy in the room.

No matter how progressive society will become, biology will always manipulate identity. Not only will women continue to solely bear the burdens and experience the intimate joy of childbirth and nursing, but they will also experience other aspects of their biology that differ from men.

While menstruation is an obvious example of this gender-specific biology, boys and men also experience gender-specific moments in their physical lives. A man's biology includes the development of physical strength and broadened shoulders, the growth of sexual maturity and its responsibilities, and the challenges of particular health issues—prostate cancer, heart disease, and so forth—later in life. In addition, many men voluntarily terminate their fertility through vasectomy. These are biological moments in a man's life. If religion exists to enrich, celebrate, and add meaning to life, then the denial of gender-specific biological moments eliminates opportunities for greater spiritual depth, for men and for women.

In addition, new studies of brain development show the myriad ways that men and women differ biologically in how they process information, respond to life, and relate to others.[26] We also cannot fail to notice that we socialize our boys and girls differently, almost from the moment of birth.[27] No baby can be raised gender neutral (go and try to buy baby clothes that are neither pink nor blue—good luck!), nor should they be, and our practice of Judaism should celebrate these differences rather than ignore them.

We should also not forget that the most brutal form of gender specificity—sexism—is still alive and well, among even the most enlightened communities. Despite our best intentions and our highest, and most ethically pure, beliefs, we still see major inequalities in every area of society, both Jewish and secular. While women may be filling the pews and populating programs, the Jewish community still has a thick glass ceiling, and some of the most important doors remain closed. In the summer of 2006, the Jewish People Policy Planning Institute gathered the top leaders of Jewish organizations to plan for the future of the community, and they invited not a single woman. Writing in reaction, Steven M. Cohen and Shaul Kelner describe the extreme paucity of women at the top of almost every Jewish organization:

> Over the years, we have conducted eight separate studies, both quantitative and qualitative, of gender equity in the Jewish communal world. . . . Women are under-represented in the lay and professional top leadership of Jewish communal organizations. As professionals, women receive substantially less compensation than men performing equivalent tasks.[28]

As Susan Wiedman Schneider explains, "[T]here's still plenty of evidence that women are still being shut out. I just opened up a book called *Fifty Key Jewish Thinkers*, published in 1997, and not a single woman is included. There are still Jewish academic conferences with all-male panels, and it has been an uphill battle to make sure women are considered when leadership slots open up in Jewish organizations."[29] And the problem is not just at the top of organizations. Many of my male, associate rabbi colleagues tell stories of being contacted to officiate at a funeral or wedding because the family does not like the other clergy (senior rabbi, other associates, cantors) at the shul because they are women. At least one potential author for this book declined to write because he was not sure if he wanted to publicly state his discomfort with female prayer leadership. He knew that his opinion was sexist, and yet he still did not feel comfortable with a female rabbi or cantor. Although the Jewish community is more and more enlightened on issues of sexism, patriarchy, and androcentrism, gender bias is real, and therefore gender is still a strong signifier. While we might be able to teach, preach, and program around the evils of sexism, we will not truly grapple with its roots until we examine the men who perpetrate and perpetuate it.

Attempting erasure of gender lines will only cover persistent gender-specific behaviors and attitudes. Some of these are healthy, acceptable, and constructive parts of men's and women's lives, and we should celebrate them and incorporate them into a more relevant and personal Judaism. Other gender-influenced elements will be destructive and harmful, and we do not correct them by pretending gender no longer exists. Instead, by examining the specificity of gender, we may discover the causes of destructive tendencies and thereby correct them.

Even if we live in communities in which gender lines are faint and the manifestations of sexism a rarity, we must also consider that the underlying tendencies described by gender categories still deserve consideration. In other words, when feminists taught us to incorporate feminine styles into Jewish communal structures—collaborative decision making, non-hierarchical leadership, open discussion formats, and so forth—these consciously feminine elements appealed to many women and men. In the same vein, masculine elements—the constructive ones at least—will also appeal to both sexes, especially in a world in which our girls have more formerly male options available than ever before. Therefore, traditionally masculine styles like coaching, teamwork, rationalism, goal orientation, legal frameworks, and so forth (I am speaking in broad generalities here) will also appeal to both genders. In a post Title IX world, girls might thrive in a synagogue basketball league, and women working in large, highly structured corporations might want a hierarchical board structure. While feminism challenges us not to limit Judaism to the male, we can also see how masculine influences may nurture more than men.

Individual, family, and communal norms have changed, but we still sail in a sea of gendered expectations. Some of those winds have diminished, while others blow strongly. One goal of the feminist project is the inclusion of females, but another goal is celebration of the feminine—and the masculine—within individuals. In order to include, we can rely upon rituals, practices, and texts that sometimes are neutral and sometimes reflect gender specificity.

To return to Susan Fendrick's article about *b'rit milah*, she is not entirely a straw woman for my argument. The thrust of her argument is that feminism's transformation of *b'rit milah* has made it more inclusive, and thus gender becomes less important. Nonetheless, in one segment she does describe how addressing the circumcision itself can highlight the issue of male sexual responsibility. She quotes Elyse Goldstein, who writes, "Since we have seen how blood offers expiation throughout the Torah, can those few drops of covenantal blood be seen as atonement for male control? As cleansing of violence in a patriarchal world? The Jewish world has the potential to be a safe world . . . if it becomes a world of male sexuality defined by holiness, commitment, and responsibility."[30] In this one example, Fendrick and Goldstein show how we can focus on the specificity of male experience in a healthy and constructive way. Unfortunately, the only male-specific part of the ritual they propose is a corrective for past male behavior. Imagine a *b'rit milah* ritual that does not squelch the gender specificity of the moment and does not limit itself to critiques of male behavior, but instead intentionally celebrates a positive, healthy, and ethical masculinity. Imagine a ritual that intentionally involves male family members—fathers, grandfathers, uncles, cousins, and brothers—to welcome the boy into a supportive, loyal community of healthy male expectations. Imagine if we used that same technique for boys and girls, men and women in all of our rituals, text studies, services, classes, and meetings. Religion is a powerful tool to heal men from the limitations of past stereotypes, promote new social norms, and model male behaviors that promote the constructive and nurturing elements of masculinity.

We are different, so why not reflect that difference in what we do?

I reject the argument that gender lines have blurred so much as to be irrelevant. In fact, I believe that given the amount of change surrounding gender, that aspect of our identity is more important than ever before. Religion is at its most potent when it addresses the core values of our selfhood—ethics, love, pain, joy, hope, fear, and so forth. Gender's reach touches all of those values in some way. One of the reasons that the voice of spirituality, what I call the still, small voice, remains so faint, might be because we fail to speak or listen to this important aspect of manhood. For example, while we take a principled stand on gender-neutral God language, that stand, while admirable, might prevent some individuals from comforting, challenging, affirming, and fortifying connections to the Divine. In other words, the narrative we create in the synagogue, at camp, in the schools (day and supplemental), or at the federation event may not reflect where we actually are. The trick is to create a diverse and versatile narrative, to develop a variety of tools, ones that reflect our desires for equality, universality, and neutrality where appropriate, and others that use a healthy specificity to positive ends. The function of this book is to explore the potential for a healthy male specificity that might amplify the still, small voice in a man's life.

A New Men's Project

One of the major critiques of male specificity is the claim that the vast majority of Jewish history has been dominated by male voices. This critique argues that the existing corpus of prefeminist Jewish literature is already male specific. Why, then, do we need a new men's perspective? I call this the old masculinist problem. We could argue that men today deserve no special attention because their (our?) dominance of so much of Western civilization makes the study of men redundant.

The people who have so dominated the public sphere of Judaism for over three thousand years were certainly men, but as we have discussed, for all but the last sliver of that timeline nobody—least of all men—really considered what that meant. The men writing law, midrash, philosophy, mysticism, prayer, and history rarely considered how their gender influenced the way they functioned in the world. Where these issues did arise, they most often orbited sex differences, rather than gender differences. A rabbi might have written volumes about the differences between a man's and woman's religious roles, but did he consider what elements of those roles actually nurtured and/or starved the people involved?

As an example, the Torah provides two major commandments regarding the relationship between parents and children. In the two versions of the Ten Commandments, it says, "Honor your father and your mother . . ." (Exodus 20:12; Deuteronomy 5:16), and in the Holiness Code, it says, "You shall each revere your mother and your father . . ." (Leviticus 19:3). In the section discussing this text, the Talmud initially considers whether commandments fall differently upon sons and daughters and determines that girls are exempt. Using their typical legalistic thinking, the Rabbis determine that a woman's first obligation will be to her husband, and therefore she cannot reasonably also be obligated to her parents (Babylonian Talmud, *Kiddushin* 30b). The rest of the argument maps the topography of the commandments, their limitations and implications, all in relation to the men who must fulfill them. Noting the difference between the two versions of the commandment, the Talmud asks, "What is 'reverence' and what is 'honor'?" The answer: "'Reverence' means that he [the son] must neither stand in his [the father's] place nor sit in his place, nor contradict his words, nor intervene for him. 'Honor' means that he must give him food and drink, clothe and cover him, lead him in and out" (Babylonian Talmud, *Kiddushin* 31b).

According to the old masculinist argument, we have nothing more to learn from this text about the way that men function in the world. From the discussion about the exclusion of women from the commandment, the sexism of the text is clear. The woman in this case is an object with no say as to whom she devotes her attention and sense of obligation. Since the rest of the text concerns only men, if you want to see the male perspective, the old masculinist contends, go read the text. While the topography section does indeed concern only the men involved, it fails to ask whether the particular peaks and valleys of the commandments connect to specific parts of a man's experience. As a reader, we can gloss over the text, delimiting the bullet points of a man's responsibilities and then move on. In all of the verbosity of the Talmud, we get little about how these commandments might be specific to men, not because conflicting legal obligations force women out, but instead because the man's experience, as a man, compels him to treat his parents in a certain way.

What I propose in a new men's analysis would be to look at that topography, to examine its contours, and to see the explicit commandments as the evidence of an implicit emotional experience, in this case, between a man and his parents. When the text speaks of honor, it describes the physical and emotional care of parents as they age. This is the natural kind of sustenance demanded of a child who was once cared for by parents. We can imagine that a daughter would feel this obligation equally as much as a son, and even though the Talmud designates these obligations as exclusively for men, they do not seem exclusively masculine. But when the text describes reverence, it describes a different set of commandments, all negative. The son cannot take his father's place in public (standing) or his authority at home (sitting); he cannot speak against him (contradict) or speak for him (intervene). While these may be desires a woman faces in life, they certainly speak to the kind of Freudian rivalry in which a son chafes against his father's authority. As a son grows and struggles for independence, respect, and autonomy, these commandments guide his quest for his own authority in relation to his father's. We have no way to determine just how common this is for all men (a sex category), but we can certainly call it masculine (a gender category).

The old masculinist approach stifles a conversation that many men (and women) desire. Whether the medium is text, prayer, ritual, experience, or art, and whether the forum is independent reading, traditional study in pairs (*chevruta*), discussion, or a more formal sermon or lecture, approaching Judaism aware that part (if not much) of the experience is specifically male might open doors to further conversation. In the same way that we modern readers of Judaism use anthropology, archaeology, sociology, and psychology as tools to uncover deeper meaning in Jewish life, so too does an awareness of gender specificity become another tool toward a richer religion.

The bigger question is how this tool differs from the feminist critique that already exists. For a generation, feminists have maintained the importance of gender in their analysis. Many scholars of men's studies see it as a subset of gender studies in general, which is a construct built upon a feminist foundation. Therefore, to look at any piece of Judaism with an awareness of gender becomes a feminist analysis. How does a new men's project differ?

First of all, a complete application of a male, gender-aware thinking toward Judaism is beyond the scope of this work. Such a systematic rethinking of Judaism would be a fertile field of future thought. In this space I can hypothesize four specific ways a new men's project would differ from feminism. First, in contrast to women, whose historical experience has been one of Otherness, the men approach with an awareness of Power. How we experience that Power, as its beneficiaries, bystanders, and sometimes its victims, differs from that of women, and it would change the way we see Judaism. Second, perhaps because of the experience of Power, men have not invested the time or energy into considering gender's knife edge. Even though we recognize the split within humanity, we usually ignore it or, at best, assume it. This means we are at least a generation behind women in considering these issues.

Third, a new men's project begins with a different set of challenges. Biological research shows that women may be hardwired to form better relationships earlier. In addition, the experience of exclusion from public and literary life also may have forced women to rely less upon public, external modes of expression and more on the personal and intimate. Because the historical record has erased women so effectively, if not completely, the modern woman must look to her own experience and to the experience of other women for guidance in a project of finding meaning. Therefore, in the feminist reexamination of Judaism or of anything else, part of the analysis begins with experience.

In contrast, men have been externalizing their experience throughout most of Jewish history. Power meant that male desires and concerns could have just as easily been expressed through public rituals and texts as they could in personal conversation. An individual man could choose to push his personal experience into the private sphere, to be hidden or shared only among intimates, or to thrust that experience outside and incorporate it into a public persona. The middle ground, the sharing of experiences among men, the reliance upon the personal experience, was either squelched by the individual or co-opted by the community. If a new men's project were to ask men to reflect upon personal experience, we are asking a different kind of question. We are validating a source of authority—the private self—that most men have been trained to distrust in their quest for public authority. Therefore, while consciousness-raising groups and their Jewish equivalent, the Rosh Chodesh groups, might have been natural developments for women, these types of experience-based sharing environments might not work as well for men. In order to approach a deeper masculine impulse, one beyond the stereotype or the social expectation, we may need to begin from a different point of origin. We may need to begin outside, with a text or ritual, and then push men to articulate how this speaks to their insides, to their souls. Men are so used to externalizing that we often fail to see the soul as an authentic text. We may need to start with the external in order to approach the internal.

Finally, we have a different responsibility toward the conversation. As the inheritors of a history of male dominance, we, more than women, hold the ethical responsibility to restrain and anticipate any future impulse for domination. This does not make women into an object to be protected or whose worth is determined by men. Quite the contrary, taking responsibility for past behavior means respecting women's power over themselves. But if we end there, which would be quite an accomplishment, we do nothing to heal men of their more destructive instincts. A new men's approach would understand that the victim is not responsible for healing the perpetrator.

This last point requires further elaboration. While the relationship between men and women is not the sole locus of masculine experience, it is a major one and one that comes with special rules. A history of the abuse of power along sex lines means that when men consider masculinity, we must also consider its abuses. Masculinity itself is not inherently destructive, but history proves that it does contain destructive elements. This has special implications for men that a general feminist critique does not. As we look for the contours of male experience through men's voices today or in the textual voices of the past, we are ethically bound to apply the litmus test of abuse. When we consider our rereading and expressions of Judaism, the potential for damage demands first priority. A new men's project takes a Hippocratic oath that binds us to prevent further damage *prior* to creating future expressions of Judaism.

Certain elements of men's movements in the past have fallen into this trap. As feminism has questioned gender assumptions, we have all felt confusion and disorientation as reliable social guidelines have disappeared. Some men have responded by embracing a feminist message, diversifying their options to include not only the masculine approach to life, but also the feminine. Other men have tried or observed this route and have responded with backlash, not only disagreeing with it, but also rejecting it. The classic example of this is Sam Keen's *Fire in the Belly*, often cited as a work of the mythopoetic men's movement, but also containing a latent misogyny in the promotion of its version of masculinity.[31]

In the Jewish world we could easily fall prey to such a mistake. Especially in our postmodern American context in which we feel an enormous desire for tradition to provide all of the answers to modernity's failures, the inclination to embrace the past might lead to atavistic results. For instance, if men were to discover that a single-sex prayer environment enabled a deeper spiritual experience, some might be tempted to attend only those services separated by sex. Not only does this resemble a retrogressive Orthodox worship model with its separate lines of authority and communal power, but it would also create individual men without the spiritual capacity for joint worship. Separate prayer can be helpful, but joint worship is a central element of the modern Jewish community. A new men's project requires us to go beyond what might prove to be a comfortable male-only space. Other examples abound. Feminism has taught us much about the ways that Judaism has oppressed women in the past. In fact, feminism has been so effective and accurate that even within Orthodoxy we can see inroads into the most male-dominated aspects of community life, like divorce law, prayer leadership, and access to high-level text study.

The trick in a Jewish new men's approach would be to discover those elements of a male-dominated past that nurture men without doing harm to women. To return to the example of separate prayer environments, if separate prayer does indeed open spiritual doors for some men, we should provide that option. It nurtures the soul. But a new men's ethic requires that environment to be explicitly alternative, and separated from communal sources of power (i.e., the "Men's Prayer Circle" cannot become a de facto incubator for board presidency). In addition, the men in that group should be challenged to understand what they have discovered in the single-sex setting and to find ways to apply that same spiritual energy and strength in the mixed-sex setting.

Not only must we be wary of the slide to the same abuses of the past, but a new men's ethic requires the same vigilance toward abuse in the future. A few years ago during a national convention of the North American Federation of Temple Youth (NFTY), I led a men's prayer service. The convention had fifteen hundred participants (two-thirds of whom were female), and like most years, the leaders asked for diverse prayer options. Instead of holding different services sequentially or on alternating days, the organizers decided to hold six separate services simultaneously on Shabbat morning. But because this was the most important service of the week and they wanted to balance diversity with unity, they planned to have the members of each service march into the main convention hall during the Torah procession (*hakafah*). One of the most popular prayer options was the women's service, and for the sake of balance, a men's service was added to the program. Motivating male prayer, especially teenage male prayer, is a pretty tall order. The same distraction, fidgeting, and disinterest that boys manifest in mixed groups becomes magnified by a sense of solidarity against the spiritual purpose—like a labor union on a prayer strike. That morning, about seventy young men sat in a large circle and joined together for what was a pretty mediocre service. The words of the liturgy were on par with a typical youth service, and the music was set in keys that fit adolescent male voices, but the group felt little energy, and as a leader, I could tell that few felt spiritually engaged.

But when we reached the Torah service, we asked all of the men to rise and follow behind the Torah for the *hakafah*. We marched through the halls of the hotel, down an escalator, and into the main convention hall. We began as a chaotic and loosely organized group, but with each step I could feel the congregation behind me becoming more unified and more motivated. Our energy rose when we heard our voices bouncing off of the walls and ceilings. Our energy rose higher as we could feel the beating of footsteps all around us. Our energy rose even higher as we heard the other groups and competed to sing louder. Our energy rose higher still as we entered the hall, where most of the convention had already gathered, and we tightened our ranks in order to remain together. And finally our energy peaked as we marched to the front of the room and formed a circle of young men dancing around the Torah. The group had gone from a lackluster, barely interested lump of adolescent boredom to a fired-up, spiritually animated, cohesive community. We continued singing and dancing and passing the Torah among us. They rejoiced in Torah, community, and song. We had finally created a men's prayer service that touched the souls of adolescent boys. No small feat.

What made this happen? I cannot take credit. I had all but given up and was simply following instructions when we began marching to the main convention hall. Maybe it was the use of the body, calling to the kinesthetic learners among us. It could have been the experience of marching in rhythm, a unifying physical movement, like dance, in which the men can feel their bond. Maybe it was competition, the base male desire to display power in a large group. Or perhaps it was solidarity, the feeling of a group coming together in the midst of a larger, more chaotic group of outsiders. I cannot pinpoint the precise reason, but these guys were energized in the moment, surrounding Torah, singing words of praise to God, forming a religious community.

That's when it happened. We had been dancing in concentric circles for ten minutes or so, and suddenly two girls burst into the center circle and tried to join in. Not wanting to miss out on the spiritual energy, the girls were requesting, or demanding, access. The boys' response? They had found their energy in their homogeneity. They began pushing the girls out. My responsibility at that moment, as a leader promoting not only a masculine Judaism, but a new men's Judaism was literally to roar (it was loud in there) at the boys to pass the Torah to one of the girls and to hold their hands and dance with them. A new men's ethic requires that we demonstrate the power of masculinity—in this case solidarity, healthy competition, physical energy, loyalty—and we anticipate the potential for exclusion, domination, abuse, subjugation, and disenfranchisement.

A new men's experience of Judaism seeks to draw out those masculine elements of Jewish tradition that will nurture and support the spiritual Jewish journey today. While feminism teaches us to address gender specificity, this new men's project contains additional lenses through which to look: the experience of Power, the blindness to gender, the challenge of readdressing the balance between internal and external, and the awareness of the potential for abuse of male power. A new men's Judaism becomes in this way a tool in addition to the feminist, the psychological, the anthropological, the midrashic, the mystical, and so many other tools, for nurturance and sustenance of Jewish souls—male and female. Such a new men's Judaism will likely be based on experiences, both those articulated through generations of public discourse and the more recent experiences that will surface through new gender-aware spaces in our communities. This book is one of those spaces.

Discovering the New Men's Narrative

This book represents an opening. It is a book of autobiography, to be certain, but in the questions asked and answered, the writers examine what might be hitherto ignored elements of spiritual selfhood. Almost every writer expressed an initial discomfort or confusion with the topic, uncertain how to articulate a male experience that had seemed so assumed, so much the norm. Through the writing of this book, these men opened a door into their personal experience, which illuminates a part of larger masculinities within Judaism. In the same way I hope that readers of this book, including but not limited to men, will listen to others' experience *and* consider examining their own experience. Men have been externalizing their experiences for a long time, studying them in books and public forums. I hope this book is not only an external text for the reader, but becomes a catalyst to examine the internal text.

Because this is a book of experience, I intentionally sought and selected essays that represented the first-person perspective. I asked men to examine what it means to be a man and to be a Jew today. Enclosed in the appendix to this book is the overview statement and leading questions that each author had to work from, with the exceptions of those reprinted from other sources, chosen because they worked well as responses to these same questions. For many of the writers, these were new questions, and they reacted in a variety of ways. Some could pinpoint particular experiences that helped define their identity both as Jews and as men. Others could speak in only broad generalities. Some men could dig beneath the surface of an experience to discover new layers of meaning and direction, while others saw in the apparent events of their lives a story and pattern.

The voices in this book are not at all homogeneous or monolithic, other than all being Jewish. The experiences, opinions, and perspectives included are not in agreement and do not cohere into one overarching conclusion. With these essays I have tried to represent the diversity of Jewish life in the United States today. If the sample of essays has one major drawback, it is that it is overrepresented by Jews affiliated with synagogues. Because every editor of a collection relies in some part upon the sphere of his or her personal knowledge, this author's sphere is overrepresented by rabbis and synagogue Jews. While this may be interesting for individuals affiliated with synagogues (and churches), it leaves out the voices of so many men who have abandoned the community of the synagogue. In addition, this overrepresentation means that the experiences described herein rely heavily on the life of the synagogue. These men thus search for meaning in places like Torah study, men's groups, youth group, Brotherhood, on committees, and with their rabbis. They also search for meaning with friends, spouses, their fathers, siblings, and coworkers. While they hear the still, small voice both inside and outside the synagogue walls, the inside is perhaps a bit more common in this book than in the general population.

On the other end of the spectrum, a handful of writers chose not to write an essay, because they felt so far removed from the topics under discussion. For at least one potential writer, this was due to his estrangement from Judaism in general, and for another, his distaste for what he called "organized Judaism" (an oxymoron if ever there was one). One writer felt embarrassed to write, because the major issue of gender in his Jewish journey was a discomfort with female prayer leadership. Just as these writers excused themselves explicitly, I also must note the large number of writers who simply chose not to write. While they would probably give many reasons, at least a few likely were dissuaded by some aspect of the topic itself. All of these choices make for a somewhat self-selected group of writers, one that is closer to the center of synagogue life today than is the general Jewish population, but one that does indeed represent some diversity within the community.

This is also not a book of academic research or big-picture study. It is a book of trees, not an overview of a forest or an analysis of multiple forests. While trends and generalities do emerge from the essays within, the book intentionally shies away from drawing dramatic conclusions. We need more serious academic, social scientific research on men and masculine elements of Judaism, and we certainly need a deeper philosophical investigation into masculinity than the one contained in this introduction. That having been said, some of the writers in this book are academics, clergy, and caregivers for men, and they spend their professional lives looking for the very trends I just forsook. Interestingly, these men find meaning in their own experience of grappling with the meta-issues of masculinity. I include them not because their observations represent thorough sociological research, but because they themselves find meaning in the world of ideas.

Readers will note that this book includes the voices of three women writers. I've included them because their observations of men help us understand what might influence the way that men encounter meaning in their lives. While these women have not experienced male spirituality personally, they have observed it. In addition, two of them are in professional roles in the Jewish community and can reflect upon what they think assists and what obstructs men in hearing the voice of the soul in their lives. One of the writers, Karen Perolman, is a rabbinical student, and she adds to this the perspective of being at the focal point of a major gender transition in the Reform Movement: being in a rabbinical class that is overwhelmingly female. Such a unique perspective deserves placement in this collection. The second writer, Rabbi Jennifer Jaech, serves as the senior rabbi to a large suburban New York synagogue, one that has had female senior rabbis for over three decades. Her perspective allows us to see the way that female clergy can indeed support and enhance male religious experience. Because of the large amount of speculation surrounding the female clergy issue, this essay demanded inclusion.

Despite, or perhaps because of, this book's heterogeneity and multivocality, we can find commonalities and contrasts in the ways that men hear the still, small voice in their lives. The men differ between and within their stories. The variety tells the story of a general narrative that encompasses much of the journey for contemporary American Jewish men.

The New Men's Narrative: Hearing the Still, Small Voice

This narrative is essential for understanding the deeper meaning of these essays. We all know hundreds of men, and we have heard many of their stories. While stories can be fascinating, without a larger context in which to fit them, the lessons they teach may not form a coherent message. A narrative helps us understand how a particular experience fits into a larger context. It provides for us at least two directions of motion and momentum upon which a man can travel at different moments of life. Narrative tells us where we have come from and where we are likely to go. Neil Postman, former chair of the Department of Culture and Communication at New York University, explains the importance of narrative in finding meaning:

> I mean by "narrative" a story. But not any kind of story. I refer to big stories—stories that are sufficiently profound and complex to offer explanations of the origins and future of a people; stories that construct ideals, prescribe rules of conduct, specify sources of authority, and in doing all this, provide a sense of continuity and purpose. Joseph Campbell and Rollo May, among others, called such stories "myths." Marx had such stories in mind in referring to "ideologies." And Freud called them "illusions." No matter. What is important about narratives is that human beings cannot live without them. We are burdened with a consciousness that insists on our having a purpose.[32]

The stories in this book on their own provide a little in the way of myth, ideology, purpose, or meaning. But taken together, a pattern emerges, one that does instruct on the profound and the deep in the lives of contemporary American Jewish men. While multiple narratives surely exist for the individuals within this book, a common narrative, what we might call the American Jewish new men's narrative, begins to emerge.

It takes us back to the story of Elijah. That narrative begins with Elijah's embrace of his power. He is quintessentially masculine in that moment atop Mount Carmel, with all of the pros and cons that come with that label. He uses his power to undermine and dispel the abusive, idolatrous power of Jezebel and Ahab, demonstrating that belief in the Eternal God will prevail against injustice, corruption, and ignorance. He challenges his opponents to a competition, he taunts them, he even becomes overly demonstrative, and he prevails in every way. He also lets his power overflow, journeying into the realm of violence as he slays the 450 prophets of Baal as they descend the mountain into the valley. In all of this Elijah is a man atop the mountain, relying upon his masculine traits to achieve his ends. Victorious.

The essays in the first section of this book describe men who find comfort in the parts of their identity that align with the hegemonic masculinity of today. These are men who embrace competition, sports, building, fund-raising, fraternity, military power, and to some degree, machismo. Many of them have found ways to incorporate these elements of their lives into their Jewish identity, putting their masculinity to work in their quest for meaning. Like Elijah on Mount Carmel, they call God into their lives while achieving different sorts of victory.

But then Elijah flees mysteriously. The text seems to indicate that he flees from Jezebel's murderous rage, but this makes little sense. With God's support on Carmel fresh in his mind, why flee? I propose that Elijah is fleeing not Jezebel, but himself. On the mountain and in the valley below, he saw his capacity to wield power (and some might say to abuse it). He does not know power's limits, and he fears what it might do. Or, to go further, he rejects power. He has held the sword in his hand, he has called God's presence into fantastic demonstration, and he resists it. He flees from himself.

American Jewish men have a long history of ambivalence toward traditional male power. We have often been excluded from sources of social power in America and in most of our experience of Western history. In 322 C.E., the Roman emperor, Constantine, forbid us from holding Christian slaves.[33] In that system, slavery, while morally abhorrent, operated not as the kind of chattel market that existed in this country, but rather was a part of the class and economic systems. By restricting the Jews, Constantine effectively evicted us from the Roman agricultural economy. Since then, we have been systematically excluded from different forms of power, and in order to survive we have sought alternative sources of security. When they closed agriculture and the guilds, Jews took up finance. When they closed sports, Jews took up the intellect. When they closed access to public speech, Jews took up humor and the arts. In each of these areas, Jews found alternative methods of expression.

Ironically, we often imported into those alternative methods the same male tendencies that so thoroughly saturated the mainstream forms of masculinity. So while sports and royal competitions may have been considered non-Jewish—a myth by the way—we then transformed the pursuit of the intellectual into a competitive experience. As we studied texts, we would often compete, show off, taunt, and try to dominate our study partners, our colleagues, and our peers. The same is true of finance, humor, the arts, and every other field into which Jews were forced. Jewish men have proved the ability to bring those hegemonic masculine traits with them even into fields typically seen as feminine.

But the experiences of exclusion and otherness remain. Even the most competitive, dominant, and masculine intellectual, stockbroker, or artist knows the feeling of being on the short end of the stick if he is Jewish. Even in the twenty-first century in the United States, where we have incredible power, we still know insecurity. Some men know that insecurity in their own lives, especially if they are members of other disenfranchised groups as well as being Jewish—if they are gay, African American, disabled, deaf, Hispanic, or a member of any number of categories. And even if we have not personally felt the sting of power's abuse, every Jewish man carries the recent memory of the Holocaust, even two or three generations removed. Therefore, like Elijah, we fear power to some extent. Even our own.

This fear makes men look for alternative definitions of not just male activities, but also masculinity itself. A second group of essays represent this rejection of traditional masculinity. These writers have defined their Judaism and their identity as men by finding new ways to express the masculine. Some of these men consciously seek alternatives, finding in traditional masculinity overtly objectionable elements—sexism, most notably—while others seek that alternative more subconsciously. More than one author finds fault with traditional Judaism's exclusion of women and defines a part of their selfhood in correcting that wrong. Like Elijah, they flee the mountaintop of masculine victory and find themselves in that rejection.

But Elijah does not end up at Mount Sinai immediately. His rejection of power does not lead immediately to resolution. Elijah first heads to the wilderness, where, exhausted, he must rest beneath a broom-bush. He cannot find his way and relies upon an angel to provide him food and to guide him.

This wilderness experience is so central to the Jewish narrative. The story of Abraham begins with a going out, as God commands him to leave the civilization of Mesopotamia before he can truly establish a monotheistic life. And Abraham continues with wandering, facing the challenges, physical and spiritual, ethnic and familial, ethical and mundane, that come through the pages of Genesis. His sons have their own experiences with the wild, as first Isaac must venture forth to find his wells, Jacob flees from his brother, and Joseph grapples with the pitfalls and pits of Egypt. Then Moses leads the people through forty years (and three and a half books of the Torah) of wandering the desert. And as David grows from a soldier into a king, he lives in caves fleeing Saul. In every Jewish story, the hero, or heroes, must go to the wilderness, to the place of freedom and openness in order to find the self. This contrasts with the rest of Western folklore and storytelling. While Western myths contain men who grapple with obstacles and challenges, they always know their destination, their goal. They seek to slay the dragon, to overcome the foe, to free the princess from the tower. But these Jewish stories instead contain unknown destinations, insecurity again, and the journey for meaning and self-definition.

Perhaps this too comes through the experience of being a minority, the sense of otherness and the flimsy guarantees of a disenfranchised life. While many of these stories resemble the rejection stories—Elijah's fleeing from the mountain, Abraham's going out, and so forth—they also contain a break. The rejection stories thrust the hero into the wilderness because he (in this case) objects. He knows what he does not like, and he knows where he is going: away. But the wilderness stories contain a different narrative element. This part of the story is exile, *galut*, the place where the Temple has been destroyed, the walls have been torn down, and the Jew must find himself anew.

Often, men find themselves in *galut*. They face crisis, loss, disorientation. They grapple with addiction, illness, and divorce. They are abused,
they go to war, they lose children. They struggle to balance work and
home life, not to mention personal time. They see all of their assumptions give way as the world changes around them. They find themselves
moving to new places, doing new things, and occupying roles they never
saw as male. For many, this is painful, disorienting, and terrifying. But
this wilderness experience can also be liberating, instructive, and
redemptive. It was the wilderness after all that raised a generation of
Israelites with the faith to cross the Jordan and conquer Jericho. The
men in this book who describe their moments of crisis all find resolution
with a stronger and healthier sense of self. The wilderness instructs and
re-creates these individuals. They have found some sense of redemption.
In the pages of this book we hear their stories of the wilderness and, for
some, the lessons on how to find the mountain.

The mountain is Sinai, at Horeb, where Elijah climbs to the cleft
where Moses once stood. The mountain is the place of revelation, meaning, purpose. Elijah comes to understand there that God does not reside
in the preconceived notions. He does not find purpose and confidence in
the wind, fire, or earthquake. He finds God in the unexpected place, the
still, small voice.

Unlike Moses, who never saw the Promised Land, we do have Jewish
stories of redemption. Elijah does indeed hear the voice of God, and he
does return to the land with confidence to face Jezebel and Ahab without
fear of them or of himself. The Jewish form of redemption is not only the
achievement of victory, the slaying of the dragon, but it is the maintenance
of power with self-imposed limitations. Elijah does not return and kill the
king. But after hearing the voice he does know how to use his power when
necessary. He can rebuke the king and then walk away confident.

When David too comes out of the wilderness, he does not seize the
throne from the weakened Saul, even though he knows he could. He pro-
tects himself, waits for Saul's demise, and even refuses to annihilate his
offspring. This kind of restraint is the lesson of Elijah: to find a meaning
and sense of purpose with balance, restraint, and control.

When I teach a class on introduction to Judaism, the students invariably notice that almost every Jewish holiday or ritual contains some

reminder of brokenness in the world. On Passover we diminish the second cup of wine with ten drops, one for each of the plagues that struck Egypt. At weddings we break a glass. On Sukkot our habitations are intentionally open to the elements. And when we build houses we leave a section unpainted. The Jewish way of living is to acknowledge our lack of redemption. We continue to live, to succeed, to enjoy life, but we do so with the restraint of Elijah—the restraint of one who knows the abuses of power, who has fled, who has struggled in wilderness, and who has found meaning in the still, small voice.

We discover this same feature in the great contests of Jewish law found in the Talmud. This tremendous compendium contains a guide to Jewish practice, but it emerges from a discussion in which the victors always acknowledge and respect their opponents. The discussions may seem long and meandering, but eventually the law is certainly decided. Nevertheless, minority opinions are listed, dissenting viewpoints heard and preserved for generations to come. The classic example of this form of Jewish victory is the sage Hillel. Throughout the Talmud, this teacher and the disciples who follow him engage in legal combat with the students of a teacher named Shammai. At one point, God intervenes and declares, "[The utterances of] both are the words of the living God, but the [community law] is in agreement with the rulings of the House of Hillel." The Talmud asks, "Since, however, 'both are the words of the living God,' what was it that entitled the House of Hillel?" Answer: "Because they were kindly and modest, they studied their own rulings and those of the House of Shammai, and were even so [humble] as to mention the actions of the House of Shammai before theirs" (Babylonian Talmud, *Eiruvin* 13b). Hillel and his followers knew how to wield power and strength with restraint.

This kind of balance is reflected by a number of the essays as well. These writers find a sense of comfort with their selves as men and as Jews. They have found a voice that speaks to their souls, and they listen to it. They embrace a vastly wide variety of definitions of what that voice says and how it sounds, but they all reflect a sense of self-actualization and identity. Almost entirely, they do not pretend to have all of the answers or to have achieved some kind of supernatural revelation. Instead they recognize their confidences and their limitations. They rely on this knowledge for a sense of meaning and purpose in their lives as men, as Jews, and as human beings. As they travel through their diverse paths, they rely upon this discovered knowledge as a compass to guide them.

This sounds like the end of the story, right? We are so accustomed to stories that end with the cowboy riding off into the sunset, victorious after overcoming the unbeatable obstacles. But again, this is not the way the Jewish story ends. Even though the Hollywood version ends with the moment at Sinai, the Torah continues for three and a half books of instruction in the desert. In the same way, after Elijah's moment of revelation, God instructs him to take a disciple, and Elijah encounters Elisha plowing in his field. The precious knowledge of God needs to be passed on to the next generation. The teacher needs a student.

This relationship, between teacher and student, is a holy one, and it represents the culmination of life experience for many of us. The foundations of Judaism as we know it today are from the study circle, in which the rabbi sat surrounded by his disciples. The experience of this relationship, learning over a text, became the central route to the encounter of God after the Temple was destroyed. This relationship between teacher and student grew to such importance that it became a competitor, or sometimes a replacement, for the father-son relationship. The Talmud imagines many scenarios in which the needs of a father and a teacher compete for the attention of a student or son. In one section the father and the teacher both lose their wallet.

> His lost object and the lost object of his father—[he should seek] his lost object first. His lost object and the lost object of his master (*rabo*)—his first. The lost object of his father and the lost object of his master—his master's first. Because his father brought him into this world, and his master taught him wisdom that will bring him into the world-to-come. (*Mishnah Bava M'tzia* 2:11)[34]

Here the debate is over particulars about lost objects, but the details stand in for larger questions about loyalty, obedience, and intimacy. In Judaism, the experience of learning and teaching is as sacred and emotional as that of parenting.

The importance of that relationship comes through a number of the essays in this collection as well. As the men included here sought meaning and guidance in life, they frequently found it in their fathers, but just as often, if not more, they found it in teachers, therapists, mentors, bosses, and coaches. Judaism understands that some essential part of men's development depends upon connection with older, role-model men who are not their fathers. As Robert Bly teaches in *Iron John*, men crave some transition from boyhood to manhood overseen—or initiated —by another, non-father, man. Psychologists describe how male development depends upon cycles of disengagement, which often lead to the discovery of mentors to fill roles previously occupied by parents and friends. But even these relationships often end in disengagement or with what Stephen J. Bregman calls "power over violations" in which the man needs to break away from his mentor. "Agents of disconnection learn how to disconnect others, and how to twist themselves out of relationship, to 'succeed.'"[35] This experience of growth through relationship with first parents and then nonparent mentors comes clearly through the essays herein. For many men it is the core of their Jewish experience.

These different pieces of the Jewish new men's narrative are not necessarily sequential or comprehensive. Men may experience any or all of them in various orders. However, they point to fundamental elements of the male experience. This book contains brief glimpses of key spiritual elements in Jewish men's lives. In some ways the selection is narrow— mostly white, Reform, variously affiliated, upper-middle-class, North American, and almost entirely male—and in other ways highly representative—those same limitations describe the center of the male part of the American Jewish community. The stories and lessons herein show us what Judaism means, how men see themselves as men, and where are the routes to meaning in their lives.

While the essays are descriptive, not prescriptive, they will give us insights into strategies and tactics that may help the liberal Jewish community better serve its men. Communal leaders, if we are sensitive, feel the needs of our members. We see the statistics and count the bodies, but we also form relationships and try to help Jews achieve spiritual fulfillment. The question is how? All kinds of anecdotal evidence show us that we have not been doing so well with men. That failure goes back over a hundred years and is deeply rooted in the culture of American religion. Recently it appears that we are failing even more spectacularly. The interpretation of that appearance depends on the attitude of the beholder. Is it because the proportion of women in more visible and authoritative roles—like the rabbinate—has finally achieved the goals of the women's rights movement, or is it because we are finally recognizing the needs of men as men? Regardless, the best way to understand and serve men is to remind them that they are, indeed, men. To use the language of masculinity, manhood, and maleness. To reflect upon that experience in life and to build on commonalities and differences that that factor presents for Jewish men. We do not have that conversation often. This book hopefully will help incite it.

I have used the narrative of Elijah—success, rebellion, confusion, enlightenment, and mentorship—to describe different perspectives on masculinity and Judaism. Those are broad categories, and the individuals who have contributed to this book help further define them. At the beginning of each section I introduce some of the categories represented by the different essays. As these essays are autobiographical, they contain the intricacies and idiosyncrasies of individuals. Other readers may find other key ideas; indeed, others—including the writers—may wish to categorize them entirely differently. Of course, that is possible, and I encourage the reader to use these texts as a jumping-off point for further discussion. As each man travels his path in search of meaning, he finds different landmarks, maps, and guides to help him along the way. Some he sees as important, others minor. These authors have chosen to tell us a bit about where they have found direction, meaning, and expression, and for this we should be grateful. My introductions—the framework of this book—may be based on the journeys of the writers, but taken together they tell a different story. Each man in this book struggles to find meaning and purpose in his own way. As I have listened to these writers, I too have discovered my path. They are my teachers, my guides, and my mentors. As I introduce and react to their stories, I find myself telling mine.

Notes

1. Susan Faludi, in her book, *Stiffed*, explores in detail the ramifications of changing economic and social conditions on male self-image and behavior. She explains how the rapid economic shifts of the twentieth century undermined many of the values traditionally associated with masculinity: "A social pact between the nation's men and its institutions was collapsing, most prominently but not exclusively within the institutions of work. Masculine ideals of loyalty, productivity and service lay in shards. Such codes

were seen as passé and their male subscribers as vaguely pathetic. Loyalty meant you were too slow or too stupid to skip out on the company before it skipped out on you. Productivity was something corporations and their shareholders now measured not by employee elbow grease but by how many employees the company laid off. And service meant nothing more than consumer assistance, exemplified by a telemarketer trapped in a cubicle, a phone glued to his ear, his have-a-nice-day conversations preformulated and monitored. Such a profound and traumatic transformation affected all men, whether they lost their jobs or simply feared losing them, whether they drowned or floated in the treacherous new currents" (Susan Faludi, *Stiffed: The Betrayal of the American Man* [New York: William Morrow, 1999], p. 43).

2. The landmark General Social Survey by Duke University found that in a comparison of data from 1985 and 2004, every measure of social isolation rose. The number of people who claimed to have no one with whom to discuss important matters tripled in that time. The average number of confidants dropped from three to two in that time, and most social networks became more centered on spouse and family, with fewer and fewer non-kin ties (Miller McPherson, Lynn Smith-Lovin, and Matthew E. Brashears, "Social Isolation in America: Changes in Core Discussion Networks over Two Decades," *American Sociological Review* 71 [June 2006]: 353–75).

3. Male depression has been a misunderstood phenomenon for many years, but recent work by psychologists like Terrance Real and others argues that the standard criteria for diagnosing depression is based largely on symptoms exhibited mostly by women. They posit that male depression has always been common but that it is now becoming more prevalent. In addition, men are more likely to squelch their emotional lives in chemical or behavioral addictions, showing higher rates of alcohol and drug dependencies. They also are much more likely to actually complete a suicide, because men seem more willing to use more violent means (Terrence Real, *I Don't Want To Talk About It: Overcoming the Secret Legacy of Male Depression* [New York: Fireside, 1997]).

4. Many studies have noted higher rates of antisocial and maladaptive behavior with a wide variety of negative health effects. Men die on average seven years earlier than women, and they have higher mortality rates in every age range. They are more likely to delay seeking medical treatment, and when they do finally seek such treatment, they tend to take longer to recover from similar illnesses. Men engage in more violent and risky behaviors as well (Ronald Levant, *Masculinity Reconstructed: Changing the Rules of Manhood—At Work, in Relationships, and in Family Life* [New York: Dutton, 1995], pp. 208–29).

5. Brian Fogel and Sam Wolfson, *Jewtopia: The Chosen Book for the Chosen People* (New York: Grand Central Publishing, 2006).

6. Full disclosure: my research with young Jewish men was done under supervision from Barden and the then director of youth programming, Rabbi Andrew Davids.

7. For more information about gender imbalance in the Reform Movement's programs, see *The Gender Gap*, URJ Press, 2008.

8. E. Anthony Rotundo, *American Manhood* (New York: Basic Books, 1993).

9. Steven M. Cohen and Arnold M. Eisen, *The Jew Within: Self, Family and Community in America* (Bloomington: Indiana University Press, 2000), p. 206.

10. In response to the assertion "I want to become more involved in Jewish life," 69 percent of girls said yes, while only 58 percent of boys agreed. To "B'nai Mitzvah was a graduation from Jewish life," 48 percent of girls said yes, while 57 percent of boys agreed. And to "My Israel experience enhanced my connection to Jewish life," 81 percent

of girls agreed, while only 59 percent of boys responded in the affirmative. Either girls really are more interested in and affected by Jewish activity, or boys are just more honest about their lack of interest (Charles Kadushin, Shaul Kelner, and Leonard Saxe, "Being a Jewish Teenager in America: Trying to Make It" [Boston: Cohen Center for Modern Jewish Studies, Brandeis University, 2000]).

11. Rona Shapiro, "The 'Boy Crisis' that Cried Wolf," *Forward*, January 5, 2007.

12. Abraham Joshua Heschel, *God in Search of Man* (New York: Farrar, Straus and Giroux, 1955), p. 3.

13. Michael S. Kimmel and Michael A. Messner, *Men's Lives*, 6th ed. (Boston: Pearson, 2004), p. x.

14. Kevin Sack, "Poll Finds Optimistic Outlook, but Enduring Racial Division," *New York Times*, July 11, 2000, A23. In a national poll that asked, "Has too much been made of the problems facing black people, has too little been made, or is it about right?" 10 percent of blacks said, "Too much," while 33 percent of whites said the same. When asked, "Who has a better chance of getting ahead in today's society?" 57 percent of blacks said, "White people," while only 32 percent of whites said the same. These kinds of splits were consistent throughout the survey.

15. Shawn Zevit, foreword to *From Your Father's House . . . Reflections for Modern Jewish Men*, by Kerry M. Olitzky (Philadelphia: Jewish Publication Society, 1999), pp. xi–xiii.

16. Robert Bly, *Iron John: A Book about Men* (Reading, MA: Addison-Wesley, 1990).

17. Levant, *Masculinity Reconstructed*, p. 5.

18 William Safire, "On Language; Linguistically Correct," *New York Times Magazine*, May 5, 1991.

19. Deborah Solomon, *New York Times Magazine*, June 13, 2004. Walker replied, "I don't agree with that. The feminist movement came into being because women were fundamentally in pain and unable to develop to their full potential. And men are similarly hampered by this masculine ideal, in which they are expected to repress their emotions."

20. Some academics refer to this as pro-feminism, but that sounds more supportive and less participatory. What I suggest here is that men actually participate in the feminist project.

21. W. E. B. DuBois, *The Souls of Black Folk* (1903) (New York: Vintage Books/ Library of America, 1990).

22. Judith Plaskow, *Standing Again at Sinai* (San Fransisco: Harper and Row, 1990), p. 11.

23. Susan Fendrick, "Jewish Feminist Ritual and Brit Milah," *Sh'ma: A Journal of Jewish Responsibility* (March 2005): 6.

24. "The New Israelite Temple Association constitution of the Hamburg Temple," December 11, 1817, in *The Rise of Reform Judaism: A Sourcebook of Its European Origins*, by W. Gunther Plaut (New York: World Union for Progressive Judaism, 1963), pp. 31ff.

25. I speak in careful tones here, because transgendered individuals feel a disconnection between the particularity of their gender and the anatomical sex. While deemphasizing gender in ritual would provide a more flexible and open ritual space for the transgendered, the trade-off is the ability to address a central area of identity for the vast majority of men and women.

26. Louann Brizendine, *The Female Brain* (New York: Morgan Road Books, 2006).

27. Carol Gilligan, *In a Different Voice: Psychological Theory and Women's Development* (Cambridge, MA: Harvard University Press, 1982).

28. *Forward*, June 23, 2006.

29. Aron Hirt-Manheimer,. "The Reluctant Man: A Conversation with Susan Weidman Schneider," *Reform Judaism*, Fall 2006, p. 88.

30. Elyse Goldstein, *ReVisions: Seeing Torah through a Feminist Lens* (Woodstock, VT: Jewish Lights Publishing, 1998), p. 121.

31. Sam Keen, *Fire in the Belly: On Being a Man* (New York: Bantam Books, 1991). Keen carefully distinguishes between his idea of the metaphoric WOMAN that, in his words, binds men's psyches and the real women with whom men interact. As he tries to "free" men from this bondage, the reader can easily slip from the metaphoric to the real, where resisting psychological enslavement becomes subordination of the female. A passage illustrates: "We are haunted by WOMAN in her many manifestations. She is the center around which our lives circle. WOMAN is the mysterious ground of our being that we cannot penetrate. She is the audience before whom the dramas of our lives are played out. She is the judge who pronounces us guilty or innocent. . . . She is the goddess who can grant us salvation and the frigid mother who denies us. She has a mythic power over us." Most of *Fire in the Belly* does not concern women, but Keen puts this obsession with the female at the front of his book and describes the discovery of a new manhood as a reaction to it. That posture, for me, is too oppositional.

32. Neil Postman, *Building a Bridge to the Eighteenth Century: How Our Past Can Improve Our Future* (New York: Vintage, 1999), p. 101.

33. "If any one among the Jews has purchased a slave of another sect or nation, that slave shall at once be appropriated for the imperial treasury" (Laws of Constantius, August 13, 339, quoted in Jacob Rader Marcus, *The Jew in the Medieval World: A Source Book 315–1791* [Cincinnati: Hebrew Union College Press, 1990], p. 5).

34. *Tosefta Horayot* 2:5 offers a parallel story for the question of whom you would redeem from captivity first, the father or the teacher. Again the teacher comes out on top.

35. Stephen J. Bergman, "Men's Psychological Development: A Relational Perspective," in *A New Psychology of Men*, ed. Ronald F. Levant and William S Pollack (New York: Basic Books, 1995), p. 79.

PART 1

TOP OF THE MOUNTAIN: EMBRACING MASCULINE IMAGES

INTRODUCTION

In Philip Roth's masterpiece, *American Pastoral*, the Jewish protagonist is the tall, blond quarterback of the high school football team, who eventually marries Ms. New Jersey. He succeeds in every measure of American masculinity. Therefore, from his 1950s community he earns the nickname "the Swede." Of course.

What Roth knows is that American Jewish men typically have struggled with the stereotypical identifiers of manliness. We have ingrained the message that by virtue of being Jewish, we are simply not manly. And if we do succeed in the typical categories, somehow that must negate our Jewish identities, like "the Swede." Even in a post-Koufax, post-Israeli-soldier, post-Jewish-bodybuilding, post-Jewish–*Gun's and Ammo*–reading world, the popular imagination rejects the notion of Jewish men as stereotypically manly. So Roth's character still resonates deep in the soul. When I told some friends that I was editing a book about Judaism and masculinity, they responded, "Must be a short book."

But this is a false dichotomy. People are much more complicated than that. We have always had our exemplars of manliness. When Elijah stood atop Mount Carmel, he challenged the prophets of Baal in their own game. Playing by the rules of his day, he emerged victorious beyond anyone's wildest expectations. Not only did Elijah's God show up as a spontaneous fire, but the Eternal One did so against the laws of physics—which of course is not a problem for God, but it sure makes an impact when fire erupts from a sacrifice soaked with twelve jugs of water.

Elijah then continues to act within the expected behavior of his day, behavior that fits the stereotype of manliness all too well. He marches forth from the mountain to slay his opponents in the valley below. While this grisly response might offend our modern sensibilities, Elijah was simply playing by the rules. This is what a victorious prophet did. And in a religious context, this sort of behavior worked. In an agricultural society dependent upon rain for water (Israel has no Nile upon which to rely), religion was about proving the trustworthiness of a deity. The Elijah story exemplifies competition at its best, and if God emerges victorious over the other gods, so too does Elijah become Da-Man versus the prophets of Baal.

Today, many men continue to find meaning in the typical rules of masculinity. (Fortunately, synagogue softball teams do not celebrate victory by massacring the team from the Episcopal cathedral across town.) But what is typical masculinity? Even though—to paraphrase Supreme Court Justice Potter Stewart on obscenity in 1964—we all know it when we see it, an exact definition eludes us.

When I was a young man in the B'nai Brith Youth Organization's male division, the AZA, we used to read the mission of AZA at every meeting. The document made reference to the purpose of creating "manly men." At that time, in the haze of adolescence, we equated manliness with toughness, coolness, athleticism, charisma, and, most importantly, facility with women. These characteristics seem so obvious, and they each describe a wide range of personalities. What may seem charismatic to one might be boorish to another and awkward to a third. And these are just the ideas of a bunch of upper-middle-class, white, presumably straight, suburban Jewish kids in Miami during the 1980s. Each of those descriptors can modify the expectations of behavior for every aspect of what we call "manliness." Even though the coolest guy in my high school was the president of the windsurfing club, let's not forget that during the 2004 election, the Republican party made John Kerry look effeminate as he cut back and forth on a sailboard.

Academics have written volumes trying to describe masculinity, and the consensus, as described by scholars Michael Kimmel and Michael Messner, has been to point instead to "masculinities." While scholars of African American men struggle with images of the "Pimp" and "Badass," Latino scholars look at machismo.[1] Scholars see different images of masculinity in different regions of the country and world, in different contexts and at different life stages. Many of these scholars also recognize the destructive potential of masculinity and try to delineate the borders of healthy male identity and behavior. Robert Moore and Douglas Gillette, in their book *King, Warrior, Magician, Lover*, examine the folkloric ideals of masculinity and discover a volatility within adolescent male behavior in which manly norms like competitiveness can overflow into destructive action like violence. For each of the types, they see an adolescent, dangerous variety of masculine behavior, and a mature, healthy option.[2]

In this discovery of a diversity of masculinities, the types of Jewish masculinity have remained largely fixed in the imagination. Most scholars agree that Jewish men typically have been viewed as non-manly, effeminate, weak, and bookish. These are stereotypes, and while they certainly describe some Jewish men, they hardly describe most—not today and not ever. But the stereotypes have enormous power over the imagination, and they occupy a large part of the public portrayal of Jewish men. In a study of depictions of Jewish men on television, Maurice Berger describes six categories, none of which seem so flattering: "the exotic or vulgar ethnic, the subordinated or passive schlemiel, the validated Jew, the neurotic, the inferred Jew, and the feminized Jew—cynically defined to undermine or ameliorate Jewish manhood."[2]

Even the manliest of Jewish men must use these stereotypes as a reference point and construct his own ideal of masculinity, and thus self-image, from that start. No matter how tough, strong, or athletic a Jew becomes, he remains aware that his Jewishness describes an alternative definition. He might rebel against this Jewish stereotypical definition and create his self-image in reaction. Nevertheless, somewhere along the line the stereotypically manly Jew asks himself if he has actually become "the Swede."

The Jewish men who embrace the markers of stereotypical masculinity find ways to do so in conjunction with their Judaism. Like Sandy

Koufax, whose legend only grew because he refused to pitch the 1965 World Series when it fell on Yom Kippur, these writers refuse to relinquish Jewish identity in order to succeed by the typical measures of masculinity. Instead, many of the writers in this section enter territory typically defined as manly—sports, military service, fraternity (in this case Freemasonry), leadership, finance, and the image of the Israeli ideal man—and bring home a spiritual experience.

We begin with two essays on sports and the way that by embracing athleticism two men—indeed, two rabbis—Ben David and Stephen Wise, find personal meaning. Charlie Niederman's essay begins with the story of his military service and then shifts to his personal rejection of the stereotype of Jews not being manly. Michael Freedman describes the experience of a particular all-male environment, Freemasonry, that enhances meaning (and the role of Judaism) in his life. Using some of the most powerful male language I have ever seen applied to Judaism, Dana Jennings, a convert, exhorts his Jewish sons to take their religious obligations seriously and to step up their participation in Jewish life. And finally, Mark Criden describes the role of a synagogue administrator in the language of hunting, relying upon the masculine concern with the chase for his source of meaning.

Also in this section are essays that start from the other direction, starting their journey certainly within Jewish terrain—prayer, song, wedding dancing, youth group, religious education—and then applying a masculine overlay to that behavior. In an excerpt from his book, *Searching for My Brothers*, Rabbi Jeffrey Salkin begins with the myth of the Israeli man, desert hardened, tough, and liberated from the emasculated image of the Diaspora Jew. Matthew Stern describes how male song leadership in the Jewish camp environment provides a role model of testosterone-rich means toward Jewish ends. Jason Freedman and Bobby Harris also apply masculine methodologies, in this case the male-only fireside discussion, to the Jewish camp environment, and in the process he leads a group of counselors to a much deeper sense of self and spiritual commitment. David Bergman proposes a new look at a familiar and old ritual: Jewish *simchah* (celebratory) dancing. Comparing it to the mosh pit of a rock concert, Bergman explains how all-male dancing creates an entirely different experience from that of mixed group. Finally, Avram Mandell, in his role as the director of education for a synagogue, considers how he can use the lessons of masculinity to more successfully reach both young and adult men.

As we view these two groups of essays—those that start in the masculine and end in a meaningful Judaism, and the reverse—we find the result is the same: men who have found ways to stick with the masculine norm and find spirituality in the process. These men follow Elijah's lead. They climb the mountaintop, accept the terms of society, and then find religious meaning in those terms.

These essays represent a small slice of Jewish society. The stories they tell can help us understand how better to speak the language of masculinity, albeit with a Jewish twang. If the still, small voice can be found in such stereotypically manly behavior, then communal leaders, teachers, and clergy should learn how to engage that behavior so that other Jewish men, those currently on the outside, the "Swedes" out there, can find a connection to Judaism through what they already do best.

NOTES

1. See the section entitled "Perspectives on Masculinity" in Michael A. Kimmel and Michael S. Messner, *Men's Lives*, 6th ed. (Boston: Pearson, 2004).

2. Robert Moore and Douglas Gillette, *King, Warrior, Magician, Lover* (San Francisco: HarperSanFrancisco, 1990). The division between adolescent masculine behavior and healthy adult manliness begs the question of how a man crosses that line. More specifically, do rites of passage help control masculine behavior and channel it to the constructive? Does the uninitiated remain in a stew of uncontrolled adolescence? This conversation, which is beyond the scope of this work, raises fascinating options for a redefinition of bar mitzvah.

3. Maurice Berger, "The Mouse that Never Roars: Jewish Masculinity on American Television," in *Too Jewish? Challenging Traditional Identities*, ed. Norman L. Kleeblatt (New York: The Jewish Museum, 1996), 93-107.

CHANNELING THE PASSION OF MY *ZAYDE*

Stephen Wise

My *zayde* would usually point at me and instruct me to sit to his immediate right hand. My *bubbe* would settle down just for a moment on his left, though it seemed she would always be hopping up and down to run into the kitchen to check on the matzah ball soup or stir the *cholent*. Then the rest of the family would slowly find their way around the large table. As my family grew, we had to extend the table, but I don't remember there ever being a "kids" table, because my *zayde* always wanted me beside him. He would stand up and welcome everyone formally, even though these were his children and grandchildren. He talked a little about the significant events that had happened to his children and grandchildren since last Passover, highlighting the *simchas* and *mazal tovs*. Then he always concluded with the following blessing: "I pray this year that we have peace in Israel and peace in the whole world." That was the start to every Passover seder at my grandparents' house. Clearly my grandfather was in charge. He knew all the songs and melodies, all the prayers and readings. He opened the book at page one, and we read each word until the final back cover. He always asked me to lead the singing or would ask me to explain a passage.

When I think of a Jewish role model, it was my *zayde*, Zalman Berholz. He taught me to love Judaism. He taught me to drink in the melodies and rhythms. He honored those who knew the most *yiddishkeit* and inspired everyone to learn more. I don't consciously remember thinking about becoming a rabbi at that point, but years later after, I finished graduate school at Brandeis University and thought about my formative Jewish moments, it was my *zayde* singing prayers with a huge smile on his face that warmed my soul and pushed me toward my chosen career.

It's a different world today. Engaging men into Jewish life might take more than only seeing Jewish male religious leaders who love being and doing Jewish. As a rabbi I want to project more than simply the image of a man who leads the congregation in prayer and officiates at life-cycle events. I also want to be a man who enjoys sports, loves going to the movies, and doing physical activities. I play ice hockey once a week, and when congregants found out, they were amazed. I went to the Boca Raton city hall to promote the building of a new ice skating facility here in town, and when a reporter found out that I play hockey, he thought it was so outrageous he wrote an article about it for the *Sun-Sentinel*. I was proud to see the headline, "Hockey-Playing Rabbi Heads Synagogue." It opens people's eyes to Jewish leaders who also take part in typically masculine activities such as ice hockey. It's a great release for me, and I truly enjoy the sport. I love the competition and the action. In fact, when I was calling some potential members to join the synagogue, they heard that I played, and we had a long conversation about hockey. As a result of this personal connection, they're now looking to join the temple community. As one of them stated, "I want a Rabbi I can relate to."

Our Brotherhood also sponsors a softball team in the local ecumenical men's league. We play all the different churches in town each Saturday evening. These are all men of faith, who come together for friendly competition. We begin each game with a short prayer, usually led by a clergy member, but if one is not present, one of the players steps forward and says a few words. It's usually about asking God to keep us safe and free from injury and allowing us to play competitive sports among fellow men. It's an excellent example of deeply committed religious individuals getting together to play spirited sports. The fact that our clergy also love to play simply shows that we are ready to get down and dirty and engage in athletic activity as one of the boys. Off the pulpit we can have colorful conversations in the dugout, whether relating to Judaism or simply life. There was one ballgame that had a short rain delay, and we were sitting in the dugout watching the drops fall and waiting to see if the game would continue or be called. Rabbi Dan Levin stood up and did a quick and fun analysis of the week's Torah portion and how it related to a rain-delayed softball game. It was a great moment, guys in their cleats and uniforms with their gloves on, talking a little Torah and then finishing up their game of softball.

A few weeks ago I went to see the movie *Borat: Cultural Learnings of America for Make Benefit Glorious Nation of Kazakhstan*. I saw it with two other rabbinic colleagues, not because we wanted to learn anything, but because we wanted a fun night out watching a hilarious movie. In the following weeks as more and more people saw it, jokes from the movie started filtering through the synagogue walls. This movie seemed to appeal mostly to men. The women we saw it with thought it had some funny moments; most of the men I talked to couldn't breathe, they were laughing so hard. The especially poignant scene of two hairy naked men wrestling through the lobby of a hotel sent me howling into a fit of giggles. With the guys at shul, we can chuckle together about the outrageous scenes. It's male humor—the quest to see Pamela Anderson, the potty humor, the drunken fraternity boys—and it's fun to see a Jewish comedian making the world laugh. There are also some lessons to be drawn from the movie, such as the anti-Semitic stereotypes in the movie that expose people's deeply held beliefs. Borat's bumbling sexist and homophobic persona disarms people into revealing some of their own sometimes close-minded attitudes. Using clips in my ninth grade high school class prompted some interesting discussions about Jewish humor, boundaries, and the danger that it might reinforce people's deeply held bigotry. The boys in the class were so excited to see Borat on the TV in religious school that they quickly brought their chairs to the front of the room and engaged in the discussion like I had never seen before. Sometimes allowing boys to be boys, to laugh and shout out movie lines and have fun, sets a masculine tone to religious studies and Jewish life that can be both inspiring and enticing.

That is what I hope to do—to channel my *zayde*'s passion and love for Judaism into the new modern Jewish man, who can play hockey, laugh at Borat, and yet engage in Torah and lead the Passover seder with wisdom, insight, and humor. That is the new Jewish man for the twenty-first century.

ON RABBIS, RUNNERS, AND RIVERS

Benjamin David

People wonder where the men are. For years, my Judaism consisted of following my father to the JCC gym on Sunday mornings, to houses of mourning on occasional weeknights, and to committee meetings before dinner, where my brothers and I would wait outside, and, depending on the mood, play our Game Boy, talk hockey, or ignore each other completely. As I remember it, each of these locales were teeming with men, men moments before a basketball game or just removed from a loved one's funeral, men perpetually introducing me to new expressions of manhood with their tears, their angst, their relief, their distinct laughter or silence. The world that was the Judaism of my youth, as I see it now, was populated to a tremendous extent by men.

In time, my brothers and I became men as well. One day we were pale-faced and unsure. The next day, or so it seemed, each one of us were married, motivated, and dependable. Before this ever happened, however, we were boys. We may have been the rabbi's boys, but we were boys nonetheless. And so, on weekends, it was not uncommon for our house to become something of a gathering spot for other boys far and wide. A football game could be organized in minutes. And it often was. Hoagies could be devoured in seconds. And they often were. Secrets carefully kept. Bonds forever tightened. We became accustomed to the cadence of this life. When everyone returns to my parents' house now, for Thanksgiving or seder, with each of us now beginning a family of our own, I see that this fraternity we quietly (or not so quietly) built in growing up, at the synagogue, at home, and at camp, is still strong, stronger than ever perhaps. Particularly now, it provides in such important ways. Once upon a time it granted security and rhythm in a world sometimes without these entities. Now it allows us to bring to our own burgeoning families an understanding of terms such as "partnership" and "care." Between watching my father provide for others and establishing true camaraderie with my brothers and our friends, I would like to think that I know what it means to be a partner. I know what it means to care. At long last I may even know what it means to be an adult member of our own Jewish community: sensitive, patient, compassionate, endlessly committed to the community itself.

I have indeed brought each of these lessons not only to my family, but to my rabbinate. I bring to my synagogue days now those earlier days not only within my house and the religious school, but amidst the football games and hiking trips and young summers away at places such as Camp Harlam and Israel. All these years later I suddenly find myself not on the outside, but inside the committee meetings, inside the houses of mourning, part of the JCC basketball games I once only watched with eyes wide and curious. These places once seemed so foreign to me, so grown-up, so wonderfully layered as I observed from the side. I sensed this complexity then. I truly realize and appreciate it now.

I would like to think that my rabbinate consists to a great extent of attempting to help others precisely because of these early moments, these early encounters that I will always carry with me. Alongside my father I witnessed loss and struggle and celebration. Now I devote my time to helping others as they negotiate loss and struggle. I help them to contextualize celebration. I help them as I have been helped, teach them as I have been taught. Those who have taught me, these many models and guides, my father and others, I sometimes wonder what they have in common. How is it that each of them reached me? Maybe it is because they had all claimed their own unique sense of Torah from the paneling of history, bringing the words of our tradition into their relationships, their moments of struggle, their moments of introspection and celebration. Maybe it is because I saw with my own eyes how they crafted an earnest Reform Judaism that speaks so directly to those same ideas that speak so directly to me, a Judaism that calls us to be sons, grandsons, brothers, friends, husbands, fathers, students, teachers in every sense.

As much as I may teach or guide, however, I know well that my days primarily consist of learning. If there is any one shared lesson taught by these various mentors, from my father to my grandparents to my many colleagues, it is that we are a community of learners. We are blessed with opportunities to learn. New perspectives on Judaism. New perspectives on fortitude and survival and scholarship. The idea that mitzvot indeed come in various shapes and sizes. I believe more and more that we can bring our own unique self, a male self, the sense of fatherhood or brotherhood, the sense of story, to our Judaism and to our Jewish community, just as our ancestors brought their unique selves to the Tabernacle so many years ago.

To this end, a colleague and I recently founded RunningRabbis.com, an initiative based on the idea that each of us should run to find our own mitzvot. After all, Judaism has never been about complacency! As Ben Azzai teaches in *Pirkei Avot*: "Run to do the least of the commandments as you would to do the most important" (4:2). Indeed we must actively seek out those Jewish ideas and practices that speak directly to us, specific causes and ideals we are ready to make our own, whether it be creative worship or Hebrew literature or Israeli history or Jewish yoga. As for us, we're literally running, and we're doing so for the sake of social action. (Yes, rabbis can run). Our group has grown. We've run multiple marathons together and raised thousands for local community groups, particularly those that work to improve the lives of children. The Running Rabbis, by simply bringing others together for Sunday morning 5Ks in the name of causes ranging from breast cancer research to the support of inner-city youth, have helped remind people that Judaism can happen and mitzvot can happen just about anywhere—in the synagogue, in Central Park, at your local diner, in your living room, at the soccer field, at the office, at the beach, or while driving carpool. Whether at evening jogs or full marathons, we find ourselves surrounded by community, our own Running Rabbis team. As a community, a congregation of sorts, we run not only for our own well-being, but for the sake of other communities, children we may never meet, patients we may never meet, the needy, the homeless, those whose lives we hope to improve by virtue of our own actions on this day, now, together. To me this is social action with a capital "A."

Perhaps all of this is a male idea, perhaps not. I will say that in 2006, of the 397,000 individuals who completed a marathon, over 61 percent were male. Of the 37,869 people who finished the New York City Marathon last year, 25,548 were male. People wonder where the men are. If we are out running, biking, golfing, or fishing, then why not do so as Ben Azzai advised, for the sake of the commandments? Why not bring our words, as husbands and partners, sons and colleagues, learners and teachers, as bearers of story and carriers of experience, to the words that are our tradition?

The Talmud's (Tractate *Chulin* 7a) teaches that every river flows in its own direction. Because I grew up in a household where different modes of creativity were valued, different senses of humor were valued, and different brands of expression were valued, I now appreciate the fact that we as a broader people have thrived and will continue to thrive because each of us brings to this, our peoplehood, a sense of the unique. Community only grows stronger as a result of diversity. Who we are, or more importantly who we can be, as learners, as parents, as fathers and sons, only grows stronger as a result of this diversity, this distinct sense of narrative each of us carries about the community and shares with one another. The very notion of brotherhood, as I found in my house and continue to find in the broader house that is Reform Judaism, is that it also grows stronger as a result of our miscellaneous stories. I also know that these many rivers, all of these rivers, rivers of personality and justice and learning and commitment and heritage, in the end they lead to a vast and deep sea of holiness.

FINDING MY WAY AS A JEWISH MAN

Charlie Niederman

My own family offered few if any Jewish male role models. My father never taught us anything about Judaism beyond a few Bible stories, nor did he talk much about what, if any, religious education he received. He emigrated from Hungary with his family when he was a boy, and his father, after owning a series of small businesses, settled on pig farming. My mother, born in the United States to recent German Jewish immigrants, had, among her nine siblings, only three brothers who were observant Jews, and only one had a close relationship with our family. She despised organized religion but was an unqualified supporter of Israel, primarily, I think, for its then socialist values. We did observe Chanukah, knew what Rosh HaShanah and Yom Kippur were about, and each Passover had at least one seder from the Manischewitz Haggadah. We lived in rural eastern Connecticut, and the rationing of gasoline during World War II left us fairly isolated until I was about twelve. Then we, my younger brother and sister and I, had a three- or four-session encounter with religious school arranged by my father at the Orthodox shul about twelve miles away. The man assigned to teaching us, who were so far behind the others, made no secret of his disdain. But I do have good memories of touch football at recess.

My next Jewish experience was as a cadet for four years at the Coast Guard Academy. The cadet corps of approximately five hundred averaged about a dozen Jewish cadets. Saturday was a day of room inspections, close order drill, and parades, before liberty was granted in the afternoon. That left us as Jews to find religion on Sundays. We could get out at eight in the morning for church liberty instead of waiting for regular liberty at ten, so for years Jewish cadets were allowed to sit in on bar mitzvah class and rehearsals at the local Conservative synagogue. This became my first formal religious schooling—mostly skipping the *alef-bet* and learning the morning prayers by rote. Later, as an officer, I attended some High Holy Day services at military chapels when ashore.

My first personal religious education came when my future wife felt it was important that she convert to Judaism. After the discouragement that most would-be converts encountered forty years ago, she and I were directed to a Reform rabbi who had recently served as a navy chaplain. He insisted that we take the conversion course together as a couple. It was the first time that I felt completely comfortable with my religion. It was an intellectual exercise more than a spiritual one and also a cultural journey for my wife. Much later, a decade ago, we studied together for our adult bar and bat mitzvah ceremonies.

The Judaism we experienced in our own family has been egalitarian, especially so since we had four daughters and no sons. Support of equality for women has been important to me throughout my life. Over the last forty years I have welcomed the rise of women in Reform Judaism. In Judaism, as in other spheres, sharing power and leadership with women never seemed to be a threat. One of our daughters even became a Jewish educator. As men now absent themselves from Reform Judaism and most other religions, the issue seems to be far more related to us as men than to the rise of women.

Being a Reform Jewish man suits me. There is fulfillment in being part of a movement that accepts a broad spectrum of religious belief, feels strongly about social justice and humanitarian causes, and welcomes those who wish to be part of its Jewish community. As our family moved around the country during my coast guard career, we joined four different congregations, our current one for the second time. I have had seven male rabbi role models: young, old, scholarly, spiritual, and politically active. They differed in many ways but had in common a dedication to Torah and social justice and morality based on halachah. I see my own dedication to Judaism as more intellectual than spiritual. My beliefs are probably shaped more by rationalism than by spirituality. However, understanding Torah at deepening levels and appreciating Talmud and the process by which it has developed are important to me, as is Jewish history.

Certainly there is not much in my own background that is stereotypical, which leads me to question the validity of the stereotypical Jewish male. The stereotype often portrayed is the self-absorbed, emasculated intellectual made neurotic and vulnerable to domination by women by his "Jewish mother." However, this is generally invalidated merely by looking at the Jewish men around us.

For Ashkenazic Jews, the ideal male for centuries was the gentle, studious, and sensitive Talmud student. Although some of these ideal men may have had the means to support themselves, the economics of their society in the shtetl and beyond would dictate that they were a minority. There were far more Tevyes, the milkmen, butchers, and tailors, than rebbes. Most of us are descended from those who served in the farms, trades, and professions that made the society self-sufficient. The ideal did not predominate.

As American Jewish men, any of us may identify with some parts of the stereotype just as we might identify with the stereotypes of our profession or hobbies. The Jewish American stereotype has little applicability to Israel and probably does not predominate in other parts of the Diaspora. It also would be alien to most Jewish men prior to World War II. An example that applies here, although I more often use it to dispel prejudices based on sports stereotypes, is elaborated well by Jon Entine in his online article "Jewish Basketball Giants" (www.aish.com). Entine explains that during the 1920s and '30s the basketball scene in Philadelphia and beyond was dominated by the South Philadelphia Hebrew Association SPHAs. He quotes Paul Gallico, sports editor of the *New York Daily News* in the 1930s, who wrote, "The reason, I suspect, that basketball appeals to the Hebrew with his Oriental background is that the game places a premium on an alert, scheming mind, flashy trickiness, artful dodging and general smart aleckness." Entine adds, "Writers opined that Jews had an advantage in basketball because short men have better balance and more foot speed. They were also thought to have sharper eyes, which of course cut against the stereotype that Jewish men were myopic and had to wear glasses. But who says stereotypes have to be consistent?"

Jews also excelled in boxing, though often not under Jewish names. The popularity of sports with Jewish men in the first four decades of the twentieth century is based on sports as a vehicle to escape the poverty of the inner city. Today many Hispanic and African American boys in the same economic conditions aspire to the same goals, although their traditions and myths bear little similarity to those of Ashkenazic Jews.

American Jews, even those who claim to be ethnic and not religious Jews, are still influenced by the traditions and myths from our immigrant past that are passed from generation to generation. We are even more the product of our specific American Jewish experience. The Reform Jewish Movement itself owes its nineteenth-century origin to a uniquely American view of Jewish Enlightenment that originated in Germany and was spreading across Europe. As Reform Jewish men, if we are anything stereotypical, we are Jewish Americans living in an era of unprecedented acceptance.

In my dealings with other men, especially as a manager, it is important to me to encourage each to rise to his potential and in many cases exceed his own expectations. It applies to the Jewish men I try to influence. Teaching about masculinity and Judaism is often best done by example. Showing pride in Judaism and not allowing fear to govern how we live convey both Jewish and masculine values. Fairness and integrity are also masculine and Jewish values that are best conveyed by example. As Jews, there is a place too in our masculinity for compassion and dedication to family. Conveying these values to other Jewish men gives them the tools to examine the values in their own lives.

Struggling solely to dispel a stereotype that is overly inclusive is in many ways a vain effort. It can be more productive and time-honored to ponder, strive to understand, and live up to what was posed by Hillel (*Pirkei Avot* 1:14): "If I am not for myself, who will be for me? And if I am only for myself, what am I? And if not now, when?"

MY JOURNEY INTO JUDAISM AND FREEMASONRY

Michael Freedman

My Jewish education, like that of most young men of my era, began at home, continued through Hebrew and Sunday school, and was put on hold during my high school and college years. It was during this early period that the basic Jewish precepts of valuing education, giving charity, and repairing the world in which I resided were inculcated in my young impressionable mind. Although I was a willing, yet passive recipient of these values, it would not be until I was made a Freemason that I would actively practice these values and truly experience the joys that they bring.

I had watched my father dress in his best suit of clothes to go to the monthly Lodge meetings since I was a child and remembered vividly the time he was home recuperating from his heart attack when he was visited by a courtly, immaculately attired, mustachioed gentleman who brought a box of candy and the well wishes of his Masonic brethren. Thus, it was natural for me to approach my dad to sponsor me for Lodge membership once I was an adult and on my own. My father was my guide through my initiations into Freemasonry. As I was entered, passed, and raised through the three degrees and became a Master Mason, I was enthralled with the history and traditions of Freemasonry. There was so much to learn—art, architecture, history, and especially the allegories and symbolism that Masons derive from the Hebrew Bible.

The building of King Solomon's Temple at Jerusalem is central to the history and tradition of Freemasonry. In recounting the story of the Temple in its erection, with attention to the details of its construction, internal and external appointments, and the stories related to the architects and craftsmen who toiled with determination on this structure, Freemasonry enhanced my knowledge, understanding, and appreciation of the history of the Jews beyond the religious-based education of my youth. In addition, the tale of the building of the Temple was replete with inferences to architectural terms and features as well as the form and uses of the tools of ancient and present-day operative stonemasons. Indeed, the tools of the operative mason serve as allegorical symbols for the speculative Freemasons of today.

Speculative Freemasons promulgate the notion of making good men better men. In so doing, they imbue their fellow brethren with a sense of appreciation of art and architecture, the belief in a Supreme Being, and a strong connection to the egalitarian principles upon which the United States of America was founded. It may be assumed that the principles of liberty, equality, and fairness, as well as a commitment to help their fellow man, are what prompted our founding fathers to rebel against tyranny and were first learned in the Masonic Lodges to which many of them belonged.

The cementing of the bonds of fraternalism for the common good of all—a Masonic tenet—parallels the concept of repairing the world, or *tikkun olam*, as taught in the traditions of Judaism. Freemasonry teaches that for a Lodge to flourish, all private animosities, if any should exist within it, should give way to peace and good fellowship. Furthermore, brethren are admonished to promote the useful arts, to practice moral virtues, and to improve all that is good within the individual. Through Freemasonry, I found an avenue for applying this idea. By supporting Freemasonry in general and my Lodge in particular, I have been an integral part of an independent organization that fosters the original ideals that my fellow brethren in Freemasonry (George Washington, Benjamin Franklin, et al.) followed in order to found this great nation. Such men saw in Freemasonry that man was able to govern himself and to promote a free and empowering democratic lifestyle. With education, equality, and diligence, man was able to achieve his personal pursuit of happiness. Similarly, by practicing the teachings of Freemasonry and exemplifying the notion of equality within and without the Lodge room, I have been better able to pursue my profession, coexist with my neighbors, love and empower my family, and try to inculcate these values in my students. I saw Freemasonry as my set of tools with which to repair the world as it lay before me.

Tzedakah, or giving to others, another theme of Judaism, is also central to the tenets of Freemasonry. Organizationally, there are established Masonic charities that individual Masons and their Lodges support. These include homes for the elderly, support for orphans and at-risk youth, and the many hospitals and burn centers operated through the benevolence of the Shriners (an adjunct Masonic body). Charitable funds are an integral and legislated part of Masonic institutions and Lodges. However, charity, in the Masonic tradition, is not limited to monetary contributions. Concern for brethren in need, *chesed* in Judaism, includes caring, visiting, counseling, and supporting brethren in their hour of need. Such support is not made public, but offered with great circumspect and consideration for the brother. Interestingly, and unlike my experience with charity that is often associated with synagogues and many Jewish charitable organizations, the Masonic Lodge does not solicit charitable or other funds directly other than regular dues and initiation fees.

I was fortunate to have affiliated with a Masonic Lodge that boasts a large, active membership consisting of men of all ages, occupations, education, and backgrounds. A large contingent of these men are Jewish and, as such, have served and continue to serve as role models for me. They have taught me that in spite of their humble beginnings, Jewish men can be successful in life, well-respected members of society, and leaders in and out of the Lodge. I have learned to respect the wisdom and expertise that comes from experience and diligence rather than from privilege or diplomas. I have seen all men, but especially Jewish men, being treated as equals in the Lodge room regardless of their profession, religion, or social standing. Fine men in my Masonic Lodge expended the human capital that enabled me to become a better man and a leader.

My Masonic experiences have offered me an outlet through which I am able to routinely and daily apply the attributes of learning, giving, and helping that were taught and shown to me in my Jewish upbringing and education. I was fortunate to have been guided through both my Jewish and my Masonic experience by my late father, who was always the "wind beneath my wings." For sixteen wonderful years we, father and son, were brothers in the Lodge room and good friends forever. Both my Masonic and my Jewish education have contributed to a greater fulfillment for me as a man, a citizen, and a contributor to our society. They have kept me from growing old in spirit and from losing touch with younger people and people from various occupations, backgrounds, and beliefs. Both experiences have and continue to contribute to my intellectual and emotional welfare.

A LETTER TO MY SONS

Dana Jennings

Dear Drew and Owen:

In today's culture, we like to think we have shattered most taboos. We talk to our children about sex, about drugs, about mental illness. Still, strangely, I don't hear much talk between fathers and sons about God, about faith, about Torah, about what it means to be a Jewish man. As the two of you stand proudly at the brink of full adulthood, I want to start that conversation.

As a Jew-by-choice, I feel like the man who falls in love with a brilliant and beautiful woman who is taken for granted by those who have known her for a long time—think Cinderella with a *kipah*. I don't want either of you to ever take Judaism for granted. Though you may not understand it as such now, being a Jew is a gift. *An absolute gift.*

But it's a gift that too often is abandoned in the back of the spiritual attic. We're struggling through a time when Jewish men are vanishing of their own volition from our communities. It saddens me to watch them shun their birthright, letting it rot and grow brittle like the leather on their grandfathers' *tefillin*, treating Judaism as if it were an ethnic accessory to be shrugged on and off at will . . . as just another entrée in the cultural buffet, rather than what it truly is: a profound covenant with the God of Abraham, Isaac, and Jacob.

We are trapped in a culture that sends the message that men of faith are sissies; the man who prays with heart and soul is somehow suspect. Well, boys, I'm here to tell you that real men pray and sing and study and walk *humbly* with their God.

As a man who has been stunned wide awake by Judaism, by Torah, I want the two of you to know soul-deep that real Judaism can suffuse each moment of each day—if you let it. You need to understand that some mornings when I pray I feel barely tethered to this earth. You need to understand that when I read that 20th-century prophet Abraham Joshua Heschel, he almost always carries me back with him to Sinai. You need to understand that when I look at the Hebrew script of Torah, I don't see mere letters; I see the ancient, transcendent tents of Jacob billow and snap.

Sure, it can be frustrating to be a man of faith in this culture of hollow desire. It is easier to obsess over how the Knicks and Lakers are going to do this season. To ooh-and-aah over the latest sleek idols made by BMW and Porsche. To admire your very expensive pecs in the mirror. To buy your season tickets to the local synagogue, and only show up for the big games—you know, Yom Kippur and Rosh Hashanah, and maybe the occasional bar or bat mitzvah. I don't want you to become men who think that Sunday morning softball and dropping the kids off at Hebrew school—drive-by Judaism—is what makes a Jew.

We are slaves to the culture of the self. To get ahead, we are told to brag, to polish our images into a kind of Golden Calf. But, boys, we were not made to praise ourselves. We were made to praise *Adonai*, made to praise all Creation. We have to let Torah—that holy turpentine—strip the varnish of falseness from our souls. We have to admit—and this is hard—that our mewling, pathetic self is not why the universe exists. Only in humility can we be open to the awe that the Holy Breath should inspire. In the same way that the Eternal contracted to make room for Man, so Man must contract his ego to make room for the Eternal.

There are so many ways to avoid the big questions, to shun God, to lead a Teflon life. Drew and Owen, don't become one of those men who spurn our tradition to chase wind: the candy-apple-red Hummer, the third home in Aspen, the trophy wife. The goal is to be the opposite of wanting. It's your souls that matter in the Economy of Holiness.

Our people survived slavery in Egypt, the razing of the Temple, pogroms and persecutions beyond reckoning, the Holocaust. But I put this question to you, my sweet Jewish sons: Can we survive a future of Jewish fathers who buy a new suit, sheepishly show up as strangers on bar or bat mitzvah day, awkwardly pass the Torah on to a still-unformed 13-year old—and then never come back?

That very real image nearly makes me weep. I know some would write my deep feelings off as the zeal of a convert. But, boys, there's one last thing you need to understand: In this day and age, we're all Jews-by-choice.

THE LOVE OF THE HUNT

Mark Criden

Those who know me as a synagogue executive director with a background in law and investment banking think I'm all about money. These people would largely be right, but money qua money is never in my sights: I'm a hunter with a mission.

A hunter, of course, always has a mission. But while your garden-variety shark pursues the prosaic—putting food on the table or keeping the wolf from the door—my task is positively Talmudic. Like any organized religion, Judaism centers on the Divine: there is no food without Torah. But the Mishnaic Rabbis keenly understood God's balance: there is also no Torah without food. So while it is the Torah that puts Jews in the pews each week, those like me need to ensure there are pews. Our rabbis, cantors, educators, youth directors, and teachers bring us Torah. As the hunter, it's my duty—my mission—to provide the food.

What I hunt—the fruits of my labors—puts the "organized" in "organized religion." Religion without organization has no center, no home, and no house—whether of worship or books or assembly. Rootless religion is internal, dependent for survival and success on the hearts of each believer. Of course, this is too much to ask any individual to bear—to carry on the traditions, customs, and teaching of our forebears. It takes a village, a home, and a community—in short, a synagogue—to ensure that Judaism flourishes.

My beloved grandfather, the kosher butcher Abe Hoffman, taught me the importance of synagogue and schooled me in the business of hunting, too. His lessons were those passed down by hunters through the ages: be strong, be resolute, be straightforward, be direct, be prepared, be successful. Provide for the woman in your family and community. Disdain pussyfooting and bullshit and half-measures, he taught, channeling the Orthodox rebbes of his shtetl youth. This is what God demands of us; this is what it means to be a Jewish man.

No flies with honey for me.

These skills brought success in earlier careers. But then I became a Reform synagogue professional and discovered that members of our tribe are ambivalent about their hunters. It's not the delicateness of this balance between Torah and food that causes mixed emotions; it's the aggressive, primitive—and heavily phallocentric—nature of hunting itself. Sure, many of our greatest parables involve testosterone-heavy tales of money, resources, sacrifices, and territory: Moses leading his followers to better real estate, Abraham offering up the Isaac tax, Solomon's judicial brokerage. But for every admiration of David or Judah Maccabee, there's the counter-tale of Esau, the very paradigm of the rube, or Cain, the apotheosis of bad male behavior.

But bad or not, hunting is quintessential male behavior, and one that runs headlong into Reform Judaism's great tenet of inclusiveness. Generally, "inclusiveness" is like cabbage: you can fill it with anything you want. But this very flexibility creates two problems for me as a hunter. First, my value as a hunter—and, frankly, as a man—depends on my success, which turns on the sharpness of my spear. Classically, religion has proven a formidable whetstone. Traditional Judaism—my grandfather's Judaism—speaks with the force of the Bible and the expectation that we obey God's rules, where unquestioning belief, fidelity to ritual, and life lived according to commandment hone devotion and polish commitment. Reform Judaism, however, designed as it is to make Judaism more accessible, softens the Torah's blow, turning commandments to suggestions. While Orthodoxy contains the kernel of its own survival—halachah—Reform Judaism carries the seeds of entropy. Hebrew?

Optional. Kippot? Optional. Kosher? Optional. What to the Orthodox speaks of the Divine—building a temple, tithing—to the Reform Jew speaks of the proposal. An Orthodox rebbe can speak of a need, and the flock should follow, however grumbling. But when a Reform Rabbi speaks of a mitzvah as a commandment, the congregants, trained in the voluntary nature of their faith, are not forced to pay heed. To them, mitzvot equal good deeds, entirely and totally discretionary.

The challenge this poses—to make Reform Judaism so compelling, so magnetic, so overwhelming that its members will want to provide this elective support—is largely the province of our clergy and teachers, although as their hunter, I often ask whether our worship experience is absorbing, our community caring, our adult education classes captivating, and our cultural programs spellbinding. I remind them that excellence gets people to love a place, to support its mission, to provide its resources. Mediocrity sends the crowds to the door early and finds their charity at the SPCA instead of the shul.

The second problem is more personal and thus more difficult. As I look around the fields today, I see many female spear-carriers, as the bright line between male and female roles has dimmed in recent decades. Women are hunters, CEOs, and soldiers, and men are househusbands and nurses. To be a man today is to recognize and struggle with the male and female aspects of us all, the solar and lunar, the yang and the yin, the provider and the nurturer. The honored manly stoicism of my grandfather's generation is now deplored; to be a man today is to share feelings and to share roles. This complexity of choice, this very permission to explore all facets of our personalities, is at the very core of Reform Judaism.

I know it takes both X and Y chromosomes today to make Reform Judaism compelling and that sharks come in both male and female varieties. But—now again channeling my grandfather—I wonder what will ever overtake hardwired biological imperatives. While a woman without a spear is still a woman, and a man who doesn't bake cookies is still a man, the converse is not yet true. Society questions the femininity of the woman who refuses to cook and the masculinity of the man who won't hunt. So, while I hear the modern chorus coaxing me to get in touch with my feminine side, when I go to work, I have to man up. I have to don traditional male garb and hunt.

SEARCHING FOR MY BROTHERS: JEWISH MEN IN A GENTILE WORLD

Jeffrey K. Salkin

The Eternal Jew and His Paper Route

It was the summer of 1967—the summer after Israel's stunning victory in the Six-Day War. I remember a Catholic kid at the school lunch table, hearing about the swift Israeli victory, turning to me and saying, "Hey, you guys can really fight!"

On the Golan Heights, maybe. On the Suez Canal, maybe. But back in the middle of Long Island, I was not doing so well against a bunch of Catholic school–educated hoodlums. I had a job delivering newspapers, and the anti-Semitic toughs who hung out at the bottom of my street used to gang up on me.

In order to deliver my newspapers, I had to engage in various forms of subterfuge. I constructed an elaborate network of routes to deliver my papers. I would cut through people's backyards, tunnel through hedges, leave the newspapers at back doors. I would wait until my tormentors would go in for dinner, and then excuse myself from the dinner table and go out to my deliveries. I would then have to weather the complaints of my customers. They somehow thought that an afternoon newspaper should come to their doors, in fact, in the afternoon, and not in the early evening. I lost customers because of it. I was afraid to tell them what was wrong. Once or twice, my customers watched me being beaten up and tormented and found it rather funny. Once, I called the mother of one of the kids on the block, and, doing my best imitation of a woman's voice, tried to pass myself off as the mother of one of the bullies, asking that he be sent home for dinner. Oddly enough, it worked. That is, until the mother on the other end of the phone asked me how my (that is, the other mother's) job interview went. I hemmed and hawed. They actually knew each other! This was a possibility that I had never anticipated! I abruptly said to her, "I don't want to talk about it . . ." and hung up.

So, if one Jewish boy's life is a metaphor for anything, my experience that summer was a metaphor for Jewish history in exile. I was working as a classic middleman, selling goods. In doing so, I was beset by anti-Semites. I was tormented under the watchful and uncaring eyes of neighbors. I constructed elaborate routes of escape. I "suffered" economically due to my victimization. I had to resort to subterfuge and masquerade (over the telephone) in order to "survive." And that my telephone persona was that of a *gentile woman* is simply too funny and ironic even to analyze.

No American Jewish parent wanted a weakling for a son that summer. My father yelled at me: "Go out there and fight those kids!" The hidden translation: If they can do it in Gaza, you can do it on Long Island.

Luck smiled upon me. One day, I discovered that an Israeli teenager was living with a family in my neighborhood as an exchange student. This guy was right out of central casting—well tanned, a *kibbutz* hat, and sandals. As the hour for newspaper delivery would approach, I would sometimes go out on my bike and look for him. Sure, I wanted to hear all about Israel. But I was also hoping that he would hang out with me, walk my route with me, and, if necessary, defend me against my tormentors.

I was the Diaspora Jew who needed the Israeli Jew to defend me. If there had been a contest for poster boy to illustrate contemporary Zionist theory, I would have won.

"Go out there and fight those kids!" my father had yelled. I can still hear him. I could not have known back then that my experience had a particular parallel in the life of Sigmund Freud. In *The Interpretation of Dreams*, Freud writes about how the episodes of childhood often make their way, in well-concealed form, into adult dreams. Freud recalls an incident in his youth when he was ten years old. His father used to take him on walks and tell him that things were much better now than in the old days. The older Freud recalled that when he was a young man, he went for a walk one day with a new fur cap on his head. A Christian came up to him and knocked the cap in the mud and shouted: "Jew! Get off the pavement!" "What did you do?" Freud asked his father. "I went into the roadway and picked up my cap," the older man replied.

The elder Freud's behavior was guided by the way that Jews had lived their lives for centuries in Europe—through the pattern of docility and acquiescence. It is significant, therefore, that in adulthood, Sigmund Freud and Theodor Herzl, the founder of modern Zionism, lived on the same street in Vienna. For Herzl would come to reverse the elder Freud's need to step into the roadway to retrieve his hat.

Zionism as a Masculine Fantasy

Zionism is not *only* the nationalistic enterprise of the Jewish people. It also has a larger significance. Zionism is also a rebellion against the image of the emasculated Jew. It represents a break in the history of Jewish meekness and docility. For Jews, statelessness was the equivalent of frailty; to have a state was not only to come home geographically, but also to come home spiritually and psychically to a new understanding of Jewish strength.

Undestand how the fathers of Zionism transformed their movement into a masculine fantasy. Theodor Herzl had been a member of a dueling fraternity at the University of Vienna. Later, he would found his own Jewish fraternity at the univesity. It had one purpose—to show that Jews could brawl and drink just like any other people.

Herzl fantasized about dueling and defeating Austrian anti-Semites. A duel was not just a duel. Dueling was the symbol of masculine privilege and male honor in Europe. As the late historian George Mosse has written, to duel meant having the same social status as your adversary. As with today's ghetto toughs who will fight if they believe that they have been "dissed," one of the most frequent causes of dueling was the denial of one's due respect. The worst thing was to be called a coward. The dueling scar was a badge of honor. The duel was an accepted part of the lives of military officers, students, politicans, and businessmen—as well as Jews, who used it to disprove the cowardly stereotype of the Jewish man.

That stereotype had gained new power in the aftermath of the infamous Kishinev pogroms, initiated and organized by the local and central authorities, during Easter on April 6–7, 1903. Forty-nine Jews lost their lives and more than five hundred were injured; seven hundred houses were looted and destroyed and six hundred businesses and shops were looted.

In his famous poem, "In the City of Slaughter," the great modern Hebrew poet Hayim Haman Bialik eulogized the victims of Kisinev. He described the "lecherous rabble" raping Jewish women. And yet,

> . . . Note also, do not fail to note,
> In that dark corner, and behind that cask
> Crouched husbands, bridegrooms, brothers, peering from the
>   cracks,
> Watching the sacred bodies struggling underneath
> The bestial breath,
> Stifled in filth, and swallowing their blood!
> Watching from the darkness and its mesh
> The lecherous rabble portioning for booty
> Their kindred and their flesh!
> Crushed in their shame, they saw it all;
> They did not stir nor move;
> They did not pluck their eyes out; they
> Beat not their brains against the wall!
> Perhaps, perhaps, each watcher had it in his heart to pray:
> "A miracle, O Lord—and spare my skin this day!" . . .
> The *kohanim* sallied forth, to the Rabbi's house they flitted:
> "Tell me, O Rabbi, tell, is my own wife permitted?"

Bialik sneered at pious Jews who could not defend their women. He mocked those Jews who could only hope for a miracle and would emerge from refuge to ask whether their wives were now permitted to them. The wives of *kohanim*, descendants of the ancient priesthood, could not have sexual relations with their husbands if they had been raped. Tragic questions like this would arise after the Holocaust, when Jewish men found that their wives had been drafted into service in the brothels of the SS. Reb Ephraim Oshry, an authoritative decider of post-Holocaust questions of

Jewish practice, indeed permitted husbands to resume relations with their defiled wives.

Bialik futher lamented how

> . . . The heirs
> Of Hasmoneans lay, with trembling knees,
> Concealed and cowering—the sons of the Maccabees! . . .
> It was the flight of mice they fled,
> The scurrying of roaches was their flight. . . .

Oy, the poet would ask himself, how is it possible that the descendants of "real men," the Hasmoneans who were descended from the Maccabees, could not fight back? These are Jewish men? Recall that when cartoonist Art Spiegelman drew his famous comic book series *Maus*, the story of his father's experiences in the Holocaust, he chose to depict the Jews as mice. Bialik's poem became a clarion call against Jewish oppression. It sparked political Zionism. Never again would Jewish men—or Jews in general—be passive.

In an odd way, Zionism was a kind of Jewish self-hatred. Jews actually imported anti-Semitic stereotypes from the general culture. In 1898, the Zionist thinker Max Nordau distinguished between the coffee-house Jew and the muscle Jew, and proclaimed that muscular Jews would replace the weak, effeminate Jews of the Diaspora *shtetls*. The new Jews were to be "deep-chested, sturdy, sharp-eyed Jews." As historian David Biale noted, the early Zionist congresses published postcards with illustrations that contrasted the virile young farmers of Palestine with old, frail Orthodox Jews in the European Diaspora. Nordau would propose a physical education program for Jewish youth—a program that would build new Jewish bodies to house the new Jewish spirit.

The lionization of the new Jewish man had its ramifications in the early Zionist movement. The early Zionists freely spoke of *muskeljudentum*, muscular Judaism. They believed in revitalizing Jewish manhood. Such a masculine emphasis impeded Jewish women's involvement in Zionism on an equal basis with men. It took an assertive Hadassah movement to trumpet the notion that Jewish women had an equal role in the building of Jewish nationalism.

It also had its effects on early Zionism education. When the early Zionists confronted the totality of the inherited Jewish past, they made choices as to what literary and spiritual areas would be emphasized in the newly settled Land of Israel. In the process, they exalted aggadah, Jewish lore and legend, over halacha, Jewish law. Why? They associated halacha with Eastern European yeshivot, with the ghetto, with weakness, and with pale-faced Talmud students who, let it be recalled from Bialik's poem "In the City of Slaughter," could only ask halachic questions and could not defend their own women. Aggadah, lore, was romantic and inspirational; halacha was the worship of a dead system.

A New Jewish History

Modern Zionism would create a new way of reading Jewish history. The Zionists saw Jewish history as a three-act play. Act One was Jewish history in antiquity. This was a positive time, the period of the Hebrew Bible, an era of national power. Zionism loved biblical heroes such as Samson, Saul, and David, because they were men of power. Zionism loved the Maccabees, and borrowed their name for the Maccabiah Games, the international Jewish athletic competition that would prove that Jews use their bodies and not just their minds. In Zionist curricula, the Maccabean revolution became the paradigm of a Jewish national liberation movement.

Act Two was *galut*, exile. That act began on the ninth day of the Hebrew month of Av, in the year 70 C.E., when the Temple in Jerusalem was destroyed. *Galut* Judaism was a religion of passivity. The Psalmist had proclaimed that "God neither slumbers nor sleeps." Zionists read that verse and laughed. God had been sleeping all along! And so, instead of applying the text to God, they applied it to Zionist defense organizations. The Hebrew terms of the Bible took on new meaning. When Israel developed its own machine gun, it was named the Uzi, "my power." It is an interesting name for a gun. When the term *uzi* is used in the Hebrew Bible, it always refers to God. God is *uzi*, "my power." No longer. Don't rely on God. Build guns. Prayer won't help you.

Zionists saw exile as bodily pollution or physical disease. Vladimir Jabotinsky was the revisionist Zionist who was the intellectual *zeyde*, grandfather, of Menachem Begin, Benjamin Netanyahu, and Meir Kahane. He founded the militant Betar movement, named for the fallen stronghold of the messianic pretender, Bar Kochba. Jabotinsky often juxtaposed the Yiddish-speaking "Yid" of Europe with the Hebrew-speaking "Hebrew" of the Land of Israel: "The Yid is ugly and sickly; the Hebrew has masculine beauty. The Yid is easily frightened; the Hebrew ought to be proud and independent." Jabotinsky admired masculine power so much that his youth organization smelled slightly of fascist youth organizations in Europe. Ironically, German Jewish youth organizations in the 1930s borrowed, ever so slightly and even subconsciously, from German youth organizations of the same period.

Act Three was the homecoming to the Land of Israel. To make *aliyah*, the emigration to Israel, was to undergo nothing less than a masculine transformation. The great Israel poet Uri Zvi Greenberg would write of "masculinity rising in the climate of the land of the prophets / And I was born in Poland a soft child of Judaism and my father's oldest son."

In *galut*, the text for study was Talmud. In Israel, the text for study would be the land itself—its flora and fauna. There, *tiyul haaretz*, touring the land, would replace rabbinical literature as a subject of intense intellectual scrutiny. And if there was going to be any kind of traditional text study, it would be the Hebrew Bible. The Hebrew Bible was the text of national power, written for the most part by ancient Israelites who had their own kingdoms. The Jews of the modern Land of Israel were no longer "Jews." That term was for Europeans. The Bible never called its characters "Jews." The new Jews would be powerful biblical "Hebrews" once again.

In the words of the old Zionist song *"Anu Banu Artz"*: "We have come to the land, to build *and to be rebuilt by it*."

JEWISH MUSIC, JEWISH MEN

Matthew Stern

During the summer of 2006 I attended Hava Nashira, an annual convention of Jewish musicians from around the country, at URJ Camp OSRUI in Oconomowoc, Wisconsin. For almost a week, I toted my guitar around the camp to various workshops and sessions at which the greats, such as Dan Nichols, Debbie Friedman, and Jeff Klepper, shared some of their insights regarding Jewish music. My attendance at this convention prepared me for a rewarding summer of song leading at URJ Camp Harlam in Kunkletown, Pennsylvania. At URJ camps across the country, "song leading" describes a kind of music director–like position at a summer camp. Song leaders stand in front of the camp community daily at meals and services and during programs, usually with their trusty guitar, and attempt to create a meaningful musical and Jewish experience for the participating campers. From personal experience, I can tell you that this is much easier said than done.

At Hava Nashira, I participated in the URJ Camp Song Leading track, where a group of mostly college-age students worked with Dan Nichols and Cantor Rosalie Will-Boxt to prepare for a challenging summer of music. The sessions were partly discussion about various aspects of song-leading technique and partly demonstration and critique. The group of song leaders consisted mostly of men, which was notable, but not necessarily surprising. As the week unfolded it was interesting to see how this particular phenomenon would affect the nature of camp song leading across the country in the coming summer.

In one of the demonstrations that took place over the week, an all-male group of song leaders used their ample supply of testosterone to their benefit. From the initial shocking strum of the seven guitars that formed a circle, everyone in the room instantly understood that we were about to take part in a powerful musical experience. After about ten minutes of red faces, popping veins, stamping feet, and borderline-intimidating eyes, the entire group—song leaders and song session participants—practically collapsed, hyperventilating and sweaty as a result of singing four traditional Jewish songs with intense spirit. The seemingly brute male force that the song leaders had presented affected the entire mixed-gender group. In my experiences at summer camp, if campers are similarly captivated at the end of a *Shabbes* song session, I have successfully completed my job. Needless to say, Dan and Rose beamed during their critique of the group of song leaders. It was even pointed out in the evaluation of the all-male group that their abundance of testosterone impacted very positively on the song session.

While some people see a dearth of men's involvement in Judaism, the song leader position does not follow this trend. At Hava Nashira '06, roughly 65 to 75 percent of the URJ Camp Song Leading track was composed of men. One camp, as mentioned before, had a staff of seven male song-leaders, and no females. Similarly, at URJ Camp Harlam '05, the song-leading staff was composed of four men. The following summer, there were six male song leaders and two female song leaders. Don't get me wrong. I don't have anything against female song leaders. I believe that they are perfectly capable of exercising their role, as the all-female song-leading staff at URJ Camp Harlam aptly proved in the summers of '02, '03, and '04. So, if female song leaders can get the job done, why is there such a predominantly male song-leading community in the Reform Movement today? Perhaps a certain degree of manliness contributes to the effectiveness of Jewish music.

In taking a look at Jewish music on the whole, there are certain generalizations that can be made. The history of the Jewish people, wrought with hardships, persecution, and estrangement, demands a culture that can make the Jewish people internally strong. In times of plight and difficulty, the Jews had to do their best to stay together and build off of each others' energy. Jewish music, one of the many emblems of Jewish culture, must reflect this. The passion involved in the fervent prayers of a Chasidic community, the emotional tears of visitors to the Western Wall, and the enthusiastic celebrations occurring at Jewish summer camps across the United States on Shabbat evening during song session all illustrate the essential unity that Jewish culture provides. All of these examples of Jewish music can be characterized by zeal, sweat, enthusiasm, and, perhaps, testosterone.

It makes perfect sense that the leaders of Jewish camp music in America are predominantly male, because they are communicating a culture that lends itself to masculinity. For thousands of campers across America, *ruach* has been translated into jumping up and down; the Sabbath bride is welcomed with clapping hands, strong strumming of guitars, and notes that are too high to be sung without turning red. The Jewish community has come to understand all of these crucial and tangible symbols of Judaism and spirituality in a masculine light. Suddenly, Jewish male energy is something that is important, real, and ultimately essential for the continuity of Jewish culture. Jewish males can provide the *ruach* that the culture demands.

Interestingly enough, at Camp Harlam, the song leaders seem to embody one of the few central displays of strong Jewish identity. Since so much of Jewish music harkens to Hebrew, Torah, Talmud, and values, the two tend to become one in a camp setting. So, at camp, I find myself attempting to embody strong male identity and strong Jewish identity in order to meet the terms of my contract. I would always be *that* counselor who got excited about *shiur* (a daily period of Jewish learning). I find myself to be one of the few members of the community who dons a tallit for services on Saturday morning. In addition, I don't know many counselors other than myself who spend all of Shabbat wearing a *kippah*. Is it an accident that the evening staff activity of studying Talmud once in a while was attended by six people, four of whom were song leaders, in the summer of '05?

This same group of strong Jewish role models then stands in front of five hundred children after dinner on Friday nights with guitars and headset microphones, almost looking like rock stars. The camp sits and sings *Birkat Hamazon* (Blessing after Meals) together in anticipation of the thirty to forty-five minutes of raging excitement that is about to ensue. After the last "amen" is stated, the benches immediately go up on the tables to allow more room for dancing and roaming around, and the entire camp begins singing together joyously. Some groups are doing choreographed dances together, jumping and spinning in circles, while others just bang on tables and laugh with each other. The energy in the room increases, sweat accrues, my voice regularly gets shot, and the camp loves it.

This past semester, I learned, for the first time, about gender norms and their importance throughout history. One of the most prominent ideas in the course I took was that the ideal male American Jew is a feminized ideal. Rather than being strong, athletic, and stubborn, most of the males in the American Jewish community are gentle, cerebral, and sensitive. Take a look, for example, at the culture of American Jewish women who swoon for Jon Stewart of *The Daily Show*. Similarly, Tony Curtis is considered extremely attractive by the average Jewish grandmother of today. Neither of these celebrities are appealing because of their looks, but more because of charming, suave personas and obvious intelligence. Perhaps camp song leading, as a part of the Reform Movement, is subconsciously attempting to avoid this stereotype by infusing song sessions with sweat, volume, and ultimately, testosterone, something that is not generally considered attractive in the Jewish community.

I know that my role as a college-age, male religious school teacher is one that is invaluable to the education team at my synagogue of employment. As a male, I will be able to connect with some of my male students in a way that a female teacher simply could not. In 2004, I was sought out as a one-on-one Hebrew tutor for a male student primarily on the basis that I was male. Jewish male youngsters simply lack ways to identify with an institution that has become predominantly female in the course of Americanization, and thus the Reform synagogue is struggling to find ways to appeal to them. I don't believe it's necessarily an accident that eleven out of sixteen students in my Hebrew school class are male. In an environment of forced attendance, lots of Jewish males are placed in the classroom with the male teacher, in the hope that they will open up to their religious education, and to the institution as a whole. Male participation goes down once the requirement to attend is taken away, though. It cannot be a coincidence that there were only two male bunks in the ten- to eleven-yearold unit at camp during second session '06, while there were four female cabins. The concentration of males in the song-leading staff serves to work against this and successfully promote Jewish values in the masculine light that the Reform Movement idealizes.

I feel important and significant as a Jewish male in the Reform community, in the same way that I would hope every Jewish male in the Reform community would feel. Any Reform Jewish male who is committed to the Jewish faith or can at least identify with it on some level has the unique opportunity to aid in the "re-masculinizing" of Reform Judaism in America. Simply by reaching out to Jewish youth and being a role model for Jewish young men, we can help broaden Reform Judaism to encompass and appeal to everyone. I see this working on some levels already, especially at Camp Harlam, where having male staff is so essential to the culture of the camp. As Jewish men, we are able to be role models for youth, who will be able to do the same when it becomes their turn to take the lead. Hopefully, the future holds a Judaism that's cool enough for ten-year-old boys not only during song sessions, but also in worship, study, and action, where it truly matters.

TEEN BROTHERHOOD

Jason Freedman and Bobby Harris

Twelve high school Jewish guys gather in a room at a NFTY (North American Federation of Temple Youth) conclave and talk about their fears, regrets, and aspirations. One teen speaks about his struggles to stay in school and how badly he wants to lead a normal life. Another reveals his secret—he's shy and desperately wants to fit in. Another talks about how much he misses his brother who passed away a few years before. Many of them have never even met each other before. Yet they're staring deeply into each others' eyes, unafraid of judgment and eager to support one another.

Eighty male camp staffers arrive at camp for a week of orientation. Twenty-four hours later they're having a discussion around the campfire: "When did I first start to feel like I was becoming a man?" Four peer leaders start the conversation, "stepping up" to share their personal stories—the only other sound is the crackling of the fire. The eighty young men then break out into smaller groups, where everyone can share his own story—and by the time the groups rejoin, the counselors have their arms round each other—connected male energy. They no longer care about being "cool." In fact, they've redefined "cool" in terms of "brotherhood"—the overwhelming sense of men's acceptance and community.

Having run the young male bonding program at temple youth group conclaves and Reform camps six times as part of a "separate gender" program, we now know that it *is* possible to create an environment that enables young men to express what's really going on in their lives. In our American culture, confiding our inner thoughts may be perceived as unmasculine, but our camps and youth groups can become places where young men feel safe enough to talk about their troubles, apprehensions, and regrets, sometimes for the first time. They perceive their overworked and overstressed parents as too immersed in their own concerns, and fear that sharing their vulnerabilities with friends might result in a backlash of ridicule.

Given this reluctance, the key to successful young adult discussion programming is establishing a social climate in which it's okay for teens to reveal their doubts and personal weaknesses. To create the environment, we enlist peer leaders who have the maturity, charisma, and credibility to demonstrate to the group how to be real, open, and vulnerable. They join us in a pre-program discussion based on Jewish texts. Sometimes we use the biblical story of how King David acted immorally by impregnating Bath-sheba—a married woman—and then conspiring to have her husband killed in battle. In the end, David is punished for his sin. This affords us the opportunity to discuss the most distressing regrets in our own lives, and what we'd do differently if given another chance. Other times we use the Hillel quote in *Pirke Avot*—"In a place where there are no men, try to be one"—to examine such questions as: "Where am I on my path toward becoming a man?" and "What was my defining moment when I realized where I was on my path?" We also talk with the peer leaders about how difficult it is for guys to be open with each other, and explain that they'll play a special part in the program because they're perceived by others as role models. After the orientation, we say, just as you've been able to be open, supportive, and trusting of one another in this small group, you'll be able to model openness, support, and trust in the large group.

It's program time. We choose the King David story. The large group is asked the questions previously asked of their peer leaders. Everyone is silent. All of a sudden one of the peer leaders stands up to answer. He's been preparing himself since our pre-program discussion, but he's still visibly nervous. In emotional tones he tells the group about the time he cheated on his best friend and how much he regrets it. There's no preaching about cheating, morality, etc.—he just ends by saying what he would do if his friend gives him a second chance. The other group leaders follow, sharing equally powerful stories.

Just a few minutes ago the teens were hanging out and playing ultimate Frisbee, but now there's a new energy in the room. The young men are amazed by the raw honesty, impressed by the risk their peers have taken in sharing their stories.

The larger group is now divided into smaller group sessions where each person can share his story. The emotional floodgates open. Two hours fly by as they speak candidly about their lives with unprecedented intensity.

Afterwards we regroup and finish the King David story. We talk about how David repented and all the great things he did with his second chance—and what it means to leave a legacy. King David left us his passion for music and prayer. The psalm we sing before the *Amidah* is David's way of saying that he wants to overcome his own selfish needs and trusts God to "open up his lips in praise." We talk about Gandhi's quote, "Be the change you want to see in the world," and how it applies to us. And we acknowledge how different and good it feels to overcome inhibitions and "be real" with others. We suggest that everyone continue to look beyond his inhibitions and join us in song.

Slowly we join in a friendship circle and sing "A *na na na na . . . Adonai. . . .*" The awareness is palpable—we're in the midst of a life-altering experience.

Later, one camp counselor reveals that this program has "changed the way I live my life. I realize that . . . put[ting] people down [to] get a laugh . . . I don't have to do it anymore . . . the laugh that I get is not worth the hurt that I could cause to that person: . . . I [am now] more sensitive to that. It's weird, even talking about it now and hearing me say that that one program really changed me . . . but I can't deny it, it's true . . . it really did!"

Our young men may not show it, but they're asking to be engaged in Jewish life. They deserve safe Jewish environments where they can be themsleves. And when they experience the joy of being themselves, they will always want to return.

A FUNNY THING HAPPENED
ON THE WAY FROM THE MOSH PIT

David Bergman

When I was in high school, I was an angry young man. I was interested in a wide range of music, from jazz to alternative, and had a mild affinity for punk rock music. Although I rarely had the money or the inclination to do so, one night I went to a punk concert and had an amazing experience doing things I'd hardly thought possible. At this concert, with its incredibly loud, syncopated music, I joined a mosh pit—a swirling mass of (mostly) other angry young men bouncing in time with the music, hurling and slamming our bodies into each other with incredible force. I even mounted the stage, saluted the musicians, and leapt—in a glorious stage dive—into the waiting arms of my comrades.

The mosh pit was largely self-selective—only men (though there could have been a small number of women, I don't recall any from my experience) who were so inclined joined this odd dance that was unquestionably violent, but utterly devoid of malice. That night I experienced something I had only witnessed in anthropology documentaries: a kind of out-of-body ecstasy brought on through wild, raging dance. I was completely sober (a claim I could not make for my comrades), yet the combination of the music and the dance made for something truly incredible.

And a funny thing happened on the way *from* the mosh pit: I found myself talking to my male friends about what had occurred and how I experienced it. In doing so, we deepened our connection not just to the experience itself, but to each other. Any prior knowledge I had about such experiences was irrelevant. I didn't need to know about the ritual to feel its power—I *did* the ritual and I *felt* its power. The knowledge came through the doing and provided the toehold for further exploration and conversation with my friends.

Dancing a hora is not so dissimilar—with one major difference: I don't experience the same ecstatic state when doing so with a large number of women. As a man, an *inclusive* hora is inherently unsatisfying because it requires restraint—the way I am inclined to dance is too violent, not communal enough, not sensitive enough, too aggressive. And yet, *exclusive* (that is, male-only) horas exhibit the very same quality of wild abandon that is characteristic of the mosh pit.

Most of my male Jewish contemporaries do not have and have never had these kinds of experiences in a Jewish, let alone a punk rock, context. To begin with, most of my contemporaries are functionally illiterate Jews, who can scarcely name the five books of the Torah, let alone describe the components and order of a worship service. It is thus no surprise that these factors, in turn, have led to a gender-biased disenfranchisement from Jewish rituals. And the distance from rituals, I believe, is a contributing factor to the breakdown in civic cohesion among men, which further undermines efforts to bring Jewish men together in a religious context.

I am certainly not the first to note the low level of Jewish literacy among my contemporaries—both male and female. It is suggested by the Jewish Population Survey and is posited, in part, as the impetus for Rabbi Joseph Telushkin's *Jewish Literacy*.[1] *Why* this has occurred is less important than *that* it has occurred, though I think it is closely tied to the fading importance of the Holocaust, moral ambivalence about Israel, and our position, largely, as third-generation American Jews increasingly removed from the tight-knit communities of the "old country."

Men's disconnect from Judaism is also a manifestation of liberal Judaism's ambivalent relationship with ritual. Firstly, liberal Judaism tends to perceive traditional Judaism as antediluvian, misogynistic, and oppressive of individuals and individuality. At the same time, many of the observable affectations of traditional Judaism (around which there are great rituals)—*kippot*, tallit, tzitzit, and *t'fillin*—are traditionally donned by males. Thus, liberal Judaism discourages men from observing these rituals because doing so would be a tacit approval of the outdated, misogynistic, and oppressive elements of traditional Judaism. While women are free to adopt the rituals associated with these items (as an act of gender empowerment), men are similarly encouraged to discard these rituals, thus refusing to participate in the oppression of women.

This, too, is derived from the values we express in our civic lives. After all, Thurgood Marshall rightfully argued in *Brown v. Board of Education* (1954) that separate cannot be equal. And if separate is inherently unequal for African Americans and whites, then it stands to reason that separate is similarly unequal for men and women. Jewish men, like white people, therefore have a special obligation to ensure an equitable distribution of power and authority. What exactly this means, however, is just one of the many challenges facing contemporary Judaism.

Additionally, women devalued their traditional role in Judaism, while elevating the role of men. This was an almost wholesale adoption of the male-normative Jewish experience. In liberal Jewish circles, the result was that women were *free to adopt* the tallit, yarmulke, and *tfillin* (and the rituals associated with them)—the very same cumbersome rituals men were newly free from. As time went on, the connection from man to man and father to son became virtually devoid of Jewish ritual content.

And going back to the mosh pit, I am struck by the value and the power of rituals, but particularly Jewish ones. I am amazed at how well Jewish rituals bind people together with common experiences and how effectively they can provide the toeholds that lead to deeper knowledge and the space through which men can have meaningful interactions with other men. Ritual practices—much like the elaborate ritual of the Passover seder—function as pedagogic tools and offer a multitude of opportunities for deeper exploration. Jewish rituals bring together fathers and sons, teachers and students, veterans, neophytes, and peers, in incredibly meaningful ways. Ritual is not a panacea. And it *can* become unfeeling and cold. But we must not discount how critical it can be for communication and transmission of our traditions and ethics across generations, as well as within them.

I believe that men have lost something in Judaism, or rather, that we have forgotten what we once knew. Ultimately, the greater inclusion of women in Jewish practices has made for richer traditions. Men *can* learn from women . . . and we do. But we can't learn everything from women. Men *can* experience things with women . . . and we do; but we can't experience everything with women. But while men—at least men of my generation—don't have a problem talking to women, we *do* have a problem talking to other men. And here again, I am struck by the simple and powerful role that rituals can play.

I doubt my own father, for example, has ever put on *t'fillin*. Jewishly, he hits the big ones: he usually hosts a seder, he goes to services on Rosh HaShanah and Yom Kippur, and, of course, he lights a *chanukiyah*. But that is about it for Jewish ritual. He is neither terribly knowledgeable about it nor inclined to explore it. And while he exhibits many of the philosophical and ethical traits of Judaism that I value so strongly, these are not exclusively Jewish either in content or in their combination. But more to the point, we can't get together and do philosophy the way we might do a ritual. When we see each other, we can't exactly do ethics the way we might do a ritual. And while we have secular family rituals, these have a limited capacity to deepen our relationship to each other and to our world.

So my father and I don't talk, or we talk about things that don't matter all that much. We spend time together, but we don't really connect. And I am constantly left with the nagging suspicion that there is more *there* there if only I could figure out how to get at it. And as we lead our separate lives with our separate daily activities three thousand miles apart, I can't help but wonder if having more Jewish rituals in common would make a difference. I mean really, would it matter a whit if he'd taught me to lay *t'fillin*? If we went to a minyan together? If we had these rituals in common, could we then have a real conversation? Yes, I think so. And as I play with my own son and we go to shul on Saturday mornings, will it make any difference for us? God, I hope so.

Notes

1. Joseph Telushkin, *Jewish Literacy* (New York: William Morrow, 1991), p. 9.

FUNNY MAN

Avram Mandell

I recently attended the National Association of Temple Educators conference. It was wonderful to gather with so many of my fellow Reform Jewish educators to meet each other, to learn, and to pray. We share many interests and most importantly a strong commitment to educating Jewish youth. Yet when I looked around the room, I realized there is one thing that we do not have in common: unlike most of the conference attendees, I am a man. I encounter this phenomenon, that of being one of few men, in my own congregation as well. Inevitably, women outnumber men at services and in meetings. Judaism, in its traditional practice, is male-driven in many ways, yet when I look around our Reform community today, I see mostly women. Somehow, men have become a marginalized population in the Reform Movement.

Growing up in the early 1970s and '80s I can only remember one male teacher throughout my eleven years of congregational education. But having only female teachers did not hinder my religious school experience in any way. I remember that through second grade my educational experience was fairly positive. At age eight, I wanted to learn Hebrew and go to religious school three times a week like my older brother and sister. My mother, aware of how her children's religious school involvement required a tremendous commitment on her part, pushed me to solidify my motives. She believed that Jewish learning should not be taken lightly and should come from a place of authenticity. My mother told me that if I began attending religious school three days a week in third grade, I would obligate myself to attending through confirmation. At the young age of eight, I made a pact with my mother and myself that I would continue my Jewish learning through age sixteen. Over the subsequent eight years, I occasionally wavered in my interest in religious school and, at times, wanted to stop attending religious school altogether. However, during those times, I reminded myself of my promise to my mother and remained true to our pact.

My mother, a secular, female, Jewish intellectual, was a driving force behind the active Jewish participant I am today. I was also fortunate enough to benefit from my father's strong influence in my Jewish identity as well, as I watched him bless my siblings and me on Friday nights, lead our Passover seders, and teach me to build a sukkah on our deck. I grew up celebrating Shabbat every week at home and either going to services or studying Torah in my family's living room. Of additional significance, though, is that in the course of my path from childhood to Jewish adulthood, I was able to excel in Jewish settings by asserting traits that are associated with traditional conceptions of masculinity. Part of my success in Jewish communal settings comes because I have sought out communities that value my more quintessential male traits. One of the factors that has encouraged my active participation in the Reform Jewish community is that I can be funny (although you would not know it from this essay). Humor and wit are appreciated in Jewish circles, and being funny is something that receives immediate positive feedback; many successful Jewish leaders are known for these qualities, especially Jewish men. Had I attempted a career outside of Jewish communal settings, this quality may not have been met with such success. Bill Gates, for example, is not known for his humor—but Rabbi Chaim may be able to count on a renewal of his contract if his board received feedback that their congregants loved the Rav's humorous and insightful High Holy Day sermon. Jewish humorists not only find acceptance in Reform Jewish life, they are able to experience accomplishment while participating in their communities.

My ongoing interactions with the Reform Jewish community have reaffirmed my identity as a funny man—a quality that is part of my self-worth and self-value. Abraham Maslow, the twentieth-century American Jewish psychologist, addresses this phenomenon in his Hierarchy of Human Needs. Maslow asserts that after physical needs are met, such as food, water, shelter, and personal safety, humans must experience "self-esteem, confidence, achievement, respect of others, and respect by others," in order to reach the highest point of human development: self-actualization.[1] For me, part of that self-actualization came from my ability to be funny. Ironically, as a child, I spent many of my synagogue days in the religious school principal's office, waiting to be reprimanded for being a class clown. This behavior, which was seen as negative and inappropriate as a child in the classroom, is the same behavior that I perceived as gaining me acceptance and success as an adult. I am glad I stuck around at the synagogue despite those many weekday afternoons in Dr. Flexner's office. Starting in seventh grade I went to Baltimore Hebrew University's High School program and just kept going. As a man, I want to feel confident in who I am and in my knowledge of my environment. I want to be able to actively and wisely participate in whatever situation in which I am involved.

For graduate school I wound up going to seminary. Choosing a graduate school that would guide my professional choice was an involved process. While living in New York City, I took graduate courses at Bank Street College and Hebrew Union College–Jewish Institute of Religion. The first nudge was from my mother, who suggested I audit courses to help me get an edge in the admissions process. The second push was from the dean of HUC-JIR New York, who graciously allowed me to audit the course (he had been my older brother's NFTY youth group advisor), and the final push was from the professor whose course I audited. At the end of one of her lessons she pulled me aside and said, "You should apply to this program." After she agreed to recommend me, I agreed to apply. It was the gentle nudges, the mentors pointing me in the right directions, and people willing to give me opportunities that brought me to the field of Jewish education as a professional. It sounds quite simple, but it worked.

Having a master's degree in Jewish education does not make me the most scholarly of Jews, but it does make me confident in my Judaic knowledge and also allows me to be confident in my Judaic practice. I have given much thought to my observances, and I continue to scrutinize them. I enjoy being asked questions about my Jewish practice and thoughts, because I have a strong knowledge base from which to draw. This confidence comes from family practice and encouragement, my father's pursuit of Jewish learning, my mother's active participation and constant questioning of Jewish beliefs, my own learning, and familiarity with practice and customs. Take these elements away and I would be nervous to be around Jewish learning. Despite all my training, I was recently in a Hebrew literature workshop and felt like a second grade math student trying to understand college calculus. I was worried the teacher would call on me to read, revealing publicly my inadequacy when I made a mistake or could not remember the definition of a Hebrew word. I cringe at the idea that congregants might experience these feelings, whether at services, Torah study, or a synagogue lecture series.

My sense is that the kind of activities and experiences that are prominent in most Reform congregations do not offer the average Jewish male opportunity for self-actualization. Recall that Maslow's definition requires *self-esteem, confidence, achievement, respect of others, and respect by others.* For generations, traditional synagogues have offered these experiences to men through such typically male opportunities like leading weekday services, serving as the *gabbai* (the one who ensures the Torah is read correctly), being honored with *aliyot,* leading Torah study sessions and fellowship discussion groups, building the sukkah, holding Brotherhood breakfast meetings, and singing with fervor and pride. While some men in the past have found a sense of success through these opportunities, many men have not, and today most men do not. And when we talk about creating new opportunities, today we innovate more for women. Through women's study groups, the women's Passover seder, Rosh Chodesh meetings, and other temple auxiliary groups, women who find achievement in building social relationships or helping support social relationships can more easily find accomplishment in the synagogue context. Men, however, have less opportunity for the kinds of activities that *they believe* will lead others to respect them and offer them confidence; in short, men are granted less opportunity for success.

I stayed involved with congregational life in college because my mother told me that teaching religious school was a good way to make money. As a young teacher, I was not involved with any groups or activities other than the occasional youth group event. Post-college, I continued to teach but was also looking for an extended family. Since the age of seventeen I have always lived away from my family. I was looking for community, people to care about me. That is actually a lot harder to find in the Reform community than in other denominations that have mastered reaching out to the stranger. For example, every time I have davened at an Orthodox shul, I have been approached by a congregant asking me if I had a place for *Shabbes* dinner. There is not a Reform tradition of inviting over anyone you do not recognize to your house for dinner. Even so, it was the comfort of the prayer service and the potential of meeting warm and inviting Jews that kept me coming back to the synagogue. My experience was unusual in this regard though, as it is often tough for single men, or even young men who are part of a couple, to find warmth, comfort, and acceptance in a Reform synagogue community.

As a synagogue professional who works with a wide range of Jews on a daily basis, I have observed two categories of men who do find Maslow-style fulfillment in Reform synagogues. The first are Successful Businessmen and Lawyers (SBLs) who serve on boards of trustees. These men would prefer not to have "check-in" or sharing time during the meeting and would rather that the rabbi skip the *d'var Torah*. These men desire to approve last month's minutes, show their expertise in budgeting or policy analysis, grab a cookie left over from last Friday's *Oneg*, and head home before their wives fall asleep. The second category consists of Learned Jewish Males (LJMs). These men were either raised Orthodox, went to yeshivah for a year, studied in Israel in college, or are the products of rabbi-fathers. Men in both categories have a clear sense of what it means to be successful in the Reform Jewish community. They can make sure business is in order, or they can come to Torah study and worship services.

As I try to involve both types of men, the SBLs and the LJMs, I often wind up confused, because these two groups have conflicting definitions of success, making it hard for me to meet both of their needs for self-actualization. The stereotypical SBLs, who are generally less familiar with liturgy, biblical writings, and Jewish history than the LJMs, feel ignorant and "less than" if I try to involve them in things like Torah study. My SBLs will come away feeling subpar to the rabbi or the ex-Orthodox *yeshivah bocher* in the committee meeting.

Yet I have come to realize that these men do seek some sort of measure of accomplishment. John Gray, relationship therapist and author of *Men Are from Mars, Women Are from Venus*, states that a man's sense of self is defined through his ability to achieve results. Men are competitive creatures who are looking for quantifiable realizations. If I am an SBL (which, as my bank account will testify, I am not), I will be able to measure my success by the salary that I make or the title in front of my name. But, at least at synagogues that I know—and likely at most Reform synagogues—we have removed any type of competitive spin on davening or Torah knowledge, and thus it is difficult to even be able to measure accomplishment in those areas. To make matters worse, many of these highly accomplished men walk into the synagogue and the rabbi will use a word in Hebrew or Yiddish that they don't know, or a Torah story will be referenced, and they will be ignorant of some crucial detail. For this reason, I wince when I hear rabbis or other Jewish professionals using the phrase, "We are all familiar with. . . ." Upon hearing that, the Jewishly ignorant but brilliantly successful media tycoon member feels defensive and unconfident.

I see this problem in the religious school as well. "Little Evan loves coming on Wednesdays and learning Hebrew, but he is not into the dance or the art programs you provide on Sunday. He's a very good student in his secular school, and he has never had a problem before in a school setting—what are you going to do about it?" This is a common scenario I hear from parents. Learning Hebrew is a definable and objectively measurable skill; learning Torah stories and Jewish values is less easily quantifiable. Many goal-oriented students love learning Hebrew but do not derive satisfaction from the Judaic studies courses. The objectives of the former are made clear to the students, and it is evident whether the student knows the entire *alef-bet* or has six more symbols to master. It is apparent when a boy reads a prayer with fluency and when he has mastered the required vocabulary. In contrast, he cannot easily measure the amount of understanding or compassion shown when visiting the sick in expressing the Jewish value of *bikur cholim*.

Spirituality is another one of those areas that offers no quantification. It is not competitive and is not viewed as macho, and thus many men do not experience success in the "spiritual" environment. By contrast, in Los Angeles there is an inter-synagogue softball league. The synagogue at which I work has two teams because of the number of interested participants, 95 percent of whom are male. It is easier to feel successful in softball because a man can be clear on what the expectations are and how he will be evaluated. Camaraderie and exercise might be a part of the formula, but there is nothing ambiguous to the American male about what constitutes the evaluation of America's second favorite pastime. For many men, the sanctuary is not a safe environment because it does not offer clear expectations of how to succeed in spirituality.

When working with Jewish males I try to create opportunities for them to succeed at the synagogue. While I do not have a formula, I strive to assess each situation and group to determine what will constitute success for them. Is it playing football during recess, or is it refereeing the game? Is it fun games and activities in the classroom, or is it students showing off their intellectual knowledge through deep discussions? Is it learning Hebrew so that adults can be more competent in services, or is it engaging the comedians of the congregation to help write a humorous Purim skit? Is it raising money for social action projects, or is it the physical labor involved in moving one hundred boxes at a food pantry? Is it building the synagogue's communal sukkah, or is it participating in a *Havdalah* drum circle?

Drumming is an instant male win. It is impossible to be out of tune and nearly impossible to be off rhythm. There is immediate success, gratification, and mastery, and it is just as easy to stand out as it is to blend in, depending on the preference of the drummer. Other examples include softball, classes where everyone is a beginner, classes that clearly state prerequisite knowledge needed, classes that allow people to advance, camping trips, talent exhibitions, and social action events with clearly stated objectives, goals, and expectations. "Come to Torah study—everyone welcome" is not an attractive title to the goal-oriented male. Instead, men are more attracted by something like "A Happy Wife Equals Happy Life: Learn five tricks the Torah offers to make your marriage work; for men only. No knowledge of Hebrew necessary." The skill level should be made evident, and what objectives will be accomplished should be stated.

Reform synagogues should create opportunities that offer men a clear sense of how to be "successful" in each opportunity. Such synagogues should program events with more immediate gratification and avenues for success. Professionals can look to the secular world with which men interact as a model for bringing more men into the synagogue. In order to engage and empower men in synagogue life, Reform synagogues need to create opportunities for men to show proficiency, for men to share with one another in a safe environment, and that allow for growth and development of the male spirit in a positively competitive and, yes, nurturing environment.

I am currently a synagogue programmer, community builder, and professional nudger. As the director of education for a seven-hundred-family synagogue, I plan events that I would like to attend personally. This helps fulfill my needs as an active male in the community and hopefully reaches other men as well. While I'm still working on creating a Men's Shabbat in Vegas trip, in which we would donate 10 percent of our winnings to *tzedakah*, with the assistance of my colleagues I have implemented a drum *Havdalah* experience, organized a social action trip to Mississippi, and encouraged our students to attend summer camps, at which men customarily seem to flourish. I am now the one reaching out to other men who are members of our temple community. I am constantly on the lookout for the father who is hanging around religious school a little early to pick up his child or the easily bored male student who needs more stimulation than the traditional classroom experience offers. As for my personal sense of accomplishment in synagogue life, I drum as a way of praying, whenever I can—once a month during our musical Shabbat service and every Sunday morning with the children. I play on the softball team for the sense of camaraderie and male bonding. I bring in interesting and engaging guest teachers to our community retreat, and I still try to make people laugh and feel at ease when they step foot onto the grounds of our temple.

NOTES

1. Abraham H. Maslow, "A Theory of Human Motivation" (1943), originally published in *Psychological Review* 50: 370–96.

PART 2

FLEEING AHAB AND JEZEBEL: REFUSING TRADITIONAL MASCULINITY

INTRODUCTION

After Elijah finishes off the prophets of Baal, he does the strangest thing. Hearing that Jezebel, the queen, wants his life because of the massacre, Elijah flees as far south as possible. Even though it makes sense to flee a murderous queen, I still find this odd. Elijah has just proven his power and his connection to God. If he is faithful, how can he question God's ability to protect him?

Instead, I propose that Elijah flees something else. I submit that Elijah has experienced the apex of his society's definition of success, and he rejects it. He has seen his ability to win the competition, to bring the fire of God, to massacre the prophets, and he fears it. He no longer wants to play by those rules.

In the introduction to part 1, I mentioned Philip Roth's character from *American Pastoral*, "the Swede." Wildly thriving in all of the stereotypically masculine ideals, this character is given a name by Roth that denies his Jewishness. But as the plot continues, we see the Swede suffer the pain of a daughter who becomes a homicidal, bomb-making Vietnam War protester. After she disappears into hiding, the Swede eventually meets one of her war-movement handlers at a hotel. In that scene, this young woman challenges him to have sex with her, and when he refuses, she graphically masturbates. Roth has created a character, the Swede, that embodies every ideal of American masculinity, but then uses a series of women—first the daughter who revolts against his quiet suburban success, and then the handler who demonstrates his impotence by penetrating herself, and then much later in the book his beauty queen wife who has an affair with the neighborhood geek, an architect—to vitiate those same ideals.

While the authors in the first part of this book find meaning in traditional forms of masculinity, others, like Roth, rebel against them. They follow the path of Elijah who fled traditional patterns of power to find a new way of being. The men in this section ignore, abandon, or even reject the systems and established modes of masculinity, and in so doing they define a piece of their identity. The rejections tend to follow three possible paths. First, they refuse to abide by the way that traditional masculinity treats other men and women. They want no part in what I have called the destructive elements of masculinity. Second, they reject the standards and options of traditional masculinity as being too rigid for themselves. Following the message of "Free to Be You and Me," Marlo Thomas's emblematic women's movement creation, these men want options previously open only to women. And finally, some of the men in this section rail against what they see as the problematic masculinity within Jewish systems. They seek to transform Jewish institutions, and perhaps Judaism itself, into new models of male behavior and gender relations.

These three types of refusal of traditional masculinity—against the traditional masculine interpersonal behavior, life options, and Jewish systems—can all cause a sense of disorientation and psychic struggle. This is the fertile ground of religious inquest, and Judaism has a great deal to offer the man who defines a part of self through the denial of antiquated social norms of manhood. The authors herein describe how that process works and how the tools of Judaism can lead them to a new definition of masculinity.

Mike Rankin's essay begins on a naval ship during the Vietnam War. While the soldier is a persistent stereotype of masculinity, Rankin describes the way that a makeshift Yom Kippur service helped redefine his attitude toward warfare. Rabbi Douglas Sagal also redefines a stereotypical area of male behavior, the sport of boxing. As he describes his experiences as a boxer, we see how Sagal finds a style of masculinity that defies expectations. Rabbi Joel Soffin, Rick Recht, and Wilson Baer, each in his own area of experience—as a rabbi, a Jewish rock musician, and a high school student, respectively—all find in Judaism values that defy traditional masculinities. Rabbi Marc Rosenstein, the director of the Galilee Center for Value Education in Israel, reexamines the myth of the new Jew created by the early Zionists and asks whether its validity holds today. Michael Kimmel and Jon Crane, both academics, see in the embrace and intellectual exploration of egalitarianism a route to a meaningful Jewish existence. Rabbi Max Rivers and David Segal, a rabbinical student, both articulate the feeling of alienation they experience while witnessing the exclusion of women and the way that their Jewish experience depends upon a more just and inclusive community. Beth Kander examines the way that stereotypes of masculinity and Jewish masculinity become lodged in the female Jewish imagination, even though reality rarely bears this out. Finally, Karen Perolman, a rabbinical classmate of Segal's, describes the experience of being a woman in a majority-female class of rabbis and ponders the way a glass ceiling functions for men. She argues that a different norm of male behavior might be necessary in order to include men in the ranks of future Jewish participation.

Each of these essays investigates a different aspect of the masculinity question, but they all conclude with the need for change in the way that men see themselves and promulgate future expectations of masculinity. Like Elijah, who rejected the version of manhood he so successfully employed on Mount Carmel, these writers refuse to rely upon traditional norms. We find in their essays suggested criteria for the promotion of a new masculinity and the experiences that might motivate a shift to such a radical reconstruction of identity.

A JEWISH VIETNAM VETERAN
IN A TIME OF WAR

Mike Rankin

Since the beginning of the Iraq war, I've thought a great deal about my service in Vietnam. I've done so as a combat veteran, as a Jew.

As often as I can, I speak of my Vietnam experience with my fellow Jews, hoping they will understand what we went though over there and what our young men and women are going through now in Iraq and Afghanistan.

We Jews teach with stories. These are mine.

Yom Kippur, 1965, I was Jewish lay leader aboard a navy destroyer off the coast of Vietnam just north of Danang. I had a "congregation" of about fifteen sailors, all of whom knew far more about Judaism than I did. There were no women on navy ships in those days. Had there been, they would have been as much a part of the congregation as the men. They would have shared everything we shared, felt the exhilaration and terror of combat as we felt them.

The ship's captain had promised us an hour or two to hold a service *Kol Nidrei* evening, but late in the afternoon the ship went to battle stations. An Australian base camp south of Hue was under attack from a North Vietnamese unit, and we were to fire around the perimeter of the camp to drive them away.

The firing continued all *Kol Nidrei* night and through most of the next day. After much loss of life on both sides, the NVA regiment withdrew. We secured from general quarters, and the captain allowed the Jews on board to gather on the fantail of the ship for a brief service. The other sailors stayed away, giving us a rare time of privacy and quiet.

We had no prayer books, so we stumbled through a group chanting of *Kol Nidrei*. We remembered *Avinu Malkeinu*, some of the *Al Cheit*, the *Sh'ma* and *V'ahavta*, and other parts of the Yom Kippur liturgy. The seas were too rough to have chairs on the deck, so we stood through the service.

After *Aleinu* and *V'ne-emar*, we said aloud the names of family and friends we wanted to remember in our *Kaddish*, our prayer of affirmation and remembrance for those we loved and lost.

"And we also remember all who died in battle this day," one added softly.

When *Kaddish* was over, the sailor who had added the names of those killed in the fighting picked up a coronet he'd brought to the service. Wrapping his prayer shawl tightly around his shoulders, David turned toward the sandy beach. As the sun set over the lush green hills, he sounded *t'kiah*, the first of the shofar calls. Then *t'ruah* and *sh'varim*. Then a final, prolonged *t'kiah g'dolah*.

We stood in silence, lost in the emotion of the moment. Slowly we removed our tallitot and *kippot* and returned to the mess decks. The evening meal had almost ended, but the ship's cooks had saved a "break the fast" for us.

We felt the presence of God that Yom Kippur afternoon. Not a Yom Kippur has come and gone since then that I do not remember it. Shipmates tell me it is the same for them.

We knew that on that Day of Awe God was with us and was commanding us to turn from the obscenity of war toward peace.

Some of our group returned home to join the Vietnam Veterans Against the War. One went to Ethiopia with the Peace Corps to help eradicate smallpox. Others found their own ways of healing. For we had sworn an oath that Yom Kippur afternoon: if we survived, we would do all we could to build again, to teach others what we know, to try with the time we had remaining to find goodness and meaning in this life.

This was the most powerful religious experience I'd had until that date. I believe it still is.

My Jewish identity was strong, though I had not attended Hebrew school. There was no Hebrew school and no synagogue in my small Arkansas town. Mother was my one Jewish teacher. It was enough—the identity was formed, and it was strengthened that Yom Kippur. Years later, when I became active in Reform Judaism, serving on URJ boards and commissions, I remembered well all she had taught me. I only regret she did not live to share the joy of Jewish activism with me.

With friends and fellow veterans, I went back to Vietnam in December 1996, to celebrate my retirement from the navy and the Veterans Administration, where I'd been a VA physician for eighteen years, caring for men and women who'd served in all our nation's wars from World War II to the First Gulf War.

My retirement party was held at a hotel bar in Saigon where we had gone as young warriors to get drunk and to get away from the sound, smell, and fear of battle. We toasted absent friends, reminisced, had dinner, and returned to the cruise ship.

The next day we sailed to Danang and took a bus north on Highway 1 toward Hue.

The bus made a rest stop at the Hai Van Pass, the highest point on the highway, and a painfully familiar site. As a navy medical officer, I served with the navy aboard ships and with the marines in country; my marine base camp was near the pass.

There is a souvenir shop there now, but our old bunker complex was still standing, half a mile up a fairly steep trail. I could go there alone while the tourists stayed below to use the facilities and buy postcards and T-shirts.

I walked up the path and to the bunker, now almost covered with brush and vines. The memories flooded back. I did what Jews do when visiting the grave of a loved one. I placed a small stone on the entryway to the building. I said *Kaddish* for my comrades who did not return and a *Mi Shebeirach*, a prayer for inner peace and healing, for those who did.

Walking down the trail, I encountered a young Vietnamese boy, about ten years old. Glowering at me, the old enemy, he took an aggressive boxer's stance and punched the air vigorously.

I grinned and waved to him.

Surprised, he lowered his fists, grinned, and waved back.

Then I knew why I had returned to Vietnam. I felt the presence of God on that narrow path, as surely as I had on the fantail of my ship that Yom Kippur afternoon.

There is peace now in Vietnam, with open discussion, even friendliness between old adversaries. Can that peace not one day come to Israel, and indeed to the entire Middle East, Iraq included?

In the spirit and words of our Torah and our prophets, may that troubled part of the world become a place where fields of hope are renewed, where all the inhabitants—Jews, Christians, Palestinians, Shia, Sunni, Kurd, and others—feel a sense of pride and ownership in the land of their hearts, where all may live in freedom and peace. If we will it—and work for it—it will be more than a dream!

Kein y'hi ratzon. So may this prayer be God's will. Amen.

MY LIFE AS A BOXER

Douglas B. Sagal

As I reach forty-five years of age, my career as a boxer is inevitably winding down. In the sport of boxing, forty-five is not only old, it is ancient. Boxers who pass thirty are considered in middle age, and at thirty-five, most professional careers have ended. I know that the sport of "white collar" boxing, boxing for middle-aged men, is popular somewhere, but the gyms I frequent have no executives and lawyers and hedge fund managers putting on the gloves, just young, hungry kids, and me.

I have engaged in the sport of boxing now for close to sixteen years. I have spent countless hours learning and perfecting punches and footwork, I have run miles upon miles while doing "roadwork," and I have sparred many rounds.

I wish I could say, as many older people do, that I got into boxing to relieve stress, or lose some pounds, or tone up, but that would not be true. The fact is, from a young age, I have wanted to be a fighter. My wife calls it my adolescent fantasy, and I suppose she is right. Other teenage boys were gawking at skin magazines on the shelf of the local drugstore, while I lusted after glossy copies of *Ring* and *Boxing Digest*.

As a kid in suburban New Jersey, I never had the chance to live my fantasy of becoming the middleweight champion of the world. I took tennis lessons and acted in school plays, but despite surreptitiously visiting YMCAs and health clubs, I could not find anyone who would teach me to box. I would later be schooled by men my own age who had grown up in the hardscrabble towns around my affluent suburb and discover that while I was playing tennis and preparing for high school achievement tests, they were competing in the Golden Gloves and Junior Olympics. Our worlds were so different, the chance of our paths crossing was practically nonexistent.

While I was in rabbinic school, I finally began to follow my long-delayed teenage dream. I found a gym with a heavy bag and learned the basic moves that make up the boxer's arsenal of punches. Soon after rabbinic ordination, I discovered a boxing gym and persuaded the owner to teach me along with some of the younger men he trained. Cleve, my first trainer, was an elderly African American gentleman who ran a gym in a small city about twenty miles from my home. Crippled by arthritis and diabetes, he still could hit the heavy bag with a resounding "thwack." It was from Cleve that I first learned to box, and I revere his memory as much as I do my early teachers of Torah.

Cleve seemed to live hand to mouth, and in addition to bringing him small quantities of food, I invited him to join us for our family seder one Passover. I am probably the only rabbi who entertained the president of my congregation and my boxing instructor at the same seder table.

Cleve did not have many students, and sparring opportunities were few. He didn't want me to spar on my own, but I was eager to try out my skills. One night, without his knowledge, I persuaded the owner of a local karate gym to allow me to spar with some of his students. I learned quickly the number one rule of boxing training—that you never, ever, ever spar without your own trainer present. I was badly beaten. I left the gym with my head ringing and my ribs bruised. To make matters worse, later in the evening, I had to attend our congregation's annual meeting! All I recall from that particular meeting of our synagogue community was my fervent hope that the bruises would not show.

Cleve left town to live with his daughter, and I began training at another gym. I stepped up my training, rushing from teaching midweek Hebrew school to the gym, and I sparred more frequently. During this time, the word began to spread about the "boxing rabbi" who both

preached *and* punched. Local newspapers did stories, including one entitled "Why Is This Fight Different from All Other Fights?" Because of this
notoriety, I helped charitable organizations raise funds by participating in
boxing events.

Occasionally, I have been asked how I can square my participation in
boxing with the rabbinate, a profession that teaches peace and reconciliation. My answer is that boxing, properly done and properly conducted,
is a safe sport. I have seen boxing coaches show much more caring for
the fighters under their tutelage than some coaches of suburban sports
such as baseball and gymnastics, whose drive to win causes debilitating
injury to their students.

Over the years, as my rabbinic career has taken me to different cities,
I have trained in several gyms and had the privilege of learning from different instructors. I have sparred frequently, mostly with young people,
occasionally with people closer in age to me. I have helped train young
adults for the Golden Gloves tournaments and Junior Olympics and have
even sparred more than once with heavyweight contender Gerry Cooney,
whose boxing skills are amazing to behold.

I have trained in gyms from New Jersey, to Connecticut, to Chicago.
One of the wondrous aspects of the sport of boxing is that rank amateurs
like myself train alongside the top professionals. I have trained along with
Andrew Golota, Angel Manfredy, famed female boxer Wendy LaMotta,
and current heavyweight contender Monte Barrett. I have been taught by
men who train champions. In no other sport is there such a close proxim-
ity between the pros and the mere enthusiasts. How common is it for a
golfer, say, to practice his putts alongside Tiger Woods?

Perhaps the greatest discovery of my boxing career has been that boxers are remarkably gentle and kind individuals. Virtually every great
fighter I have ever met is humble, decent, and generous. Some of the
finest persons I have ever known are in the sport of boxing.

Other men my age yearn for the perfect drive or the satisfying sound
of a tennis ball hitting the sweet spot of the racket. I still marvel at the
sight of a beautiful left hook and the sound of a crisp jab smacking the
heavy bag.

Currently, I train in a small but busy gym in Newark, New Jersey. My
coaches are patient with me, the oldest person at the gym, and are trying

to persuade me to participate in something called "Masters Boxing," which seems to be made up of people my age as crazy as me. I spar with kids young enough to be my bar mitzvah students. Just the other day, I met a newcomer to the gym, a young man of twenty-six or seven. Ten years ago, he was state champion, no mean feat in a state with many excellent young fighters. His pro career has not been successful, and so he has returned to the gym to train with his old teachers. Sitting with me in the locker room, he reached into his gym bag and pulled out a cracked leather belt with a brass plaque, his trophy from years ago. He held the belt as reverently as I hold a tallit or siddur. We were quiet. He told me of how he intended to turn things around and "get more fights," as they say in the boxing world. I wished him luck and admired his belt. I told him how proud he should be. He silently nodded and slipped the belt back into his bag.

At my age, I am slowing down considerably. Boxing is a taxing sport, and without speed and stamina, a boxer cannot defend himself. Witness Evander Holyfield, exactly my age, who is genuinely endangering himself by entering the ring in a quest to regain the heavyweight crown.

I never quite achieved my teenage fantasy of the middleweight championship, but I have come pretty close to experiencing the life of a fighter and, in truth, loved every minute.

THE REAL MAN

Joel Soffin

You may find this hard to believe, but the very first superhero was Jewish —both parts of him.

Who was this first superhero? It was none other than Superman. And how do we know that he was Jewish—both he and his alter-ego Clark Kent? Simple: his fathers, Jerry Siegel and Joe Shuster, were both Jewish.

It seems strange to think of Superman as being Jewish, doesn't it?

Now Clark Kent—that's a different story altogether. We might imagine him as a member of the Jewish community. He's a writer who wears glasses. He's a *nebbish*—an often frightened, incompetent, and powerless man who bumbles along in a non-threatening and reasonably sweet way.

Why would Superman's creators have divided his character into the mighty and the meek? Siegel and Shuster were living out their own ambivalence about being Jewish men in America, following the biblical tradition of separating Ishmael from Isaac and Esau from Jacob: the real men from the Momma's boys. Maybe they were struggling with the American definition of what it means to be a real man and saw themselves as not measuring up to the standard in some way.

A red-blooded American man is a protector, a provider, and a pillar. He defends his family and his community in any way necessary. He provides a good standard of living. He is independent and invulnerable. Big boys don't cry. No pain, no gain. Winning isn't everything: it's the only thing. Stand up like a man.

You can almost hear Abraham speaking these very words to Isaac. In the Torah portion Abraham wakes up his son early in the morning; he's taking him away from home. Isaac is not permitted to ask any questions. His father is strong and powerful, and when he has his mind set on something, it's best not to challenge him in any way. So for three days they walk along in absolute silence, two men being the way men are—strong and silent.

Then it is time to bind Isaac on the altar and to sacrifice him. Some say that Isaac was thirty-seven years old when this happened, so he had to go along with his father's plan of his own free will. Why didn't he protest? He was trying to be a real man. Why didn't he cry? Big boys don't cry.

Our wrestling with images of what it means to be real Jewish men goes back to the very beginning of our history. And the wrestling continues to this day.

A man is a protector. He is strong and brave enough to defend everyone around him, especially his parents, his wife, his sisters, and his children. He is all-powerful and even aggressive and violent if the need arises. All of this is done without evidence of any fear or anxiety.

This description of a real man haunted me for a long time. When I was a young boy, walking home from religious school at the temple that was two blocks from my house was a terrifying experience. Bullies would chase me home; I would barely escape them as I raced through the door to my house.

My younger brother was the fighter in the family. At times, it was he who protected me.

And then there were my early trips to Manhattan just after I got married. I felt an enormous burden as I imagined taking on the role of defending my wife if we encountered any threatening situations away from home. Now I could no longer run away, as Jacob used to do. I had to stand up like a man and face whatever dangers there might be. To be honest, the mere possibility gave me nightmares.

I never played football when I was growing up. Jewish boys just didn't engage in physical contact sports—we might get hurt. When my sons were learning to be more aggressive on the soccer field, I wasn't so sure that was such a good thing. Being so violent didn't seem to be the Jewish way.

How did we become a people who talked and reasoned without resorting to physical violence—whose heroes were not Samson the wrestler, but Hillel, the man of patience and kindness?

The beginnings of an answer can be found in this true story told by Sigmund Freud. One day, as he and his father were taking a walk together, his father said, "When I was a young man, I went for a walk one Saturday. I was well-dressed and had a new fur cap on my head. Someone came up to me and with a single blow knocked off my cap into the mud and shouted: 'Jew! Get off the pavement!'"

"And what did you do?" asked young Freud.

"I went into the roadway and picked up my cap," was his father's quiet reply.

This interchange had a dramatic impact on Freud. To feel like a real man, he would have to identify with someone other than his own father.

And yet, his father was acting in the way that he had learned from his own father. This had become the Jewish way to respond to such acts of aggression. Why? Because it was vital to the very survival of the Jewish community.

The rabbis realized as far back as two thousand years ago that our people were too small in numbers and too weak to take on the powers that ruled over us. Each time we tried to do so—against the Romans at Masada or Betar—the consequences were catastrophic. Our people were nearly wiped out.

As Aviva Cantor has explained, during the Middle Ages, when we lived in separate, tightly knit communities, the rabbis developed a new understanding of what it means to be a real Jewish man. Violence was prohibited under virtually any conditions. Even if we might have won a battle or two, the powers-that-be would take revenge on our community as a whole and the suffering would be unbearable. No violence was accepted within the Jewish community either, lest it spill over onto our behavior outside.

And so the rabbis taught: *Aizeh hu Gibor?* Who is strong and a hero? He who is able to control his passions and not yield to the temptation to strike back. Who is the real Jewish man? The *talmid chacham*, the one who studies the Torah and the Talmud. Through his studies, the spiritual hero will save the Jewish people from destruction.

This is the same attitude expressed by the ultra-Orthodox in Israel today who seek exemptions from military service, claiming that they are defending the country by being part of God's army in the yeshivah.

But we don't live in such isolated communities anymore. We live in the aftermath of the Holocaust, with the words "Never Again" ringing in our ears. So it is time we take back more of the protector role. Think carefully: have you ever risked your life and your well-being to save someone else? Have you ever put your life in danger for another person?

There was one time I did so. In April of 1987 I visited refuseniks in the former Soviet Union. I didn't know whether it was safe to violate Soviet laws and bring them medicine and record their stories, but my wife and I and one other couple went anyway. I had nightmares of never returning to my sons, but the trip had to be made regardless. Never again would our people suffer if we could defend them.

Returning to the U.S., I felt heroic, sensing for the first time what it meant to be a real Jewish man. I had taken back my power as protector in a Jewish way.

Men are also taught to play the role of provider. We Jews often define ourselves in terms of the work we do. When we meet new people, we quickly inquire about their career or occupation. When we speak with our children about what they want to be when they grow up, the conversation centers on job choices, not on Jewish sources of self-worth and self-esteem. We do not ask if they seek to become a *tzaddik*. We ask whether they will become a doctor or lawyer or accountant.

This breadwinner role narrows our identity as whole human beings and sometimes transforms the workplace into a battleground. Our coworkers become our competitors rather than our teammates. We have to look out for number one and keep our own upward progress ever in mind.

Worst of all, this makes us vulnerable.

The truth is that we have little control over our lives as breadwinners. There is nothing we can do to offset the fluctuations of the economy or the changes in economic policy introduced in Washington. We have all the responsibility and so little of the power. And worst of all, we can't talk about it openly to each other.

Have you been laid off, this year or last year? Are you afraid your job is in jeopardy? As Frank Pittman has written: "When we lose our work, we lose our dignity, our network, our purpose, our structure, and we live in a state of shame. It's nice if our family loves us anyway, but we [feel] that we haven't earned it and don't deserve it"—that we have failed as men.

In the days of the *shtetl*, this problem was much less intense. If a person lost his job, even for an extended period, he did not lose his identity or his manhood, for that depended primarily on whether he was a *talmid chacham*, a man who knew Torah, or a *chasid*, a pious man who shared his overflow with the community.

And, finally, there is the man's role as pillar. "Real men" keep their emotions and feelings deeply suppressed, don't open up to anyone about their inner lives, and resent the questions asked by spouses and children. "Real men" are never unsure of themselves. We don't say: I don't know—not just about directions, but about anything. We fear being ridiculed as weak, or rejected as wimpy. Interestingly, keeping quiet is a kind of power. It draws everyone else to us as they struggle to discover what we're really thinking and feeling, and erects a wall between us and our families. We remain isolated and alone.

Once again, in the *shtetl* it was easier for men to express their feelings. In those days, according to Aviva Cantor, "most Eastern European Jews believed emotions were made to be expressed, whether in words or in tears, both to achieve communication and as a catharsis. . . . Boys were never told to be brave or to be a man. They were expected to cry when [they were] hurt or unhappy."

Holding our feelings in so tightly also harms our physical health. The life span of men is seven or eight years shorter than it is for women, partly, I believe, because of this suppression of feelings. It is thus vital for us Jewish men to open ourselves up to one another, to share our real thoughts and feelings, to find some company on the common journey of Jewish manhood.

Centuries ago, Hillel taught: *"B'makom she-ain anashim . . .* in a place where there are no real men, *hishtadayl l'hiyot ish . . .* you, you strive to be a man." I would offer this version of Hillel's teaching: In a time and in a place where some think that to be a man is to be strong, silent, invincible, and invulnerable, we need to think differently. We need to remember that to be a real Jewish man we must be strong enough to conquer the temptation to run away and hide behind our roles as protector, provider, and pillar. We must be strong enough to share our feelings, to ask for help and support, and to find our real self.

BLESSED TO BE A JEWISH MAN

Rick Recht

What does it mean to be a Jewish man today? It's funny. When I was asked this question I thought, "No problem. I'm Jewish. I'm a man. Shouldn't be difficult to talk about my perspective on my role or self-perception of being a Jewish man." I found it interesting, however, how completely empty my mind went, staring at my blank laptop computer screen on a flight home from Florida. Flat line.

When I was a young boy growing up in a relatively Conservative congregation, no one really talked about what it meant to be a Jewish male versus a Jewish female. Aside from circumcision, the most apparent differences seemed to be the *m'chitzah* (separating wall) between the men and the women at services, the *t'fillin* that we men wrapped together during morning services, the minyan counted by the number of males (females not included), and the fact that there were virtually no female rabbis or cantors.

Looking back, I see how each of these areas of difference implied a kind of exclusiveness or power—a privilege that was transparent to me and my friends. It was just there. Just like the color of our white skin, just like our middle-class economic status, just like our privilege as males in the power structure in the United States. It was just there, and no one really told us. No one told us what to do with it. But we did feel it. I did. I remember feeling a sense of fraternity hanging out with all the older men on Sunday mornings wrapping *t'fillin* and after services kibitzing over bagels and lox. Just me and the guys. I even remember feeling a bit excited about knowing there were mitzvot that only men could do. Even though I learned about the mitzvot exclusive to only women, those mitzvot seemed different. Of course, I also knew that if you wanted to be president, or the Jewish equivalent—a rabbi—you also appeared to have to be male. So, as a young boy, probably by the time I was thirteen, even though I thought it unfair, I considered myself lucky to be male.

It was more than a decade before I truly started taking a deeper look at myself as a man. I had graduated college at USC in Los Angeles, moved back to the Midwest, and had been touring for several years playing at secular rock clubs, colleges, and fraternities around the country. I was essentially living on the road in a bus with a group of guys witnessing, virtually every night, the relatively alarming interaction between male and female audience members, often intoxicated with alcohol, drugs, exhaustion, or all of the above. Although, as a male, I understood and had grown sadly accustomed to witnessing this type of behavior, there was something in my consciousness, something in my stomach and my heart that twisted and ached when I was in these disturbing atmospheres. I decided to take an anti-bias class facilitated by the National Conference of Christians and Jews and started reading self-exploratory books about what it means to be a male in our society. The class and the books helped to bring my emotions to the surface and lead me deeper into my personal history to explore who I was and how I wanted to actively live my life as an adult male.

At the time, I was on the road about three weeks every month and taught guitar to a few students when I was in town. One of my students was a director of a Conservative Jewish day camp in St. Louis, who, after having no luck finding a song leader, decided to try to learn guitar herself to provide some song leading at her camp. She took guitar lessons from me for over a year, hinting here and there about me becoming a Jewish song leader. I had never worked with kids, didn't know any Jewish music, and was touring in a relatively successful rock band. I was totally uninterested. That being said, the summer rolled around, and after deciding to take a couple of months off from the touring circuit, I realized I needed a job. How bad could song leading be! So, I took the job and started practicing Debbie Friedman songs like there was no tomorrow. My guitar student, the director of the camp, my boss, quickly became my mentor. She was an incredibly talented public speaker and had a wonderful way of creating such exciting, meaningful, and relevant connections to Jewish living. I was blown away! This was a Judaism I had never experienced before. This was a Judaism I didn't know existed before and one that I absolutely loved. In the first few weeks of camp, I discovered that I had found my calling in life. Working with Jewish youth, writing Jewish music, and most importantly, becoming a Jewish educator became my life's passion. All summer, I wrote Jewish music for the kids at camp and learned from the camp director more and more beautiful dimensions of Judaism. She and I became very close friends as we met almost everyday to reflect and create together. After the summer, I went back out on the road with my band. But there was something inside of me that was permanently changed by my summer at Jewish camp. I gave the guys in my band notice, came home, built a studio in my basement, and recorded my first Jewish CD, *Tov*. The following summer, I hit the road as a Jewish rocker, playing fifty Jewish summer camps from coast to coast. And so started the beginning of my career as a touring Jewish musician. I also started dating my guitar student, the camp director, my mentor. She's now my wife, Elisa. It really happened just like that!

So one day I was touring in a rock band, staying up every day till five in the morning, living in a bus, traveling from city to city, playing in the most wild, bizarre and disturbing scenarios you can imagine. The next day I was taking anti-bias classes. And the next day, I was a Jewish musician singing at a summer camp learning about the beauty of Jewish music, Jewish values, community, interaction, teaching, and learning. It really felt like it happened that quickly. It happened so quickly that these three life experiences naturally overlapped in my mind, forcing me to reconcile my old band experiences with a new self-knowledge about my role as a male and my new life as a Jewish role model, teacher, and learner. That reconciliation started happening as I was learning about an aspect of Judaism that I had never been aware of before. I had never understood how much of being Jewish surrounds concepts of *tikkun olam*, the repair of the world. It was this *tikkun olam* that I could relate to and hold onto as a link between my old life and my new life. It was this *tikkun olam* that I felt passionate about and felt I could express in my original Jewish music. And years later, it was the concept of *tikkun olam* that would lead me to draw the connection between my personal aspirations to improve the world and the importance of acknowledging the power, privilege, and impact I have as a Jewish male engaging in these efforts to make a difference.

More than twenty years later, I'm sitting here on this airplane, thinking about how many female rabbi and cantor friends I have now, how many female youth group directors, Hebrew school principals, camp directors, Hillel directors, Jewish musicians, and executives in the Reform and Conservative Movements I know. So, it seems like the power and privilege structure may have changed quite a bit. And where does that leave me as a Jewish male?

Well, answering this question honestly, it makes me feeling genderless. At first glance, it's hard to see my "maleness" having any weight in my role as a Jew today, since as a child my entire perception of being a Jewish male was based on what female Jews couldn't be or do. My first reaction to realizing how genderless I feel as a Jewish male is not feeling sad or upset. After all, throughout my life, I was barely aware of any difference in my role of being a Jewish male in the first place. So, what's left?

What's left is that I'm still male. I'm still a white, thirty-something, upper-middle-class male in the United States. I'm a lot more aware now than I was as a child. I am crystal clearly aware of the power and privilege I have as a white male in this country, where we are, just over the last few years, warming up to the idea of women occupying high leadership positions in our government, earning similar wages, and receiving appropriate benefits for maternity leave and child-care considerations.

As white males living in the United States with such blatant privilege and power, we have an obligation to acknowledge our unearned, "given" position of access. As Jews and as human beings, we have a responsibility to engage in bettering the world in which we live, and as males in the United States, we have an amplified opportunity to use our access in positions of privilege and power to expedite the changes we are capable of creating in this world. One of the greatest ways we can strive to make these changes is to use our unique position to advocate for greater access for women in meaningful leadership roles both in the Jewish and secular worlds. Given that more than half of the world's population is female, it seems only logical that a female perspective is critical in addressing issues that affect the female population. Including women in every way possible is how we ultimately guarantee that we are all officially "sitting at the same table," maintaining a fair and balanced dialogue, and achieving our greatest potential in making productive decisions for both men and women. Together, the synergy of all of our talents and perspectives give us much greater strength to effectively engage in true *tikkun olam*. Sharing power and ensuring women equal opportunity result in a greater good for all of us. If all of the power in the world were a pie, then giving women more access will just create a larger pie for us all to share.

When I departed from my life as a secular rock musician to become a Jewish rock musician, I never could have imagined how much Jewish values would ultimately affect both my music and, more importantly, my self-perception. This change in the way I view myself has led me to experience and understand more fully not only what it means to be a man, but what it means to be a Jewish man in our world today. As males, we need to realize our real self-image and self-esteem not through exclusive access or physical or authoritative dominance, but through true sharing, caring, and achievement with our female counterparts. It may be difficult to give when we could just take, but this is our mandate. This is our purpose. This is our role. God put us on this planet to struggle together, to grow together, to love each other, and to use our higher intelligence to supercede our animal instincts to dominate, by establishing bridges between each other, both men and women, Jews and people of all faiths and cultural backgrounds, as we fulfill our true destiny as caretakers of our planet and all living things.

I see myself as an educator with an opportunity to use the magical and mystical medium of music as an incredibly effective tool for communicating the beautiful lessons of Judaism. As a Jewish male in this capacity, I see myself as having amazing opportunities to encourage men and woman to realize not only the responsibility, but the capacity we have to change our world when we do so collectively. My views on equality are profoundly informed by Jewish values and the influence and inspiration of the Jews I am surrounded by in my life as a touring Jewish rock artist.

With music as the bridge, I am able to help unite Jews from a variety of denominations, people from a variety of faiths, and people from a variety of races, ethnicities, and cultures. I am blessed to live the life that I am living, touring from coast to coast, singing and celebrating these kinds of beautiful differences with community after community. This is what my Judaism is all about!

As the plane begins to land here in St. Louis, I'm looking out the window through the clouds thinking I may have just discovered that my "maleness is, in fact, actually a significant part of my role as a Jew. My "maleness" uniquely informs me and infuses my teaching, learning, and personal growth with a special strength and sensitivity that allows me to actively make a positive impact in this world. When I visit synagogues today in my travels, I look out at the young boys in the audience and wonder how they will define their identity as young Jewish men. I hope that they will not define their roles as Jewish males based on mitzvot exclusive to males or positions of religious power still dominated by Jewish men. As their eyes look up to me, I hope to share with them a spirit that gives them the confidence to find completion as males only when standing side by side in unity with the young women who surround them. This is our contemporary reality of what being a mensch is really all about. As a Jewish people this must be our collective realization, that men and women working together in unity is the only way we can truly achieve our greatest potential as human beings and the only way to fulfill our mission to leave our world in a better place than it was before we arrived.

When I lay down tonight next to my wife, Elisa, I will feel incredibly blessed for my health, my family, my friends, and my career. And now, for the right reasons, I will feel blessed to be a Jewish man.

GROWING INTO JEWISH MANHOOD

Wilson Baer

As I embark into the world of manhood, I find myself pondering many models of Jewish masculinity. Before I began to prepare for my bar mitzvah, Judaism and Jewish observances and values, and even my Jewish identity, seemed very clear. But as I become an adult, I can see greater complexity in Judaism as more and more personal questions enter the picture, and I want to make decisions thoughtfully and with deliberate intent. Some questions that I consider are abstract, and some more concrete. I wonder what profession I might have, if and when I should start a family, and what type of leader I should be. Not only do I contemplate such questions in general terms, but I also wonder how I should consider them through the lens of Jewish values and my Jewish identity, as well as my identity as a man, and how these should relate to one another. Furthermore, I also identify with other groups of people, and this only complicates the matter.

Growing up, Judaism has always been a big part of my life. If you knew me, then it would quickly become obvious that I am Jewish, not because of physical traits or apparel, but because of the way that it governs my life, the things that I say, the choices that I make, and the fact that I openly connect my actions with my Jewish identity. But are my views of a Jewish man and the sort of Jewish man I will become influenced only by Jewish men or by others as well? I imagine that a few decades back, a young Jewish boy had plenty of male Jewish role models to consider through the neighborhood and local extended family. Today, on the contrary, I think my views of a Jewish man and what I must become are influenced not only by Jewish men, but by Christians and atheists, since my father is not Jewish, and by women as well, particularly by my mom, who is Jewish. I do know that as I look toward those other groups and Jewish men around me, I find that my religious Jewish values and observances are more my own mix and that both the men and women who have been a part of my life have influenced my mensch-i-ness, or rather *menschlichkeit*. I would define *menschlichkeit* as my personal values, practices, and ways in which I interact with others. My religious observances, in contrast, pertain solely to Judaism, but my *menschlichkeit* relates more to my secular life, although it includes Jewish values.

The mix of Jewish religious observances that I feel drawn to developed from my earliest education, when I learned only the basics of Judaism. At that time, I did not consider the religious roles of a Jewish man. Then as I grew older, I discovered that by mixing observances and values into a conglomeration by which I try to live my life, I have begun to embrace Judaism and make it my own. I love studying and questioning the Jewish laws and texts, and by developing a religious identity in this way I leave much room for change. As I learn more, which happens almost daily, whether my learning is Jewish or secular, to my liking or not, my religious identity and values develop and change. In this way, all of my Jewish family, friends, teachers, and rabbis, as well as all of my religious experiences, allow me to grow as a Jew.

The development of my own religious Jewish identity, however, is very different from what I believe I have gotten and continue to get from the role models of the Jewish men in my life. The first Jewish man who was a part of my life was my grandfather. However, he has not had a major influence on my Jewish life, nor does he now, in a spiritual or religious way. My grandfather is a judge, and most notably I learn about Jewish values of compassion and justice through him. I doubt he realizes these as Jewish values though; rather, he sees them as human values.

About seven years ago, however, I met the first observant Jewish man in my life, now my stepfather. Through my stepfather, I have been able to begin to learn the ways of a Jewish man. The most influential example of his Jewish values for me was when his mother was living very close to us during the last two years of her life. He would visit her several times a week, or even more frequently when she was ill, and always talked about his love and care for her. There were many reasons why he did this, and all have their roots in Judaism. First, from his Jewish upbringing, he knows always to care for someone who is ill or even just to keep someone company who needs it. Secondly, his care for his mother was done in return for all of the kindness and care that she had shown him through-out his life and his duty to "return the favor." Finally, the single most pow-erful thing that he said with regard to all of his time spent with her was, "She was worth it," showing the Jewish value of each and every life and doing everything possible to help keep that person alive or, possibly more importantly, in good spirits. Again, however, his influence on my actual religious observances has been and continues to be limited. He is not the most observant Jew I have ever met and does not teach me Jewish prac-tices—more likely the other way around. But it is his role model of *men-schlichkeit* that I admire and try to emulate, as he has absorbed that model from others and I now absorb from him.

And what does my non-Jewish father, who does celebrate Christmas, but truly considers himself an atheist, bring to the equation? The biggest way that he impacts my values is through his acceptance. When he and my mom were together, he appeared to my young eyes as practically a Jew. He came to every service that we went to, celebrated every meal with us (though maybe just for the great food), and even one time when my mom and brother couldn't go to services, my dad brought me to the synagogue for Simchat Torah, and we both danced around the sanctuary. My dad did all this, and all that he asked in return was to celebrate Easter, mostly for his mother, and Christmas, both in a wholly secular way. Now that my par-ents are divorced, he still remains accepting, and he has even helped us with celebrating holidays. When we have been with him during Passover, he has served us every type of potato imaginable so that my brother and I can keep Passover. And when we have been with him during Chanukah, he has requested that we bring a menorah and candles so as not to put our celebration on hiatus. In these ways, my dad has influenced my values of tolerance and acceptance of others, which demonstrates how many Jewish values are really human values we all should try to embrace.

But as a Jew, and as a man, I feel that I have a responsibility to fulfill a duty. As a man I have to lead others in a proper way, but as a Jew, I must live by certain values that have been outlined for me. As I combine these two ways of life and try to find a way to do this properly, two things come to mind. First, I understand that as I observe those around me, I often incorporate principles I want to emulate into my own value system which then helps guide my development as a person. I must be a person who combines different ideas and make one composite blend that is appropriate for me. I must be myself and who I want to be, a person who is willing to uphold values that I have chosen, even as others may challenge them. This is made much easier by the second idea: the Jewish values of acceptance and compromise, which allow me to blend and balance all of these diverse concepts, experiences, lessons, practices, and customs into a powerful and meaningful combination.

As a Jew, I feel that I need to uphold the faith and rituals of my people, even as I also identify myself with many other groups of people. As a Jew, I need to represent the Jewish people. I am a Jewish man in my opinions and values, and some of my deepest values are respect and tolerance for others. As a man, I need to care for and lead others, but as a Jewish man, I have even more responsibility not to tolerate discrimination.

When I speak of myself as a Jew, I am almost always accepted, but in those times when I am not, I have to choose which model of manliness to follow. Sometimes I feel like following the stereotypical image of a manly response of one who has been insulted, which usually involves anger and aggression. But as I have watched those around me from whom I have derived my *menschlichkeit*, I have learned that this is at best not productive, and often counterproductive. So I have learned to try to explain calmly and without anger why Jews should not be viewed with negative stereotypes. Although any sort of intolerance angers me, my Jewish image of a man compels me to use reason and patience and even compassion in response to such challenges. By responding in this way, not only do I fulfill my responsibility to face down intolerance, but I model a Jewish way of doing so that teaches the other a different example of manliness.

When people think of what it means that someone is a Jew, they mainly think of the religious rituals and observances, but not of Jewish values. So many people know of the holidays and perhaps even about the services, but being a man is something that is outlined by Jewish values. To be a man, I believe, one must not only be of a certain age, but be an appropriate leader, and one that people can emulate. In this way I feel a duty to be a leader to those around me, whether they are Jewish or not, in my religious observances, my Jewish moral values, and my *menschlichkeit*.

THE NEW JEW

Marc J. Rosenstein

(based on Galilee Diary, January 21 and 28, 2007)

My father came from a traditional home; my mother's father was a social-ist. Both were Zionists who toyed with the idea of *aliyah* in the mid-1940s and who also brought their Zionism to their involvement in Reform synagogues. So for me, the synthesis of Reform and Zionism was natural, taken for granted. My parents, and Rabbi Robert Samuels, then assistant rabbi at North Shore Congregation Israel in Glencoe, Illinois, encouraged me to participate in the Eisendrath Israel Exchange (EIE) program. That real-life, intensive experience of Israel confirmed my Zionism—and my feeling that of all the different flavors of Zionist I could be, I was definitely a Reform Zionist. Over the years I visited Israel numerous times, to work, to study, and several times to serve as a coun-selor for Reform youth programs. Each time I discovered new facets of the country and of myself, and struggled with my ambivalence about where I should live as a Reform Zionist. Finally in 1990, my wife and I decided it was now or never, and we moved to Shorashim, a small com-munity in the Galilee affiliated with the Conservative Movement. We have never looked back. Tami is a speech clinician working in early inter-vention. I direct the Galilee Foundation for Value Education, which does informal educational programming in the areas of pluralism and Jewish-

Arab cooperation. My rabbinate is not pastoral, and I never preach. But I derive great satisfaction from the feeling that I am teaching the Torah as it was meant to be lived, as I seek to use education to make Israel the utopia I believe it must be.

> . . . Taking each others' pictures with the distinguished dead at
>   Rachel's tomb
> And Herzl's tomb and Ammunition Hill,
> Weeping for the beauty of the heroism of our boys
> And lusting for the toughness of our girls . . .
>
> —Yehudah Amichai, "Tourists"

Zionism was more than simply a movement to obtain land and statehood. It was a revolution against the Diaspora—and against the perceived nature of Jewish identity in the Diaspora. The Zionists sought to create a New Jew, who would be strong, brave, and natural, freed of the neuroses and fears of ghetto life. This direction in Zionism can be seen as reflecting a trend in European thought of the late nineteenth and early twentieth centuries—a feeling that European society was decadent and weak, cut off from its roots in blood and soil. Young intellectuals in Europe envisioned a New Man. So did, a little later, the Soviet Union.

In our case, the New Jew was expected to be some kind of a new hybrid, bringing together the virtues of rootedness in the soil; suntanned, muscular good health; simple morality and a sense of honor; courage and military prowess; a proclivity for wholesome, honest, physical labor; commitment to his community and his people; and some kind of Jewish cultural distinctiveness. While there was a certain amount of rhetoric, from the early twentieth century, about equality between the genders, which was certainly in keeping with socialist ideals, a lot more imagination and interest was focused on the New Jew than on the New Jewess. And the memoirs of the early pioneer women are full of frustration and even bitterness at their relegation to the laundry, the kitchen, and the nursery. I think that while there was a theoretical commitment to gender equality and the liberation of women from their traditional roles and status, the image of the New Jew was definitely a masculine, "macho" one. Those cute girl soldiers, it turns out, are mostly secretaries, teachers, and social workers in the army; and those *chalutzot* (pioneer women) spent an inordinate amount of time in the kitchen. American Jews cling to the image of Golda Meir as a nice Jewish grandma. But from closer up, it looks like she achieved her success in politics here by "acting like a man" among the men who built and ruled the country.

Israel, as it developed, incorporated a number of cultural influences that perpetuated traditional gender roles: perhaps first of all, the emphasis on defense, on the necessity of military thinking, skills, and prowess, on the culture of the army, generated a definition of the ideal Israeli male as "fighter" (a word transliterated into Hebrew phonetically to refer to a military "type"). Even six decades into statehood, the sense that we are under siege continues to be a part of our collective consciousness, and the combination of universal conscription and years of reserve duty (for men) to some extent convert the whole country into a barracks, dominated by buddies, comrades in arms, who enjoy an earthy, backslapping sense of esprit de corps that shows up in just about every social setting, and that is unquestionably masculine/macho in tone. Note that the opposite of a "fighter" is a "jobnik"—one who has a desk job or other noncombatant role in the army. Even though many men may be happy to get such assignments, traditionally it is not considered something of which to be proud. Another not-insignificant factor is the predominance in Israel of populations that represent premodern cultural backgrounds, societies that were and are extremely patriarchial—for example, Jews and Arabs from the Middle East, Ethiopian Jews, and Jews from ultra-Orthodox communities. These cultures are very much alive and present all around us, and even those who have grown away from their roots often find it hard to break away from deeply ingrained values and habits.

Meanwhile, of course, Israel is not immune to the cultural currents that flow around the globe. The small, close-knit society of the pre-state *yishuv* has grown into a modern state, diverse, divided, integrated into the world economically and culturally. Even in the most traditional communities, like the Arab villages, the increasing availability of local options for higher and vocational education means that young women are not consigned to working in local sewing shops until their marriage at twenty-one, but can aspire to a more satisfying intellectual and professional life path. And so, willy-nilly, men too have to readjust their expectations and their roles. These shifts often cause a great deal of personal suffering, and there are reversals and backlash. But the wheels of change seem unlikely to stop turning.

And while it is still true that Israel feels that if it does not remain the alpha male in the neighborhood it could disappear—and that feeling trickles down to an emphasis on traditional masculine virtues and male dominance throughout society—still, nothing is as simple as it used to be: Israel's entry in the Eurovision song contest in 1998 was transsexual pop diva Dana International. And in 2002 a popular film, *Yossi and Jagger*, dealt with a homosexual love story set in a combat unit in the army. Periodically the media cry *gevalt* over statistics that seem to indicate a decline in interest by high school seniors in combat units—and increased numbers of kids who find ways to opt out of army service altogether. The courts have found in favor of men who sued over prospective employers' use of their army record as a criterion for hiring. And now it seems that the traditional path from military to political leadership exemplified by people like Yitzchak Rabin and Ariel Sharon is no longer taken for granted; both our prime minister and our defense minister rose to their positions through civilian channels and are not military heroes or even veterans of elite units. It is interesting that while the army remains perhaps the most sacred of Israel's sacred cows, its centrality as a unifying and leveling force, its role as melting pot and identity builder have diminished over the past several decades. There are probably at least several reasons for this shift: the disillusionment over the Yom Kippur war; the feeling of failed leadership in the wake of the first and second Lebanon wars; globalization and the rise of individualism and materialism at the expense of the willingness to sacrifice for the nation; the realization that not all existential threats can be solved by force . . . These can be seen as disturbing trends, signs of disintegration—or as indications of the maturation and "normalization" of Israeli society. In any case, the decline in the centrality of the army experience in life and culture has helped open up the definition and expectations of male identity.

I remember, as an EIE student over forty years ago, being very much impressed and moved by the heroic sabra image: the ideal of the relaxed, straightforward, brave, idealistic young men—my high school classmates—and the subject of all the sad poems and songs of Memorial Day. This seemed to me the height of authenticity, just as it had to Jews seeking to shed the stereotype of the "Old Jew" sixty years earlier. Later, coming on *aliyah* in my mid-forties, I experienced certain pangs of guilt and/or disappointment that I had not paid my dues, had missed out on the formative experience of the army. And thus, it was with great ambivalence that I waved good-bye to each of my children at the induction center as they went off to serve in combat units: torn between feeling proud, feeling "really Israeli," and feeling terribly anxious—but beyond that, wondering if, at the bottom line, the Zionist dream was really to build a society in which patriotic pride at seeing our children put on uniforms would be such a central aspect of the culture. Is the solidarity of the tank crew really superior to that of the *chevruta* study partners in the yeshivah? How did we get to the idealization of strong young men instead of wise old ones? Are we still, somehow, prisoners of conceptions of authenticity that originated in early twentieth-century western Europe? Are we products of "the security situation"—or are we, by playing out these conceptions of heroism and strength, actually helping to create that very situation? If we are so powerful, then why are we powerless to change the reality in which we live? Or are we stuck in a narrow and macho understanding of what power is?

We will, I believe, continue to mature as a society. As the culture evolves, I believe we'll reach a time when we'll look back with a bemused smile at the masculine ethos that characterized our first sixty years. Ironic as it may sound coming from a Reform Zionist, I look forward to a softening of our resistance to the culture of the "Old Jew"—a renewal of our connection with the traditional understanding that redemption comes "not by might, and not by power, but by spirit" (Zecharia 4:6).

JUDAISM, MASCULINITY
AND FEMINISM

Michael Kimmel

In the late 1960's, I organized and participated in several large demonstrations against the war in Vietnam. Early on—it must have been 1967 or so—over 10,000 of us were marching down Fifth Avenue in New York urging the withdrawal of all U.S. troops. As we approached one corner, I noticed a small but vocal group of counter-demonstrators, waving American flags and shouting patriotic slogans. "Go back to Russia!" one yelled. Never being particulary shy, I tried to engage him. "It's my duty as an American to oppose policies I disagree with. This is patriotism!" I answered. "Drop dead you commie Jew fag!" was his reply.

Although I tried not to show it, I was shaken by his accusation, perplexed and disturbed by the glib association of communism, Judaism, and homosexuality. "Only one out of three," I can say to myself now, "is not especially perceptive." But yet something disturbing remains about that linking of political, religious, and sexual orientations. What links them, I think, is a popular perception that each is not quite a man, that each is less than a man. And while recent developments may belie this simplistic formulation, there is, I believe a kernel of truth to the epithet, a small piece, I want to claim, not as vicious smear, but proudly, I believe that my Judaism did directly contribute to my activism against that terrible war, just as it currently provides the foundation for my participation in the struggle against sexism.

What I want to explore here are some of the ways in which my Jewishness has contributed to becoming an anti-sexist man, working to make this world a safe environment for women (and men) to fully express their humanness. Let me be clear that I speak from a cultural heritage of Eastern European Jewry, transmuted by three generations of life in the United States. I speak of the culture of Judaism's effect on me as an American Jew, not from either doctrinal considerations—we all know the theological contradictions of a Biblical reverence for women and prayers that thank God for not being born one—nor from an analysis of the politics of nation states. My perspective says nothing of Middle-Eastern machismo, I speak of Jewish culture in the diaspora, not of Israeli politics.

The historical experience of Jews has three elements that I believe have contributed to this participation in feminist politics. First, historically, the Jew is an *outsider*. Wherever the Jew has gone, he or she has been outside the seat of power, excluded from privilege. The Jew is the symbolic "other," not unlike the symbolic "otherness" of women, gays, racial and ethnic minorities, the elderly and the physically challenged. To be marginalized allows one to see the center more clearly than those who are in it, and presents grounds for alliances among marginal groups.

But the American Jew, the former immigrant, is "other" in another way, one common to many ethnic immigrants to the United States. Jewish culture is, after all, seen as an ethnic culture, which allows it to be more expressive and emotionally rich than the bland norm. Like other ethnic subgroups, Jews have been characterized as emotional, nuturing, caring. Jewish men hug and kiss, cry and laugh. A little too much. A little too loudly. Like ethnics.

Historically, the Jewish man has been seen as less than masculine, often as a direct outgrowth of his emotional "respond-ability." The historical consequences of centuries of laws against Jews, of anti-Semitic oppression, are a cultural identity and even a self-perception as "less than men," who are too weak, too fragile, too frightened to care for our own. The cruel irony of ethnic oppression is that our rich heritage is stolen from us, and then we are blamed for having no rich heritage. In this, again, the Jew shares this self-perception with other oppressed groups who, rendered virtually helpless by an infantilizing oppression, are further victimized by the accusation that they are, in fact, infants and require the beneficence of the oppressor. One example of this culture of self-hatred can be found in the comments of Freud's colleague and friend Weininger (a Jew) who argued that "the Jew is saturated with feminity. The most feminine Aryan is more masculine than the most manly Jew. The Jew lacks the good breeding that is based upon respect for one's own individuality as well as the individuality of others."

But, again, Jews are also "less than men" for a specific reason as well. The traditional emphasis on literacy in Jewish culture contributes in a very special way. In my family, at least, to be learned, literate, a rabbi, was the highest aspiration one could possibly have. In a culture characterized by love of learning, literacy may be a mark of dignity. But currently in the United States literacy is a cultural liability. Americans contrast egghead intellectuals, divorced from the real world, with men of action—instinctual, passionate, fierce, and masculine. Senator Albert Beveridge of Indiana counseled in his 1906 volume *Young Man and the World* (a turn of the century verison of *Real Men Don't Eat Quiche*) to "avoid books, in fact, avoid all artificial learning, for the forefathers put America on the right path by learning from completely natural experience." Family, church and synagogue, and schoolroom were cast as the enervating domains of women, sapping masculine vigor.

Now don't get me wrong. The Jewish emphasis on literacy, on mind over body, does not exempt Jewish men from sexist behavior. Far from it. While many Jewish men avoid the Scylla of a boisterous and physically harassing misogyny, we can often dash ourselves against the Charybdis of a male intellectual intimidation of others. "Men with the properly sanctioned educational credentials in our society," writes Harry Brod, "are trained to impose our opinions on others, whether asked for or not, with an air of supreme self-confidence, and aggressive self-assurance." It's as if the world were only waiting for our word. In fact, Brod notes, "many of us have developed mannerisms that function to imtimidate those customarily denied access to higher educational institutions, especially women."[1]

And yet, despite this, the Jewish emphasis on literacy has branded us, in the eyes of the world, less than "real" men.

Finally, the historical experience of Jews centers around, hinges upon our sense of morality, our ethical imperatives. The preservation of a moral code, the commandment to live ethically, is the primary responsibility of each Jew, male or female. Here, let me relate another personal story. Like many other Jews, I grew up with the words "Never Again" ringing in my ears, branded indelibly in my consciousness. For me, they implied a certain moral responsibility to bear witness, to remember—to place my body, visibly, on the side of justice. This moral responsibility inspired by participation in the anti-war movement and my active resistance of the draft, *as a Jew*. I remember family dinners in front of the CBS Evening News, watching Walter Cronkite recite the daily tragedy of the war in Vietnam. "Never again," I said to myself, crying myself to sleep after watching napalm fall on Vietnamese villagers. Isn't this the brutal terror we have sworn ourselves to preventing when we utter those two words? When I allowed myself to feel the pain of those people, there was no longer a choice; there was, instead, a moral imperative to speak out, to attempt to end that war as quickly as possible.

In the past few years, I've become aware of another war. I met and spoke with women who had been raped, raped by their lovers, husbands, and fathers, women who had been beaten by those husbands and lovers. Some were even Jewish women. And those same words—Never Again—flashed across my mind like a neon meteor lighting up the darkened consciousness. Hearing that pain and that anger prompted the same moral imperative. We Jews say "Never Again" to the systematic horror of the Holocaust, to the cruel war against the Vietnamese, to Central American death squads. And we must say it against this war waged against women in our society, against rape and battery.

I see my Judaism as reminding me every day of that moral responsibility, the special ethical imperative that my life, as a Jew, gives to me. Our history indicates how we have been excluded from power, but also, as men, we have been privileged by another power. Our Judaism impels us to stand against any power that is illegitimately constituted because we know only too well the consequences of that power. Our ethical vision demands equality and justice, and its achievement is our historical mission.

NOTES

1. Harry Brod, "Justice and a Male Feminist," in *The Jewish Newspaper* (Los Angeles), June 6, 1958, p. 6.

STAGES OF JEWISH MEN

Jonathan K. Crane

Pirkei Avot (5:21) describes the growth and development of men as follows:

> A male at five years, for Scripture. Age ten, for the Mishnah.
> Age thirteen, for the commandments. Age fifteen, for the Talmud.
> Age eighteen, for the wedding canopy. Age twenty, for pursuit.
> Age thirty, for strength. Age forty, for understanding.
> Age fifty, for counsel. Age sixty, for being an elder.
> Age seventy, for gray hair. Age eighty, for might.
> Age ninety, for being bent.
> Age one hundred, it is as if one is dead and passed and ceased from
>   the world.

This text would have young boys learn and grow in a linear fashion, following the chronology and complexity of Jewish textual tradition. As men age, they take on different endeavors and ultimately achieve social stature and admiration before succumbing to biological limitations.

However admirable this linear version of a man's life is, this idealized notion of (hu)man development does not conform to reality. While this version provides clear benchmarks, boundaries, goals, and logic, who could follow this life plan to the year? In my experience and in the lives I have observed, Jewish male aging is different.

A second model of male development speaks less in terms of linear age than in broad stages. Commenting on this verse from Genesis— "Joseph dwelt in Egypt, he and his father's household, and Joseph lived 110 years" (50:22)—the Rabbis reflected:

> Moses spent forty years in Pharaoh's palace, forty years in Midian, and served Israel forty years. Rabban Yochanan ben Zakkai worked as a merchant forty years, studied Torah forty years, and served Israel forty years. Rabbi Akiba was an uncultivated person for forty years, studied Torah for forty years, and served Israel forty years." (B'reishit Rabbah 100:10)

The time frame of "forty years" is famous in the Jewish tradition because the Israelites wandered the desert eating manna for forty years. During this time, the generation who experienced slavery in Egypt died, and the younger generation came into adulthood. In a sense, the time frame of forty years represents a paradigm shift, a change from one mindset to another, as much as it is a change in one's bodily experience.

So, too, modern Jewish men go through paradigm shifts and, as the midrash teaches, usually we experience three. Most Jewish men emerge from boyhood with an education, values, and early employment. Then they embark on paths—career and personal—that take them to new places, and then, for one reason or another, they focus their energies onto Judaism and the Jewish community.

This pattern is reflected in my own life. My childhood was shaped by my family. My father, perhaps because he converted to Judaism, takes the intellectual issues of Judaism seriously and has always relished home rituals. His passion for understanding what it means to be a modern Jew reflects modernity's drive to put religion into intelligible terms. In some ways my own curiosity of our tradition emerges from his incessant questions regarding reasons for this or that ritual or value or text. My mother, too, instilled in me and my brothers a passion for learning and careful thinking, and an undeniable love for home cooking. My parents modeled an egalitarian partnership in which everyone's needs and interests were taken seriously and cared for with tenderness.

As a teen I became involved with the Reform Jewish youth group, NFTY. I quickly realized that by participating in all things Jewish with them, I would be one of a few Jewish men in a sea of Jewish women. In some circumstances, especially in leadership cadres, I found myself to be the sole Jewish man. This was as true in the temple youth group as it was at the regional and international leadership levels, and in other Jewish youth groups as well. Through these experiences, I became cognizant of the impact of egalitarianism on my life.

I continued this appreciation of gender when I matriculated at Wheaton College in Massachusetts (the same school my mother and grandmother attended) a few years after it switched from being a women's school to a coeducational institution. The school conscientiously infused all aspects of its curriculum, social and dorm life, athletics and leadership, with awareness to gender issues. As nothing was beyond the purview of such questions, I became convinced—and rightly so, I believe—that a healthy community wrestles with gender issues on an ongoing basis. Gender-critical reflective conversation continues to help me connect and communicate with women (and men!), if only to hear the plethora of voices in Jewish and non-Jewish communities.

I also saw how ongoing concern about gender would influence my personal life. My parents and my brothers have always modeled for me matters of the heart. A Jewish man, they teach, values his partner's well-being and happiness as much as his own. Albeit in different ways, my brothers and I take our wives' professional and personal pursuits seriously. This attitude is not unique to our family: I see many men in their twenties and thirties actively supporting their partners, male and female alike. Men want to partner with similarly ambitious people. This model of egalitarianism in one's home mirrored the new gender attitudes I learned and observed outside the home.

In parallel to the midrash above, I experienced a paradigm shift after emerging from college. My early experiences inspired in me a desire to resolve conflict. This desire partially stemmed from the way in which I understood gender relations and egalitarianism. Then, when I started to think seriously about my professional aspirations, I realized that as a rabbi I could probably be more effective at reducing certain kinds of conflict. This led to a further decision to earn a Ph.D. in modern Jewish ethics so that I could teach future communal leaders to address inevitable conflicts with moral maturity. These choices were paradigm shifts for me, from a childhood observing general issues of conflict and egalitarianism, to a career working from within a Jewish perspective.

In this new stage of life, I see the same new gender attitudes shaping my career. Jewish men are not the only ones who decide to become Jewish academics. Even though few women have gained substantial recognition in the field of modern Jewish thought and ethics, they tend to offer more explicit gender critiques than do men. This does not surprise me. Rather, it encourages me to stretch my own thinking and contributions to be similarly concerned about gender-related issues. The advancement of female scholars shapes my career in other ways as well. While third-generation feminisms emerge in the academy, I am part of a generation of men raised in multi-gendered schools, workplaces, social events, and homes. Indeed, my generation, by and large, celebrates the rise of Jewish female scholars. This brings, however, greater competition for particular academic spots, and while this may benefit knowledge generally, for the individual aspiring academic increased competition is, well, more competitive.

New gender norms in academia can also offer different opportunities for a man than in previous generations. Academic careers can reasonably flex as a family grows, and because my earning potential will be fairly limited (unless I write a best seller), I, along with many other male academics of my generation, may need to consider being a primary caregiver at some point and return later to academic work. Today's Jewish male scholars often have a curriculum vitae punctuated by periods of nonacademic activity. Of course, female scholars have long done this with great panache; I hope to live up to their benchmarks. I will not be surprised if in the next generation the notion of being a lifelong academic will be a historical relic. Perhaps this may be the case for many professions, especially in Jewish communal organizations including synagogues wherein "family values" are culturally and structurally integrated.

These kinds of changes in the professional trajectories of Jewish men and Jewish women reflect, I think, broader acceptance of diverse notions of Jewish masculinity (and femininity, of course). This broader acceptance creates greater options for how a Jewish man chooses to express or apply himself. Especially since the 1960s, a question arises whether it is reasonable to speak of only one form of Jewish masculinity at all. Perhaps as Daniel Boyarin, Howard Eilberg-Schwartz, David Biale, Jonathan Schofer, and a slew of other modern scholars have argued, there is a spectrum of contemporary masculinities prevalent among Jews.

Despite this greater variety of Jewish masculinities, we often typecast, categorizing Jewish men according to profession (the businessman, the clergyman, the academic man, the medical man, the political man, the family man, the shul and *beit hamidrash* man, the entertaining man, etc.) or by hobby (sporty-types who enjoy discussing or playing sports, intellectual-types who read voraciously, host-types who bring people together, and text-types who center their lives around texts—liturgical, legal, and midrashic). Even though many Jewish men would rather define their Jewish masculinity through a variety of engagements and attitudes, I find that Jewish men are nonetheless typecast by fellow men and, more often, by Jewish women. In casual conversations, I hear men (and women) described typologically (particularly by profession), and I see audiences nod with understanding. I am uncertain whether this typecasting is good or bad, but I think it follows an ancient and ingrained practice in Judaism to differentiate (*l'havdil*) this from that. On the other hand, I do see a tension between typecasting and the modern trend of (frequently) changing jobs, career tracks, location, and (Jewish) community and of a general openness to differences.

However difficult it is to maintain a personal sense of identity in this age of constant (egalitarian) shifting, I see Jewish men finding comfort in continuity, *Jewish* continuity in particular, much like it says in the midrash. I am no exception: after having invested in my education and pursued what I naïvely thought was going to be a world-changing career in conflict resolution, I have opted to work and live primarily within a Jewish context. It is in this stage of increasing personal connection and relationship with Judaism that I find myself becoming more, well, me. Its vast textual tradition, colorful communities, and rituals ground me in profound ways. The constancy Judaism provides enables me to enjoy modernity's changing challenges. I think the relationship is reciprocal inasmuch as I and many others bring to our Jewish living a heightened sensitivity to gender issues: we are changing Judaism even as it solidifies us.

I feel I am not alone in this experience of becoming more at home in Judaism. I have seen Jewish men and women around the world live something like the midrash's three stages. They take time to attend to personal issues like investing in their educations, pursuing vocations, and caring for families. Once they, men in particular, reach a particular stage professionally or familially, they tend to show up more frequently at synagogue and other places of Jewish learning. After a while, these men begin to express eagerness to serve their communities in leadership roles, as philanthropists and as stalwart participants.

It is rare, in my experience, to see Jewish men who take their Judaism seriously disappear completely from their communities. To be sure, this is not a hard-and-fast rule; some Jewish men yearn throughout their lives to dissociate themselves from the organized Jewish world. Nevertheless, I have found Jewish men in the United States and Canada, India and China, England and South Africa, take increasing interest in Judaism and their Jewish communities as they age. Something profound about Judaism and their Jewish communities entice men to seek ways to be involved. Perhaps it is for companionship, as my great-uncle told me, who at ninety-three still loves going to Torah study for the communal learning and so he can socialize with younger women—those in their eighties. Maybe it is for continuity, as those in far-flung places want to maintain something familiar from their Jewish childhoods. Perhaps aging men find increasing meaning in Judaism because they experience their approaching mortality as an inspiration to connect with what has not faded through the millennia. Maybe older men find that there is profound wisdom in the Jewish tradition and deep joy in the community beyond their (perhaps far-flung) ken.

It seems that Jewish men do not experience life linearly nor exclusively among other men. Rather, there are liminal moments in a Jewish man's life when he reconsiders his life, livelihood, and participation in the Jewish community. Even though these moments in a man's life arise idiosyncratically, they should be welcomed as benchmarks of being and becoming Jewish men.

GROWING UP JEWISH AND MALE

Max Rivers

My earliest memory related to being a Jewish male happened when I was about three. I remember walking to my grandfather's Orthodox shul. (I was raised in the Reform tradition, which is why this incident stood out in my mind.) It seemed odd, all these grown-ups, all dressed up, walking together in a herd through the dirty city streets. In the clean, pristine suburbs where we lived, grown-ups never walked. They drove everywhere. But I liked it. It seemed silly and out of the ordinary, like a party.

This festive mood changed abruptly in the dark, woody interior. Something mysterious and scary was happening as we entered the inner chamber. There was a low gravelly growl coming from men standing scattered around the main area of the room, swaying with their eyes closed, holding books and wearing what looked like beautiful white dresses over their dark suits. Occasionally, one or another of them would change his low moan into what sounded to me like a loud groan of pain and then would subside back into the group growl. I looked up at my father to see if he was going to help these men who were in such pain, but before I could figure out this mystery, another more confusing one swept over me.

I had been holding my mother's hand, and in such a strange place as this, that hand felt like my lifeline. Suddenly, my mother was drawn away from me, through a door that led up a dark flight of stairs. Other women were also moving in this direction, and as I had become accustomed to, I began to follow. But I was suddenly grabbed from behind and looking up, I saw my uncle holding me, laughing. I reached out to my retreating mother and was about to cry out when my father came up and wrapped me in one of the beautiful white dresses like the other men were wearing.

Up close, it was made of silk or satin, with crisp gold embroidery, and lots of soft tassels to play with. Then a satin cap was put on my head. I had never before been permitted to wear anything so soft and sensual. I remember looking up at my mother's retreating form, while fingering the tassels and holding onto the silky cap, then looking to my father's outstretched hand and feeling a tremendous conflict. One which it seemed must be resolved immediately, which was of immense importance, and of which I had almost no understanding.

That is where my memory ends, except for a flash of another image. I am sitting next to my father, surrounded by the moaning swaying men dressed darkly and draped in shining white talises. I crane my neck to see my mother up in the balcony, peering down at me through wooden bars. I remember that it seemed like something was very wrong with this separation.

I looked up at my father and at the other men, and back at the women cloistered away, looking for some sign that they too saw the injustice or felt the indescribable wrong that seemed so apparent to me. But seeing no such validation, I did something with those feelings. I have come to believe this kind of dilemma is often the case with little children. When their innate sensibility is contradicted, and the adults (or sometimes other children) around them don't seem to agree, they make the assumption that something must be wrong with them. And some precious part of them gets stored away forever (or until such time as it is brought back up into the light, and reclaimed). And this is just what I did.

It wasn't until recently that I uncovered this incident of my own Jewish history. I was seeking to reestablish a connection with the Jewish community after some twenty years as a self-described "anti-Semitic Jew," and in following that path I attended a service at a Reform synagogue that had rewritten their prayer book to remove sexist language.

As the service began, the cantor, a woman, came out and, before beginning, removed a beautiful white silk talis from its case, kissed the tassels, and draped it around her shoulders before taking her place in front of the congregation. I found myself staring at her the whole service. I felt myself fighting back tears the whole service long, and on the quiet ride home, I could feel something inside, healing.

Somehow, during that service I came to realize that what I had done with the wrong that I'd felt thirty years ago was to take it on myself. If I felt something was wrong, but neither my mother nor my father seemed to even notice, then it must be something wrong with me. It must be right to separate men and women this way, for men to pray out in the open, clothed in silk and satin, while women hid behind bars. And my feeling bad about that must be a flaw in me.

But seeing a woman and a talis together, proudly praying, leading prayer, brought back that little boy's feelings of rage and disempowerment. And gave back the man a little of his faith in his feelings for justice and equality.

STANDING TOGETHER AT SINAI?

David Segal

Every year when we recount the revelation of Torah to the Israelites at Mount Sinai, I wrestle gender and Judaism. In her pioneering work, *Standing Again at Sinai*, Judith Plaskow focuses on a verse from this episode. Moses's words to the Israelites, uttered three days before the revelation, are emblematic of the impediments to a feminist reclamation of Jewish memory and tradition: "Be ready for the third day; do not go near a woman" (Exodus 19:15). The problem, writes Plaskow, is that "at the very moment that the Jewish people stands at Sinai ready to receive the covenant . . . at the very moment when Israel stands trembling waiting for God's presence to descend upon the mountain, Moses addresses the community only as men. . . . At the central moment of Jewish history, women are invisible."[1] Plaskow justifiably asserts that "there can be no verse in the Torah more disturbing to the feminist than Moses's warning."[2] One can play interpretive games with the text and try to explain away the difficulty, as many scholars (the Rabbis included) have done. Ultimately, however, the Bible presents profound challenges to feminism and to women.

The more I think about and live this narrative, the more I realize how profoundly it challenges men, too. Moses's women-wary admonition, now part of our collective religious memory, also alienates me and potentially anyone who identifies as a pro-feminist man. I cannot feel fully involved in a Judaism that does not give voice to the prayers, hopes, and sufferings of my family, friends, and neighbors—women and men. To be sure, my exclusion is subtler and less immediately disenfranchising than women's, but it, too, undermines feminist progress.

This issue is complicated for me, personally. My maleness allows me to be present, at least physically, in Jewish male-only settings. It grants me the strange privilege of being approved to enter a "traditional," gender-segregated synagogue to experience prayerful *male* community, even though that setup is ultimately incompatible with my egalitarian theology. In a minyan that doesn't count women, I—though ambivalent—count. Sometimes, I feel like an impostor.

This discomfort became manifest during the year in Israel I spent as part of my rabbinic studies at Hebrew Union College–Jewish Institute of Religion (HUC-JIR). In the weeks leading up to the High Holy Days, our class visited a traditional, Sephardic synagogue in Jerusalem for a *S'lichot* service. The male students accompanied Cantor Eli Schleifer, Director of HUC's Cantorial Music Program in Jerusalem, into the main sanctuary. The female students went with the women faculty into the women's gallery, a distant balcony blocked off by a thick lattice wall that blocked their view almost completely. The service was a fascinating and educational experience, as the men of the congregation chanted back and forth, each trying to outdo the other in vocal gymnastics, volume, and prayerful intensity. I began to get caught up in the spirit of the moment—until I remembered the women of my community. They were crowded into a stuffy space and could barely see, let alone hear, the men below. Suddenly, my experience changed. Instead of a place for prayer, the synagogue and service became for me an anthropological experience. I could appreciate it as a kind of living museum of Jewish culture, but I could no longer fully participate in it as a worship community. In addition to ruining my female classmates' *S'lichot* experiences, the sidelining of the women shut *me* out—not physically, but spiritually.

I picture myself standing at Sinai, ecstatically lifting my hands toward God's imminent revelation, yet mournfully directing my eyes toward the distant disenfranchised—our mothers, our wives, our sisters, our daughters. I don't know where to stand, or if I even want to be there. How can I be a Jew with integrity if I condone, even tacitly, the exclusion of half of my community? Moses's warning threatens to rob me of the fullness of my Jewish experience, questions the integrity of my Jewish identity, and challenges my rightful place within the Jewish community. How can I, in good conscience, stand in the presence of God while the women stand apart?

All of this matters to me because *my* liberation from the yoke of oppressive gender barriers is bound up with women's liberation. As a man, I am bound by societal expectations about how men should act and what we should care about. "It is time, therefore," as Judith Plaskow said almost two decades ago, "to recover our history as the history of women and men, a task that will both restore our own history to women and provide a fuller Jewish history for the Jewish community as a whole."[3] Thus, we *all* have a stake in Jewish feminism, for the sake of our Judaism and our selfhood.

Yet, at the same time, I have sometimes felt excluded or overlooked by the feminist movement and feminist initiatives. I have been told more than once, upon questioning my exclusion, "Now you know how women have felt for thousands of years." This response is understandable and somewhat true, and I feel conflicted about how to respond. On the one hand, who am I to tell women not to react in anger or defensiveness at a man who wants "in" on "their issue"? On the other hand, maybe it is not just "their issue." As a man, I struggle to find a way to be involved in feminist progress in a sensitive and productive way.

This issue has taken on an ironic new dimension for me as a rabbinic student at HUC-JIR, where women outnumber men. This demographic shift has begun to appear in all corners of liberal Jewish life, and many Jewish organizations are scrambling to figure out what to do about the "disappearing Jewish male." The exodus of men from Jewish life is unfortunately a foil to the successes of Jewish feminism in Jewish life. It is normative in our communities now for girls and women to be actively encouraged to find their own voices, assert their individuality, and not let old-fashioned gender barriers fence them in. And God forbid that it should be any other way!

As a case in point, at a recent rabbinic mentorship meeting at HUC-JIR, I was reminded of the community and support that the Women's Rabbinic Network (WRN) has provided to women in the rabbinate since 1975.

A female rabbi at the meeting enthusiastically invited all the female students to attend the upcoming WRN conference. At that moment, a male rabbi within earshot of me whispered to his colleague, "When are we going to start the Men's Rabbinic Network?" While wholeheartedly supporting the vision and goals of the WRN, I still find myself asking why there is no parallel organization for men. We assume because of gender/power dynamics that the Central Conference of American Rabbis (CCAR) addresses male rabbis' needs. But as a man in the rabbinate I will also need an organization specifically charged with the development of a meaningful support system, the monitoring of issues that affect men in the rabbinate, and the advocacy of programs that further awareness of these issues.[4] Yet these issues are not considered "men's issues." The healthy and long overdue assertion of women's autonomy, needs, and aspirations might be healthy and long overdue for men as well.

Judith Plaskow remains my inspiration and guide. In the opening pages of *Standing Again at Sinai*, she includes a striking dedication: "To my son, Alexander Gideon Plaskow Goldenberg." That she would dedicate her foundational work of Jewish feminism to her son is in itself a profound statement. And just below this dedication, Plaskow quotes Adrienne Rich's *Of Woman Born*:

> What do we want for our sons? . . . We want them . . . to discover new ways of being men even as we are discovering new ways of being women.

This sentiment resonates strongly with my experience as a son in the Jewish community. I was fortunate to have strong role models in both of my parents, who showed me the importance of independence and cooperation. They were both actively involved in my upbringing and education, Jewish and otherwise. They both made deliberate professional choices that allowed them to be present for their children, such as working from home or avoiding business travel and long hours at the office.

Unfortunately, my educational experiences were not always as enfranchising or supportive. I remember presentations in high school and Hebrew school on women in the sciences or women in Jewish history, pep talks to assure girls that they could be engineers, rabbis, or anything they set their mind to. In college, not a month went by without an event sponsored by the Organization of Women Leaders, the Association of Women in Science, or some similar group to assure young women that all doors were open to them and that the dream of having both career and family was not out of reach. I worry that we boys were taken for granted in a subtle way, as if our sense of autonomy and self-worth would develop without nurturing. I would have benefited from being told early on—as the girls were—that I have a responsibility, together with my eventual life partner, to define the balance of family and career that will be fulfilling for me and my loved ones. Indeed, I want to dedicate myself to my future family and career. While the difficulty of work-life balance is repeatedly communicated to women from an early age, men are assumed to get it on their own—or, unfortunately, not to get it at all. I want paternity leave when I have children, and I want some flexibility with my hours so I can be involved in my children's upbringing. And it is frustrating to me that these are not seen as men's issues. Why is this kind of discourse about men still marginal, among men *and* women?

One of the greatest successes of the women's movement has been the empowerment of women to discover themselves anew and to take responsibility for the shaping of their individual and collective identity. Unfortunately, we continue to take the same qualities for granted regarding men. We assume that what has been so hard-won for women comes naturally to men, and we have yet to challenge the strict gender roles that still rule men's lives and choices. Now it would be wise to learn from the women's movement how to find our own voices, to "discover new ways of being men."

I hope that Jewish men are ready to take up this task of reinventing ourselves, to own it as women do. I hope that we will be willing to make the necessary sacrifices, to ask for help and offer support to our peers, and to hear the voices we may still be silencing—including our own. I pray that we remain focused on the goal, a vision of mutuality that promises empowerment and spiritual fulfillment for all.

Notes

1. Judith Plaskow, *Standing Again at Sinai: Judaism from a Feminist Perspective* (New York: Harper & Row, 1990), p. 25.

2. Ibid.
3. Ibid, p. 31.
4. Paraphrased from the WRN's list of goals, http://www.womensrabbinicnetwork.
org/index.cfm?fuseaction=about.

HE SAID, SHE SAID

Beth Kander

Jewish men? What do I know about Jewish men? I'm not one, and while I have lots of Jewish friends and lots of male friends, I have a proportionally small representation of Jewish male friends. I haven't dated a Jewish guy since college (rather a touchy subject with some members of my family). In sum, I am far from being an expert on the Jewish man.

And I'm not alone.

A few years ago, I participated in an exercise. In order to protect the identities of the other participants, I will simply set the scene by saying that we were a group of at least marginally Jewishly identified twentysomethings. The session facilitator divided us by gender and then instructed the males to write "Jewish women" at the top of a sheet of paper, and the females to write "Jewish men" at the top of another sheet of paper. She then gave three minutes for each gender-group to collectively come up with a list of word associations about the other gender. The women quickly filled the page with adjectives:

Short.

Hairy.

Cocky.

Career-obsessed.

Cheap.
Neurotic.
Mama's boys.

It was not a very nice list. There were a few kinder descriptors thrown in there, such as "good with kids/good fathers" and "smart," but they were far outweighed by the harsh critiques and condemnation of what seemed to be the ladies' two basic stereotypes of Jewish men: nebbishy Woody Allen types and self-important lawyer types. I didn't contribute anything to the list, positive or negative, but not for any reason other than that a few particularly enthusiastic women were so quick to feed their contributions to our designated scribe that the rest of us never even needed to open our mouths. However, I cannot exonerate myself: most of the words I would have said were on that list, called out by someone else in the group.

The facilitator asked us to share our words. Laughing nervously, we did so. The men in the room snickered at a few, rolled their eyes at others, and most had their arms crossed by the end. Somewhat wounded by the women's initial attack, the men were then happy to strike back and share their choice words for Jewish women ("whiny," "high maintenance," and "JAP," to name a few). Their list was shorter, but no kinder.

"Interesting," said the facilitator. "You know, I didn't ask you to list stereotypes; I just asked you to write down words you associated with Jewish men or Jewish women. Why do you think everyone was so harsh?"

We all sat for a moment, reflecting. I thought, what if she had asked us to think of *a* Jewish man and describe him, rather than describe "Jewish men"? My mind went immediately to my father, and words to characterize him came quickly: kind, funny, loyal, trustworthy, family-oriented, intelligent. A mensch. That's my dad. I also have two younger brothers, both Jewish men, both of whom could be assigned plenty of positive adjectives. Of the Jewish male friends I do have, some are grassroots political organizers, some starving artists, several are nice Jewish boys seeking nice Jewish boys. They live outside of the boxes the other women and I created in that list.

Why *were* we so harsh, the men to the women, and the women to the men? Reexamining the list, it was just as often not what we said but how we said it. Leaving anti-Semitic physical descriptors aside, we could have couched almost every attribute listed in a more positive manner. Instead of "career-obsessed," why not "hardworking" or "successful"? Instead of "cheap," why not "fiscally responsible"? Perhaps the exercise would have been just as upsetting if it had been word associations about just "men" and "women," rather than adding the Jewish twist. However, as it stood, it was a painful realization to witness the level of specificity with which we could cut each other down. Do Jewish women hate Jewish men—and vice versa?

Maybe it's like the "n" word, or the reclamation of the word "bitch" (a train I never did board, but I certainly have friends who are passengers). Within our own group, it's all right to tease and generalize and vent our frustrations about "our men" or "our women," but we're protective of one another outside.

Or are we? I'm not so convinced. I've overheard Jewish guys laughing with non-Jewish male friends, joking, "Yeah, well, you know how Jewish girls are." I have insider knowledge that Jewish women do the same thing, particularly when tearing apart their Jewish ex-boyfriends. The fact that half my family tree is non-Jewish has earned me the comment from *more than one* Jewish guy that I have "a certain level of *shiksappeal*"—and that's meant as a compliment.

Meanwhile, as we self-sabotage, others are wearing rosier glasses as they gaze at Jewish people. I came across several articles recently about the phenomenon of non-Jews utilizing J-Date, the popular Jewish dating Web site. Specifically, the surge is non-Jewish women seeking Jewish men, extolling the masculinity they see Jewish men as embodying. Their profiles explain how Jewish men appeal to them because they are more loyal, more trustworthy, better providers. They are the ones converting "neurotic" to "sensitive," and "cocky" to "secure" . . . and speaking of converting, J-Date responded to the growing contingent of non-Jews-seeking-Jews by adding "willing to convert" as a box that people can add to their profiles.

These guys they're talking about sound pretty great. Smart, sensitive men who provide for their families? Is that not masculine? Is it less masculine, and therefore somehow less appealing, than motorcycle-riding fallen Catholics who can't commit? (Purely to pull an example out of thin air, of course).

In our allegedly enlightened era, might it be time to start glorifying stability over shock value—and thereby begin to redefine masculinity? Whether or not the stereotypes are true, whether or not they apply to any given individual, might the paradigm shift be under way wherein the-Jewish-men-who-make-good-fathers replace the gentile-bad-boys as the epitome of masculinity? Could be. Seems like at the very least, it's time for Jewish women to come up with a nicer list of words to describe Jewish men . . . and vice versa.

THE GLASS FLOOR

Karen Perolman

"Look! It's snowing," someone called out, and we all looked up. Through the glass ceiling of the Hebrew Union College–Jewish Institute of Religion's New York campus we saw the small flakes of snow descending from the sky. As the conversation quickly moved to the possibility of a snow day and getting hot chocolate before class, I recognized the irony of the situation. Here we stood, six female rabbinic students watching the snowfall through HUC-JIR's glass ceiling.

Growing up female in the 1990s I frequently heard about the "glass ceiling" I would eventually encounter. Often at an *Oneg Shabbat*, older women would tell me that as a woman, I would be able to look up and see all the possibilities available to me, but I would then have to break though the glass to access them. Secretly, I always wondered if I would receive some sort of "rite of passage" hammer in order to break the glass or if I would be expected to use my fists. As a teenager, when I told people that I wanted to be a rabbi, many would respond, "I didn't know that women could be rabbis!" or "Talk about a gender reversal!" The Judaism of that generation conformed to strict gender roles: women stayed on the ground, advising youth groups and presiding over Sisterhood meetings, while men led on the bimah, serving as rabbis and cantors. Those same older women at the *Onegs* even told me that *my* glass ceiling would be embossed with Jewish stars. Choosing to pursue a traditionally male career was progressive, I knew, and there would be challenges to overcome, but I felt as if I could follow any career path I wanted. Doctor, scientist, politician, rabbi—they were all the same in my mind. And when I closed my eyes and dreamt of life as a rabbinic student, I saw rows and rows of men and one bouncy ponytail sticking out with a pink *kippah* pinned to the top.

Over the past two years, as news of the "men's crisis" has crept into my inbox and my consciousness, I have begun to think differently about the idea of a glass ceiling. As a second-year student at HUC-JIR, my awareness of this phenomenon grows when I look around my classes and count twelve female students and only seven male. When the entire school gathers together, there are easily two women for every man. My Hebrew class in the Year-in-Israel Program contained exactly ten women and one man.

Rewind to a hot July day in the summer of 2005. I was standing in line at the HUC-JIR campus in Jerusalem waiting to receive my new student packet. Everywhere I gazed there were women, mostly young, and many looked just like me. There were dozens of bouncy ponytails. A few males sprinkled the crowd, but if I quickly scanned the room I could swear that I had just signed up for a women's yeshivah. Later that week, speaking of the large number of females at our *ulpan* orientation, Rabbi Na'amah Kelman, director of the Year-in-Israel Program, quoted feminist and women's rights activist Gloria Steinem: "We're becoming the men we wanted to marry." My entire Year-in-Israel class, fourteen men and forty-one women, struggled with the gender shift, thinking of the upcoming year we would collectively experience. While I had expected to be in a female minority, I instead found myself in a large group of women. Publicly, we joked about the drought of men, the failure of our movement to retain males after their *b'nei mitzvah*, and the small numbers of males at NFTY events. Privately, many of us worried that the dearth of men would become the death of men in our community. Male congregants would continue to exist as fathers and husbands and bar mitzvah boys, but women would exclusively control the leadership of the Reform Movement.

How will this gender switch impact the next generation of Reform Jews? Should I be more mindful of my male sixth grade students? Should I encourage my male friends to pursue the rabbinate? What should I be doing to help change this pattern? As a future rabbi, I feel nervous for what is to come. These questions will remain with me as I enter the rabbinate, a female leader in my community. While I am elated that women have begun to burst through the glass ceiling, I recognize my commitment to help reverse the trend of the disappearing man.

But today in January 2007, I'm sitting in my apartment in Brooklyn watching Katie Couric, the first woman to host the evening news. I'm reading about Nancy Pelosi, the first female Speaker of the House of Representatives. I'm flipping through *Lilith* magazine's feature article about the retirement of Sally Priesand, the first female Reform rabbi, ordained more than thirty years ago. The urgency of this gender equality crisis feels far from these pioneering moments in women's history. So perhaps as women are breaking through our glass ceilings in the public arena, in the private arena men have their own glass floor. The sky may be their limit, but it is the ground where they are needed.

PART 3

GOING TO THE WILDERNESS:
SEARCHING FOR IDENTITY

INTRODUCTION

W hen Elijah flees Mount Carmel, he does not proceed directly to Mount Sinai. He simply flees. At this point all he knows is his rejection of the methods of power that are the norm of his society. The text tells us that he makes his way as far as Beersheba, leaves his servant there, and then continues into the wilderness. He finds a broom-bush, lies down beneath it, and prepares to die. He is in complete confusion and despair. At what might seem the moment of death, an angel appears and provides food and water. But this is not enough to convince him that he must carry on. One meal cannot spring him from the pit of his bewilderment. But after the angel repeats the miracle, Elijah realizes he must make his way to Sinai (I Kings 19:3–8). Something happens in that moment where he discovers a new direction. The wilderness can do that. At first it appears terrifying, but then it can be life-giving.

We find this message elsewhere in the Bible. After Moses sends twelve spies to scout the Promised Land and ten of them return filled with fear of their future Canaanite enemies, God punishes them with the decree that the generation of slavery shall die in the desert. The wilderness becomes a place of fear and death. But the punishment also means that a new generation, born in the desert, will arise without fear, and they will take the land of milk and honey. Thus we wander for forty years (and not, as the joke goes, because Moses refused to stop to ask for directions).

The message of this text is clear. The wilderness inspires an attitude different from civilization. Elijah can discover new options under a broom-bush. He can consider that a different form of Power might be possible and then proceed to Sinai in order to find it. The Israelites of the desert generation will differ from those slaves raised in the confines of Egypt. A great empire like the one along the Nile may offer the tremendous opportunities of technology, society, arts, culture, education, and power. But those opportunities come burdened by expectations, rules, restrictions, and a limited field of reference.

The wilderness, while it may be terrifying, teaches the opposite lesson. In the wilderness, old rules fail and fall, allowing the society or the individual to discover newer, healthier, more robust forms of behavior.

Just as Elijah and the Israelites needed the experience of wilderness in order to transform their faith and social structure, so too does the individual man often need a similar experience in order to (re)discover his life's path. In his foundational work of the Men's Movement, *Iron John: A Book about Men*, Robert Bly posits that every man needs an initiatory experience in order to truly become a man. Bly believes that initiation must come from an older man—not a father—who forces the boy through a trauma into a new understanding of male behavior.

> The job of the initiator, whether the initiator is a man or woman, is to prove to the boy or girl that he or she is more than mere flesh and blood. A man is not a machine only for protecting, hunting and reproduction; a woman is not a machine only for protecting, gathering and reproduction, but each carries desires far beyond what is needed for physical survival. William James praises "the number and fantastic and unnecessary character" of the human being's wants.[1]

The initiation transforms childish wants into adult, mature, healthy lifelong desires. By coming through the initiatory experience, the individual redefines his or her old assumptions and finds new tools for interpreting and responding to life's demands.

Robert Moore and Douglas Gillette describe four male archetypes—the king, warrior, magician, and lover—that can each function in a destructive immature form or in a healthy, productive, and ethical mature form. They see the need for initiatory transformation as essential to correcting some of the great inequities of the world. "How well we transform ourselves from men living our lives under the power of Boy psychology to real men guided by the archetypes of Man psychology will have a decisive effect on the outcome of our present world situation."[2] The same could be said for the future of Judaism.

While Judaism has formal initiation rites—namely bar/bat mitzvah and confirmation—these are rarely the moments of personal transformation described by Bly, Moore, and Gillette. Men today find initiation, crisis, and wilderness at many points in their lives, often long after their teen years. This may be a function of the recent slide of adolescence into the twentysomething years, or it may say something about the ineffectiveness of contemporary ritual, or both. In addition, the role of initiator can be found in the archetype described by Bly, a non-father adult man, but more frequently men today are finding initiators from a variety of personae. Regardless, this initiation experience remains crucial to personal development for many men.

The essays in this section describe different moments of crisis, wandering, loss, and then the road to salvation, redemption, understanding, and security. Like Elijah, whose flight from Carmel led him to the Negev and Sinai deserts, some of these men found themselves sleeping in the dirt beneath a broom-bush. They sometimes needed angels to provide food, water, and direction. But they all made it through the wilderness to a new destination. That experience can instruct us about how contemporary Jewish men are transforming their lives. It provides inspiration for other men undergoing similar experiences and begs community to consider ways of incorporating new opportunities for initiation into Jewish life. These essays span a variety of the common facets of men's lives today—relationships, work, son-hood, fatherhood, community, and, unfortunately, addiction—and the ways that each of these experiences contain the potential for confusion and redefinition.

The first essays grapple with issues of relationship. Two essays begin after marriage, with divorce, and describe the experience of self finding that led both writers, Stuart Debowsky and Rabbi Dan Moskovitz, to seek new male communities and new definitions of masculinity. Norman

Cohen also describes how his study of Torah eased his journey through divorce and family transformation as well as his passage through the deaths of his mother and father and the serious illness of his son. Finally, Rabbi Victor Appel's description of his journey to acceptance of his identity as a gay man highlights the importance of community and support for men wandering through the thickets of sexual identity.

Rabbi Steven Z. Leder approaches the subject of work and describes how his life as a rabbi often leaves him gasping for air, which leads him to the ritual of *mikveh* as a source of redemption. Rabbi Simeon Maslin describes a journey to Jerusalem to close the eyes of his dead father and along the way considers how he grew to understand a relationship that began with abuse. Paul Schoenfeld also addresses his relationship to his father and how the need to adjust his unrealistic expectations re-creates the relationship. Scott Sager and Yigal Rechtman both describe the challenges of modern fatherhood and the ways that this role forces them to reexamine their relationship to Judaism. In the case of Sager, as the primary caregiver, he must relearn Jewish home rituals, and for Rechtman, he reconsiders his identity, since he was raised in Israel but now raises his children as Jews in the Diaspora.

Rabbi James Prosnit and rabbinic student Neil Hirsch both explain the need for community. Prosnit does so by writing about the men's group he formed at his synagogue and the variety of ways they have explored Judaism and their lives. In contrast, Hirsch discovers the need for male community through the disorienting experience of watching female rabbinic students prepare a presentation of *The Vagina Monologues*.

This section also contains an anonymous essay by a man who suffered from food addiction and the way that the Big Book of AA and the 12-step process helped him redefine himself and his relationship to Judaism. Another rabbinic student, Owen Gottlieb, explains how the discovery of a men's ritual, the *Kiddush L'vanah*, inspired him to reconsider the way that rituals help him define his selfhood, particularly his masculinity. And finally Lary Bloom describes how his desire for personal transformation led him to seek out an initiatory experience from his past, as a soldier in Vietnam. His essay, perhaps more than most of the others, describes how his transformation is ongoing.

Each of these essays displays an alternative route through the wilderness and offers multiple examples of ways that Judaism can help or hinder the process. They show how contemporary Jewish men grapple with life's challenges and what communities can do to assist in those challenges. These moments of crisis are the most obvious ways in which individuals desire transformation, but they are by no means the only times men feel the need for initiation. While the more common examples of initiation (e.g., bar mitzvah, fraternity hazing, military indoctrination) are not in this section, these essays provide emblematic lessons for us all.

NOTES

1. Bly, Robert. *Iron John: A Book about Men*. Reading, MA: Addison-Wesley, 1990, p. 55.

2. Robert Moore and Gillette Douglas, *King, Warrior, Magician, Lover* (San Francisco: HarperSanFrancisco, 1990), p. 145.

UNDERSTANDING MANHOOD

Stuart Debowsky

Within the period of about a year, I divorced my wife, lost not one but two jobs, and, in some ways, degraded my sense of self-respect. It was only then, around age thirty, that I taught myself about "being a man" and standing on my own two feet—for the first time. I can still remember the realization that I needed to find an inner strength. I can also remember talking to God at length for the first time in many years. And, I remember wanting my own father to teach me things again. Mostly, though, I remember crying (literally sobbing, more than I ever had previous to then as an adult) in total disbelief that my life experience had not prepared me to handle the challenges ahead; I felt small, weak, and humbled by the maturity that needed to occur in order to be healthy and move forward.

Like other men, I would imagine, my solution started with an accounting of what I possessed in my life, a list of things that I could count on to make my situation better. In many ways, I actually found comfort in those who counted on me; my family looked for me to rebound, and my friends struggled to understand the situation and seemed to *rely on me* to make it better for them! Foremost, however, I realized that my role as a part-time high school youth group director at the synagogue compelled me to continue to model a positive young adult's life and reinforced my belief that (oftentimes) the teacher learns from the students. In the teenage world, gender roles are overemphasized, planning for the future is exaggerated, and those in my group constantly looked to me as the conduit toward a better understanding of the adult world. We held "guy's night out" events (the teenager-appropriate kind!) and participated in weekend retreats on manhood, all meant to self-define our masculinity. The participants were half my age and to my profound surprise, my struggle for identity was just as prevalent as theirs! It was primarily in this position, as the role model to so many impressionable young men, that my own sense of responsibility was underscored; this was the moment when I acknowledged that being a man sometimes meant seeking out personal fulfillment for others to witness and from which to draw strength, even if it meant showing the vulnerability that life imposes along the way. I was never alone on the journey toward that realization.

Still, I decided to endeavor toward an independent definition of manhood, one that would be a consistent touchstone for the future, wherever that was to take me in the coming years. I knew that I had to demarcate my own path, as my own man, to grow confidently.

Although it may seem clichéd to find my "answers" in the synagogue (don't only desperate people look for wisdom in religion?), I cannot deny the instant "community" I found in our temple's informal Saturday minyan service, and ironically I connected with a number of the parents of my youth group members. This casual group of men and women—professionals and retired, some wealthier than others—was truly accepting of me as a fellow adult and appreciative of the modeling I had done for their children. It was here that I reconnected with three key elements of the life I aspired toward. First, I took on a newfound appreciation for Torah and the writings of our people; I found the teachings comforting and extraordinarily modern in dealing with the complexities of adult life. Next, I learned the value of taking time to stop, meditate, and reconsider things. There is something about devoting a Saturday morning purely for yourself, to take stock of things, which provided a powerful perspective on the way my life was changing. And lastly, perhaps most importantly, I discovered the value of persistently seeking out a number of mentors of my own, as a developing man. Somehow, I had lost sight of the concept of identifying a few people, perhaps at the next stage of life, and spending the time to understand their experiences. I wondered when I stopped relying on my father's wisdom, all too sure that I had gotten all that I could from him. Sadly, I realized that my development did not leave room for humility, as gregarious confidence seemed to be my own secret to success. I found myself realizing that I needed to take a closer look at the truly fortunate men of the minyan community—those who had balanced individual wealth with a sense of personal peace. Thankfully, the synagogue had a number of people—all with a variety of outstanding personal qualities and diverse levels of accomplishment—who could be studied and treasured as models to glean from. In truth, it felt like a very "Jewish" experience to pass along knowledge (or receive it, anyway), and I know that I am a better man as a result of being the lucky beneficiary of contemporary wisdom and the humor that only age provides.

I stand taller today than ever before, in many ways a product of all that broke me down at that dark time in life, and certainly due to those who cared enough to build me back up. I owe my life to men like my father, who made me see my strength, and to those who acted like fathers when they certainly had children of their own to raise; they taught me the value of brotherhood, in a global sense, and they showed me, through the model of their lives, that life is a very long path to travel. I do not consider myself "manly" by any stretch of the definition, forever apathetic to discussions on automobiles, electronic gadgets, and just about anything related to being outdoors. I am, however, more prepared these days to be a responsible member of my community, a loving husband and father to my own (unborn, as of yet) children, and a more confident professional when challenging situations come my way. I asked God for this insight, and I have made myself the promise to represent this serenity to the generation that comes after me, perhaps at the same synagogue minyan group. For me, understanding manhood required expanding my circle. To be a man translated to accountability. It meant to love what others loved in me.

MALE MYTH #101:
MEN DON'T ASK FOR DIRECTIONS

Dan Moskovitz

In the spring of 2003, I found myself lost—which is to say that I was lost and without a direction or compass in life—and by being lost I found the man I truly was and discovered a path toward the one I wanted to be.

It was in April of that year, the day before Pesach, that my marriage of eight years ended. I'm a congregational rabbi, and the day before Pesach is a big event in our preschool. Each year I dress up as Moses, and staff in hand, I free our preschool students from the bondage of their class-rooms and lead them on a harrowing journey across the desert of the playground, to the Promised Land of our social hall. That morning, they would have to free themselves. Moses himself was in need of salvation.

My ex-wife and I met in college, married a week after graduation, and lived a grad student's life through the six years of rabbinic school and my first year in the rabbinate, with no children, a rented apartment, and mostly borrowed furniture. When our marriage ended, there was little to divide up (she kept the cats, thank God!) and even less to mourn—it was as clean a break as one could possibly make—the saying, "they grew apart" described us well.

That night, freed from a bondage of the spirit, I was alone for the first time in ten years. Sleeping on a friend's sofa bed, with a bar cutting into my ribs, I was free, but I was lost. Like my ancestors before me, like Moses himself; I was in the desert. I had been on a path my whole life, a path toward marriage, family, and a career. Somewhere along the way I realized that the path I was on was not leading in the direction I wanted to go, but I took comfort that I was on the path. Momentum is a very powerful force; it is so often easier to just keep heading down the road than to stop and change direction. Even if you don't like the direction your life is headed in, as I felt about my marriage years before it ended, it is so easy to say to yourself, "Follow the road; at least you're moving."

That is why Judaism makes such a big deal out of the process of t'shu-vah, of turning and repentance on Yom Kippur. If it was so easy, we wouldn't dedicate a whole holiday to convincing us to do it. A student asked his rabbi, "Rabbi if you are going down a road all of your life and you discover that you are headed in the wrong direction, what do you need to do to change course?" The rabbi responded, "If you want to change the direction of your life, all you have to do is turn around."

That morning the road disappeared, the traveling companion was gone, the destination just vanished. I was lost in the desert and didn't know which way to turn; all of my compass points had vanished. Laying on that sofa bed I remember looking up at the cottage cheese ceiling of my friend's basement and wondering, "Now what? Where do I go from here?" I was lost, and since men don't get lost and they don't ask for directions, what I was really feeling was, "I have failed as a man."

So much of our identity as men is tied up in our accomplishments, on the sports field, in business, in our stock portfolio, getting best seats at the baseball game or a better table at the restaurant. But more than all of those combined, getting and keeping a wife are viewed by many men as their greatest accomplishment, in part maybe because it seems so improbable at the outset; because it actually involves another person, we can't do it alone. It is how we were raised; Jewish tradition has taught us since Adam and Eve, "it's not good for man to be alone" (Genesis 2:18).

I remember during my frantic search to find a place to sleep other than my buddy's sofa bed, I visited a national chain of "furnished corporate apartments." When I walked into the lobby and inquired about an application from the female receptionist, I felt like I should have been issued a sign, "Male Failure, Recently Divorced"—in fact that might have been what she stamped on my form when I turned it back in. As I sat in the indestructible lobby furniture, I realized that there were three other guys in the lobby as well, all filling out similar forms. I looked them over and they too looked like they had been sleeping on a friend's sofa bed for a week and living out of their hatchback—which I guess made the sign idea totally unnecessary.

In the same moment that I noticed them, they each looked over at me and gave me that subtle guy head nod that says, "Yeah, buddy, I know what you're going through." It was a head nod that could have knocked me over, if my indestructible lobby chair had not been built out of solid oak and cinder block. "Yeah," I said to myself, "I bet you do." It was the most comforting head nod I had received in a lifetime of head nods.

In the lobby of some massive apartment complex, in the middle of my desert, I found my traveling companions. When I thought no one could understand what I was going through, in the knowing nod of a sofa-bed disheveled head I found acceptance, understanding, and friendship. When you're lost and walking in the desert, the greatest feeling in the world is to discover the way out, and the second greatest feeling is to realize that you are not alone. I was in the company of men—I was not alone!

To get out of the desert, you need three things: a traveling companion, a destination, and a map on how to get from where you are to where you want to be. The ancient Israelites had Moses, each other, and God; their destination was the Promised Land, a land flowing with milk and honey, and their map was the Torah. At the moment, I had three guys in a lobby, but I am a Jew—my people had survived the desert many times before, I could do this, it's in my blood.

The Rabbis teach that the Israelites wandered in the desert for forty years before reaching the Promised Land. This period was necessary to unlearn all the bad habits acquired in Egyptian bondage and to learn not only the words of Torah, but how to *live* the words of Torah.

Forty years seems like a long time to find yourself and reclaim your manhood, but I figured I would give it as long as it took. The first lesson I would learn about what it means to be a Jewish man would be patience, patience with myself.

For my map I drew inspiration from my wandering Jewish ancestors, beginning with Torah. I am a rabbi and have read the Torah beginning to end many times, but I had never read it through the eyes of a divorced man trying to find his way out of the desert. That is the remarkable thing about the Bible. It never changes, but we do. The text has been the same for thousands of years, the stories unchanged from when I learned them in Hebrew school, and yet every time I read it I find that it speaks to me and connects with me differently. It is like a mirror; our reflection in the glass makes no lasting impression on the mirror, but what we see reflected back to us makes a profound impression on how we see ourselves. This reflection led me to other sources, books, and articles on being a man; they were not easy to find, but slowly, with the help of the Internet, I assembled my map.

For traveling companions, I assembled a group of men, men from my congregation. They were all in their own desert of one form or another. Some had gone through divorce, some had lost parents, some were out of work, some discovered their home was now an empty nest, and some were dealing with the challenges of raising children, providing for a family. Everybody has a desert they want to get out of.

We started by meeting in my living room once a month, getting to know each other and affirming that this was a safe place to share our stories. It began with a simple but powerful exercise: we had to introduce ourselves to the other guys without saying what we did for a living. As men, we so often define ourselves by what we do, how we provide for our families. It's probably deeply connected with our hunter-gatherer nature, and it certainly feeds our competitiveness with each other.

I felt that this group would work only if we could retrain ourselves to change this damaging and isolating pattern. We had to teach ourselves to see other men as brothers, with good things to give and to receive.

I also established four ground rules that I had gleaned from reading. I copied them and handed them out to my brothers.

1. Confidentiality—what happens in Vegas stays in Vegas, what is said here stays here.
2. No put-downs of others or talking about people by name who are not here—wives or bosses, present and former specifically.
3. Hear each other out; let a man finish. The emphasis is on listening to each other speaking from our hearts, rather than interrupting

with argument or well-meaning advice. We get plenty of that in our normal lives.

4. You don't have to speak, but when you do, use "I" statements, no bullshitting, say what you mean and what you feel, and don't talk too long.

I made study sheets from the books that I read, I connected them to the wisdom of our tradition from Torah and Talmud and midrash, and there in my living room, of my unfurnished, not so corporate apartment, we studied and we journeyed out into the desert together.

Our topics were obvious—if only by how uncomfortable it was to talk about them at first. Why we work so hard. What kind of fathers we had, what kind of fathers we are. Being a husband. Health, sex, money, God, power, friendships. If a topic made us uncomfortable to think about talking about in a room full of men, it became a topic.

We'd look back on where we had been, and we'd imagine where we would like to be headed, how we would like to change course in our lives. And we did that very unmanly thing—when we felt lost, we would ask for direction, first from the text, and when that was not sufficient, we would ask it from each other. Each man's desert was another man's well-learned map, and from our shared experiences we helped each other find our individual Promised Lands.

We have been meeting for four years now The group has changed some; members have come and gone and come back again. But change was the whole point. Some have found their Promised Land, others are still in the desert. But in either case none of us are wandering around alone. For me personally, I found myself and have begun to assemble the answer to my question, what does it mean to be a Jewish man? This essay is part of that process, and so is my incredible wife and our newborn son. One day, he too will find himself lost—for all men get lost—and in that moment, though hopefully long before, I will teach him how to ask for directions, just as I learned from my brothers. And he will discover, as I have, that "in the company of men," you are never truly lost—indeed, you can be found.

ETZ ḤAYYIM HI:
IT IS A TREE OF LIFE

Norman J. Cohen

The defining metaphor for the Jewish people is the Exodus from Egypt and the ensuing journey through the desert to the mountain and ulti- mately the Promised Land. One one level, it is the paradigm of the life journey of each and every one of us, as we move from Egypt, *Mitzrayim*— that is, *metzarim*, the narrow places, the places that oppress and limit us—to the openness of the desert and its potential for liberation. We, like our ancestors, must throw off the yoke of confinement, that which ties us to the purely material and immediate, and move into uncharted territory which offers a glimpse into eternity.

The crowning moment in the paradigmatic journey of our people took place at Mount Sinai. After having the yoke of Egyptian oppres- sion removed from us, we exercised our newly found freedom by accepting the Yoke of Heaven, or *malkhut shamayim*. This sealing of the covenant between ourselves and God should have been the cul- mination of our journey; it should have taken place at the end of the trek through the desert. Yet it occurred close to the outset of the forty-year sojourn in the wilderness, in the third month of the first year, and, we ask, Why? Why did God give the Torah to the people of Israel so early on in their journey, when they still must have been in utter shock from the events surrounding the escape from Egypt and the parting of the waters of the Red Sea.

Sinai, however, was never the ultimate goal. *Matan Torah*, God's revelation of Torah to Israel, was to be perceived not as an end but as a means. In order to survive the desert and somehow make their way to the Land of Israel, the people needed the redemptive vehicle of God's word. It was the Torah which would enable them to overcome the aridity of the desert, the moments of fear and doubt, and the loneliness of the journey.

The struggle for survival in the desert has a way of sapping all of one's belief and strength. No wonder then that only a short time after passing through the Red Sea, when they were inundated by its waters, which had cleansed them from the Egyptian experience and carried them closer to the Land of Israel, and when they had uttered their song of redemption to God (*Shirat ha-Yam*, Exod. 15:1–21), the Israelites found themselves without water (Exod. 15:22). Whatever they had experienced at the Red Sea, the sense of God's presence and power, a moment of uplifting song, dissipated in the course of three short days in the heat of the desert sun.

We, like the Israelites of old, try to survive in the prosaic interval of our lives, in the long stretches between the rare moments of uplift that we feel. Like the Israelites, we search desperately for the source of our own salvation on the journey of our every day. We, too, long to reach the nearest oasis in the hope of drinking from its salvific waters.

Ironically, when the Israelites did come upon an oasis, its waters were too bitter to drink (Exod. 15:23). It, therefore, was called Marah (Bitterness). However, upon hearing the complaints of this fledgling people, Moses cried out for help to God, who showed him a tree, a piece of wood. And Moses took the wood and threw it into the water, which somehow transformed the bitter waters of Marah into waters of sweetness, waters of salvation (Exod. 15:24–25).

Commentators from Rashi onward have continually wondered about this miraculous tree whose wood could make the bitter waters sweet. As Gunther Plaut notes, trees like the oak contain tannin, which can neutralize the alkalinity of water, thereby causing the bitter matter to sink to the bottom.[1] Yet, if we do not take the text literally, understanding it instead to have symbolic power, then perhaps it is not important to know the type of tree intended by the biblical writer. The rabbis know this very well, as they demand that we listen to the words used by the biblical writer. The Exodus text does not read *va-yareihu etz*, "God showed Moses a tree," but *va-yoreihu etz*, which means, "God taught him a tree." And what tree might it have been that God taught him which enabled him to make the bitter waters sweet? Of course, it had to have been the Torah, the *Etz Ḥayyim*, the Tree of Life.[2] What allows the rabbis to interpret this narrative so symbolically? The words which immediately follow in the very same verse in the text (v. 25): "There God gave them a statute and ordinance," i.e., the Torah.

For the rabbis, as for us, the Torah is the vehicle that transforms the bitter waters into waters of salvation. In order to survive the desert journey and all of its trauma, in order to traverse the distance between Egypt and the Promised Land, we Jews have only one means at our disposal—the Torah given at Sinai, which we have carried with us in all of our sojourns. It is the *Etz Ḥayyim*, the Tree of Life, which can provide us with *mayyim ḥayyim*, the life-giving waters for which each of us searches.

To be sure, the forty-year journey through the desert was fraught with many moments of suffering and doubt for the Israelites. Even after their experiences at Marah as well as Sinai, they constantly complained about the lack of food and water and longed to return to the fleshpots of Egypt. Contentious and rebellious in the face of the hardships of their journey, they resorted to shaping an image of a golden calf which would guarantee that God was in their midst, at the very moment that Moses was receiving the Torah. Even after the revelation at Sinai, the people of Israel continued to show their vulnerability and lack of faith, despite possessing God's commandments.

Yet most powerfully it was God's word that would enable them to survive, and even flourish as a people. They would experience the fresh, life-giving wates of the oasis and eventually reach the Promised Land of their ancestors, as God had guaranteed, if they would imbibe the power of the words of Torah which they possessed. One again, they would sing a song of redemption, as they had done at the shores of the Red Sea.

An Individual's Journey: The Blessing of Torah Study

As it was for the Israelites of the desert generation, so it is with each and every one of us, their progeny. We live through the heat and the aridity of our own circuitous journeys, in the hope of occasionally experiencing those moments of true spiritual uplift that can keep us going. Like them, we too come to Marah and find that the waters there are bitter, but we continue to believe that we will survive despite the frustration and anger.

My personal journey began as a child growing up in a liberal Orthodox home in New York City, attending Hebrew school five afternoons a week, and wondering why I couldn't play ball in the schoolyard like all of my other friends. Nevertheless, I actually enjoyed learning Hebrew, although I usually would not admit it to anyone, and I especially liked being able to participate in Shabbat and holiday services at our synagogue. The melodies used by our hazzan, which to this day filter in and out of my consciousness, and the way the rabbi and certain individuals in the congregation made me feel a part of the community probably account for the reason why attending services was never perceived as a chore. Shul became an oasis, a place where I was refreshed. And I drank the sweet waters of Torah and imbibed the sweet melodies of worship and felt something special. It was as if I were sitting at home when I was in shul, especially when I went with my grandfather.

My paternal grandfather, whom we affectionately called Shorty (he was all of four feet, ten inches tall), had everything to do with my Jewish feelings as a young teenager. The times I accompanied him to shul on Shabbat afternoon, sitting next to him during the *se'udah shelishit* (the mystical third meal of the Sabbath, which is understood as a taste of the messianic banquet) and the afternoon study session between *Minḥah* (the afternoon service) and *Ma'ariv* (the evening service), were mystical to me. I especially recall watching his face as the rabbi or some other person interpreted the text being studied in a particularly intriguing way. His face shone with a light that could only be described as that which emanated from Moses as he descended from Sinai (Exod. 34:29). It was obvious to me that he was transformed by the words of Torah which he had experienced, and all I wanted was to feel the same way as Shorty did.

Those moments of studying midrashic texts or *Pirkei Avot* with my grandfather's friends on Shabbat set me upon a path which was irreversible. I sensed even then just how important studying Torah would be for me, knowing indeed that it would become the focus of much of my religious experience.

My journey to serious study of Torah and to an earnest commitment to Jewish life was, however, to be rather indirect. Following my bar mitzvah, I became less enamored of the Orthodox synagogue which I had attended and somewhat disenchanted with the Hebrew high school in which I was enrolled. The narrowness of the approach to such issues as the need for people to choose what is important to them and the lack of openness to students who asked questions about basic theological assumptions dampened some of my enthusiasm for study and for Judaism (in this case Orthodox Judaism) in general. The result was that I dropped out of Hebrew high, opting instead to spend my free time in other ways.

The conduit back to Jewish involvement, however, surprised even me. Since some of my friends had begun to participate in a Zionist youth organization called Young Judea, I decided to join. I remember well the first meeting I attended; I was shocked to see my friends doing Israeli dancing, something I swore I would never try. But the upshot was that six months later I became a member of the National Young Judea Dance Group, which was followed by an ever increasing involvement in the movement. In looking back on those years, I still am amazed by the impact that YJ and the Zionist dream had upon me, and how it transformed my life. The sheer joy I felt as a Jew who loved Israel and resonated with the vision of a Jewish state was (and still is) indescribable.

My Young Judea experiences led me to Israel during my junior year in college, where I continued as a chemistry major at the Hebrew University. A funny thing happened, however, on the way to Terra Sancta and the HU chem labs: I realized that I enjoyed my classes in Hebrew literature and classical Hebrew texts much more than my science courses. The immersion in text study during that year in Israel impelled me to change my academic focus when I returned to the States. I became a Hebrew studies major and continued on in a master's program following graduation. I finally had begun truly to understand the passion my grandfather had for grappling with Jewish texts, and I was bent on spending my life doing just that. My study and teaching at the Hebrew Union College –Jewish Institute of Religion has given me the opportunity to share my love of Torah with many others, just as Shorty did with me.

I remember the first paper that Rabbi Borowitz assigned to us in the introductory course in modern Jewish philosophy/theology. It was entitled,

"How do I Experience God's Presence?" After struggling with the topic for some time and trying to characterize how I felt when I prayed and how (or even if) prayer helped me to sense God's presence, I realized that more than in any other context, it was in the exhilaration of studying Torah and trying to find personal meaning that I felt a true sense of both grounding and uplift at the very same time. For me, Talmud Torah is the path to sensing a closeness with the divine; with feeling the Shekhinah's presence. By imbibing the power and the beauty of the words of Torah, in finding insight into who I am and what I can become, by becoming one with the text, I too, found my way of transforming the bitter waters of Marah.

Between Moments of Pain and Faith

The journey through life is never smooth. It is fraught not only with the day-to-day problems of making ends meet, confronting the challenges associated with our professions, and working at our relationships with those whom we love, but also with the pain of illness, tragedy, separation, and loneliness. These experiences frequently dominate our lives; they can set the tone for the whole journey.

As it is with all of us, my life journey has been like the trek through the desert which the Israelites experienced. There have been times of heightened joy and exaltation, moments of poetry and beauty, but they do not come every day. The test, in truth, is how to survive and make the best of all those prosaic moments in between.

In fact, my personal path has been marked by four major events which brought me great pain. Four times have I come to Marah and tasted the bitterness of the water; there my faith in life's essential goodness and in the reality of the power that makes for wholeness has been challenged.

While I was still a rabbinic student at the College–Institute, my mother died of cancer at a relatively young age. Her extended suffering over several years, the physical pain she had to endure, and the toll it took on her were very difficult for me to witness. After all, I knew her to be a wonderfully warm, sensitive, and most giving person, and she surely did not deserve what life had meted out to her. There were moments when I could not understand why this had happened to her. (I surely felt like the

Israelites in the desert when they wondered why they had been brought out to the desert to experience death.) During that period, what I found most comforting was my study at the College–Institute. It provided me with a grounding that allowed me to see things in a larger perspective. The worldview of our traditional texts, which emphasizes the importance of each individual and the place of each person in the continuum of the human experience, made me realize how much my mother had given us. She touched my soul in the deepest way and was a most powerful model of integrity, warmth, and humility for me. In fact, she was the one who encouraged me to apply to rabbinic school, and that experience gave me a great deal of desperately needed sustenance. Studying Torah at HUC–JIR nourished my soul at a time of doubt and anger. I would even say that writing my rabbinic thesis while my mother was in the final months of her life literally kept me going, though the journey was so dark.

I had the same basic feeling while going through the trauma and pain surrounding the breakup of my first marriage. In the bleakest moments, when I was most disheartened and all I had to look forward to most days was returning to my small sublet with its rented furniture and its windows facing the gray wall of the apartment building on the next block, I craved the comforting haven of my classroom. The joy of studying and teaching allowed me at one and the same time to feel my passion for life, to connect in a basic way with other people, and (most of all) to regain a sense of purpose and focus. The most difficult moment in the entire process of separation and divorce was probably the day I left permanently the home in which my first wife and I lived with our three young children. The irony, however, was that I had to teach an adult education class in a local synagogue that very evening. And almost miraculously I found that the pain of crossing that threshold and moving on to a new and frightening place in my life was somewhat lessened when I became immersed in a midrash that touched my very soul and gave me hope. Like the children of Israel when they set out into the desert, not knowing with any certainty if they would survive but hopeful that God would lead them to an oasis, I could only think of the prophet's words: "All who are thirsty come to [drink of] the water" (Isa. 55:1). The words of Torah, and those who relished the study of Torah, refreshed me when I most needed it.

I have never ceased wondering how at any given moment of Torah study the text has jumped off the page and taught me about myself as a human being. This was certainly true all the years that my father suffered as a stroke victim and I struggled with the burden of watching him bear his pain and trying to be there for him. The stories of characters like Esau responding to his father Jacob's needs when he became dependent upon his son in his old age, while Jacob was nowhere to be found (Gen. 27), Joseph's willingness to respond to his father's request that he visit his brothers in Shechem even though it was fraught with potential pain (Gen. 37), and Isaac and Ishmael coming together at the cave of Machpelah to bury their father Abraham (Gen. 25) became mirrors of my own life during the years of my father's infirmity and subsequent death. Immersing myself in these ancient biblical stories and filtering them through the prism of my life experience helped me to understand better who I was as a son and brother, and what my life journey as part of a family was all about.

Similarly, when our seventeen-year-old son Ilan was stricken with lymphocytic leukemia, and I thought that everything in which I believed was shattered the moment this innocent child began to suffer the pain of his treatments, one source of real solace came from the community of students and teachers of Torah of which I am blessed to be a part. The darkness and fright of those early days of Ilan's illness were dispelled by the warmth of a community committed to Torah, just as the words which Israel received at the mountain enabled them to traverse the perils of the forty-year journey. The caring that I felt from my students and colleagues at the college taught me about how a community can provide spiritual nourishment to its members. The individuals studying to be rabbis, cantors, and educators at the college, and the faculty priviledged to share their love of Torah with them, became a well of comfort and strength for me. Every day they shared with me the power of their belief in God, the source that makes for healing and wholeness, and for that I will be every grateful. They helped to lift my spirits by being living vehicles of Torah and its optimistic view of the world.

We Each Need a Teacher, a Mentor

I learned that we can neither navigate the bitter waters nor survive the arid sands of the desert by ourselves. In Moses, the Israelites had a model of faith and action, and a mentor and advocate who taught them that they could take the first steps into the Red Sea and survive. At moments of heightened fear and anger, Moses showed them how to find salvific waters in the midst of the parched desert. All of us, even those of us who are priviledged to serve others in the Jewish community, need to feel the guiding presence of individuals who by virtue of their own life journeys can affirm for us that a path does exist and that we have the ability to find our own way.

I have been exceedingly lucky in my life. My grandfather, Reb Ḥayyim Barukh, Shorty, taught me not only what it was to be a passionate, devoted, and practicing Jew, but he touched my soul with his love of Torah. In so doing, he helped me to shape the course of my life and find supreme joy through the study of God's words. Likewise, several of my teachers at the Hebrew Union College–Jewish Institute of Religion, among them Rabbi Eugene Borowitz, modeled for me what a life of Torah is all about. They exemplified how a Jew had to live if the words of Torah resonate through one's being, while enabling me to find my own path and expression. They extended their hands to me, thus strengthening my own. As Moses empowered his people by word and deed, so, too, my teachers and my students have given me gifts of self which have shown me the way from one oasis to another. The waters of Marah need not remain bitter if we are fortunate to be touched by individuals of faith and caring.

With that debt of gratitude in mind, I dedicate this essay to Rabbi Eugene B. Borowitz on the occasion of his seventieth birthday. It is dedicated with much reverence and affection. For over twenty-five years, I have benefited from his wisdom, insight, spiritual passion, concern, and guidance. I am proud to say that he is my teacher, colleague, and friend.

NOTES

1. Gunther Plaut, ed., *The Torah: A Modern Commentary* (New York: Union of American Hebrew Congregations, 1981), p. 497.

2. Mekhilta de-Rabbi Ishmael, Vayassa 1.

ALL THINGS POSSIBLE

Victor S. Appell

By the age of fourteen, I knew two things about myself. I knew that I was gay, and I knew that I was Jewish. Though not yet sure how these two parts of my life would coexist with each other, I knew that they were inexorable parts of me. I somehow knew that I could not be one or the other, and I could not be one without the other.

In 1974, there were no Gay-Straight Alliances in high schools. The few images of gays and lesbians in the media relied more on stereotype than reality. The gay rights movement was only a few years old, and in a couple of years Anita Bryant would begin her crusade against it. Yet a ninth grade assignment made it seem as if all things were possible.

My ninth grade social studies teacher, Mr. Cerqua, required that we read the *New York Times*. Each student in the class had a subscription, and each day I picked up my copy at my school in the Bronx. Back then, the *New York Times* was not the production it is today. There were no special sections for each day of the week. Rather, there were two sections, A and B.

While Mr. Cerqua wanted us to read about current events in the *New York Times*, each week I turned to one very small advertisement that held within it the promise of my future. Each Friday, on page two or three of section B, churches and synagogues placed advertisements announcing the times of their services over the weekend. While the majority of the ads were for churches, a number of synagogues also took out ads. Most of these were large ads from large temples.

But at the bottom of the page there was a small three-line ad that read, "Gay Synagogue: Friday Night Service," followed by the time and location. Every Friday, when we picked up our paper in class, the first thing I did, as discreetly as possible, was turn to the second section to make sure the ad was still there. In doing so, I was making sure the gay synagogue was still there.

Even as I read the ad week after week, some part of me could not believe what I was reading. I studied the small ad looking for some hidden clue. Maybe they were just happy Jews I thought, not gay like me. At fourteen, I knew I was years away from going to the gay synagogue. From their small ad, I knew it could not be a large synagogue, and so I prayed that the congregation survived until the Friday evening when I could go to services.

After ninth grade I continued my subscription to the *New York Times*, if only to make sure that the gay synagogue was still in existence. Week after week, and eventually year after year, this little advertisement became my lifeline. In high school I became active in the North American Federation of Temple Youth (NFTY). I was president of my youth group and then went on to become a regional president. In the summers I worked at a Union for Reform Judaism camp. I began to think that I wanted to become a rabbi. And all the time, I waited until I could go to the gay synagogue.

That opportunity finally presented itself in my senior year of high school, three years after I had seen the ad for the gay synagogue for the first time. It was Thanksgiving weekend. That Friday I made a plan to go to the synagogue and stay over at a friend's home. The synagogue, Congregation Beth Simchat Torah (CBST), was on the west side of Greenwich Village. I had never been to this part of the Village before and got terribly lost, wandering around the meandering streets, too afraid to ask anyone for directions.

The synagogue was located in the Westbeth Artists Housing Project, a former factory that had been converted into lofts for artists. The building took up the entire block, and finding the synagogue was no easy task. Finally making my way into the courtyard, I found a long ramp leading up to a gallery space that the congregation rented.

My heart was beating as I walked up the ramp. I had waited for three years for this moment, and now it felt as if it were taking me three years to walk up that ramp. I walked in just as services were beginning. Someone greeted me at the door and handed me a name tag and a siddur. I quickly found a seat. There were perhaps a hundred people in the room, mostly men, and all gay. Never before had I been in a room with gay people. The service was foreign and much more traditional than I was used to from my NFTY experience. The melodies were different, and some of the rituals unfamiliar.

After services, there was an *Oneg Shabbat*. And then it happened. One of the greeters that evening, a man named Sy, came up and welcomed me with a kiss on the cheek. My first public act as a gay man was going to a gay synagogue, and my first "gay" kiss happened at a synagogue! I am quite sure I blushed. Even though I had waited so long for this evening, I was so nervous that all I wanted to do was leave.

It would be another year before I returned. But return I did. It was at the gay synagogue where I grew up and became a gay Jewish man. I became active at CBST, and to this day several of my closest friends are people I met there over twenty years ago. My parents would join me every year in June for "Family and Friends Shabbat," and my mother became friendly with the mothers of my friends from the congregation. In the many years before Hebrew Union College–Jewish Institute of Religion was admitting openly gay students, CBST was where I was able to lead services and give *d'vrei Torah*.

I have often thought about that first night at the gay synagogue, the years of waiting to go there, and of coming out in a religious context. At a time before positive gay role models, at a time when Anita Bryant was making headlines, simply knowing that such a thing as a gay synagogue was possible gave me the hope that I would not have to sacrifice one part of myself for another. As a teenager, there was a place I could go where those headlines were rejected, and where I could meet gay men and women who were indeed happy and living full lives, unlike the sad images portrayed by the media.

Most gay people do not come out in a synagogue or church. However, coming out in a religious context can have a profound effect on a person. It is difficult to like yourself, to have a positive self-image, when much of society would tell you that what you are is abnormal or that your are a sinner and would seek to deny your civil rights and make your expressions of love against the law. Coming out in a religious context challenges all that. We can learn, in synagogues that welcome us, that what we are is good; that we can love and be loved; that we are created, like everyone else, in God's image; and that God loves us with an unqualified love. Religion has the ability to transform us. With people not only hating us but trying to make us hate ourselves, we desperately need places where we can learn to love ourselves.

A couple of years after my initial visit to the gay synagogue, the first national march for gay and lesbian rights was held in Washington D.C. It was in October of 1979. CBST had chartered a bus to take members down to Washington for the day. The bus left at around six in the morning. My father, not wanting me to ride the subway alone at that hour, went with me to the Upper West Side to pick up the bus. Needless to say, I was the only gay man that morning being put on the bus by his father! Though I may have been a bit embarrassed, it was proof that all things were possible.

CLOSING A FATHER'S EYES

Simeon J. Maslin

None of the classic rabbinic texts prescribe that a son close the eyes of his father after death. Nor would I have agreed to do so in the more familiar ambiance of an American funeral home. But I was in Jerusalem, a beardless, jet-lagged American, not having slept more than an hour or two since receiving the long anticipated phone call thirty hours earlier.

My father's body had been entrusted to an ultra-Orthodox burial society, whose particular practices dated back over two hundred years and were not, I was told, subject to question.

Sensitive to my exhaustion and vulnerability, my brother-in-law offered to substitute for me and to do whatever had to be done in the privacy of the society's preparation room. I had decided, though, that I would not allow any modernist notions to intrude on the grief of my Israeli Orthodox family. And so, as I had done so often while he was alive, I allowed my father's traditions to prevail over my sensibilities and followed the young chaftaned chasid into the preparation room for the ritual closing of the eyes.

Usually I sleep quite soundly on long flights, but, as tired as I was after the long hours of cajoling, rushing, and dumb luck that culminated in my being the last passenger to board that 747 out of Kennedy, I needed those flight hours, insulated from any distraction, to come finally to some understanding of the frayed but powerful bond that linked me to my father.

Years earlier an analyst had told me that I would never have an honest relationship with my own children until I confronted my father about the "abuse" that I had endured as a child. My father was a powerful man, whether leading an admiring congregation with his dramatic tenor renditions of the liturgy or beating his terrified, sobbing son for some dereliction. But he never allowed his still threatening hand to touch me after my bar mitzvah, and slowly I began to love and even revere him, initially through sheer relief but in later years as I came to understand the degree of his impatience and frustration and the intricate ambiguities of our relationship.

I recalled how often during my childhood he would use me as an excuse to get away from home for a few hours. We would go fishing in a small rented dory, which he would row with choppy muscular strokes far beyond the safety of the Winthrop breakwater toward Graves Light. Out there on the ocean, this garrulous, eloquent, and monumentally impatient man would sit silent and immobile for hours, a taut line suspended from his index finger, teasing the sinker along the rocky bottom while his carefully baited hooks sought out the flounder and cod.

I could never bring myself to impale the squirming bloodworms on my hooks, and so he did it for me. And then, after catching enough fish for the neighbors and ourselves, he would haul up the anchor and row in toward shore, encouraging me to join him in his lusty rendition of familiar rubrics of liturgy. There must have been days when we returned without fish or song, but I can't remember them.

All around me on the 747 people slept or read as my mind wandered back to that day half a century ago when I brought home a Batman comic book instead of my monthly Superman. Whenever I did a satisfactory translation of a chapter from the weekly Torah portion and the commentaries, my father would give me a dime for comics, baseball cards, or candy. Once a month on the day when it arrived at Sinky's I would buy my Superman. I knew that my father read it too because I often found it on the hamper lid in the bathroom. But the day that I switched to Batman, he grabbed it from my hand, shook it in my face, and demanded to know why I read such cheap junk.

I tried to explain to him that Batman was more exciting because any person could be Batman. He slapped the booklet across my face and shouted that he didn't work so hard every day so that I could throw away his money on stupid comics. "But, Dad," I cried, "you read Superman." Mistake. He tore the booklet into shreds and warned me never again to bring such drivel into our home. He threatened to ban baseball cards too if I didn't start paying more attention to my Torah studies. I took a chance and bought a Superman with my next dime. Two days later I found it on the hamper lid. Not a word. From that day on I thought of Superman as Jewish and Batman as "goyish."

If my seatmates had been awake, they would have wondered why, learning back with my eyes closed, I suddenly began laughing. It was that incongruous dichotomy—Superman Jewish and Batman "goyish." (What did they use for the circumcison? A blowtorch?) The Red Sox must have been Jewish too, because my baseball-loving father would never take me to a Braves game. Again, he used me as the excuse to escape from home. "The boy loves baseball. Who else is going to take him?" But only the Red Sox. We were there at Fenway the day that Jimmy Foxx, Joe Cronin, and Jim Taber hit consecutive home runs. We delighted at the arrogantly fluid swing of "The Kid," Ted Williams, my father always reminding me that his middle name was Samuel. And then there was "Doc" Cramer; with a name like that, how could he not be Jewish?

Even that remarkable duo of Sain and Spahn couldn't attract my father to Braves Field. He knew the stats of all his Red Sox and once kept his bedside radio on over the Sabbath so that he could listen to a crucial, late season game between the Sox and the hated Yankees. The Yankees weren't "goyim" like the Braves and Batman; they were more like the "rich Reform Jews" in Back Bay and Brookline.

My mind raced ahead a few years to the day when I came home from graduate school to tell my parents that I had decided to study for the Reform rabbinate and that I was leaving for an interview in Cincinnati that evening. My mother announced simply and coldly that I could expect no support from them if I became a Reform "goy." Conservative maybe but Reform never! And then she refused to discuss it. In later years she would tell people that I was "doing post-graduate work in the West."

My father argued with me for the entire afternoon. He admitted to me his great respect for Stephen S. Wise and Abba Hillel Silver, respect as Zionist leaders and orators but not as rabbis. Rabbis were steeped in Talmud and were the guardians of sacred tradition. My grandfather, great-grandfathers and as far back as we knew were rabbis, "real rabbis." How could I turn my back on all of that? Didn't I know that Cincinnati with its Hebrew Union College was like Sodom? They led people astray; they were apostates. He quoted chapter and verse to me—Torah, Talmud, Maimonides—to prove that I was making a terrible mistake. He was passionate in his attack, but he didn't yell at me. He argued and quoted through the entire afteroon, until I told him that I had to leave for Logan to catch my plane.

He walked with me to the bus stop, pleading every step of the way. "You haven't given it enough thought." "Yes I have, Dad, all summer." "And you never discussed it with me?" "I discussed it with my teachers; I knew how you would react." "Don't do this to your mother." "I'm not doing it to anyone, Dad. This is what I believe, for myself."

The bus came into view, a few blocks down Shirley Street. "Can't I change your mind? At least wait another week. Please. . . ." "No, Dad. My mind is made up. I'm sorry." The bus was rolling to a stop as he reached into his pocket and pulled out his wallet. "Do you have enough money? Probably not. Here, take this." He handed me fifty dollars, and I left.

I sat weeping in the darkened cabin of the jumo jet, grateful for the deep sleep that had overtaken my two seatmates. Why had he terrified me so as a child? Didn't he realize that half a century later I would remember his strap and the stinging impact of his right hand as clearly as his soul-stirring chant of Kol Nidre? The sacred melodies and the profane thrashings were intertwined in my memory as, he once taught me, the souls of father Jacob and his son Benjamin were intertwined—forever bonded and beyond exorcism.

I thought back to the day a dozen or so years ago when I delivered a lecture in Jerusalem on prophetic values in contemporay Judaism. I carefully avoided telling my father about the lecture because I intended to be very critical of the way that the Orthodox religious establishment ignores the ethical imperatives that are the heart of biblical prophecy. I didn't want him to hear me denigrating the community of which he was very much a part.

Somehow my father found out that I would be lecturing, and he told me that he would be there. He had other appointments that afternoon, but he would set aside the hour for my lecture. I couldn't dissuade him. "After all, how often do I get to hear you speak? People tell me you're good, and I've never heard you except on tape." Not my fault, I thought, as I began considering whether I could soften some of the more critical paragraphs of the lecture out of deference to an aging father. But no, I decided; he has his strong opinions and I have mine. He's been warned; it's his choice.

From time to time during my lecture, I looked at him, sitting on an aisle seat toward the rear of the hall, ready as usual to dash. He was attentive but expressionless. When I finished, during the customary applause before the questions, he quickly rose and made his way to an exit. But before he went out, he turned to me and raised his hand in a gesture of enthusiastic approval, his thumb and forefinger in a circle as he waved goodbye. I was baffled; I knew that he had to have disapproved of most of my message. Yet how to interpret his gesture?

That evening I called my father and I asked him what he had meant by that sign of approval. Had he really agreed with my critique of Orthodoxy? "No, no, certainly not," he answered. "I didn't agree with most of what you said. But I loved the way that you said it!" The message and the messenger, the chanting and the beating, the daily study of Torah and the Red Sox, father and son, obverse and reverse—the same coin, stamped and scored with rigor, yet indestructible and eternally precious.

And so I followed the young chasid into the preparation room where two older chasidim were completing the enshrouding. All I could see of my father was his face; his head and neck were wrapped in white linen. Next to his head was a tiny mound of sand on a white paper. They told me to take a pinch of the sand and to drop it into his eyes. Actually the eyes were almost completely closed, but one of the hassidim moved back the eyelids so that I could deposit the sand. "Why?" I asked. "*Minhag atik*," they answered impatiently—an ancient custom. No reason.

Then they told me to close my father's eyes. Gently I laid my right hand on his face, my fingers covering the sightless eyes. I paused and looked into their deep blueness. Those eyes had guided me through the sea of the Torah and through the ocean swells off Winthrop to the deep-hidden fish. They had revealed to me the esoterica of Talmud and Midrash along with the kabbalistic numerology of R.B.I.s, E.R.A.s, and the length of the foul line to Fenway's "green monster." They had introduced me to the grandeur of Jerusalem and the awesome beauty of the Judean wilderness long before he or I actually saw them. And they had exposed me to a father's fallibility, so that I might one day be able to live with my own.

I was taking too long. The oldest of the chasidim impatiently put his hand over mine, forcing my reluctant fingers to close those eyes forever, as he intoned verses from the Psalms. I let my hand linger for a moment and then I was satisfied. I left the preparation room having done what I hoped I might do some day. I understood.

YEARNING FOR FATHER

Paul Schoenfeld

My father is almost eighty-six years old. Last week he learned that he has inoperable lung cancer.

My sadness surprises me. I thought I was ready for this moment. I thought that my anticipation would spare me from grief. But no, expectation does not provide protection.

As an adult, I have always felt distant from my father. We speak different languages. He is a scientist, a technician, an engineer who likes facts, symbols, numbers. I am a psychologist who lives in the world of people.

Not too long ago, he said to me quite earnestly, "You know, Paul, you have done pretty well for someone who doesn't know anything." I understood exactly what he meant. I know little about physics, mathematics, chemistry. I thanked him for his compliment. He had meant it sincerely.

My father didn't go to father school. He went to engineering school.

He has limited interest in his grandchildren. He has limited interest in me. His autobiography included only a few pages about his family. We are a back story, a counterpoint to the real challenge of his life—work. For the last five years he has been writing a book on the history of neuroscience at Rockefeller University, where he has been employed for thirty years. He is probably one of about ten people interested in this topic, but it filled his days for years.

Why is it that we sons are so often disappointed in our dads?

I am like all sons. Even though my hair is gray and thinning, I want to be recognized, appreciated, acknowledged, greeted, and feted by my father. I want him to see the real me. I want him to be my Moses, and I will be his people Israel. I want him to be my Torah. I want him to teach me, coach me, inspire me, and guide me when I am lost. I want him to give me courage when I am afraid and to hold me when I am lonely. I want his wisdom to pour forth into my soul so that I will know who I am.

But how can he live up to my expectations? He does not even have a *tallit* to give me when he dies. What will I have of his that I can pass on to my children?

Once my father stood tall, larger than life. He held my small hand when I crossed the street. On Sunday mornings we drove to the bakery together. He bought bagels, cream cheese, lox, pickled herring, smoked whitefish, and a box of brightly colored Danish pastries. We laid the delights on our big table for the family to admire. How I savored those Sunday morning feasts.

When my father paid the bills, I would hide under his desk in his office. Did he know I was there in his sanctuary? This is how I would get close to him.

Today, in his sun-drenched Florida apartment, he is small, shrunken, visibly short of breath. As always, I listen as he talks. We discuss logistics —twenty-four-hour care, help needed, health care directives. "I had an interesting life," he says. He looks peaceful, reflective. We hug and say goodbye.

As I drive away, I imagine myself at the *shiva minyan* with the other mourners, who, like me, yearn to touch and find our fathers deep within our Jewish souls.

AT THE END OF MY DAY

Scott Sager

Last night as I lay in bed, just before sleep, I prayed. Every night I give thanks to God for giving me another day of this crazy, challenging, imperfect life and my two children, who are such a part of it. My prayer always begins the same way but soon meanders through the day that has finished. Yesterday was Shabbat. We stayed home and ordered in Chinese food, rented a movie, and left lo mein under the sofa. Sometimes we go to services and afterwards eat sushi with friends or go to the community dinner. Sometimes Shabbat eludes us, forgotten in a rush of birthday parties, soccer games, or out-of-town guests.

Last night I prayed for peace between my children. We lit candles at home. I am stingy with candles and only use two. We put them in the tin candlesticks from my mother-in-law and her mother before, or the brass ones that come from my grandmother. My daughters both want to light the candles. They both want the last turn sipping the grape juice so they get the biggest gulp. They both compete for the inside of the challah, leaving a cavernous hole after tearing out their share. I am stingy with the challah too, trying to dole it out so there will be enough left for breakfast on Monday.

My wife is often not home when we light candles. She works a demanding, never-ending sort of job that involves a BlackBerry, travel, and obligatory cocktails or dinners. I try to remember her mother's tradition of the women putting napkins on their heads as the blessings are said. When my daughters were younger, before they knew the blessing for the candles, I would say it. I knew this was traditionally done by women, but there are very few of the usual gender divisions in our home. I am responsible for the cooking, the shopping, and the laundry, and my wife brings home the money.

I have almost no childhood memories of Shabbat observance to work from, rebel against, or reproduce. I remember very rarely being at my grandmother's lighting candles. There in the same small apartment where my father and his brothers were raised, my sisters would stand with Grandma, and it would be a quiet moment amidst the swirling smells, the aroma of the dinner to come seeping out of the kitchen, the plastic smell drifting up from the covered furniture, and the smoke from the match with its one clear note of sulfur, a scented punctuation that we were together.

Last night I asked God for guidance. My religious education was barren. In many ways I was unprepared to raise Jewish children. From the first Tot Shabbat I took my oldest daughter to through today when she is in sixth grade, I am still learning the rituals, the weekly and yearly order of Jewish life. My understanding of holidays grows every year as my children bring their celebrations home in another clay candlestick or tie-dyed matzah cover. I learn bits of history that seem so striking to me, that the Torah was written mostly by four authors, for example, or that Chanukah was in part a conflict amongst Jewish sects and not simply a successful rebellion. I am learning the fundamentals of Judaism only now, in the middle of my life.

I asked God for patience to face what I have brought on myself. I am the one who's around, what is called the at-home parent or primary caregiver. I have been a social worker and a preschool teacher, but with my wife's career and schedule, we faced choices. I couldn't earn enough to support the family on my own, but she could, so either we needed full-time child care or I would be the parent to stay home. It has not always been easy, but I have come to embrace my role and its importance. We never questioned wanting our children to know they were Jewish, but making it happen has fallen to me. I schlep them to religious school; I attend the *Mishpacha B'yachads* —activities that include parents; I take them to Purim carnivals and *Shabbatons*. I organize the Passover candy sale and bring my daughters with me to cook for our synagogue's home-less shelter. I make sure there are candles in the house and a loaf of bread on Friday nights, and I take the girls to Shabbat services when I can. I do all this so they will be able to choose how or if to express their Judaism when they are grown.

I remember as a teen going to a bar mitzvah at a Conservative synagogue and feeling at a loss at how to participate, the Hebrew way beyond my abil-ity and the rituals exceeding my knowledge. At family seders, my younger cousin, raised in a Conservative home, took over chanting the Four Ques-tions in Hebrew at an early age, while I was relegated to the low-status Eng-lish translation. My father's phylacteries, which I never saw him wear, were mysterious, unfathomable relics to my young eyes. Even today, I shun wearing a tallis out of fear I will somehow do it wrong. There are many lit-tle ways I find myself not knowing how to be a Jew. This is what I hope my daughters will avoid; at the least I hope that they will have a foundation they're comfortable with and confident in if they choose to learn more.

In the darkness I prayed for a fairer world. My sensibilities have clearly been formed by my upbringing, including the liberal humanism so integrated into the Reform Movement I grew up in. The thought that my daughters wouldn't be allowed or encouraged to participate fully in our religion has never occurred to me. My eldest sister was among the first to become bat mitzvah at our synagogue. My daughters should expect no less. We have friends who are Orthodox. Their eldest child just had his bar mitzvah, a joyous affair centered on his reading Torah. Their second child, a daughter, will simply have a party, a glorified twelfth birthday cel-ebration. These different gender roles offend my parental pride. I feel certain my daughters are as capable as any boy. Just as I expect them to have equally worn fields to play soccer on as the boys and the same opportunities in their professional lives as any man, I can tolerate no marginalization in their religious world. As their mother has pursued the career of her choice, and their aunts and grandmothers each in their own way have too, I expect the choice to be theirs. As I, a husband, and we, a family, have supported my wife's path, I will look forward to no less from whomever they find for partners in their lives.

There is so much I mean to bring up each night with God. I always mean to ask for a watchful eye on my children to cover for all the times I can't be there to protect or guide them. I wish their world to be happy and safe. Although I taught them about strangers, I have avoided their questions about bad things that happen to kids. I have hesitated to tell them about the Holocaust. I won't listen to the news when they are in the room, not wanting them to hear about the murders or violence in their world. But I can neither keep the world out nor keep them out of the world, something I sometimes think of as a fatherly failing.

These larger issues mix with smaller ones, like who didn't practice their instrument and that I have to get more conditioner. How did my older daughter find out about *South Park* and *The Family Guy*? When will we find the time to cook a pumpkin and make a fresh pumpkin pie? Have I harmed my children by not buying organic milk all the time? The evening went by and we didn't play the game I had promised, nor did I read to them as long as I said I would. Another day has slipped by.

I prayed that I would be a better father tomorrow as sleep found me at last.

AS NATURAL AS BREATHING

Yigal Rechtman

My son is to become bar mitzvah this year. I have never been called to the Torah in the sense of "having" a bar mitzvah. I am the skipped generation of men in my family, never having learned to chant Torah. Now, a year after my daughter has become bat mitzvah and with my son on his way, I feel there is a special meaning in raising two Jewish children in a non-Jewish country. My origins were the opposite—I was raised in a Jewish country yet did not particularly identify as a *Jewish* child.

I was raised on a kibbutz in Israel during the 1970s and 1980s. When I was a boy, my perception of what it meant to be Jewish was different than what it is now. In my mind there was nothing about me that was "Jewish." My father had chosen to walk away from Judaism, which in his mind was associated with being a "Diaspora Jew" and had nothing to do with being the new Zionist that he became. Growing up, I didn't think about my identity. Although my educators were consistent and persistent in explaining the importance of a Jewish state after two thousand years of life in the Diaspora, the significance was somewhat lost on me. As a young person, I couldn't really fathom my place within the history of a Jewish nation, a Jewish clan, or even a Jewish family. I was who I was, and I had two sets of grandparents who were young and available for discourse—so what other "past" did I need to explore? I did not yearn to understand the significance of being a Jewish boy born in a Jewish state and speaking the Hebrew language. It was as natural as breathing.

As a boy on the kibbutz I was exposed to the existence of other religions ("Funny," I used to comment, "they took off on Sunday of all days to go to pray"). Yet "they" all seemed remote and distant from our flow of life. I knew that my family and community purposely shielded me from some of the "others" that were out there, but there wasn't much need for it—everything about our life was in Hebrew, it was in Israel, and it was Jewish, by definition.

So I never had a bar mitzvah. There was a secular celebration of our seventh grade year, which roughly corresponded to me and my classmates becoming of bar and bat mitzvah age. Most of us—definitely not the girls—did not read from Torah and did not bother with learning customs that were perhaps our parents' but certainly not ours. The only echo of the ancient coming-of-age rituals was when my dad, half-proud and half-joking, said, "I am now exempt from the responsibility of this one," a blessing traditionally said by fathers over their thirteen-year-old sons. For us children, there was no need to define ourselves beyond what we already intimately knew to be true: we were Jewish. That's all that mattered.

Fast-forward six years. I was enlisted in the Israeli army at age nineteen. The most memorable Jewish identity moment came to me when toward the end of my service, in classic catch-22 fashion, I became the N.C.O. of a small base in northern Israel. It was theoretically a demotion. I was being sent away as far as possible from the dubious privilege of being the right-hand man of the platoon's officer. Life could not have been better the last six months of my service. I had regularly scheduled visits home, I had time to study for the entrance exams for college in the United States, and I got to interact with a steady stream of reserve soldiers who came in rotations of three to four weeks at a time. One personal aspect that I adopted into the life of "my" small army base was to display the Israeli flag, making sure to have a flag raised at all times. Large army bases often had this detail taken care of, but at smaller bases flags were generally only raised during ceremonies or as part of other "official" business. I insisted that a flag be flown every morning. During my service, I started to think that ultimately every little bit of what we were about had to do with the greater good of the Jewish people. The blue and white flag became the embodiment of this idea.

The reserve soldiers rotating through my base came from a variety of places and social circles of Israeli society. I got to meet men from all walks of life and figure out how to get along with them. I quickly become a de facto human resources manager as issues and requests came up. In this role reversal, I, the twenty-year-old, became the supervisor of men twice my age. This brought to me a sense of personal confidence but also a sense of humility as to my limited abilities to be in that position. As the common wisdom on our small base was to involve headquarters as little as possible with our affairs, I became at times the last word in decisions that affected people significantly older than I. I tried to approach matters such as health, fatherhood, financial stress, and the wish to just go home to be with one's family with as much sensitivity and respect as I could, despite my relative lack of maturity.

As an N.C.O., I let several military standing orders fall by the wayside. There was a relaxed uniform dress code and, as some of the men were accomplished cooks, an elaborate emphasis on meals rather than standard army fare. But in two areas I insisted we follow protocol: clean water and the proper raising of the Israeli flag. In retrospect, this period at the end of my service contributed to my feeling of being part of the Jewish people. It was there that the internalization of my Jewish identity began, and I located myself on the spectrum in the sea of nations and languages. The fact that this realization came to me as a man among other Jewish men is significant. I suppose this was a maturation experience in which I not only saw the variety of Jewish men and their differences but also saw how we were all connected, drinking the same water and working toward the same independent state, embodied by a flag flying high.

At the end of my army service, I came to the United States to study. The hours at the army base studying for the standardized tests paid off, and I was accepted to a computer science program in the Northeast. Following graduation, I became a computer consultant and then a staff accountant at my father-in-law's accounting firm. Meanwhile, I got married and with my wife began raising our daughter and son. Early in my children's lives I had to rely primarily on memories of how child rearing should be. My parents were in Israel, and phone calls were at premium cost. As much as I tried to stay in touch, it was the day-to-day lessons I had to bring forth from within me, from my recollections to the raising-a-family mode that I was suddenly in.

I had one prime source of these family-raising templates. I am sure that my parents were the less-conscious part of that internalization of family-raising style. To a great degree, when it came to raising one's family I think that I looked up—consciously—to how my grandparents did it. My maternal grandfather Alec is a life-loving, devoted father who lives his days with a bright outlook and sensitive touch. My paternal grandfather Solly was a more reserved type. Solly impressed me as the "provider" type for his children and a center for his family, a strong person. In my attempts to develop my own image as a father, I took to heart how my two grandfathers raised their own families. One common thread for the three of us, my grandfathers and I, was in the embracing of communal life, embodied by the shul, or, as I now know it in my contemporary American jargon, the synagogue.

Grandfather Alec has been a role model for me as someone who can talk to anyone. He continually searches for common ground, making connections with people of all ages and types. Grandfather Solly was also a communal being, a community organizer and activist, and someone who cared much about the Jewish people and their place in the world.

Moving from life in the kibbutz to membership in an army unit, I never had to worry about belonging. As an Israeli-born boy, I always sensed the right to belong, and so I didn't have to seek it out. But now a father and a man in a foreign country, I harken back to images of two men who were in the same position half a century ago: my grandfathers. I recall how with pride I told both grandparents Solly and Frieda that I was a member of a synagogue, and how important it was for me when my grandmother Yaffa died to make sure that her *yahrzeit* was recorded and an acknowledgment sent to my grandfather Alec. In this transformation, from a boy who did not have to question his Jewish identity to a man who had to proactively engage in defining it, I matured. Real or perceived, the images of my grandfathers, like a backwards generation skip, are what I can hold before me as I go through this process of defining myself as a Jewish man and father outside of the Jewish state.

I use these images of my grandfathers, as well as the love that I felt from both my parents, to try and define my new-but-old Jewish identity. I aim to mix the values my parents instilled in me—love of other human beings, openness to new ideas, and the importance of being a mensch—with values more lofty than day-to-day acts, that of belonging to a group, being a member of a nation, a membership that transcends time and physical boundaries. So I bring this fusion of past and present to my role as a parent, and I watch my children soak it up. I never know for sure how much they take in and what they will reject in an act of self-definition. I trust that most will stick even as they find that some of my ideas and hopes do not fit theirs. Yet I cannot help but imagine that we are part of a constant and continuing stream of lights. I imagine life itself and national identity in particular as a stream of sparks, each flickering for some time and lighting others while they live. Some illuminate for a long time with bright light, warming others, while others are just moving along with the direction of a flame. And my hopes for my children are that I can bring the warmth of the past to the forefront of the next wave of sparks, their future.

I feel as if these steps are all connected. First there was the unquestioning identity I grew up with. Then there was the emergence of my own identity as I was exposed to varied types of Jewish people and their lives. Now it is my time to reflect upon my past, including my role models and their lessons, and to project their lessons upon the future I am creating with my own children.

GALLOPING HORSEBACK, ZEN JUDAISM, AND LEAPING FOR THE SKY

Owen Gottlieb

My father was a Jewish cowboy. He was a woodsman and an expert marksman, rode horseback, and came home each summer from deep-sea fishing trips out of Montauk with bins full of three-foot-long bluefish. The bins of crushed ice and fresh fish would sit in our North Jersey driveway, and neighbors would drive over for fish for their freezers. His truck had a C.B. radio and a green and white sticker on the side window showing his membership in the P.I.P. Club—the Palisades Interstate Parkway Club. When drivers broke down on the side of the road, he'd jump-start their cars for them or radio in for assistance—even on nights, back in the 1970s and early '80s, when crime in New York was at its height, before there were cell phones, when breaking down on the roads often meant peril. He was a big, warmhearted bear of a man who cut a rug on the dance floor, jitterbugging with my mom. He took my brother and me trout fishing in the rivers and brooks of upstate New York and to the Doctor Who sci-fi conventions we loved.

My father often drove me home from my modern dance classes. After trying gymnastics, I had finally convinced my parents that I really did want dance lessons. Eventually I'd end up in a troupe in New York. Leaping in the air was my specialty. Dad was proud. When I wanted to quit dance because I was being typecast, he told me, "Don't you quit. Dance is your ticket." Dad looked out for my cousin who moved to the States from Israel after fighting in the Yom Kippur War. Though he'd never been to Israel, it was clear that part of Dad's heart was there, with the tough Jews. He worked hard all day Saturdays. When the rabbi gave his eulogy two months after my bar mitzvah, he told the story of how Dad had noticed all the overgrowth on the synagogue grounds and had volunteered to come by on a Sunday with his chainsaw to clear it out. I couldn't bring myself to dance for years after I lost him.

I'd been a seeker, a questioner since my earliest memories. But in the years after my father's death, I stopped asking questions about Judaism. For a long time, I didn't even know where to begin.

Then, during my first year at college, I found myself at the Hillel House, exploring once again. One afternoon I even visited the rabbi's study. He asked me about my Judaism. I talked about fighting anti-Semitism, a cultural, political, ethnic Judaism. The rabbi called it "vigilance." I didn't tell him that I stopped searching for God when my father died, but I think he knew. And then, he asked me a question: "What about the fun stuff?" I didn't quite see what he was getting at. He talked about *nigunim*, dance, ritual, and literature. And the more I met with him, sitting in the sculpture garden of the arts center, walking in the woods (as he told me Reb Nachman did), or in the little Hillel House, the more I discovered his wisdom. He was the first to start me on my path to meditation, first with Zen meditation, before I would eventually, years later, turn also to Jewish meditation. I'd come to him with questions about ethics and love and life, and he'd share his wisdom. And then, one afternoon he answered one of my questions with a concept culled from his decades of Talmud study. In hearing his explanation, I came to understand a sage answer to a question about life that had kept me pondering and wrestling for years. Perhaps it was then that I first saw the connection between his wisdom and his deep knowledge of Jewish texts. Beyond his vast life experience, he was drawing from the life experiences of our ancestors and his own remarkable teachers. I realized there was a treasure chest of ancestral wisdom to be plumbed. All this was happening in the forests of New England. And as the year progressed, my experiences of having a first understanding of God-in-nature began to blossom around me in the woods and the rivers. I don't think the rabbi mentioned God once. I just came to understand. That understanding was the beginning of a new journey.

Thirteen years later, living in Jerusalem for my first year of rabbinic school, I traveled from minyan to minyan, seeking. There were the "trad egal" Carlebach minyanim in friends' apartments. We sat on floor pillows, drumming, chanting, men and women dancing and praying together, warming our potluck dinner on Shabbat hot plates, and singing together late into the night. Some Shabbat mornings, I'd walk around the corner to the Sephardic shul in Rehavia, where the melodies were infectious and the Torah scroll resided in a magnificent vertical case. Twice I davened in the Ugandan style led by a Conservative rabbinic student from Uganda, once in an Ashkenazic shul with the *yekkes* and Chasidim side by side. Once with the Bratzlav Chasidim in Meah Shearim, where the prayer was like an ocean in which I was carried by waves. Once with the Bratzlav Chasidim in Baka, where a single verse of *L'cha Dodi* transformed into a twenty-minute ecstatic dance. This was not an academic exercise for me, nor was it simply an anthropological expedition. It was a chance to learn, but it was more than that—because I was searching. I was searching for something mysterious and cloistered, something ancient and guarded, hidden in the stones, locked in the little cubbyholes and nooks of our ancient city, nestled in the flowers blossoming on my Rehavia balcony, sheltered under the wings of the hummingbirds. Something our forefathers whisper to us in the quiet night. What it means to be a Jewish man. When to be a scholar, when to be a warrior; when to hunt and when to meditate; when to nurture and when to compete; when to defend and when to oppose; when to protest and when to pray; when to stand up and when to lie down. I continued to search.

And at the very end of my year, just before I left Jerusalem to return to the States, I finally discovered that there were other men on a similar search. Word reached me that men at other progressive seminaries had been meeting in small circles together each month recovering the observance of *Kiddush L'vanah*, the men's ritual sanctification of the moon, which dates back at least as early as the Babylonian Talmud. A group had formed in Philadelphia, and a few students had brought their practice to a new group in Jerusalem. They shared their experiences and journeys with one another and embedded those discussions in ritual—in the ancient and primal ritual of being together, reciting blessings, and physically leaping toward the moon. The leaping, historically has been referred to as a "dance." The description of the ritual echoed within me, because for as long as I could remember—in the dance studio, on the gymnastics mat, off of ski moguls—I had been leaping for the sky. These men were mixing the immediate, contemporary questions of male identity with the primal rites handed down to us. And by the end of that year, I understood the power of that mix. I had been delving into the primal all year. But the ideas of building a bridge between the primal, hidden ritual to today's life, that was the key with which I was to depart from the city. I had found them too late to join them in Jerusalem. They were about to disperse across the States. But their vision of reinvigorated Jewish men's ritual is one that has stayed with me.

I believe those men had found a path. They had found a way to wrestle with the questions that Jewish men ask. They did not feel the need to justify a private men's space nor justify reaching back into the more primal, perhaps less "dignified" or scientifically understood ritual of reaching out toward the celestials. In fact, it is this mysterious aspect of ritual in particular that allows for the unlocking of the deeper longings within a man's soul. Because of my exploration of ritual thus far, I know that in the coming years, delving into rituals such as *Kiddush L'vanah* will lead to the discovery of deeper questions and perhaps, on occasion, even the glimmer of some ancient answers. As Jewish men, we must reclaim the heritage of our rituals for the modern world, and in so doing come to understand ourselves anew: leaping for the moon, looking to the stars, our cowboys and our hunters, our dancers and our seekers, our brothers, fathers, uncles, and sons will find new ways and ancient ways to seek out their truths—together.

READY FOR REDEMPTION: A *MIKVEH* EXPERIENCE OF PERSONAL HEALING

Steve Z. Leder

"You can't put one *tuchus* in two chairs," was my father's not-so-quaint way of summing up times like the High Holy Days for rabbis. On one chair there's my own inner search for meaning among the ruins of last year's regrets and next year's promises. On the other, my responsibility to help lead thousands on their own inner journey—not to mention making the kids' school lunches each morning and cleaning up after the dog. Guess which chair wins?

One way or another though, I do find time to prepare for the High Holy Days. I check the prayer book to make sure I know all my parts and have my glasses adjusted so they don't slip down my nose when I preach. My robe and *tallis* are dutifully dry-cleaned, and my sermons are carefully rehearsed from the *bimah*.

But in the midst of all these technical preparations—and in the midst of getting the synagogue cranked up for another year of holiday celebrations, religious school, adult education, study groups, the men's group, the fund-raising, the late summer weddings, hospital visits, funerals, meetings, memos, and phone calls—there's not much time for personal reflection. In fact, even during the actual High Holy Day services I'm usually too preoccupied to do much serious praying and thinking.

The truth is these annual rituals of mine have more to do with being a rabbi who works during the High Holy Days than with being a Jew who prays. Any rabbi who tells you he or she can do both is at best an optimist and at worst racking up another white lie to add to next year's Yom Kippur confession.

I've confronted a lot of joy and sadness as a rabbi. Weddings, babies, miraculous recoveries, hugs from children, tears of joy—there's plenty of good to go around. But so too open wounds in the hospital, brain tumors in young fathers, divorce, murdered children—you name it. The problem is staying connected to it all. I can go from a wedding to a funeral to a bris in one day without thinking very much about it. It's not that I'm insensitive—just busy.

In part, I make my living helping Jews face sorrow. But it's their sorrow I help them through and during the High Holy Days it's their self-scrutiny I try to facilitate, not my own. Yes, I've faced a lot of things as a rabbi, but it's not very often that I face myself. I'm no different from most people—rabbis, salesclerks, attorneys, bus drivers, doctors, tailors, teachers, and parents—we're all so busy living that it's hard to feel truly alive.

There was, however, that one afternoon the week before Rosh Hashanah thirteen years ago at the *mikveh*. The *mikveh* in my town is tended by a woman named Lillian, affectionately known among rabbis in town as the "Mikveh Lady."

I knew traditional women used the *mikveh* after menstruation, and others used it for conversions to Judaism, koshering dishes, and occasionally prior to Shabbat or the High Holy Days, but I had never actually been in one before. After witnessing the impact it had on the young woman I just converted, I was curious.

Looking at Lillian, I wondered, "Could I use the *mikveh*?"

"Of course," she said warmly as she let me in.

Lillian hangs around a lot of rabbis, and she's seen the power of the *mikveh* at work in many people's lives. She knew more about what was in store for me than I did.

"Take your time," she said with a knowing smile.

"Take your time," I thought to myself. Rabbis so seldom get to take their time at anything they do.

I showered, brushed my teeth, trimmed my nails—the Law requires that nothing come between me and the water that would surround me. Then, naked and alone, I entered the square, silent, blue-tiled chamber —built to talmudic specifications—to immerse myself three times and recite blessings.

I descended the seven steps, one for each day of Creation. Standing shoulder-high in the water, I gently lowered my head and pulled my knees to my chest. Floating in the warmth, I felt linked to generations of men and women who also sought refuge, sought God, sought themselves in the *mikveh*. Suspended in the liquid silence, I was suspended too in an eternal, infinite moment.

To my dismay I sighed a sigh of sorrow. A sigh for all the unfinished business of my life. A sigh for my grandfather who I had not seen in thirty years—still alive, but cut off from me in some twisted family conflict I vaguely recall but do not understand.

A sigh for my brother, my little brother whom I could not protect from the harshness of the world. A sigh for my lost loves—where are they now? Where am I now? Another sigh for Israel—how far I am from her again this year. Will my wife's cancer ever come back? A sigh because I should be better, do more, study more, give more, write more, read more. What kind of a father am I? What kind of a man am I?

Distinct and separate demons awakened all at once, psychic baggage never unpacked, weight never shed nor even noticed, but heavy to bear. My sorrows pushed deep into the background were magically released to the untelling, all-knowing wates, to God.

The week before Rosh HaShannah 5748, I left that small, quiet place slowly, having uttered my High Holy Day prayers for the very first time in peity and truth. I left ready for redemption.

Now I go back each year, curling like an embryo beneath the still water, making peace with my longings, reminding myself of Lillian's advice: "Take your time, rabbi. Take your time."

IT BEGAN WITH
A SIMPLE INVITATION

James Prosnit

"I am writing to a small group of men in our congregation who I thought might be interested in being part of a men's spirituality discussion group. No, I'm not interested in a Jewish version of Promise Keepers or the Million Man March, but I do think that there is an interest out there among Jewish men to discuss issues of faith and spirituality; tradition and family; career stress and a search for balance—all in a Jewish context and framework.

I sent the letter to about sixty men in the congregation. Some were active in our Brotherhood, some served on the Temple Board, but most had not been all that involved in synagogue life. I knew them through their wives or children, but they themselves had never taken a particularly active role in the congregation. Of the sixty I invited over half attended. We had struck a nerve and maybe even a need.

Five years later the Men's Spirituality Group at Congregation B'nai Israel continues to be a source of connection and conversation for many of those original attendees and for several others we have added along the way. To be sure there was some drop off and attrition—a dozen or so didn't return to the second meeting. But each month a faithful group of men gather in someone's home to discuss and share insights and concerns that few would have suspected possible from a group of men in a pretty mainstream suburban Reform congregation. Sports, technology and the office may provide metaphors for the conversation but they are never the topic of concern.

In that first meeting there were a number of questions as to what we meant by spirituality. I remember someone did a typical "man thing" and found a dictionary and began looking up the word. Someone else suggested that focusing on a dictionary definition was the antithesis to the spirit of spirituality. So without agreeing on a formal definition, we've tried to open ourselves up to the possibility that our being together in pursuit of the spiritual is enough. In that way, we've tried to be more than just a study group. Men can be good students, but not necessarily the best sharers. While a traditional or modern text is frequently a springboard for conversation we try to see ourselves in the text and open up to what it says about us as individuals.

As an example we spent a year looking at the biography of Moses. We focused on his story through biblical text and midrash, considering things like his initial hesitancy to accept God's call, his anger, his leadership, his lack of relationship with his children and his risk of burn out. In each instance such teachings provided a guide for our own story telling and for reflection on the challenges that men face in their multiple roles today. We've read Rabbi Jeff Salkin's book *Searching for My Brother* and sections of both Rabbi Lawrence Hoffman's book *The Journey Home* and *Seven Prayers That Can Change Your Life*, by Leonard Felder. We dabbled in some Jewish mystical texts using Mindy Ribner's *Everyday Kabbalah* as a source and even found time for a guided meditation or two. The group is diverse so some love those exercises and others giggle, but the relationships forged over time have created a trust that enables those who facilitate each session to experiment without fear. While I lead several sessions each year, I always think we're at our best when responsibility and ownership of each meeting is shared among those who attend. I am regularly impressed by the abilities and thoughtfulness of the men involved to find ways to integrate conversations about their spiritual lives with their more worldly pursuits.

It's a good group for me personally. Rabbis need to find time for some spiritual sharing and I think the men involved are intrigued to hear me express the questions and doubts that have been part of my Jewish journey. Of course, there are some boundaries that separate me from the others. I can't complain about the aspects of my job that drive me crazy. I choose not to reveal too much about my family. Aside from that, however, I'm pretty open and while some in the group may have a hard time getting beyond my title, others see me as a fellow searcher with just more expertise in this area of study. I may not be "one of the boys," but I do feel comfortable as a participant as well as a facilitator.

In his book, *The Journey Home*, Rabbi Hoffman uses the metaphor of a "connect the dots" game to provide a perspective on Jewish spirituality. He writes, "Life is very much the process of connecting the disparate dots of daily events that befall us. These dots may be ordinary or monumental; planned or unexpected; joyous or disappointing; elating or tragic." While the patterns we create are uniquely our own, the template is shared not only by the men who are present each month, but by Jewish men throughout the generations. Our men's group has provided a valuable way for those involved to see themselves as part of a much larger unit of connection. That has been its spiritual and congregational success.

WHAT *THE VAGINA MONOLOGUES* CAN TEACH YOU ABOUT BEING A MAN

Neil Hirsch

During my first year as a rabbinic student at Hebrew Union College–Jewish Institute of Religion (HUC-JIR) in Jerusalem, at the end of *Shacharit*, a classmate of mine—Micol—stood up to make an announcement. She explained that our class would be putting on a production of *The Vagina Monologues* and that women would be able to pick up photocopies of the audition material soon. I was wrapping the straps of my *t'fillin* around their plastic cases as she made this announcement. I remember doing a sloppy job that day.

The Vagina Monologues on my rabbinic school's campus? The idea of it made the hair on my arm itch.

After some deliberation, I made an appointment with Micol to air some of my concerns.

"It's twofold," I said. "For some reason, the idea of presenting *The Vagina Monologues* at HUC-JIR does not feel right to me. First, we are a Jewish seminary. Can we really appropriately put on a show that has no direct Jewish content?"

"I see your point with this, and I've been thinking about it myself," Micol responded. "We can talk about this, but what's your second concern?"

"HUC-JIR is supposed to be an institution that promotes and exemplifies egalitarianism. In everything we do at this school, and in Reform Judaism writ large, men and women are supposed to be equal. I realize this hasn't always been the case, and now it still isn't. Look at our class—we're two-thirds women and one-third men. I thought the point of *The Vagina Monologues* was for women to express their voices in the face of non-egalitarianism. So, I cannot seem to figure out why it is appropriate for us—as a Reform Jewish seminary—to present this show. This just doesn't seem like feminism as equality, to me."

Micol nodded politely, thinking about my argument. In retrospect, it was me who did not know all of the facts.

As the meeting continued, Micol and I brainstormed a solution to give *The Vagina Monologues* a Jewish twist. Micol and I decided that we wanted a program outside of the show that would address gender issues in a Jewish context. We would have a potluck Shabbat lunch and study session. The study session would address a topic directly applicable to both the men and women in our class and the relationship between the genders. This turned into a successful Shabbat text study on *Eishet Chayil*, "Woman of Valor," taken from Proverbs 31, a text traditionally sung by a husband to his wife at the Shabbat table. The unadulterated version leaves something to be desired to egalitarian ears. I have trouble accepting an enumeration of a woman's worth in which the wife is esteemed because "her husband is prominent in the gates" (Proverbs 31:23). Nonetheless, in our session we looked at it all, including its different interpretations and variations, trying to figure out what we single, nearly married, or married students would do when faced with the opportunity to praise or be praised in such a fashion.

Micol and I ended our meeting in disagreement about whether or not *The Vagina Monologues* was unfair to men, as I felt at the time. She did not think that the show was inappropriate in its one-sided portrayal of men. She was not alone. The show has moments of real anger over the treatment of women in our time. The production offers women an outlet for that anger. It seems as if there is a slight attempt to show that not all men bring on hurt; however, the characterization of men in the majority of the work is not friendly.

But as the women began to rehearse the show, and as I heard through the grapevine about the rehearsals, I learned that the value of *The Vagina Monologues* lies not in the actual show but in its preparation. In fact, whether or not the show is unfair to men is beside the point. The purpose of the show lies in the opportunity for women to come together and share experiences, to discuss concerns, to explore issues that are distinctly female. Through the women's meetings and rehearsals, my female class-mates had an opportunity to bond through the sharing of similar experiences. They derived strength from one another during this time, and it was apparent to many of us in the community outside of those meetings.

As an individual on the outside, I was jealous of my female classmates who participated in the show. I was jealous that the women of my class were worried about their gender and had the opportunity to explore what being female means. During this time, I came to understand that men need to have a place where we are able to discourse on the meaning of masculinity. I am not suggesting that we institute *The Penis Monologues.* That would be reactionary and would not be honest as to how men relate to one another. How men relate to men and how women relate to women are two different animals. When we try to bring men together, it must be honest and in a place where men feel comfortable, whether that be on a softball field, over a game of cards, or in front of a grill with beer in hand. We need to make sure that we are allowing ourselves this time, which I do not think my fellow male classmates and I did often enough while in Israel. No matter what form these meetings take, and no matter whether these are frequent or infrequent, the time needs to be treated as sacred.

Setting up meaningful meetings is part of the solution, but we also need to bring the solid contemporary male role model out of the wood-work. Now on the threshold of my adult life, I am learning to be the man I will be and the rabbi I will be because of the male role models I had in my family and among my clergy. While some of my female counterparts might have chosen to attend HUC because of their exposure to strong, female Jewish leaders, I am at rabbinic school because I grew up with strong male role models among my clergy. These men were talented ora-tors, writers, and scholars. They were also athletic, enjoyed good rock 'n' roll, and knew their cars. They could also be humble, sincere, and com-passionate. They were spiritual and religious, and passionate about

Israel. They were family men in a contemporary sense—they stood in partnership with their wives. I take pride in the example set for me by my male rabbis, and I hope to continue in their footsteps.

There is no silver bullet answer for how to be Jewish men together. The best we can do is be honest about two things: men need time to be together as men, and the Jewish individual—no matter the gender—should be committed to fulfilling an image of a strong man and a strong woman who are able to stand side by side one another in partnership.

A JOURNEY THROUGH RECOVERY

Anonymous

In 1954, when I was born, I was not a very typical baby of the generation. My dad was fifty-four at the time; he came here from Russia in 1914 at the age of fourteen and spoke broken English. My mom was so out of touch with herself that she didn't even have a clue she was pregnant. She had a multitude of mental and physical illnesses. I felt from a very early age on that there was something wrong with me, and I was told many times it was because I was fat. No matter what the situation, it would be different if I was not fat. If I didn't eat so much, then I would feel better.

Every adult in my life reinforced this fact. I ate too much, that was the problem; I needed to eat less to feel better and to be better. They all told me that if I just would eat less then all would be fine. Every fiber of my being ached for the day when I could eat less and be okay with that. I tried with all my soul to eat only certain portions or to avoid certain foods altogether. But every time I went back to those foods and felt like a failure. I begged God for the kind of life I saw in others and wanted for myself. My parents were older and much less well off economically than other people. My mom would tell me every day that she hated my dad and the only reason she stayed in our house was because of me. My dad would tell me every day he hated my mom and the only reason he stayed here was because of me. I remember that I was all of about three or four when they started doing this. My parents could not do the things with me that I saw other parents doing. My dad was old enough to be my grandfather and then some. My mom was very obese, and she was out of it mentally.

I wanted Rob and Laura Petrie, or the Cleavers, but got something very different. We rented an apartment in a very nice area, and I was jealous that my friends came from houses that their parents owned. I was jealous that they got new cars and we had ten-year-old cars. I was jealous that they had things I didn't have. I asked God for things like vacations, but we went nowhere. I asked God for thinness, but got fatter. I begged God for the things I thought were so important, but I didn't get them. I spent a lot of time wishing I could be someone and somewhere else. I was never at any time happy with who I was.

At the age of eight I was put on diet pills, and then when I was nine they changed them to another diet pill, with the same result. I was going on about fifteen minutes of sleep a month, but I didn't overeat. I lost weight. Until the pills wore off. Then I would eat Illinois and most of Wisconsin before I came up for air.

I went to a Hebrew school in the area that was Orthodox. My Hebrew stinks now and was horrible then. When they would tell us things in English I loved it. But the praying and the *Chumash* were all in Hebrew. It really bored me, and I was not one to want to do things I was not good at. Many of my friends were Orthodox, and for some reason I do not understand, every time they would have a meal or a gathering at their house, I was asked to leave. I felt like I was purposely excluded from their activities. Once again I did not make the cut because of something I could not control. I felt like I was never good enough or religious enough for the rabbis at my Hebrew school or religious enough for the friends who were Orthodox, and it made me feel bad. I blamed God. It seemed to me that in the area of God there was no way I could ever be good enough to earn God's love. I was not quite up to God's standards. My Hebrew stunk. The services may as well have been in Chinese. They bored me. I could not wait for them to be over so I could eat. I hated going to Hebrew school, and I hated shul even more. I felt shut out. I felt like there was no point in trying. I stopped. I didn't care anymore about any of the Judaism at all. If they didn't want me and I was not good enough—then screw them.

When I was twenty-two years old my mom died, and when I was twenty-four my dad died. I was broke and alone, and I was about six hundred pounds at the time. I hated doing it but I begged God for things and girls and a way out of the hopeless life I had. I was suicidal and wanted the death everyone had promised would come soon enough. If I was going to die, I wanted it to be right away, and I wanted to make sure I had a belly full of food. I was living with a friend, and my life was pathetic. From the time I was a child, weight had defined me, and it had mastery over me. The fat on my body was in charge of who I was and who I was not. Food was Pharaoh, and I was its slave. Resentments, fears, dishonesty, guilt, shame, and remorse were the taskmasters. I lied when the truth would have been better. I was in pain all the time from the contact dermatitis that plagued me. I was defined and emasculated by the fat. I could not sleep in a bed, as I could not lay flat and breathe. My legs were open from the ulcers caused by the edema in my lower legs. The swelling was so profuse that I could not wear socks, as they would get soaked from the puss that ran down my legs. I had dime-sized ulcers on the back of my legs, and I have the scars and the discoloration there today to remind me how far I have come.

When I was living that way I knew it was not good or normal, but I didn't really understand the way out. Later in my life someone told me the first rule of the hole is to stop digging. The pain was out of control. Loneliness and despair were all around me. I remember that on Saturday nights when my friends would go to places to meet girls and socialize, I would often buy large amounts of candy and things like that to binge on. When I was driving back home, with the car seat broken and the steering wheel cutting me in my overhanging stomach, I would beg God to help me eat only some of the food and to save the rest for some other time, because I really wanted to be out with girls and do the things that I saw them doing all the time. I wanted a life. I wanted to be happy. I wanted to be anyone else. I looked at the outsides of people around me, and from the surface I assumed that they had everything—thinness, love, success, serenity, prosperity—of which I felt devoid inside. I was jealous. I was resentful.

I would eat a bit of the food with the TV on, and I would close the bag. The tears would stream down my face, and the crying didn't stop me from eating the rest of the food and then some. What I didn't really know at the time was that once that food was in me, I was beyond help. I didn't know until after 1979 when two loving friends came and took me to my first meeting of Overeaters Anonymous (OA) that there was a physical allergy that placed me beyond human aid. The tears would be running down my face, and it made my food salty. It seemed to me at the time that God didn't care about me at all. If there was a God, then God had decided that I still could not quite live up to the standards that were set so long ago in my Hebrew school.

When I attended my first meetings of OA, I didn't quite do what was expected of me. I felt like I was cornered. I owed so much money to people and they were the ones putting pressure on me to go, and so I resented it, and I still hung on to the idea that I could do this on my own without this OA program. Of course, I was to find out that I could not. I had many experiences that should have shown me that I could not, but that is the nature of the disease. It fools you into thinking that you don't have it. I was morbidly obese. My life was in shambles, and I still wanted to run the show. I left OA in 1981, and in 1982 I was in a hospital and they were coming to cut off my leg because I had a staph infection and cellulites were rampant in me. I begged God to save me. They weighed me at the hospital. I was 513 pounds. I was about to become an amputee, and I was scared to the core of my soul. What was I going to do now? I didn't know. The operation was scheduled, and I was terrified. I was scared, and I was hopeless. I called out to God on that bed in the hospital in a foxhole type prayer, "Please save me." By what could only be called divine intervention, a God that I had stopped believing in believed in me, and the whole thing was about to turn around.

The infection subsided, and they saved my leg.

I didn't see it at the time, but this was one of the many miracles that took me to a better place in God's world.

I went back to OA eventually and really saw the complete need to work the OA program out of the Big Book of AA (Alchoholics Anonymous). I realized that I was out of ideas, and I submitted to the direction of the 12-step program of OA.

I understood that there was no way I could stay out of the food on my own and that there were reasons that I didn't know about before, but they were very real and had affected me from the minute I was born. I saw from the Big Book of AA that I had an illness of mind and body that made it impossible for me to control this on my own, with just willpower. I thought back to when I was a little boy. People would tell me not to eat so much and I would feel better. Well, they were right. I felt anger better. I felt resentments and fears better. I felt crushes on girls better. I felt all these things and more better. And what I didn't know was that as those feelings burst to the surface, my mind would seek out the food as a way of making me feel better. I did not know that if I cannot control my eating when I ate certain food because of the actual physical craving and if I cannot keep from eating because of the mental obsession, then I am powerless over food. That is my problem.

There is nothing that anyone can do about the physical allergy that makes it impossible to stop once I have started eating certain foods that give me that "buzz," the effect that is talked about in the "Doctors Opinion" chapter of the Big Book of AA. So I am told that the mind will drive me into the food as a way of helping me to not feel the feelings of restlessness, irritability, and discontent. What if I could find a different way to feel good and therefore not set the terrible cycle in motion again? That is the OA program of recovery, and that is what I needed to do.

When I got to the line in the middle of page 45 of the Big Book of AA that says, "The main object of this book is to help you find a power greater than yourself which will solve your problem,"[1] I gulped and thought, "Oh no, here we go again with the God stuff, and I am in trouble." Someone very wisely pointed me in the direction of appendix 2 in the back of the Big Book of AA, and there it told me that all I needed was a personality change sufficient to bring about a recovery. I needed an open mind, and I needed to be willing. It told me there that if I closed my mind to the possibility of a God, then I was doomed. It told me that I needed to remember that to most people God comes slowly, not like the story of the Burning Bush. The Big Book calls this a spiritual awakening of the educational variety. That is what I have every time I go to an OA meeting or talk to someone from recovery on the phone. I have it every time I take actions to get me out of myself. I have it when I open my mind and take actions with a willingness to learn instead of the prejudice of the ego. The Big Book promises, "That feeling of uselessness and self-pity will disappear. We will lose interest in selfish things and gain interest in our fellows. Self-seeking will slip away. . . . We will intuitively know how to handle situations which used to baffle us. We will suddenly realize that God is doing for us what we could not do for ourselves."[2] I believe and live those promises. When I follow the 12 steps, the old feeling, the one about not getting what I want according to my way and my will, the feeling that there cannot be a God, that feeling melts away. Instead I have what the Big Book of AA calls serenity and peace. Because of this way of life, I am willing to take actions that seem strange at first and trigger fear—the fear of what if I do this and I still do not get what I want? The "what ifs" can kill me if I give in to them.

I have learned much in my life through the 12 steps. I have learned that there is a symphony of the heart, and it plays beautiful music when I live my life according to the directions that are in the Big Book of AA. I had to stop waiting for God to give me what I wanted before I took these actions. I had to act my way into right thinking, instead of thinking my way into right action.

There are theologians and there are philosophers as well as many people who have made it their life to think about who God is, and what God is not. I am not in that group. Here is what I know about God: There is one, and it is not me.

That is all the information I will ever really need. When I stop playing God and thinking that the world should be this or that, then I am free to do the work in front of me. Good times and bad have come upon me. No matter what happens, I will never rise above the level of human being. Every time I have problems, I need to stop telling God how big my problems are and start acting in ways that tell my problems how big my God is. I need to reach out to someone else. I need to get to a meeting of OA. I need to get out of myself and my own selfish little world and look to see who needs a call. What actions can I take? I must do God's work without doing God's job.

Today, through the way of life outlined in the Big Book of AA, I have a life that has direction to it. I know what to do each day, and when I do it, I get more in return than I ever could have imagined. From the depths of self and ego, from fears and resentments, self-pity and remorse, God has changed me and remolded me into the person I am today. The song of my soul is a symphony when I do God's work. There is such joy in giving and helping others that I cannot even imagine life any other way. I do not know much, but I do know this: God is in my heart, and when I am doing this work, I get such a feeling that tells me that I have done the work that was in front of me. When I do not, I know it too. The world looks better to me when I am not sick in self. Every day I pray. Every day I meditate. Every day I thank God for what I have, with the understanding that recovery does not mean I will get what I want, it means I will want what I have already. I feel God with me. I am filled with a sense of God's presence, and I love it. That feeling I had of uselessness and self-pity will leave me when I serve God and perform God's work well.

I have been catapulted to a fourth dimension of living through the 12 steps that is a life far beyond what words on a page here can describe. I went from death to life. I live life in a way that is wonderful. I have lost over five hundred pounds since the very beginning of my journey, and that is the least of the things that happened. I walk thirty-four miles a week. I have been married to a wonderful lady for fourteen years. I have a twelve-year-old daughter, and she is the light of my life. I live a life today that works in all areas. I believe that God loves to work through people, and the people in my life today are a mix of people in and out of recovery. Both are treasures. The people in recovery bring their unique pain and horrible nightmares to the meetings, and we share the strong bond of people who have survived a common peril. We also share the common solution. It draws us together and helps all of us. God fills me with people. The people fill me with God. We laugh and we cry. We study the Big Book together, and we learn together. It is beautiful. We function like the old minyan, and when someone is not there, we will be concerned. The tapestry of my life is stronger because of the people who weave it. Each story enhances my own, and I learn from everyone there when I see them as my teacher. Some have work problems and some health issues, and still others have marital problems. No matter what, we see the workings of God's magic in their life, and we are inspired when we see healing beyond our human comprehension.

My life was so broken when I was in the food. My life didn't work on any level. I went on my first date when I was thirty-five years old. I lived a life that was in filth and horrible self-inflicted conditions. Only God could have changed this. My financial life was horrible. My credit was ruined. Today banks call me up to try to lend me money. I own my own business. We do okay. We belong to a synagogue we love, and I have found my way back to my Judaism. I love that. Life is great. I am going to live life to the fullest because of a loving God. For that I am truly grateful. I know I will never get better by absorbing spiritual information; I heal when I transmit spiritual information. Pass it on.

NOTES

1. The Big Book of Alcoholics Anonymous (Alcoholics Anonymous World Services, 2007), p. 45; http://www.alcoholics-anonymous.org/bigbookonline.

2. Ibid., p. 84.

ONE FOOT PLANTED FIRMLY
ON THE GROUND

Lary Bloom

Several years ago, before beginning work on a Vietnam memoir, I turned to my rabbi for help.

Douglas Sagal was then the spiritual leader of our small Jewish community in rural Connecticut. He was also an amateur boxer and, as the children attested, an accomplished magician. Adults knew of a different magic: the capacity of his sermons to move even the unmovable. Here was a man with unusual powers. And for my memoir research, I needed his wizardry.

Could he help me find a rabbi I once knew, one who also had affected me deeply? This was the first rabbi to offer me what Doug had so often provided during Shabbat services—an opportunity to shed a tear.

As a young army lieutenant in Vietnam, I had been not only a long distance from home but also from Judaism. I was the product of an Orthodox education, steeped in Hebrew, Torah, and ritual and then, in the decade that followed, more than a touch rebellious.

My dog tag read "Jewish," but if such pieces of metal made necessary for identification of remains had been more specific, mine might have pointed out: "Like his father, a cynic who distrusts all religion, but like his mother, someone who knows that God surely exists, because how else could the creation of the violin be explained?" And how could I explain the phenomenon of Rabbi Ernest D. Lapp, as he was known to me at the time, but who seemed to have disappeared since?

The date was June 8, 1967. The site was Cam Ranh Bay, a supply depot on Vietnam's coast where I was stationed at the time. Rabbi Lapp had called together about twenty Jewish officers for a brief but critical meeting.

For forty-eight hours, we had all been consumed by a second conflict, one that had broken out in the Middle East: Israel against its usual enemies. What would become known as the Six-Day War was already a third over.

We gathered around Rabbi Lapp, who was dressed in un-rabbinic garb—combat boots and jungle fatigues with a sewn Star of David. He wore black horn-rimmed glasses, and though small in stature, he had a commanding presence.

As we gathered around him, we heard his compelling tale of little David, this little Israel, fighting for its life even as we, so far away, were fighting a different war. On this, Rabbi Lapp expressed a deeply personal view. He understood obstacle and tyranny in the way few of us did. He and his parents had fled his native Vienna for America in 1940, just in time to avoid becoming Holocaust statistics. And, twenty-six years later, even as the rabbi went off to Vietnam, his wife Ruth and the couple's three children went to work on a cooperative farm in Israel and were seeing, firsthand, the mobilization for yet another war.

As for the rest of us in Cam Ranh Bay, the rabbi said, there are no accidents of circumstance. We had taken the place of those we had read about in the histories of America, of the world, and of biblical times. The burdens of the struggle had fallen upon us, and it was up to each of us to make our contributions and sacrifices.

What he was doing—and I didn't understand it fully until I and everyone else in the small group took out our wallets—was collecting on behalf of the State of Israel. In a few minutes, Rabbi Lapp had nearly $1,000 from a few men whose monthly wages were meager (mine, at the time, was $260 plus $64 in combat pay). I had been under the spell of someone who spoke a language other than that spoken by politicians or historians or even the rabbis I knew to that point—a language that didn't travel from mouth to ear but heart to heart.

As my tour of duty wound down, I saw Rabbi Lapp a few more times and credited him with my reentrance into faith. It wasn't Israel that had brought me back. It was the sense that, as a man, I could confirm that for all I could learn there would remain a part of me that could not be explained—this spiritual, if not necessarily religious, certainty.

The inner struggle, however, did not end there. Five years after I returned from Vietnam, my wife Marsha—twenty-seven, a scientist, and the mother of our three-year-old daughter Amy—died of a brain aneurysm. In the aftermath of this I struggled in many ways.

Could a man, alone, raise a daughter? This was a time, shortly after the introduction of *Ms.* magazine, in which women explored new opportunities and identities. I was crossing the gender gap from a different direction, as a man who tried to think like a woman. In this, I struggled. In my revised brand of fatherhood, I assumed that my daughter needed a new mother—that a father alone was incapable of proper parenthood. I couldn't seem to deliver the two qualities that most mothers deliver in equal measure and simultaneously: great affection and the setting of limits.

I did not draw, at the time, much guidance from my religion. And my domestic choices yielded unfortunate results. I had two brief marriages that started with the great hope of "blended family" and ended in ruins. I did not understand that a child has only one mother, living or dead, and that it was my job as a father to find ways to honor this even as I led my own life. I could not begin to square my circumstances and history with any reliable spiritual measure until I came upon the little shul where Rabbi Doug became the first full-time rabbi in its long history and until my daughter Amy grew into an adult with children of her own.

As a result of all of this, I knew that my Vietnam memoir, which I have worked on even as I have published other books, could not merely become a book of military history. It would need to address the elusive sense of how I saw myself then and how I see myself now. In order to do this, it would be necessary to immerse myself in the subject and to speak to everyone still alive who had affected me at the time and many who have affected me since. This led me to ask for Rabbi Sagal's help in locating the man who'd had such impact during my tour of duty.

"Good news," he told me. Rabbi Sagal had called the Jewish Chaplains Council of the Jewish Welfare Board in New York City and asked if they knew anything about a Rabbi Ernest D. Lapp. My problem had been, I learned, that I was searching with the wrong name. Rabbi Lapp went by his given first name during his active duty years but later by his middle name—the name his friends had always called him. "Yes," the person at the other end of the line told Rabbi Sagal, "Rabbi David Lapp is here—he's right down the hallway." Indeed, he was director of Jewish Chaplains Council.

On a June day more than three decades after I first saw him, I drove to the city and found his office. He looked much different to me, of course—no longer the whirling dervish. But, yes, he remembered speaking about the Six-Day War to Jewish soldiers.

I had a picture of him all those years, but I did not know during that time of how he squared his duties to God, country, Israel, his family, and all else. Not until I listened to his recollections of war.

He told me that as often as he could he went to bases known to be dangerous. He did this because that's where his comfort was most needed, not in the relatively safe confines of supply depots. In this pursuit, he faced some opposition. His boss in the corps of chaplains, a Catholic colonel, pointed out to Major Lapp that he was one of only three rabbis serving in Vietnam. "We can't afford to lose you."

Even so, the major often flew late at night in helicopters—easy targets of the enemy. Before he went out on these missions, each time he wrote "a last letter" to his wife, just in case he didn't come back. He left the letter next to his bunk, where a colleague could find it and mail it.

As it turned out, there was never a necessity to do that. Yet something about that ritual—a ritual far different from those described in Torah—taught me about how we are to live as men, with one foot on solid ground and the other in a place that, no matter our educations or experiences, we can never fully understand.

PART 4

HEARING THE VOICE: FINDING THE SELF

INTRODUCTION

When Elijah reaches the mountaintop, he hears God's voice asking him, "What are you doing here, Elijah?" His answer, "I have been full of zeal for the Eternal, the God of heaven's hosts," shows us how he was dedicated to serving God. When the wind, earthquake, and fire pass without evidence of God's presence and then Elijah hears the "still, small voice," we see how he finds an acceptance of self, a firmness of purpose, and a vision of his future direction. When asked again the same question, he gives the same answer, but we know his zeal is now matched by his sense of security (I Kings 19:9–14).

Moses also sought that security. Even after seeing the miracle of the Burning Bush, speaking to God "face to face," serving as God's vehicle in the destruction of the Earth's greatest civilization—Egypt—and leading the people at the revelation at Mount Sinai, Moses still feels insecure. The tragedy of the Golden Calf forces him to question the foundations of his leadership, and he emerges shaken and afraid that he will be unable to lead this difficult people. When he reascends the mountain he asks God for further proof of divine protection. In the exact same spot that Elijah later stands, God passes before Moses, revealing only the back of the retreating Divine Presence (Exodus 33:21).

This kind of experience has been the goal of so many Jews throughout our history. We have sought guidance, meaning, and security through sacrificial worship, the leadership of kings, the word of prophets, the poetry of the psalms, the power of revolt, the study of law and lore, and the secrets of mystical revelation. More recent Jewish pursuits (the last five hundred years or so) have led to even more creative mysticisms, messianic pretenders, and the formation of Chasidic circles around charismatic rebbes, all against the backdrop of an ever-increasing level of legal exploration and debate. And the modern period has seen Jewish creativity blossom, in the fertile soil of the Enlightenment, the hard-fought soil of sovereignty, and the scorched earth of devastation following the Shoah. In every age, we have sought new and more creative forms of divine experience, trying to answer age-old questions of awe, ethics, and theodicy, while preserving the sacred in the midst of life's more mundane stresses. As each generation applies itself toward Judaism, they produce different ways of finding the "still, small voice" in their lives. And like Elijah—who first saw the wind, earthquake, and fire—for many Jews the discovery of God defies expectations.

We all desire a sense of meaning and purpose. We can call that many things: confidence, inner peace, the "still, small voice," or just plain old God. The name does not matter. Some of us find it, while others spend lifetimes searching (or more commonly, we succumb to superficial consumer culture and just get used to the feeling of purposelessness). What I describe here is an awareness of the soul, that part of the self that transcends physical, emotional, and intellectual needs. We may ignore our souls for a time (perhaps that is what puts us in the wilderness), but eventually the soul will demand attention. Some men know how to feed and nurture the soul, but all of us struggle with this task in some way or another throughout life.

A new men's form of Judaism would help today's men fortify their souls and find the "still, small voice." This Judaism would have structures that encourage men to continue hearing the spiritual in their lives. Such an option within Judaism would strengthen the community by reaching more men, but more importantly it would strengthen men. The question, of course, is how.

I do not fancy myself a guru, and thus I do not have the universal key to open the gates of men's souls. I do not think one key exists. Too often we imagine one kind of spiritual experience. Our modern, bureaucratic, institutional, movement-based structure promotes a kind of group-think in which the latest trend spreads like wildfire, and we begin to emulate the hottest new "spirituality" trend. Rabbi Lawrence Hoffman has written compellingly about the generations of American Judaism. He argues that in the late nineteenth and early twentieth centuries our communal goal was assimilating into an ideal of American and the embrace of many Protestant forms of worship. In the mid-twentieth century it was the blossoming of suburban lifestyles and the promotion of pediatric Judaism. The 1960s led to some rebellion against such strong suburban synagogue institutions, and the renewal and *chavurah* movements flourished as a reaction. The late twentieth century saw what Hoffman described as "seekers," and a more intimate, personal, and inward form of Judaism has become all the rage throughout the liberal movements.[1]

While the depiction of Judaism as a series of "generations" certainly does describe the major thrust of Jewish life over long periods for large groups, it obscures the diversity and depth of personal Jewish practice. People find meaning in such a vast variety of methods. While communal leaders need ideas around which to rally and toward which to direct resources, a generational approach risks ignoring varieties of spirituality.

Men are so used to declaring, "I am not spiritual" because we have excluded from the definition of "spiritual" what many men find meaningful and soulful. But these forms define different types of men and broaden what we can define as religious experience. In our state of Jewish life, where so many men feel estranged from the community and from God, we should be keen to investigate any way that a man successfully feeds his soul.

This group of essays contains some of that variety. A few of these men do embrace methods of "spirituality" that should be familiar and obvious to readers, like David Gottlieb's piece on meditation. In addition, Rabbi Meir Feldman's essay reflects a comfort with the unknown aspects of life that fits well into the postmodern mood of Jewish spirituality.

But other essays in this group reflect what might be seen as less explicitly spiritual models of Jewish soulfulness. Three authors illustrate how their spirituality and masculinity have been expressed in the connection to others: Irwin Ayes through a lifetime of service, Stephen Breslauer through community and friendship, and Jeremy Sandler through peoplehood and romance. Eugene Borowitz rejects the idea of the stereotypically "spiritual" and offers alternative models, starting with his father. Joel Eglash also writes about his father and the ways that his nonconformity shaped Eglash's Jewish identity. Richard Gartner, a psychologist, describes how Judaism aided his own journey through psychoanalysis and how it can be critically helpful to his clients struggling with their own issues of masculinity. Ellen Bresner speaks as an observer of the men in her life as she illustrates the many ways that men find Jewish meaning, especially through their relationships with women. Philip Saperia tells the story of how Judaism provided a safe haven through his experiences of anti-Semitism and, like Rabbi Victor Appel's essay in part 3, how Jewish community supported him through his process of coming out as a gay man. Finally, Rabbi Daniel Zemel considers the symbolism of a White Sox jersey he wears to Sunday school and realizes that his message goes way beyond one of masculinity to communicate a sense of authenticity and comfort with self.

That message of authenticity is at the core of finding a connection to the spiritual, to amplifying the murmur of the soul and hearing the "still, small voice." The authors in this section all describe the different ways in which they find that Jewish authenticity and marry it to their self-image as men. While two of the essays—Gottlieb and Feldman—embrace what we may consider to be an obviously "spiritual" path, the others require us to expand our definition of "spirituality." They display Jewish men finding deep meaning, purpose, and fulfillment through relationship, nonconformist father figures, healing, shelter, and personal integrity. Certainly religion includes all of those options. We would do well as a community to consider them when we aim to serve and promote the male "spirituality" of the future.

NOTES

1. Lawrence A. Hoffman, *ReThinking Synagogues: A New Vocabulary for Congregational Life* (Woodstock, VT: Jewish Lights Publishing, 2006).

THE STILL, SMALL VOICE, DROWNED OUT

David Gottlieb

There is not enough stillness, not enough silence in the life of today's American Jewish man. There are too many means of communication, too many commitments, too many appointments, and too much sheer *noise* for a Jewish man to follow the thin filament running from his head to his heart, and from there into the deepest recesses of his being. The Jewish removal from nature has precipitated our exile from the "still, small voice" that resides at our center and connects us to what is most irrevocably Jewish about us. This inner exile has come about because Judaism, born in a land of immense beauty and vast silences, had to preserve and perpetuate itself in community. Silence became an object of distrust: the silent were alone, vulnerable. Perhaps the silent had vanished. Or gone over to the worship of idols.

My own search for silence began in a kind of loneliness, dove into a deep pool of solitude, and ended up once again on the shining shores of Judaism—this time, with a deep connection to Jewish identity and practice. It was only through silence that I beheld my Jewish essence, and only through silence that I was led back to being fully Jewish.

In the late 1990s, I answered a long-unheeded call to learn to meditate. Although I was living an observant Jewish life—helping keep a kosher home, attending synagogue once a week, sending our children to a Jewish day school, struggling to learn Hebrew—I was at home neither in the Jewish tradition nor the Jewish community into which my wife, three children, and I had settled. I could not understand or read Hebrew well enough to follow the very traditional service I attended each week. It seemed that the congregation appreciated the comfort of familiarity offered by a Shabbat service so similar from one week to the next; it also seemed as though people came for reasons of community and continuity far more than for closeness to God or for enhancing spiritual awareness.

In my search for a meditation teacher, a Jewish woman of my acquaintance—a social worker—encouraged me to visit a local Zen center. The Buddhists, she said, are the ones to go to when you want to learn how to meditate. I went to a nearby Zen center, and in short order, I was transformed, undone. I had found, in the formal silence of seated meditation, a well—an oasis. I drank.

There is a distrust of silence in Jewish life, and that distrust is reflected in much of contemporary Jewish practice. Although Jewish meditation is a venerable tradition now making something of a comeback, it still is not widely taught, practiced, or understood. Our prayers are meant to be passionate; our moments of silence, though important, are few. We speak, we chant, we sing, we argue with God. We praise, thank, and petition; we beg forgiveness. It is hard, even during the silent *Amidah*, to find true silence—deep, lasting silence—or silence that is sanctified without being sad. Perhaps stillness speaks too loudly to us of the death and destruction that has haunted us—the yeshivot gone silent, the towns razed, the ashes borne into the unforgiving sky.

Perhaps the *zendo* felt right because it was simple: a plain, varnished oak floor; a row of meditation cushions along each wall; a Buddha statue in front of the wall of glass block windows at the head of the meditation hall. Perhaps it was just a relief to be in a place of worship where chatting was not an option. Perhaps I enjoyed the company of other outsiders and joining together in an effort to find and make our own community. Perhaps I loved the silence. Most likely it was all of these. Free of the intricate choreography and restless yearnings of Judaism, bathed in rigorous silence, I could finally *hear*.

For almost three years, even while ostensibly living an observant Jewish life and maintaining my efforts to become more Jewishly educated, my spiritual home was the *zendo*. Being there was something like peace on the pillow. It was not real peace, because there was torment at home: my devotedly Jewish wife could not stomach my practicing a strange religion. Judaism was not a badge or a selection from the spiritual buffet; it was an inherited treasure, a lofty and rigorous regimen, an authentic calling to lift ourselves and those around us through worship, study, and the commitment to Jewish continuity. Where was the commitment I had made to this community, this way of life?

While I understood my wife's concerns, I could not easily depart from a path on which I felt liberation was at hand. The storms at home were, I felt, brewed in her fevered mind; they were the kind of fevered grasping from which Buddhism was liberating me. People seemed shocked that I could so easily turn my back on Judaism. I found it increasingly hard to understand why they chose to remain within it.

And then, the end of my excursion into Buddhism, and Judaism's forgiving embrace, came in a most sincere, smiling, and unexpected way.

Shortly after undergoing lay ordination as a Zen Buddhist, in May of 2002, I began to become quite uncomfortable while in seated meditation. At first, the discomfort was cerebral, nagging: "Should I really be doing this?" I thought. In retrospect, perhaps it was God saying to me what God said to Elijah:

What are you doing here?

Then, over the course of two or three sittings, I had the vivid sensation of being watched—not by a person, but by a loving and patient Presence. It was here that a Jewish essence proclaimed itself to me, and it would not back away. It was friendly but unblinking, patient but unwavering. Unlike most thoughts that pass through the mind in meditation, it would not depart. It became a ghost, a shadow that hovered behind all thought and non-thought, until at last I focused on it and gave myself to it.

Meditation is difficult: thoughts arise and dance like goblins; worries emerge from their tombs to haunt you. Eventually, though, you learn to let thoughts and worries wash over you, move beyond you. It's almost like sinking into the earth, watching a train roar overhead: soon, the line of thoughts ceases to concern you, and the noise recedes. You are alone.

The Presence that came to me in meditation, however, did not, would not leave me. It caused goose bumps on my arms and a gnawing discomfort in my mind. This Presence then slowly lowered itself over me.

Wherever I refocused my consciousness, this Presence appeared. Whatever arose in my mind's eye, it replaced. I heard no voice, but I perceived the question.

What are you doing here?

And that was it.

I knew then, as I had never known before: *I am Jewish. I must learn and grow as a Jew, and I must live a Jewish life.*

I am still learning what a "Jewish life" is, but I'm learning by doing: by attending synagogue, by studying Hebrew and Jewish texts, to be sure, but also by learning how to adapt the practice of silent meditation to the appreciation of all that is Jewish. Most shockingly, even to me, it has resulted in my taking initial steps toward rabbinic ordination. There should be men who can lead our community both in song and in silence, in prayer and in meditation, in times when we raise our voices to God and in times when we merely lift up our souls.

My Jewish *n'shamah,* having grown up through the silence to meet me, now serves as my guide on a journey upon which more men must embark: seeking, through silence, to deeply hear their own Jewish essence, and to resolve to honor it through study, worship, and serving the community.

THE HOLY UNKNOWN

Meir Feldman

In many ways, my life began at thirty-eight years old, in 1998. I entered rabbinic school, finally feeling clear and excited about the path I was blazing for myself. For so long I had been clueless about what to do with my life. After college, I took a traditional route. I went to law school and then practiced law for seven or eight years, first at a large New York firm and then as a federal prosecutor in Los Angeles. But all along I felt unsatisfied. I had the sense that there was more; there was another path I was supposed to travel. Something told me there was an unknown that I was meant to discover.

In early 1996, I was listening to an NPR report about the Oklahoma City bombing case. The prosecutor being interviewed had a very distinctive voice, and I was certain that I knew her. Nina Totenberg of NPR concluded the interview by telling listeners that she had been speaking with trial attorney Beth, of the Department of Justice.

In an instant, I remembered our most important experience together. We had been two of thirty-five summer associates at our New York law firm, in 1986, ten years earlier. Beth and I and another colleague spent a day on the beach, in the Hamptons or Fire Island, I can't remember which, on a Saturday in July. We talked about lots of things, including our future plans. I explained that "I hoped to work with our firm for a few years after law school, then to go to the U.S. Attorney's office somewhere, and then . . . I had no idea what I'd do after that." My only clear idea, or hope, was that my future path would not involve the law.

Well, living on the beach in Venice, California, in early 1996, having left the law, I realized that my life path had unfolded exactly as I had imagined it out loud with Beth ten years earlier. I had spent a few years at our firm, then served at the U.S. Attorney's office, and then . . . *I did not know what*. Rather shocking—I was smack-dab in the middle of the "I did not know what" stage. For me, that déjà vu experience profoundly affirmed my journey. Even though I had *no* idea where I was headed, my choice to stop practicing law seemed more likely an act of courage and insight than a moment of brash irresponsibility.

I had no idea where I was going. Even more, I had no idea that I would become a rabbi or that Judaism would become significant, no central, to my life. If someone had told me in 1994 or even in 1996 that I would become a rabbi, I would have thought they were nuts.

First of all, with one exception, I had no Jewish ritual in my life at that time, although my one weekly ritual was on Saturday. I played in a weekly basketball game in West LA. No tallit, no prayer book, but there was a minyan, and occasionally there was an exalted high. Mostly, however, this important weekly ritual involved lots of mediocre moments. I very much looked forward to the game. I loved being outside, and I liked seeing some of the guys. But in truth, I never really understood why the game was so important to me.

Second, as someone who thought little about God, I was an unlikely candidate to become a rabbi. Surely, from time to time I had meaningful spiritual experiences. For example, after the New York Bar exam, I went to Australia for a month and spent a week scuba diving in the Great Barrier Reef. For most of us, it's inevitable that scuba diving engenders moments of sheer wonder, absolute awe—awe for the colors, diversity, enormity, power, and beauty of the created world; awe for the miracle of life. There at the Great Barrier Reef, I felt myself sharing in a vast and awesome unknown. Have you ever heard yourself breathe? It's an awe-inspiring sound. If these experiences don't generate some kind of awe-inspired feeling, then I'd say you're spiritually dead, or close to it. I had been for a long time.

Abraham Joshua Heschel and many others have said that the beginning of faith is awe. Unlike those who teach a faith of absolute certainty, our greatest teachers push us to the great unknown. We are the God-strugglers; that's how we become Israel—"the one who struggles with God." For Jews, by definition, when we embrace the struggle, we prevail in the struggle. From Heschel to Maimonides, we learn that true faith is not about certainty. True faith happens when we affirm and celebrate the grand mystery. Like Moses, at best we see only God's back, the afterglow of our sacred encounters (Exodus 33:23).

At thirty-five years old, I had a transformative experience. I was at the Brandeis-Bardin Institute, outside of Los Angeles, listening to Rabbi David Wolpe. A dear friend of mine, Marvin, a father figure of sorts, asked Rabbi Wolpe a question that changed my life. He asked the rabbi if he believed in God and if he could share some proof of God's existence. My first thought was, "What an insane question and comment!" And at the same moment, I rolled my eyes and said to myself, "This is a rabbi. You know what he'll say, Marvin. Don't be ridiculous!"

Wolpe began his response with a rhetorical question: "The first time you met your wife, did you say: 'Prove to me that you should be my wife!'?"

Of course none of us married folks adopted that approach. We shared experiences together, many of them mundane and maybe also a few sacred moments. At some point our relationship felt real. Our love became clear—it was something that didn't need to be proven. Then Wolpe continued, "After you knocked on the door, you built a relationship, which I bet at certain times is defined by great closeness and understanding, and at other times by doubt and confusion and many other emotions." He concluded by saying, "That's my relationship with God."

I was stunned—"You, Mr. Rabbi, have doubts." Rabbi Wolpe's openness, his willingness to acknowledge his *doubts*, was the beginning of my journey toward something that, today, I call faith. One rabbi's courage to question his faith opened for another the door of faith, faith in the mystery and beauty of life, faith that I and every one of us have been put here for a reason.

I had never knocked on God's door, much less tried to build a relationship. It was time to stop asking for proof on the first date. It was time to knock on the door and to step into the holy unknown.

WHAT YOU DO SPEAKS SO LOUDLY

Irwin I. Ayes

My first memories of what it meant to be a Jewish man were those of a young camper at a Jewish summer camp. Both my sister and I were in attendance. This was our first time away from home, and we were both homesick. The strange thing was that my sister had always appeared strong and self-assured. I decided to be the "big brother" and support her so that she could quickly overcome her homesick feelings and enjoy a wonderful summer. In so doing, we both felt better and had a great summer experience.

Years later, while working as a counselor at the same summer camp, I was asked to help out at a special pre-camp program for children from the inner city from the Atlanta, Georgia, area. It was only for two or three days, utilizing the camp's facilities. I was a water safety instructor and taught swimming at that time. During one session we were playing a game using a greased watermelon as you would a football. We were trying to promote and teach teamwork. We were all having a great time, but I noticed that several of the children were not able to navigate as well as the others in the water. When we stopped, I spoke to these children and found out that they did not know how to swim. This was strange for me to hear, since I was raised around water, but it wasn't strange for inner-city

Atlanta. I and a few other counselors began teaching those children how to swim. They were all great kids and thankful for the instruction. I was told, after they left camp, that one of the children I taught to swim was the son of the late Dr. Martin Luther King, Jr. Again, it was just another of life's instances with a special twist.

I became the head counselor of twelve young men whom I was to guide, counsel, and mentor. I did not realize the extent of that position. I expected a fun summer with some money to be made. I found myself being asked many questions about everything from the opposite sex, to ritual observance of Shabbat each week, to why we had to have kosher marshmallows. I taught several classes daily and was able to be a positive influence on those young men's lives. I learned to earn their respect rather than to command what needed to be done. Many of the children carried baggage from home life or school that they would not discuss with me. Some were not previously well versed in their religious studies. While I had attended religious classes leading to my bar mitzvah, my Hebrew was not good. Together we conquered that. Those who read and studied well taught the others, including me. I mentored them and was mentored by them, the impact of which was lifelong.

My parents taught me through words and actions. My father is gone now seven years, and I feel his loss as well as his presence every day. My sweet mother is doing well at age eighty-eight and is precious to me. While my parents had not been formally educated, I am truly amazed at what they learned through life experiences. We shared as a family. There was no "mine" or "yours," only "ours." Honesty is foremost, as is the hand-shake as your word. If you say you will do something, that is what you do. That is the way I operate today.

My father was and is my hero. He was all I ever wanted to be. I had not been an overtly religious person, only going to synagogue on major holidays. However, I was always taught that Judaism is not a religion but a way of life. It is a lifestyle. It is the way you treat other people, the deal-ings you have both at work and socially. It really is like the movie *The Karate Kid* in which a young man wants to learn karate to protect himself. He is frustrated by all of the work he does instead of specific karate train-ing. He finally confronts his teacher, who shows him that all of the work he had done was, in part, training for his karate.

When I lost my father, I followed the tradition of mourning and attended the minyan faithfully. There I found that, although I was not adept at reading Hebrew, I did know more than I thought. Also, the other members of the daily minyan were always available to help me and not judge me.

This allowed me to go on each day with my sorrow and, at the same time, comfort others. The ability to give of yourself and help others is the truest gift I received. When you can truly and freely give of yourself, that is when you receive. Surely we are all interested in ourselves and our own well-being, but our goal should be to help others.

For thirty years I practiced medicine as a podiatric physician and surgeon. Along the way I had several goals, including prosperity and a respected position in the community. During my years of practice I had instances of grave emergencies, but certainly, as a podiatrist, they were not like those of a cardiovascular surgeon.

In fact, I developed what I called a "limp in–leap out" outcome. Simply put, while there were the occasional serious emergencies, most of the time people came in with a painful problem that I could alleviate, and I would send them home in much greater comfort. A prayer I use to this day is that I might be able to use my talents to help relieve pain and suffering. My thought process was that if I could do my part to help others at a local level, then, with the help of others, we could collectively make a worldwide impact.

I remember the time and effort Rabbi Chapman and Rabbi Luski afforded me when they were so busy with other duties. I tried to model their behavior during every day of my medical practice. If someone needed more time to discuss family matters or general health, I would sit and talk with them. If they couldn't find the correct therapist or specialist to see, I would try to find one and schedule an appointment for them. I think I treated more things outside of a specific podiatric complaint than within. I know that I always slept well at night and have never regretted the time I spent with any one patient. Could I have seen more people and made more money another way? Yes, but I would not be any happier than I am.

When my life changed, I needed to learn to adapt. Because of some medical conditions, I began losing my acute vision. At first I had to give up surgery, and eventually had to entirely give up my practice. While it is disheartening to have to give up something before you wish to do so, I am blessed with enough vision to move about fairly well.

I am now only a few days past my second major eye surgery, and while I know that I can't ever operate again, I am blessed to be able to get around. I think back fondly on all the occasions that allowed me to help someone, whether it was a young child or an adult. I have been blessed with a great ophthalmologist and surgeon who is caring for my eyes, but mostly I am surrounded by great family and friends who continue to do for me, and they remind me of all that I am able to do for others.

It has come full circle. Hopefully I can continue to be of service to others, and just maybe that contribution, along with those of so many others, will bring more peace and happiness to this world.

BORN TO BE JEWISH

Stephen Breslauer

I was a Depression-era baby who grew up in a female-led household during World War II. For three of my preteen years, my father was overseas, and my only contact with him was via V-mail. My family was dominated by my grandmother (my mother's mother), the matriarch. Her husband was a backslapping traveling salesman, who was seldom home and escaped to the Elks Club each day he was in town. My mother was the heir to that family position. I scarcely knew my father's parents; they died when I was very young. So, although I had two brothers and no sisters, I grew up in a female-controlled environment.

We were typical middle-class, suburban, "classical Reform" Ashkenazi Jews. Our community had many Jewish families. In that era, Jews socialized only with other Jews, so by high school the friends I made at Sunday school and in youth group defined my social circle. Although I lived in an area where there was strong anti-Semitism, it never impacted on me. I attended Sunday school for twelve years, where I was exposed to biblical history and major Jewish holidays. We learned little of Jewish tradition, no Hebrew, no Jewish literature, and little Jewish ritual.

My teen years were a time of seeking and questioning. I was totally dissatisfied and unfulfilled by the juvenile Judaism I had been taught. As a part of my search for relevance in my religion, I challenged everything while in Sunday school, even the existence of God. I rejected the concept of an anthropomorphic God, a father figure residing in heaven and overseeing humankind, and the concept of an omnipotent, omniscient, omnipresent presence that foresaw my every thought and action. Rabbi Baron, who taught the confirmation class, almost did not allow me to be confirmed, because I made his life miserable by questioning everything he said and taught. He told my parents that he was not convinced that I was truly Jewish. Still I was confirmed; there was no bar mitzvah in my congregation! Throughout my adolescent years, the strongest link to my Jewish heritage was through my Jewish friends and youth group.

We lit Shabbat candles at home and observed the major Jewish holidays—Rosh HaShanah, Yom Kippur, and Passover. We lit the Chanukah candles each night, but we opened our presents on December 25; we found them each year under our Christmas tree. Our family ritual was that the tree went up on Christmas Eve and came down on New Year's Day. On Rosh HaShanah, all the Jewish boys in my class went to morning services; then we met for a game of touch football. On Yom Kippur, our parents would not allow the football game, because of the sanctity of the day.

The most positive Jewish experience I had as a young boy was youth group. Our temple organized youth activities for all high school grades. For me, the primary attraction of the youth group was the opportunity to socialize with Jewish friends who did not live in my neighborhood. As a junior in 1950, a friend and I attended one of the early NFTY (North American Federation of Temple Youth) Leadership Institutes. We took a ferryboat across Lake Michigan and then a bus to Camp Lake-of-the-Woods to attend the third National Leadership Institute. We were the first from Milwaukee and among the first from the Midwest to attend any NFTY activity. The following year we worked (unsuccessfully) with our new friends from Minneapolis to organize a new NFTY region. Although we failed, the region was finally established two years later. My experience at Camp Lake-of-the-Woods was so positive that I attended a NFTY Leadership Institute again the following year, in Haverford, Pennsylvania. Through my NFTY involvement, Judaism began, for the first time, to have a substantive, relevant impact on my life. In that environment, I transitioned from simply learning the history and archaeology of the Jewish people to becoming an active participant in the continuity of our tradition. I have a rational, analytical personality, and Judaism finally began to "make sense" to me. And my second year of participation at a NFTY Leadership Institute was truly life changing. It was there that I met my future wife, Sandra Jacobs.

By the time I left home for college, I had just begun to grow Jewishly. I "borrowed" a *Union Prayer Book* from my temple, hoping it would provide continuity and some insight in my intense search for meaning and substance in my religion. Years later I wrote a letter to the rabbi apologizing for "appropriating" the prayer book, but explaining how well it was used. I enclosed a new prayer book to replace the dog-eared one.

After college, marriage, and military service, Sandy and I settled down in Cincinnati with our two babies. Sandy also came from a classical Reform background but had richer Jewish knowledge, because her father, Henry Jacobs, was the educator, music director, and administrator of Temple Sinai in New Orleans. From the day I met him, he was a role-model and mentor for me. He had a heart of gold, cared deeply about people, and lived as an activist and "doer." He was one of the founders of NATA (National Association of Temple Administrators) and NATE (National Association of Temple Educators) and served as president of both organizations. He tried (unsuccessfully) to talk me into becoming a temple administrator.

In Cincinnati, Sandy and I wanted to affiliate with a temple, but we could not afford the dues, so we became youth group advisors. The pay was miniscule, but the job offered the attractive perk of "free" temple membership, which was important to both of us. This was my first opportunity at mentoring and becoming a role model. The youth group thrived, and I learned. My involvement as a youth group participant, and then as an advisor, was my first and strongest *positive* link to my religion. Through my involvement with the youth, I built bonds to the congregation, acquired lifelong friends in this new (for me) community, and strengthened my understanding of, and commitment to, Reform Judaism. One member of our congregation in Cincinnati was Rabbi Sylvan Schwartzman, professor of Jewish education at Hebrew Union College–Jewish Institute of Religion. Sandy and I became close with Sylvan and his wife,

Sylvia. Sylvan tried very hard to persuade me to study for the rabbinate. In fact he tutored me for a year in Hebrew and Torah. Ultimately, I decided not to enter HUC-JIR, as we had a severely handicapped child and many medical expenses. At the same time I vowed to involve myself deeply in Jewish causes, to make a difference.

Our next stop was Washington, D.C., where my next mentor was Julian Feldman, a dear friend of my father-in-law and administrator of Washington Hebrew Congregation. He hired me as youth director, again with the perk of free temple membership. My youth activities continued to be my strongest and most satisfying link to my religion and my congregation. After four years in Washington, we moved to New York to put our handicapped daughter in a special school. Again we became youth group advisors, and I moved up the ladder of temple leadership, ultimately becoming co-president of the congregation. My mentoring of youth expanded when I became director of NFTY's CNYFTY region. One of my greatest joys has been seeing many of those I advised as teenagers become lay and professional leaders of the Reform Movement.

While in New York, our daughter died of complications arising from congenital defects that had plagued her all-too-short life. At this difficult time, our congregational family was a bulwark of support and caring. Our link to Judaism, which had grown over the years, was a source of strength in dealing with our loss.

After six years in New York and the death of our daughter, we moved back to Washington and, subsequently, as "empty nesters," to Houston, nearer to Sandy's family, who lived in New Orleans. Sandy's brother, Roger Jacobs, who was beginning to climb the ladder to national leadership in NFTB (North American Federation of Temple Brotherhoods, now Men of Reform Judaism), asked me to join the Brotherhood board so we could share the "fun." For the next decade, we shared a hotel room (and midnight cribbage games) at each NFTB board meeting. While Roger and I had simply been "relatives" since I married his sister, we became good friends and developed mutual respect as a result of our time together in NFTB. He became president in 1992, and I succeeded him five years later. Although we were peers, he was, in essence, my mentor.

During that same period, I had the privilege to serve as a trustee of a family charitable foundation. This brought me in contact with Jews from all streams of Judaism and in all parts of the world. Through them, I learned to appreciate and respect many of the Jewish rituals and traditions that were not part of my upbringing and early education. Now, in my "emeritus" role, I strive to make a difference through being a mentor and role model, to help future generations experience a Reform Judaism that is richer in the nurturing and substantive content that seemed so lacking and superficial in my early years.

As I reflect on my life, I see how I have grown in appreciation of the beauty and diversity of my faith. Over the years I have embraced more and more of the Jewish traditions that seemed so alien to me as a youth. Two years ago I had the thrill of becoming bar mitzvah along with my grandson. We wore *kippot* and tallit and chanted our *parashah* in Hebrew, none of which would have been acceptable in my congregation when I was a teenager. Since becoming bar mitzvah, I have continued to wear a yarmulke at services as a warm reminder of that ceremony and of the relevance and beauty of so many Jewish traditions. I feel that my life is far richer and fuller because of its Jewish context.

A SHARED MORAL COMPASS

Jeremy Sandler

Judaism is to me something akin to oxygen. It is a vital, life-giving, fundamental part of my everyday existence—central to everything that I can become. And yet it is so second nature that rarely do I stop to consider its full meaning and importance. The fact is, most of the time, it—like breathing air—is something of which I rarely take conscious notice. Yet, taking a step back and really evaluating its importance, I know it is something I constantly carry with me and lean on for support.

Identifying Judaism's relationship to my masculine identity is complex for me because the Reform Jewish home I grew up in and the Reform synagogue I went to did not divide people based on gender. While locker rooms, classrooms, workplaces, and the broader culture fostered distinctly male and female roles, my Jewish life included rabbis of both sexes, prayers altered to incorporate the masculine and the feminine, and a home life that taught me to choose the spheres that suited me. I know being a Jew impacts the kind of husband, son, brother, and uncle that I am, but that has everything to do with being a Jewish person and nothing to do with being a Jewish man.

Perhaps the best illustration of how being Jewish impacts my life comes from the beginning of the most significant and best choice I ever made. When I met my then future wife, we were dancing at my friend's wedding. She was there as a "dessert and dancing" guest of the groom's sister. When we began talking and things began looking promising for at least the chance to get a phone number, what I like to call "relationship trigonometry" swirled into action. The calculations all pointed to something very special, and I'd be lying if I did not admit that Judaism was part of nearly every sum, product, or quotient devised by my brain. Barbara, now my wife, grew up in a Jewish home near where I grew up. Like me, she attended Holy Blossom Temple with her family. Both of us had gone to the same mainly Jewish summer camp. All of that meant shared values and shared ideas of what is special. I believe these things led us to be open and trusting in a way that let us develop a relationship that turned into a lifelong commitment. It was just over a month after our first date that we sat side by side at Erev Rosh HaShanah services. Holding hands and smiling at each other, both of us felt the same connection. A huge part of that was Judaism. At that moment, looking back on what had been important before we met each other, clearly we could each see the other as an integral part of sharing those things in the future. On our wedding day, we stood together on a bimah under a chuppah in that same sanctuary surrounded by our families. Once again, we understood how Judaism was the wellspring for so much of the bond we share.

That I have this connection to Judaism is the easiest thing to figure out. Why it exists is a much tougher question to answer. It is not because I believe Jews possess sole access to singular answers on matters of faith and religion. Collectively, Jews cannot decide on the best way to make a bagel, never mind find a synthesis between Reform, Conservative, Orthodox, and Reconstructionist branches. Our collective inability to agree on how exactly God would like us to worship contradicts the idea that Jews know *the* right path. While perhaps not as destructive as other intra-religious schisms, the divisions among Jews make it illogical to think we have any more correct answers than anyone else. Most religions have at their core tenets of love and understanding that, if followed by all, would certainly make the world a better place. What I know of Judaism's laws and precepts are generally sensible and appealing, but no more or less so to me than those of many other religions to which I do not adhere.

Given these doubts, why do I cling to Judaism? I think my strongest connection lies in our collective history. Sitting in shul, reciting a *Shehecheyanu*, or lighting Chanukah candles at home is a direct connection with more than five thousand years of our people. No matter where I am in the world, if there is a *yahrzeit* to be observed, *Kaddish* is something I can say along with any other Jews. The cadence may be different, but the meaning would be the same. For all those who came before me, I carry on the traditions of Judaism. For all those who perished in pogroms and gas chambers, I make it a priority to celebrate my own Jewishness. How could I be blessed with the freedom to say whichever prayers I want, to worship in whatever way I want, and not use it?

Having grown up in a liberal Jewish home in Canada, it was probably expected, though never demanded, that my life would maintain some sort of Jewish focus. However, I also know that now, if, God willing, we are able to have a family, it will be another generation raised with Jewish values, with children who celebrate Shabbat, become *b'nei mitzvah*, and eventually, as I was, are encouraged to understand that keeping their faith alive is an important part of who they are.

I say all this knowing that there are those who would deny my Jewishness based on my level of assimilation. I keep a Jewish home, but not a kosher one. I will work on Shabbat. I enjoy going to synagogue for services, but often the realities of modern life preclude that from happening. This is criticized by many as an a la carte approach to Judaism, one that is invalid. But I feel it is the essence of the strength of Judaism today. As I understand Talmud, Jews have been constantly reevaluating and reinterpreting doctrine and dogma for thousands of years. Modern Judaism allows that to continue on a very personal level. And in the most important ways, Jewish law and precepts govern much of what I do. Not that I am constantly evaluating decisions from a Jewish perspective. But in my professional and personal life, the ideal of treating people with honesty and respect is one I follow. It seems to me a very human concept, but one that is reinforced by Judaism and one that makes me happy with the person I am.

True, my forebears may not recognize the way I celebrate Judaism. But I'm also fairly certain the same could have been said about my ancestor's ancestors. I do know, however, that we would recognize in each other a shared moral compass. The traditions may change, but the values never do. And I feel a great responsibility to pass along that set of values, so that however Judaism evolves for the future family I will not know, it retains for them the same meaning it has for me —that is, as an equality-based religion that is vibrant and relevant not for me as a Jewish male, but simply as a Jewish person.

MY FATHER'S SPIRITUALITY
AND MINE

Eugene Borowitz

My father was as good a Jew and human being as I have ever met. Yet I wonder if people in this generation would consider him "spiritual." (I think they would respond more immediately to my mother's "spirituality," but, because it was so primally entwined with her fineness of soul, it would take more poetic skill than I have to describe it.) He and my mother attended Friday night services with great regularity, and late Saturday afternoons my dad would often take me, as a young teenager, to the temple's *shudas* (= *shalosh se'udah*), where he was often one of the youngest people present (a smallish number to begin with). I vaguely recall that his davening on these occasions seemed more perfunctory than intense. Though he enjoyed having certain rituals performed, he always managed to find ways to have more "learned" people conduct them, e.g., our Seders. Thus, I do not recall his ever having made *Kiddush*. His "study" consisted of a thoughtful perusal of the daily *Forverts* (which, in Columbus, Ohio, the mailman delivered). He esteemed learning and the educated, so my sister was long the only female college-graduate in our extended family, and the academic expectations of me were lovingly high.

His outstanding Jewish virtue, after devotion to our family, was his love of Jews, an attitude he then also applied to everyone else in the world. When as a young man he read in the Communist daily, *Freiheit*, that the Jewish settlers in Palestine were exploitative colonialists who had provoked the Arab riots of the late 1920s, he threw the paper in the garbage and became a reader of the Socialist *Forverts*. He represented the Jewish Labor Committee to the Columbus Jewish Community Council (though he managed production in a large trouser factory), and I remember sitting outside the room of one hot Council session waiting for him when the issues of refugees and Zionism were boiling. He was aroused and told the Council that he could not say what he needed to say in his English (ordinarily quite workable), so he asked for the right to address the Council in Yiddish, the only time that ever happened in that German-American-dominated august body. (I could only hear the muffled sounds coming from the room, but I could tell that he had been most passionate.) During World War II he was instrumental in racially integrating the production lines in his factory, the first time that happened at an industrial plant in Columbus. (And only the Jewish admonitions of clean speech keep me from repeating the line with which he spurned those workers who wanted segregated bathrooms.)

In the 1960s with their death-of-God agitation, I once asked my father if he believed in God. He looked at me as if that were a peculiar questions to ask and said, "Of course," as if no sensible person would do otherwise. That was that. When, some years later, he was dying of pancreatic cancer, fortunately without intractable pain, and I was walking with him in Sloan-Kettering Memorial Hospital, he quietly said to me at one point, "*Ich hob mein's getun*," "I did mine." That was as much of a summing up as he needed, as much of a statement of purpose and duty as I ever heard from him. The rest was all good-hearted deed.

By today's preferred understanding of "spirituality," I doubt that my father would qualify as a model. He certainly wasn't very self-conscious about God or his relationship to God, nor did he judge his acts by whether they made God more present in his life or that of society. People now use "spirituality" to refer to a religiosity which is more interior, more subjective, more explicitly God-oriented than my father's. I never heard him use that term or anything like it to speak to others and certainly not about himself. He probably would have shaken his head in incomprehension at it, considering it another of those American things that others found valuable but he didn't understand or value.

The gap between my father's living Jewishness and our concern about Jewish spirituality set me to thinking. If, by the American Jewish standards of his time, my father was a good Jew without our kind of spirituality, what might I learn about our sense of Jewish piety by thinking about him and some other fine Jews I have known?

Over the years I have often been reminded of my father's dedication when talking to one or another rabbinic colleague, generally not people on the national scene or of great reputation. When they talked about their work, I was moved by their simple devotion to it, the unending round of services, hospitals, simchas, committee meetings, community affairs, and more. They also complained a good deal, particularly about the heavy workload. I was, after all, a rare safe, sympathetic ear, one unlike their spouses, who they felt might already be suffering from an overload of their kvetching. Yet once the ventilation was over, what remained was their quiet determination to carry on with their rabbinic tasks as best they could. They knew that this was what they most wanted, most needed to do. God bless them, they sent me away from such encounters renewed in shouldering my own kind of rabbi-burdens, convinced that there were more good Jews in the rabbinate than our critical community—myself included—ever appreciated.

I now think of these colleagues and my father as exemplars of a classic type of Jewish spirituality. In their different ways they followed the rabbinic ideal of the *tzaddik*, the Jew whose good deeds win God's approval. Most contemporary Jews, I guess, will more readily identify this type of activist Jewishness with people who have devoted their lives to great ethical issues. That was surely my sense of some of the (apparently secularistic) colleagues who put themselves on the line in the early days of the civil rights struggle and who have tried to carry on the good fight in less dramatic ways ever since. But where the *tzaddik*-hood of ethical devotion has often been celebrated in our movement, its more ordinary, everyday elaboration deserves greater attention.

In some ways my father's activist Judaism accords poorly with his childhood, for it was tied up with another ideal Jewish type. My father grew up in the home of his maternal grandfather, awaiting for over a decade his American immigrant father's call to his wife and children in Poland to join him. Of Hershel, his grandfather, of whom my father always spoke with reverence, he particularly remembered how he stopped being the *rav* of Sokoly and instead, since he had the special *semihah* allowing him to grant others *semihah*, turned his house into a modest yeshiva over which he then presided. He was, apparently, a Jew in the classic Litvak mode, one whose spirituality took the form of study and the intellectual exercise that accompanied it. I no longer remember whether he was a *musmakh* of Volozhin or Slobodka (as I once wrote), but it was clear he was a *mitnagged* who observed the ban on Hasidism. So he was undoubtedly influenced by the classic text of Litvak spirituality, the *Nefesh ha-Hayyim* of Hayyim Volozhiner (the Vilna Gaon's disciple and the Volozhin *rosh yeshivah*). That work identifies Torah with the *Ein-Sof*, making study the Litvak equivalent of the *unio mystica* some Jews today take to be the goal of spirituality. Being a *masmid*, an unceasing student of Torah, was for such Jews a way to literally be in God's presence. Despite his love for Hershel, my father did not have the *sitzfleisch* to become a *hakham* and, though he urged education upon me, he made it clear that he thought intellect without deeds a betrayal of Jewish responsibility.

Perhaps the purest Litvak-style intellect I ever came across was my teacher Samuel Atlas. He was an acknowledged master in both philosophy and Talmud, the two disciplines he taught at Hebrew Union College. It remains one of the great regrets of my life that his understanding was so advanced and mine so rudimentary that I could not benefit from his utterly uncommon interdisciplinary mastery. Some of my other teachers, themselves dauntingly learned, also exemplified the Jewish piety of determined intellectuality. Julian Morgenstern, a leading Semitic linguist and biblical scholar of his day; Samuel Cohon, who taught theology from what seemed like an encyclopedic knowledge of Judaism; and Sheldon Blank, who meticulously attended to the words of the prophets and gently made them the standard of his life— they were all people who realized themselves most fully in the exercise of the mind. These scholars considered their subjective lives a private matter, yet their piety in and through their intellectuality was evident to anyone sensitive. *Mutatis mutandis*, they were not what the rabbis meant by *hakhamin* nor my great-grandfather's kind of Litvak, yet a single kind of Jewish religiosity linked them—and, if I may say so, is what animates the instruction at our New York School. That I followed Hershel's way was no rebellion against my father. He not only encouraged me in it but kept me a lifetime doer as well as thinker.

The more personalistic, felt piety that we today largely identify with Jewish spirituality was not without its exemplars years ago, though it was no one's spoken goal. To stay with rabbis—though some marvelous lay examples could easily be adduced—let me say a few words about a somewhat older colleague, Byron T. Rubenstein. "B.T.," as everyone called him, always seemed an unusual spirit. It's hard to know why people universally felt that way about him but perhaps it indicates that we all have a certain openness to genuine piety even if we insist it is not our own way to live. B.T.'s aura of spirituality didn't have anything to do with what he said about himself or directly urged on others. On the surface he seemed like most other good rabbis. and it didn't keep him from the life of deeds—he was the oldest rabbi (forty-something, I would guess) among the sixteen of us (and Al Vorspan) who answered Martin Luther King's telegram to a CCAR convention inviting us to come get arrested in his campaign in St. Augustine, Florida. Yet you knew he was a person of great inner depth, an unusually elegant spirit, someone whose simple wholeheartedness you would like to emulate if you ever could.

Our present discussion of spirituality has, I think, gone somewhat further on B.T.'s road by making interiority a value to be sought consciously, by struggling with how to give it adequate verbal expression, and by identifying it unambiguously with personal experience of God. These are not small gains, for in our time the subjective side of religion has not been given its due, so we are engaged in an effort to add the Judaism of the heart to that of the deed and the mind. We are learning to value not only the *tzaddik* and the *hakham* but the psalmist as well.

Some have gone even further and seek the path of the kabbalist. Zalman Schachter-Shalomi, Art Green, and Larry Kushner, each in his own way, set before us models of contemporary Jewish mystic spirituality. Within limits, I can appreciate their form of Jewish spirituality. I say that because, though I admire how mystic experience has affected them and their teaching, I have not shared their experience of merger with the

Divine. Like Buber, I find the apparent fulfillment of the self becoming one with the Ultimate less significant than standing on my own side of the I-Thou hypen, marvelously involved, yet respectful of the Other's individuality—and my own.

So I have known four kinds of Jewish spirituality in my lifetime, ones amply attested in Jewish tradition. What gives me pause in my otherwise wholehearted appreciation of the new personalistic emphasis among us is what often troubled me about one or another form of Jewish piety in the past, that emphasizing one aspect of Jewishness, they will not give proper scope to the others. At the moment, I do not see much danger that the new interiority will decrease our concern with ethics and rite. The psalmist is no stranger to the needed deed. But there is a certain American anti-intellectualism which easily co-opts subjectivity to deny or constrict the role that learning and thinking play in the service of God. Not everyone is gifted to be a *ḥakham*. Most of us would be happy to qualify as their disciples, *talmidei ḥakhamim*. What concerns me only is properly holistic spirituality, one in which, depending on temperament and opportunity, we do not turn our backs on either the doer, the student, or the believer in us, but find our way to give them a dynamic unity in our lives.

MORE JEWISH THAN EVER

Joel Eglash

Some time before she died, Grandma Ruth made me promise to her that I would marry a "nice Jewish girl." I was a teenager. When I turned twenty, Grandma Ruth died. A few months later, I would meet my future wife and life partner.

What would Grandma Ruth say of my choice of spouse? She'd certainly kvell at hearing the last name "Siegel" uttered from my mouth while introducing my wife. But when I explain what Kari is, silence might fall: I married a cantor. *Yes, Grandma, today women can be clergy.* Furthermore, I am a devout Reform Jew, live in Tulsa, Oklahoma, and am a proud stay-at-home/work-at-home dad. Who ever heard of such things?

My grandparents were *shomeir Shabbes*—they never even owned a car. Grandpa Dave davened at shul every day and ruled an old-fashioned household; everybody knew their role and accepted it without question. Their *machatonim* were Holocaust survivors (as is my mother), and my mother's father, Morris, died in 1953, two years after finally bringing his family to America. Though our daughter's middle name honors Morris, none of us ever knew him. I could only imagine what kind of man he was. As a boy, I stared at the only picture we had of him, his long legs crossed, smiling and looking comfortable on a nice chair, and imagined having a grandfather who would take me to a Brewers game, show me how to hit a three-iron, or help me with my homework. It was never to be, on either side of the family.

I knew Grandpa Dave only as a religious Jew; his personality and capacity to make conversation had all but disappeared with senility by the time I came around. As a small boy at his side in shul, he'd wrap me inside his tallis—I can still smell what it was like to be that close to him. His baritone vibrated inside of me, and I learned all the *nusach* and prayers by osmosis. I felt incredible warmth and love, though it was only Hebrew words that I ever heard come from his lips. He died when I was fifteen.

I am grateful for the variety of male influences I had growing up in Milwaukee. From rabbis to teachers to my brother, I feel lucky to have had so much experience and influence to build upon. Because of it, I believe that I was more mature than many of my peers. But to this day, my father remains my true beacon. Dad is the black sheep of his family. He inherited his father's love for the ritual traditions of Judaism but began to question God and halachah at an early age, especially after marrying a Holocaust survivor. This spiritual conflict perhaps explains best who I became as a Jewish man.

Dad became an M.S.W. and, as a JCC communal service worker, enlightened me to the purposes and perils of the world of organized Judaism. When his life and ours was turned upside down by an unexpected change in employment, he rebounded, switching careers by opening a video store. He taught me more than he realizes by succeeding while facing considerable adversity. Despite the long hours he worked to build the business, he always made time for me.

During the early years of the store, it came time for me to become bar mitzvah. For three years, we met every Wednesday night and he taught a disinterested preteen about his own brand of Judaism and life, as he had done for my sister and brother before me. Talmud to Bob Dylan, Inquisition to Elie Wiesel. I dreaded and hated most of it at the time (who wants *more* homework when you're twelve?). But as an adult, I am so grateful for this gift and plan to do the same for my child. Even so, those Wednesday nights made for some great memories: listening to good music, inventing crazy dinners from whatever was in the refrigerator, playing horseshoes, and chatting about manly things like the Packers or fishing. His lust for living was always irresistible to me, and so it was that I inherited his passion for the good things in life, like music, Judaism, family, traveling, and cigars.

Bearing a long gray ponytail and golden earring, Dad never cared about appearances. Mom stopped trying to dress him a long time ago. There are no pre-assumptions with Dad; an open mind is his way of life, but at the same time experience means everything. His open mind allows him to consider life in so many different ways. He overcame the strong influence of his parents' generational conservatism and became a product of a new age's way of thinking.

When Kari was pregnant, I mulled over what kind of father I would be. I wanted to offer my child a unique and stable childhood. Though Dad had made enough time for me while building his business, growing up a latchkey kid wasn't so easy. So I decided I would reinvent myself a little and become a stay-at-home/work-at-home dad. I had to picture myself grocery shopping during the daytime, taking baby to the mall play area, joining playgroups, working while the baby sleeps. I only briefly considered a loss of my masculine image. I figured that, given the opportunity, Dad may not have become a stay-at-home father himself, but his example allowed me to embrace this new role.

Dad never liked going to temple. To him, Judaism includes family, laying *t'fillin*, Passover seders, and visiting our Israeli relatives. After my confirmation, perhaps misunderstanding his example, I decided I'd had enough and became a "High Holy Day Jew" for a while. I started eating *treif*. I dated non-Jewish women. I went on the road with my band, sowed some wild oats.

The whole time I kept Grandma Ruth in mind. Once I became an adult, I began to appreciate both sides of the coin: my father's originality, rebellion, and self-made philosophy, and my grandparents' strongly-rooted tradition. Sitting here in Tulsa years later, watching my newborn daughter sleep, and listening to Kari sight-singing a version of *Mi Chamochah*, I feel more Jewish than ever. I spent most of the day at temple.

Like Dad, I left a career in Jewish communal service and started my own businesses. The Jewish man I have become might be called "new age" by some—an amalgam of contemporary and traditional Jewish values

—but a Jew at whom my grandparents might both shake a head and nod approvingly.

Every time I lay *t'fillin*, I take a moment to speak with my grandparents. I update them on what's going on in my life: family, friends, questions, work. They never talk back, but somehow I hear their approving voices.

THE JEWISH MEN DANCING INSIDE ME

Richard Gartner

I am a Jewish male practitioner of the "Jewish profession" of psychoanalysis who has counseled and treated dozens of Jewish men over decades of practice. Yet asked to write about my Jewishness, my maleness, and my work, I find myself at a loss to articulate how they interrelate.

How did I become a Jewish man? Who were my influences? How has Judaism informed my work as a psychoanalyst and my self-concept as a man?

I write in fragments, hoping the mosaic will reveal an image, a pattern that conveys a meaning that eludes me.

Growing up in the Bronx, I was given a desultory Jewish education until I became bar mitzvah. The teachers at my Reform synagogue (we called it temple, never shul) were well-meaning Jewish public school teachers trying to earn extra income while imparting some knowledge to children from assimilated homes who understood little about why we should care about what we were taught. Alas! These teachers knew little more than we did. Once a "Hebrew teacher" confessed that he didn't really know Hebrew and kept one chapter ahead of us in the Hebrew text. Yet, I remember my German-born cantor, who I now realize must have been a Holocaust survivor, talking about his childhood as he tutored me for my bar mitzvah. I don't remember many facts except for the star-tling detail that he owned his shroud; somehow his stories melded into those from my Orthodox paternal grandparents. The Eastern European Yiddish intonations I heard in my frequent visits to Grandma and Grandpa Gartner harmonized with Cantor Heller's Germanic accent. His stories of a rich German Jewish cultural heritage blended with theirs about the absolute need to leave a land that was sometimes Austrian, sometimes Polish, sometimes Ukrainian, but never friendly to Jews.

My paternal grandmother, granddaughter of a cantor, wise and clever, at seventeen a homely orphan, refused to marry her older widower cousin, who had four children ages four to fourteen—not because of his age or the fact that she would be raising these children, but because he refused to move to America. Instead, she met my handsome grandfather, a tall, blond, blue-eyed ironworker who was dazzled by her vision, intelli-gence, ambition, and goodness. They came to New York on their honey-moon, promptly losing the huge sum of six hundred dollars, which they had carefully saved before they married, when they put it in one of the little banks that sprang up in New York where a *landsman* felt safe to deposit his funds.

Grandpa transformed his ironworking skills as a small town laborer into ones that worked for him in New York's burgeoning light industries. His factory experiences led my grandparents into socialism. Their home was an odd mixture of old world traditional Jewish observance alongside a nihilistic view of the God that allowed poor workers to be treated badly and then ultimately allowed the slaughter of the families they had left in Europe. (Interestingly, the widower my grandmother wouldn't marry sent his four children to America, where my kind grandmother wound up rais-ing them without having to marry their father, who himself perished in the Holocaust.)

My maternal grandfather came from a working-class German Jewish family whose roots in America went back to the 1840s. He and his two brothers were put into an orphanage when his widowed mother married a man who didn't want children. Pop Pop had no Jewish education at all, although the Jewish orphanage made sure he identified as a Jewish boy. He lived there for about six years, until stepfather number one died and Great-Grandmother Frances married a third time, this time to a man who liked children. Pop Pop always refused to say a bad word about his mother's actions, and indeed he always spoke about his mother as if talking about an angel. But he never ate another banana—the daily dinner dessert at the orphanage—after he left there, and I believe the terrible temper he exhibited at times throughout his life dated to the days of his abandonment, loss, and trauma. Luckily, he also had a wonderful sense of humor, a quality that has saved many Jewish men from succumbing to their suffering.

Pop Pop became a piano maker, and among my proudest possessions are two exquisite knickknack shelves that he made from beautiful scrolled wooden music stands on old pianos. He married my grandmother Ida—who arrived here from Latvia at age one but always insisted that she was born here, a "real American"—and their middle-class home was Jewish in name and ancestry but not in custom. Still, there is that story about how during Prohibition Ida used to make cherry Passover wine in the bathtub. And, in accord with Jewish tradition, they named my mother Frances Mae in honor of two deceased grandparents: her paternal grandmother Frances—the one who had put Pop Pop into the orphanage—and her maternal grandfather Morris. Naturally, her father always called her Frances, and her mother always called her Mae.

My paternal grandparents apparently doubted that my mother was really Jewish because she spoke no Yiddish. Yet, my father was attracted to my educated, cultivated, and assimilated mother exactly because she was so foreign to his experience. As an adolescent, he had rebelled about going to *cheder* when the old man in charge beat him because he questioned some of the teachings there. He never returned.

I suppose that for my father, my mother was what Philip Roth might have called a Jewish shiksa goddess. What more could he want? Well, be careful what you pray for! My parents had such different frames of reference that they could only helplessly rail at one another's values and interests when they clashed, as they did frequently.

My parents made a home where we never doubted our Jewishness, but never embraced it fully either. The rules were inconsistent, though not unusually so among our friends. For example: We never bought German or Japanese goods. On the other hand, food at home was not kosher, though we never ate pork or shellfish in the house (except when we brought in Chinese food). And even this shaky principle had an exception: bacon and ham were somehow allowed. Despite all this, my mother insisted that the food at my bar mitzvah be kosher. We always had a large and relatively traditional seder, but my parents virtually never attended services, even on the High Holy Days. Still, they were shocked one year when I announced I was going to the movies on Yom Kippur.

Later in life, my parents became much more attached to their Jewish roots. They rejoined a synagogue and repeatedly visited Israel, connecting with long-lost cousins of my father who had migrated there. My father became active enough in Jewish philanthropy and causes that he was honored more than once. After my mother's death, and a few years before he died, my father bought a pair of magnificent silver candlesticks from a friend who had somehow preserved them when she escaped from the Holocaust. He presented them to my wife and me. Created in Warsaw, they remain a treasured reminder of our Jewish heritage, used on many holidays. While we are not consistently observant, we do light candles and bless wine and challah on Friday nights, continue my parents' tradition of making a large seder every year, and celebrate various holidays with Jewish friends.

Attending Haverford, a small Quaker college, I simultaneously drifted away from my Jewish roots and felt moved to define them better. The Quaker tradition seemed foreign, although I now see it was closer than I realized to the Jewish one I had learned so imperfectly. Honor, service, ethics—I embraced these values of Haverford and used them to help me make more coherent the moral framework I needed to articulate.

My father had learned from his own socialist father's experience. Interpersonally awkward under a genial, extroverted exterior, he nevertheless became a brilliant businessman. One of the few pieces of business advice he ever gave me was to work for myself and never have to answer to a boss. And, after some early career detours working in hospitals and other institutions, chafing under the rules and strictures of bosses whose values I questioned, I followed his good advice and went into private practice.

Later on, when I started psychoanalytic training I unknowingly—or did my instincts guide me?—chose a training analyst whose own childhood was steeped in Chasidic tradition. Having moved from yeshivot to the philosophy departments of great American universities, he went on to make unique creative contributions to interpersonal psychoanalysis. Named Ben, like my father, he was the most intellectually engaged and psychologically alive man I have ever met, and my nine years of psychoanalysis with him utterly transformed my life. Like Cantor Heller, he referenced Jewish traditions and, quoting obscure (to me) Jewish scholars, interwove Judaic ideas with his own as he valiantly confronted my resistance to being emotionally present in our own two-person universe. It was as if Martin Buber was channeled into his consulting room. Our own "I" and "thou" were all that mattered.

So, here I am, working for myself, so many Jewish men dancing inside me. Cantor Heller. Grandpa Gartner. Pop Pop. My father and my analyst, the two Bens. And all the other *"bens"* (sons) I haven't mentioned: my three uncles, my brother, my father- and brother-in-law, my own son and son-in-law, the many Jewish (and of course some non-Jewish) friends, colleagues, and teachers who continue to influence who I am.

Some visionary. Some brilliant. Some warm. Some frightening. Some frightened. Some in shadow. Some bursting in my consciousness.

As my practice developed, I began to treat a number of Jewish and non-Jewish men, including a number of clergy. Simultaneously, a progression of events drew me to treat a population of sexually victimized men. Inevitably, there were some who were both sexually victimized and Jewish, and on occasion, some of these were also clergy. The Jewish men came from all kinds of backgrounds, from the most assimilated and secular to the most devoutly traditional Orthodox. They had histories of abuse by male and female family members, neighbors, family friends, babysitters, camp counselors, teachers, rabbis, scoutmasters, coaches—in short, the same kind of assorted group that abuses non-Jewish men.

As I began to understand how socialized masculine gender norms interact with experiences of abuse, I came to see that traditional American values prevent many men from processing and healing from victimization. Men are taught to be competitive, resilient, self-reliant, independent, and certainly not emotionally needy or self-reflective. "Real" men are supposed to initiate sexual activity and want sex whenever it's offered, especially by women. For many men, these qualities *define* masculinity. Therefore, boys often can't acknowledge sexual victimization. They may assert that they weren't abused, that they weren't hurt, or that they were in charge of what happened. Being victimized or acquiescing to victimization means being "not male."

I have been led to question these values and to challenge my male patients to question them as well. And it occurs to me that age-old Jewish masculine values don't match these contemporary American ones. Traditionally, self-reflection, scholarliness, and caring are part of the ideal Jewish male identity. (We're talking in generalities here, but generalities often have their roots in some sort of reality.) Maybe my own Jewish background and identity—patchwork though it was—has made it easier for me to suggest to my male patients, Jewish or gentile, that their socialized masculine stereotypes need reexamination. This self-inquiry leads many victimized men to a kinder, more tender and compassionate view of themselves and other men, especially male victims. In essence, I am encouraging them to re-view masculinity through the lens of *yiddishkeit*. To the extent that this is a result of my Jewish background, I am grateful that it has helped so many men heal.

I try to consider how my personal path has led me to the work I do. The ethical and moral framework and family history that lead me to empathize with victims. (A friend—also a Jewish psychologist—has suggested to me that virtually any Jewish man of my generation has a personal relationship to the Holocaust and therefore also has a personal connection to victimhood.) The determination to do right by myself and my family—and patients I care about certainly become part of my family. The admixture of shyness and self-protection that coexists with a desire to connect, interact, come to a common good. The commitment to be emotionally present in my life and in the interpersonal field between me and the person who needs my help.

So many questions, but fewer answers. Isn't that what you'd expect from a work in progress?

FROM NAVIGATION
TO RECONCILIATION

Phillip A. Saperia

Eeh mutadzie juif: Goddam Jew, in local dialect. In Biddeford, Maine, of the early 1950s, those were the words that most forcibly shaped my conscious awareness of difference—of being a Jew—at the age of seven or eight. Earlier, I sensed that I was unacceptable as a playmate, but only much later as an adult did I learn from a neighbor and family friend that the local parents in Ocean Park had forbidden their children to play with the children from the two Jewish families in the largely Roman Catholic neighborhood.

Like all kids, I learned to navigate the shoals of difference both in conscious and unconscious ways. Coming from a family that casually ignored all observance except for the lighting of Chanukah candles and attending a big extended family seder, my Jewish identity was formed primarily by the experience of "outsiderness," our nuclear and extended family's positive attitudes toward a cultural Jewishness, and the local Hebrew school I was forced to attend.

Ironically, considering this ambiguity, there never was a question that this firstborn son and grandson would become bar mitzvah. Off I was, then, to the local *talmud Torah* (although I wonder if that title glorifies this three-day-a-week religious school that my sisters were not required to attend). Attending on Sunday, Tuesday, and Thursday, I also went to Shabbat morning services with the ten to fifteen men who davened in the way that was common in the Ashkenazic community of the time: fast and passionately, except when they were discussing business and gossiping between prayers.

Like a worn but familiar old slipper, I slipped into this experience with casual comfort. I came to love the very smells of the place; the undulating murmuring of prayer; the familiar and engaging melodies and *nigunim*; the warm and safe feeling of being wrapped in a tallit; the attentions and affections of the members of the minyan. All of this composed a spiritual and emotional experience that rooted me in a time and place, but also in a people and the continuing circle of their experience. This was a manly place—in that women hardly ever attended this male place. Minyanim counted men only. Still, I never have thanked God for not having made me a woman. Instead, I thank that divine spirit for restoring the breath of awakening to me each morning.

And we had Young Judaea, both in the synagogue, as well as throughout northern Maine, beyond to all New England and finally nationally. Beyond its burden-free Zionist ideology, it provided me with a completely Jewish experience, social and intellectual. Conventions and conferences provided contact with other young Jews, long debates about minor and major ideas, the joy of Israeli dancing and singing, the experience of Jewish identities, the soul-soaring experience of Shabbat among others like me, some apostate, some more fervent than I, many more learned, but all filled with the *ruach* of the time, space, and experience. Yet, the growing opportunities and unstated social pressures for male-female interaction were difficult to avoid. Since I couldn't summon the appropriate feelings and attractions, I felt uncomfortable as a man—more accurately as I imagined men should feel. I was a Jew—no question. I was a man—certainly in body. How to be a Jewish man that expressed the mix of experiences and roiling personal emergence of identity was the big question. Evolution and increment rather than intention and determined direction proved to be the path that I took—or the one that took me.

In college, starting in 1964, I learned that there were options. I discovered that thought accompanied feeling, even that feelings and beliefs could grow out of ideas. I discovered liberal Judaism and embraced feminism. I learned, but kept my distance from belief. Occasionally, I would touch base, but mostly I just trusted that religion was there and felt that I was on its periphery.

I had much more important (to me) matters to wrestle with. Those were issues of sexual identity, and they captured my inner energies and attention like never before. Of course, they were always there below the surface, but now the combination of place, experience, and hormones pushed these issues to the very top of my personal agenda and identity formation. Here the questions of manhood and of Jewish manhood were intertwined and challenged.

I set about to find myself—and devoted practically all my excess energies to this quest, as only a child of the late 1960s and early '70s could. What does it mean to be a man, a gay man, a gay Jewish man? How could I embrace all that I was? How could I reconcile the experience of Judaism, which set apart men and women and which reserved privilege for men, with my new and growing understanding? How could I reconcile my understanding of text with my new self-awareness, with my emerging acknowledgment of erotic and spiritual attraction to other men?

After graduate school and a stint of teaching in a secondary school, I found employment in Jewish communal organizations and a career in community relations—the balancing of ethnic and racial differences and the quest for community—and the administration of Jewish nonprofits. I was quite content to live a double life—the Jewish professional on the one hand and gay man on the other. Neither identity merged very much. I was "out" to only my closest friends and colleagues. Jewish politics, micro and macro, commanded my attentions, but not Jewish religion. I worked in a Jewish milieu but did not practice Judaism in any coherent or consistent way. I was Jewish by history, experience, and osmosis.

I was male by biology, by genetics and physical attributes. I lived the privilege that accrued to men but felt excluded from the fraternity that I imagined was peopled by the sports obsessed, women loving, and athletically talented. And yet I reveled in the new brotherhood that I had discovered and embraced.

In my gay life, I was similarly inconsistent. I was partnered since 1974 and living in Brooklyn, where we had a completely open social life as coupled men, including hosting an annual Pesach seder with Jews and non-Jews, gays and straights, and where I was active in local political causes and local Democratic Party life. I was on the board of Lambda Independent Democrats, a lesbian, gay, bisexual, and transgender political club, and therefore, much of my political activity had a gay context. I was out in Brooklyn politics but still closeted at work and in much of the Jewish world (or so I thought). I placed most Jewish experience, especially spiritual experience, at the margins of my life.

Finally, in 1993, in the post–Crown Heights era, David Dinkins, the then mayor of New York City, asked me to head the Mayor's Office of Jewish Community Affairs. I accepted with the knowledge that the press had a convention of avoiding the reporting of public official's private lives if those lives did not impinge on job performance. I felt safe that my secret would be protected from the light of publicity. I was free to continue my double life. But others had different ideas. I soon had a call from a colleague and fellow conspirator that a local, conservative Jewish newspaper in Brooklyn was planning to write a feature article that would "out" me and accuse the mayor of further shaming and damaging the Jewish community, this time by appointing a gay man to the position of Jewish mayoral liaison.

I contacted the mayor twice and offered to withdraw my candidacy. After all, I reasoned, why should I damage his political chances in the upcoming election? Unconsciously, I was wondering how I could handle being publicly branded as gay. Once the Brooklyn paper ran that story, it would be picked up by more mainstream papers, and given the torrent of news and reporting that surrounded the events in Crown Heights and this Administration's involvement, it easily could have become a national story. The mayor rejected my offer to withdraw. I was ready to move forward.

I decided to preempt the press and set about calling my board members and key leaders of New York's Jewish community, to tell them about the job offer, the impending story, and that I was gay. (Although I had no way of knowing at the time, the story would never run.) Aside from the fact that few were surprised and no one expressed disapproval, I felt incredibly relieved. I was liberated. For the first time in my life, I was walking into a job and walking in the world as a self-identified and openly gay man. I ran to have my ear pierced in celebration!

Although I was soon to be immersed in Jewish politics like never before, I was liberated from Jewish organizational politics and the insider concerns that accompany Jewish communal professionals. As I was liberated to be fully myself as a gay man, I began to feel fully liberated to explore the spiritual and intellectual aspects of my Judaism.

As a toe dipper, I began to attend early Erev Shabbat services at a neighborhood Reform synagogue. As I davened, I would flash back to those early formative experiences (Shabbat and holiday services, Dad's family's joyful and raucous seders, Hebrew school fellowships, and Young Judea) and deeply experience the peace of Shabbat's arrival and the formal end of the workweek. After about a year, a rabbi friend who was a fellow congregant invited me to join her newly founded progressive congregation further into Brooklyn. I just want to daven, I averred. I have no time for community building.

But follow her I did and have, for fourteen meaningful years, been part of an intentional and progressive Jewish congregation that learns, prays, thinks, eats, and struggles together with being Jewish and with being a community. I am a past president and have chaired some of its more important processes and committees.

Over time, I have joined with men, gay and straight, who model diverse forms of manhood. I have learned with acceptance that manliness is multifaceted and accessible, that Jewish manhood is also full of contradiction and potential.

My partner and I have negotiated the terms and substance of a deeply committed same-sex relationship of thirty-three years, and two years ago, we were legally married in Canada and went under the chuppah, by the shores of our beloved Delaware River, to be married by our rabbi before the Eternal, our families, and friends. My understanding of maleness and personhood has shifted. We are two males, after all, who claim for ourselves the legitimacy that heretofore has been reserved in secular law and in Judaism for men and women only. We take for granted our legitimacy and our place in all the spheres of our lives. That has been a hard-fought and hard-won sensibility. We have moved from a place of navigating difference to an acceptance and assertion of our humanness. That is both our right and our blessing.

MY MALENESS AS A JEW, MY MALENESS AS A RABBI

Daniel G. Zemel

The synagogue I grew up in was a very large, urban, Conservative congregation. It was, in those days (I was born in 1952), at the far liberal end of the Conservative Movement—women on the bimah, women counted in the minyan, bat mitzvah, organ music at services. On the other hand, the dress code at my synagogue seemed very traditional, as did the rabbi himself. On the bimah, I never saw the rabbi wear anything but a robe, and off the bimah, I never saw the rabbi wear anything but a dark suit and necktie. Growing up, I lived in the same apartment building as the rabbi—even there, whenever I saw him in the lobby, hallway, or garage, he was always wearing a dark suit. As I grew older and my interest in the rabbinate grew, I would occasionally visit the rabbi in his apartment. His wife always wore an apron. He always wore a dark suit. Such is my memory. I am not sure what this means other than that he, like all of us, was a product of his time. He wore his uniforms—both robe and suit—well and enjoyed a long, distinguished career.

On October 30, 1999, on the eve of a sabbatical that was to begin two days later, at a send-off party of funny skits and spoofs, my congregation presented me with an official Chicago White Sox jersey with my name stitched onto the back, along with number "18," for *chai*. After all, what other number should a fanatic rabbi fan wear on his back when rooting for his team? Since then I have worn that beautiful jersey to religious school nearly every Sunday morning. In fact, a kind of joke has formed around the jersey: if I am "out of uniform" on a Sunday morning and wearing a suit and tie, the assumption is that I have a funeral. Apparently, baseball attire is acceptable for weddings. I am quick to remark on those non-jersey Sunday mornings that I am the only rabbi in America who has to explain himself when he appears in his own synagogue on a day other than Shabbat wearing a suit and tie.

What explains the difference between my uniform of choice and that of my childhood rabbi? Is it our image of what a rabbi is? Is it our comfort in our own skin? The message we wish to send? The mood and temperament of the times? The differences in the communities we serve? The differences in the communities we are trying to create? The difference in the way we perceive our roles? Is it simply a matter of a different taste in clothes? All of these are certainly part of the equation. Much has been written and said about the rabbinic model of the authoritarian, remote rabbi dressed in a robe, removed from the community, maintaining distance as part of the social structure of the synagogue as well as signaling a kind of theological hierarchy—where the rabbi dressed in a priestly fashion is seen as being closer to God than the mere mortal dressed in ordinary civilian garb. All of this is simply a way of saying that rabbinic dress is symbolic.

In my rabbinate I am not overly concerned about rabbinic authority. I have a distinct sense that within my community, whatever authority my rabbinate possesses comes more from who I am as a person, the way I conduct myself, how I think and act, than from what I wear. In this sense, I might say that, in my community anyhow, there is not much there in terms of innate priestly authority, but a great deal there in terms of rabbi as role model and teacher.

The synagogue I grew up in and loved had a high bimah, fixed seating, and assigned holiday seats. I never once remember the rabbi or cantor coming off the bimah to lead or teach anything. All worship participation was from the bimah. The worship experience here at Temple Micah is different in every possible way. This new style of worship, with its emphasis on greater engagement, has become part of the expected experience almost everywhere.

Having said this, I would never dream of wearing my Sox jersey for any worship service apart from Purim. On Shabbat I wear a suit, always. I believe this reflects my attempt to express symbolically the respect I wish to express for the sanctity inherent in Shabbat. In the city in which I live, a suit is a socially acceptable way of expressing this respect. On the High Holy Days I actually wear a white robe. My sense is that for these days, the robe does not convey distance from the worshiper but again rather reflects the special nature of the holidays.

My Sox jersey is important not because I want to be seen as "one of the guys." The very thought of that makes my skin crawl and stomach ache. My clothing is important because it is an extension of who I am. I am an ardent baseball fan. I am a passionate White Sox devotee. Temple Micah knows this about me, and it is in fact why they gave me the jersey as a gift. This, I believe is critical. I make baseball references from the bimah frequently. When my team is winning (though rarely in the last twenty-five years), I suggest we chant *Hallel* to celebrate. In October 2005, upon returning directly to the synagogue from the airport just in time for Simchat Torah services after attending games one and two of the World Series, which my White Sox had won, I celebrated Simchat Torah with my congregation by marching, dancing, and singing the first *hakafah* to the music of "Go Go Chicago White Sox" as played by Captain Stubby and the Buccaneers. Clothes don't make the man; clothes are simply an honest extension of who this man is—just as they were for my childhood rabbi.

The question: what does the jersey express, and what of it is maleness? This, too, is complicated. Temple Micah now has a second rabbi. My female colleague, after seeing me wearing my Sox jersey on her first religious school Sunday morning, without fanfare, discussion, or announcement, immediately began wearing her team's jersey to religious school. The thing of it is, she really is a Cubs fan. (I struggle to keep myself in check.) This "clothes make the *man*" culture has continued, as our cantor (female) began wearing a Nationals jersey, partially as a way of showing her loyalty to our new Washington team, but also as a way of sending a signal that she, too, is part of our Micah team and with us in spirit in every possible way.

The fact that rabbis both male and female wear baseball jerseys in the synagogue might suggest that we have gone beyond gender roles. However, the commercials on television during sports events tell another story. Culturally, sports remains primarily a male domain. Further, I wonder if in the synagogue, my public affection for the White Sox as almost a kind of community-building tool works successfully within unspoken parameters. One friend has pointed out to me that baseball might be a more acceptable sport than football within the culture of the synagogue, perhaps because of the overly male dominated messages associated with football—its violence and its extremely scantily clad sideline cheerleaders.

There are other questions of maleness as well. Whereas football might be unacceptable in one way, a friend has asked me if I would be making the same kinds of informal statements to the congregation if my enthusiasm was ballet instead of baseball. This is again a question of maleness. Within the culture of the synagogue, passion for baseball is an acceptable male enthusiasm; however, similar enthusiasm expressed for ballet, for example, might appear "freaky" to kids, if not to their parents. Maleness might thus be seen as operating within a kind of unspoken synagogue culture safety zone. We might very reasonably ask the same questions about femaleness and its limits for women rabbis. At this stage in our history, do women rabbis have a finer line to walk regarding the areas wherein they can express and project their personal interests to the extent that they become part of the cultural fabric of the synagogue community? Perhaps this, too, is an area worth studying.

Over the years, more than a few new religious school parents have told me that my wearing the jersey helped their children overcome their initial fear or reluctance on their first few Sunday mornings. "We are new. We didn't even know that you are the rabbi—but then when we realized who you were and the way you were dressed, my son loved it!! The second week he came back wearing his own Orioles T-shirt to show you."

Operating within the cultural safety zone I have described, wearing the same style of clothing on Sunday mornings—albeit for different teams—has not changed who we are in our gender roles. I overhear the young bat mitzvah students talking about shoes and purses with my female colleagues in much the same way that the boys talk with me about baseball trades (which I follow) or Wizards games (which I know little about, but discuss quite happily). After all, it seems to me that if the feminist movement means anything, it means treating each person as an individual, respecting them for who they are and who they wish to be.

The question is, does the jersey do anything beyond helping some children overcome some natural early nervousness? Do girl students relate to this any differently than the boys? As already noted, girl talk and guy talk have not disappeared from the lobby of the synagogue. Clothes have become a symbolic extension of who we are and what we all wish the Temple Micah experience to be—namely a welcoming place where people can relax and feel free, confident, and themselves as opposed to judged and intimidated. What we wear helps us set the tone for the way we want our community to be experienced.

As I have written this, I have found find myself wondering why I don't see more here in the issue of sex roles or gender inequality. I am not so naive to think that our society, let alone our world, is not still rife with gender discrimination. However, I think it critically important for my worldview that I never consciously experienced a Judaism that was gender biased. My mother and my aunt each became bat mitzvah when they turned thirteen at the same synagogue where I grew up. My sister had the identical childhood Jewish experience that I did, except that she learned the trope so well that she became a regular Torah reader in our synagogue.

It therefore becomes difficult for me in general to buy into the current "favorite" topic to generate meetings, discussions, articles, interviews— perhaps even this book—that men are disappearing from congregational life. I don't see it. I don't experience it. If there are more women involved than twenty years ago—well, good. Where are there not more women? Congress? The Supreme Court? My internist until a few months ago was a woman, and believe me, I was sorry to see her leave town. I don't believe that we have a "men are disappearing" problem in American Jewish life. We are simply reflecting what we have always reflected, the culture in which we find ourselves and synagogues learning to navigate that culture within acceptable parameters.

What we do have however, is the same problem we have had for over fifty years now, namely attracting young and teenage boys to participate in Jewish life. This challenge is not new—it has simply never been properly addressed. Synagogue Judaism reflects a school culture, and at a young age, schools are geared for girls. Watch any typical group of fourth or fifth graders. Girls like notebooks, folders, pencil cases, pads of paper, sharpened pencils, decorated schoolbags. Boys gravitate toward pencil stubs, torn-out pieces of paper, and schoolbags that have been dragged through the dirt they have just been playing in. Girls organize their materials. Boys stuff theirs into bags.

My life has taught me that boys thrive in disorder. We should meet them where they are and the environments they thrive in. God turned chaos into cosmos. We need MacGyver-like figures who are Jewish teachers—Jewish role models who can build radio transmitters out of old wire coat hangers and other odds and ends. Remember that great scene in the movie *Apollo 13* when the NASA engineers had to turn a pile of notebook covers, duct tape, and other assorted paraphernalia into a square oxygen filter that goes into a round hole? We should be partners in teaching our kids real life skills. Instead, we have somehow succeeded in turning Judaism into an indoor activity. Do kids of all ages still like going outside? Could we Judaize recess? What a winner that would be! Our ancestors met God on tops of mountains, built fires, and hewed stone to forge the law. We need to get everyone outside. There is at least one Jewish educator I have experienced who teaches Mishnah from pieces of wood and midrash from roots of trees. There is an entire curriculum in Jewish theology—Creation, revelation, and redemption—all awaiting a stroll through nature.

This issue is simply another manifestation of the challenge synagogues face today. At Micah I have learned that clothes simply set a tone. I like to describe Temple Micah as an honest place. As noted above, I don't pretend to be either a priest or the Vilna Gaon. I am who I am, so to speak. Temple Micah is what it is, and as its rabbi, my goal is to strive to meet others the same way, accepting them for who they are, and try to help them become who they wish to be. Don't know Hebrew? Step right in. Can't stand creative services? I'd like to hear what you have to say. Not sure about how you feel about Israel? I am a strongly committed Zionist who believes Zionism and Judaism are inseparable, but there is nothing better than a good argument. In his great book *Zen and the Art of Motorcycle Maintenance*, Robert Pirsig writes that "quality" penetrates everything. People have an instinct for quality. People have a similar instinct for honesty and authenticity. Integrity is everything. Synagogues need to learn that lesson and apply it everywhere, as here, for example, with our young men, and accept them for who they are. Our young men too need to feel welcomed, invited, validated, and cared about, as well as free to explore who they are and will become.

These reflections are simply an attempt to provide a contemporary expression for Rabbi Shimon Gamliel, "Not learning but doing is the essential matter" (*Pirkei Avot* 1:17). Kids, especially, need much more learning by doing—and we need to offer them the requisite skills, experiences, and opportunities.

Let's play ball!

PART 5

FINDING ELISHA:
THE ROLE MODEL

INTRODUCTION

While the motif of a wizened elder is common in classic romantic literature (think of Merlin, Gandalf, and Obi Wan Kenobi), it obtains an almost revered status in the Jewish psyche. This character embodies the protective, guiding, and challenging role model. He (and sometimes she) guards ancient secrets, eternal lessons, and sacred traditions. The elder is often a shaman, a wizard, or a magician, able to offer advice from an untouchable place, remaining outside the fray of ordinary forces. Robert Bly, in *Iron John*, argues that this role fulfills a fundamental need of the male psyche. He proposes that men serve that need by an embrace of the "wild man," the Iron John character, who officiates over the initiation of the younger man.

Interestingly, the importance of this character is uneven in the Torah. In the Book of Genesis, nonfamily role models are almost entirely absent. (Who would mentor Abraham? The servant Eliezer? What about Isaac? The father who almost murdered him? And Jacob? Laban, a conniving crook of a father-in-law?) Later, we see Moses gain a role model in his father-in-law, Jethro (Exodus 18:1–12), and Moses eventually must serve as guide to his successor, Joshua. While other examples exist (Eli's relationship to Samuel, Samuel's guidance for Saul and David, Nathan's rebuke of David and subsequent protection of Solomon, and Mordecai's leadership of Esther all come to mind, as does the mentoring tone of Ecclesiastes), few of them contain the obvious emotional connections of the wizened elder in Western literature. Perhaps the biblical authors did not have a strong concept of mentorship outside the family unit, or the genre was not designed to convey feelings. Whatever the reasons, most mentoring in the Bible fails to completely convey the image of the elder role model.

The Elijah story stands out in contrast. In Elijah's relationship with Elisha, we see the devotion, compassion, protection, and generosity of the mentor-mentee bond. As Elijah sets out on his final journey across the Jordan River, where he knows he will die, Elisha refuses to leave his side despite being told repeatedly that he follows in vain. Just before the moment of death we see Elisha ask Elijah to carry his mantle of leadership, and Elijah's response, "You have asked a difficult thing," signifies at once the wisdom and the understanding characteristic of a good teacher (II Kings 2:1–18). The powerful psychological connection between these two men can serve as a positive example for contemporary Judaism, but we should not forget its uniqueness in its biblical context.

What happens in postbiblical literature is radically different. The Rabbis had such elaborate mentorship relations that the Talmud is littered with careful citations honoring teachers from generations past. We see in the Rabbinic literature stories of devotion that surpass even what might be considered healthy behavior. For example, we have stories of students following their teachers into the bathroom, and even hiding under the bed to discover their master's sexual secrets (Babylonian Talmud, B'rachot 62a). From the same period, we also see the importance of this relationship in the Christian sources, as Jesus refers to his students as disciples and they often describe their emotions toward Jesus as love. As I said in the introduction to this book, the Talmud describes the rabbi-student relationship as competing with that between parent and child.

Later, the entire mystical Jewish tradition is based on the idea of a secretive knowledge received personally from a teacher. That is why Jewish mysticism is called Kabbalah, which literally means "reception." We see the results of this mentorship in the later mystical circles that developed around charismatic leaders like the Ari, Rabbi Isaac Luria. Chasidism sprang from this relationship as well, beginning with the Baal Shem Tov, whose spiritual nurturance led to a complete genealogy of mentors. These "rebbes" became quasi-messianic leaders of their communities by developing circles of followers, who then developed more circles of followers.

We could speculate about the discrepancy between the *Tanach* and postbiblical literature (Does exile compel the need for continuity and thus students? Is the new emphasis on teachers and students a reflection of Greek and Roman influence?), but a complete analysis is beyond the scope of this book. Our focus is on how this mentor-mentee relationship in the Jewish past fits into the Jewish man's experience today. This Jewish value of the teacher-student relationship is echoed by secular research. Samuel Osherson, in his book *Finding our Fathers*, explains:

> The mentor serves very important, healthy functions in helping the younger person mature into adulthood. Dr. George Vaillant has examined in detail the lives of successful men from college through later adulthood. . . . He found that the presence of mentors is central to men's career success and to their maturation as people. . . . Men with relatively unsuccessful careers either had not discovered mentors until their early forties or had mentors only in adolescence.[1]

Many scholars like Osherson have pointed to the importance of father figures to the healthy growth of boys into men. This has led to an increased pressure on communal leaders, Jewish and secular, to hire male teachers, counselors, coaches, advisors, and clergy. While this move contains the potential for a rollback of equal employment opportunity for women, it is also a healthy acknowledgment of the developmental needs of boys.

In addition, Osherson has pointed to the role that mentees play in the lives of their teachers. A younger disciple provides the father figure with hope for the future while rekindling aspirations in the mentor that may have waned over time. This also reflects the Jewish tradition of teaching students, because the rabbis in all of those stories frequently spoke of their students as sons.

My own fieldwork on the subject came to the same conclusion. In focus groups and interviews with young men about their participation in

Judaism, a number of them spoke of a craving for Jewish male role models. For a few, the rabbi was the only adult man in their lives demonstrating a commitment to Judaism, while for many the rabbi was augmented by grandfathers and other older men in the Jewish community. These adolescent boys craved Jewish guidance from the men of their fathers' generation or younger. That is why a male youth advisor or classroom teacher in his twenties is such a hot commodity in synagogue life today.

The essays in this section echo the value of mentorship to the Jewish tradition as well as the secular literature. David Ellenson, in an article on values originally printed in *Reform Judaism* magazine, describes role models ranging from his childhood rabbi to the governor of his home state and how they affected his development as a Jew. Gary Greenebaum talks about the lessons taught by his father's example, lessons that appear to be secular behavior but which Greenebaum describes as "Talmud." Alan Moskoff takes a similar approach, examining how his father's early lessons were heavy on behavior and light on Judaism. But then he talks about how as he aged through life's stages, different rabbis and role models led him to a greater appreciation of Judaism. Doug Barden also considers the special role of family mentors, and he illustrates the way that conflicting messages from male Jewish role models, in his case a father and grandfather, can be synthesized into coherent whole.

In addition to the perspective of mentees, the essays in this section describe the importance of this relationship to the mentor. John Linder's essay exemplifies how a number of Jewish elders made valiant attempts to influence his Jewish identity, but how they all failed. He did not feel a desire to explore his soul until he was in the role of elder to his son, an experience that led eventually to his choice to return to school to become a rabbi. Alan Neuhauser also talks about the relationship between an elder and an apprentice of sorts, but his context is the Jewish summer camp, where the role of counselor is so crucial to the success of the camper's experience. Neuhauser's essay covers both perspectives, that of the developing camper and of the influential counselor.

The final two essays offer valuable perspectives whose relevance may not be obvious at first. Jennifer Jaech describes her experience as the senior rabbi at a synagogue that has had female senior rabbis for decades. She helps us understand the perspective as the Jewish leader to men and the ways in which a female senior rabbi can have success in promoting male involvement in Jewish community. And Daniel Robison offers the unique story of being a Jewish teacher in an all-male Episcopalian high school, the St. Alban's School, in Washington, D.C. He explains how his Jewish background challenges him to consider the ways he models masculinity to the boys at his school as well as his sons at home.

For each of these authors, the relationship between men and their mentors provides a fertile field for the growth of Jewish identity. For some, that growth comes through learning from an elder-type man, while for others the learning comes after being thrust into such a role. While earlier sections of this book highlighted individual paths within Judaism—the embrace of a traditionally masculine form of Judaism; the rejection of such a form and creation of a new men's model; the experience of crisis, wilderness, and redemption; and the discovery of meaning, revelation, and spirituality—these essays emphasize the importance of relationship. Whatever conclusions men will discover on their own in a quest to hear the "still, small voice," for some, that process will not be complete without the connection to another man.

Notes

1. Samuel Osherson, *Finding Our Fathers: How a Man's Life Is Shaped by His Relationship with His Father* (Chicago: Contemporary Books, 1986), pp. 47–48.

RABBI BULMAN'S KISS AND
OTHER LESSONS OF A
NEWPORT NEWS CHILDHOOD

David Ellenson

Neuroscientists teach us that the most fundamental elements of our identity are forged in childhood, and I am surely no exception. My own values are inextricably bound up with my early days as a Jewish boy growing up during the 1950s and 1960s in a tightly-knit Jewish community in the largely Christian world of Newport News, Virginia.

One of my earliest lessons as a child was to esteem and emulate individuals who demonstrated knowledge, care, and concern for Judaism. My father instructed me over and over again to show our Rabbi Nathan Bulman—an Orthodox rabbi he revered—the utmost *kavod* (respect).

One day, as Rabbi Bulman and I were studying the first paragraph of the *Amidah* prayer, we came across the phrase, "God of Abraham, God of Isaac, and God of Jacob." Rabbi Bulman commented, as Jewish teachers have for hundreds of years, that each of us, no less than the fathers of our people, must strive for a personal relationship with God. I imbibed his words and looked at the text. "There is something that troubles me," I said. I pointed out that the text said, "Abraham" and not "Abram," the name his father Terah had bestowed upon him. In contrast, the first name of the third patriarch appears as "Jacob," rather than his other name, "Israel," which he earned as he struggled with the angel.

When I asked the rabbi why this was so, he broke out in a tremendous smile and rushed over and kissed me on my forehead. His answer to the question—which was that Abraham was the name given Abram when he became a Jew, while Jacob was born a Jew—was almost beside the point. What I remember most was his kiss. Through this single act, he displayed the passion and joy involved in the study of Torah, and he embedded a love for Jewish learning and discovery in my *neshamah* (soul) that burns at the core of my being to the present day.

I have thought of that kiss often. In every teaching and personal setting in which I have found myself over the years, I have attempted to display and transmit the same love of learning to my students that Rabbi Bulman did at that decisive moment in my own life. Sometimes I am successful, sometimes not—but always I attempt to recognize the awesome responsibility I possess as a teacher. For, in the words of the rabbis, "great leaders of the Jewish people (*g'dolei Yisrael*) may spring from among those who sit before me," and each encounter presents an opportunity to touch their very souls.

Charles Olshanksy, director of the local JCC, reinforced another message I had learned from my parents: all persons have to be treated with dignity, as each of us is created in the image of God. I watched Mr. Olshansky speak politely and respectfully to everyone he met. He engaged every individual—the largest donor as well as the custodians—with the whole of his being. Most of all, he showed me that Judaism required that one love real flesh and blood people, not just an abstract ideal of humanity. Years later, when I read the words of Rabbi Tzvi Hirsch Kalischer (1795–1874) of Thorn, "Even sinners sometimes perform *mitzvot*," I identified this as a teaching Mr. Olshansky embodied—that Judaism regards fragile and finite human beings who are prone to error as nevertheless capable of being partners with God in the task of repairing the world.

This lesson remains of the utmost importance to me. In my many dealings with people, I often reflect on my own shortcomings—my lack of patience, my failure to "be in the moment" with the one who is before me, my overly excessive need for external affirmation, my misjudgments. I am aware how limited all of us are, and I often regret that I cannot live up to my highest ideal of self and fulfill the *mitzvah* of *k'vod hab'riyot* (respect for all creatures), as I feel I should.

And yet, despite the despair that often captures me at those moments of critical self-awareness and self-judgment, I see that all these weaknesses do not prevent either me or others from saying, as Abraham did, "*Hineini*," "Here I am," and being fully present in the moment to assist and support those who are in need of kindness and respect. This aspect of character calls upon me to be ever mindful of the words of Rabbi Abraham Joshua Heschel, who said that when he was young, he would first ask how smart an individual was. However, as he matured, he would first ask how kind that person was.

Growing up in Virginia during the late 1950s, I was also influenced by our then Governor Lindsay Almond's actions to challenge injustice. At that time, there were still separate water fountains for "whites" and "colored," and African-Americans and "whites" could not sit in the same sections on a bus, in movie theaters, in restaurants, or in any other public facility. The struggles that ensued in the wake of *Brown v. Topeka* seared my childhood. Senator Harry Flood Byrd of Winchester, the undisputed political leader of Virginia during this period and the architect of a policy of "massive resistance" to desegregation, vowed to close rather than integrate public schools. It was as if the Civil War had never been fought. Or, to put it more correctly, it was as if The War Between the States was going to be waged all over again. Part of the spirit of that time was captured in an obscene statement uttered by Governor Almond's predecessor: that integration—whether in schools or in public facilities—was akin to "sprinkling coal dust on vanilla ice cream. It ruins the ice cream and does the coal dust no good." I will not even repeat what my father said when he read these words and we discussed them at the dinner table.

I was then eleven years old and painfully aware of all this turmoil when Senator Byrd handpicked one of his chief lieutenants—Lindsay Almond of Roanoke, the attorney general of the Commonwealth—to serve as governor. Everyone presumed he would execute the policy of "massive resistance" that his political mentor had forged. However, in a completely unexpected development, Governor Almond broke with Senator Byrd and demanded that the Commonwealth bow to the will of the Supreme Court and the federal government and "obey the law of the land."

For his extraordinary act of valor, integrity, and steadfastness of resolve Governor Almond was literally vilified by the press and completely estranged from many of his most intimate friends. This model of character and decency has remained with me as a "profile in courage" throughout my lifetime. Since that day, whenever I read the words of Pirkei Avot, "*Bamakom sh'ein anashim, hishtadel lihyot ish,*" which I would translate as, "In a place where people no longer behave as human beings should, strive to be human," I think of Governor Almond.

During these last four years as president of HUC-JIR, I have thought often of Governor Almond's example. While I would hardly say that I have confronted moral issues of the magnitude he did, I have felt the need to offer a Jewish moral voice on a number of occasions. For example, I wrote several pieces defending the full religious and civil rights of our lesbian sisters and gay brothers that sadly elicited venomous responses, mostly from individuals outside the liberal Jewish community. Severe criticism did come my way from within our Movement early in my presidency for maintaining our mandatory year of study in Israel for all rabbinical, cantorial, and education students during a time when terrorist bombings were commonplace in Jerusalem. I will confess that I often spent sleepless nights during this period. However, I remained convinced that HUC-JIR could not surrender to the evil of terrorism a policy which seeks to transmit to future Reform leaders the classical Jewish ideal of *areivut*—mutual solidarity with and responsibility for the Jewish people.

The virtues I attach to character—kindness and love of people, courage and leadership, gratitude and fairness, persistence and love of learning—are rooted in what I learned from people in my childhood. These moral anchors have shaped my being to this day.

LEARNING TALMUD FROM DAD, THOUGH DAD KNEW NO TALMUD

Gary Greenebaum

Who are we as men? Who are we as Jews? As American Jewish men, we feel ambivalent about being American Jews. Perhaps most of all we feel conflict about being Jewish men. Our feelings are hard to sort out, difficult to understand. We are not sure who our role models ought to be. It is not clear to us what we want to be as American Jewish men.

The question "Who are we as men" makes sense only in the context of the 1980s, when men, challenged by the women's movement, have begun to rethink who we are and what we want. At last, we have become aware of our own longings as well as our own desires. It seems that some of us are only just now feeling our feelings, standing less behind intellectualized fabrications of who we are. We're stepping out of our homes and cars and offices to take a daylight look at what we *are* and not just what we *have*.

"Who are we as Jews" is a whole other question. Several men who attended the first San Francisco men's conference in 1985 said it was the first event sponsored by a mainstream Jewish organization they had attended in anywhere from five to fifteen years. One man said it was the first organized Jewish event he had attended since his Bar Mitzvah—well over half his life ago. Other men, who are involved in organized Jewish life, attended as the first event for them which dealt with issues of being men. However involved, or uninvolved, or even alienated we may feel about Jewish life, our identities as Jews seem to conintue to inform who we are as people and as men.

Who we are as Americans—as American Jewish men—adds another level of complexity to the mix. We were raised with the myth of the American male so strongly depicted for us that even when we know better, even when we can see its obvious drawbacks and limitations, we are stongly drawn to it, or at least some aspects of it.

When my brother and I were small, our father kissed us goodbye every morning when he left for work and kissed us hello every evening when he returned. If he took his leave of us in public, then he kissed us goodbye with the whole world looking on, and if we met somewhere, he kissed us then too. Sometimes it seemed a bother, but we indulged him. As we reached adolescence, we began to resist, and throughout our teen years, we refused to be kissed, first in public, then even in private.

He seemed to accept our decision cheerfully enough, and there seemed to even pass between us a sense that we all three knew that this isn't how men behave toward one another. In public, he would greet us with a hearty handshake. A safe substitute. Now, I kiss him in public. And give him a hug. And his body stiffens slightly, as though I am breaking some sort of sacred code between us. But I persist—in airports, at family gatherings, when he answers the door, and there I am. And when he stiffens, I want to shake him, and shout into his face—you taught me right the first time— we should hug and kiss, we want to and we need to. But he is the man who taught me what it means to be a man. He is the man who would tell me as he poured alcohol into my cut knees and elbows that babies cry, men don't. And when I would become so outraged, so angry at some injustice, or at how I had been wronged by the world if things weren't going my way, so frustrated that I was blithering, he would laugh and say, "You sound like Donald Duck." And when I started to grow up, he warned me, "You care too much. For other people. In the real world you will have to learn to watch out for yourself." And when it became clear that I was determined to become a rabbi, and not a businessman, it seemed, I'm sure, to him that my childish, dream-sense of how the world is and how the world ought to be was going to take precedence over a manly career—in business or in science. "All those years in school," he always says with a sigh and a shake of the head. "For all those years in school, you could have been a brain surgeon." And I always think, to myself, "A well-paid brain surgeon, you mean."

But I remember too, just after my mother died, that I was struck by how much my father knew about Jewish practices regarding death and burial. An assimilated Jew, such arcane practices seemed unlikely to be part of his Judaic knowledge. When pressed on why he knew so much, he admitted, as off-handedly as he could, that during all the years we lived in that small town in Iowa, whenever a Jew living out in the country, in some hamlet somewhere, would die, my father and several other Jewish men from our small city would travel to the little town, to insure that there was a minyan. He would travel a hundred, maybe two hundred miles, to pay respects to a man or woman he had never met.

And I remember, too, that whenever anyone we knew went into the hospital for surgery, it was always my father who went to the hospital to sit with the husband or wife or family during those excruciating hours when life hangs in the balance. He never asked if he was wanted, he only asked what time surgery was scheduled to begin.

How did I learn to care so much? For other people? Who taught me to watch out for others as well as myself? The same man who taught me not to cry. Who taught me basic Jewish values—taught them through his actions, for he did not know how to quote Talmud, and does not know what Midrash is. The same man who still cannot understand why I have become a rabbi.

My father taught me what he knew—about being a man, an American man, and about being a Jew. Sometimes garbled, sometimes contradictory, the messages sent to me by this most important man in my life left me with many spaces to fill in. But he taught me what he thought he was supposed to teach me, and he treated me as he had been taught to treat a son. If he had known Mishna, he would have taught me, "In a place where there are no men, strive to be a man." And he would have explained that being a man means being strong, resolute, knowing what is right, fearless. But his actions would have taught that being a man means being dependable, helping, caring, and involved.

Let me remind you of the story of Rabbi Zusya, who was told, "When you die and come before the Heavenly Tribunal, do not worry that they will say to you, 'Zusya, why were you not Moses?' Instead, they will require of you, 'Zusya, why were you not Zusya!'"

BECOMING A BETTER MAN,
AND A BETTER JEW

Alan Moskoff

I grew up in Middleboro, Massachusetts, a small town in the southeast-
ern part of the state. My father owned a very successful family supermarket, where he lived to work. Our house was adjacent to the market,
which was the center of our lives. My family was one of twenty Jewish
families in a town with a population of ten thousand. However, my parents made sure that I attended Hebrew School three times a week. We
attended Rosh HaShanah and Yom Kippur services at our synagogue two
towns away in Taunton, Massachusetts, where I became a bar mitzvah.
In high school I was president of my BBYO (B'nai Brith Youth Organization) youth group at the synagogue. I was different from my peers in that
I enjoyed my Jewish learning experiences so much that I can still recall a
trip to New York where a few of us stayed in the Orthodox community
for a weekend. I enjoyed the chanting and the Hebrew melodies, even
though my education was deficient in Hebrew prayer translation and
understanding.

My two closest friends growing up were Jewish males. While I was in
college, I continued to be friendly with Jewish males, because I could
bond with them easily. My closest Jewish friend and I were both married
on the same day and were unable to attend each other's wedding,

although later on, he was my best man at a subsequent wedding. One of my favorite memories was when we marched with Martin Luther King in Boston. My best friend and I also went to see Sandy Koufax pitch at Shea Stadium. I attended Shabbat and High Holy Day services in many cities, but was not motivated to learn more about Judaism as such. In my profession, I have tried to act Jewishly. My sense is to help my customers as best as I can and with understanding, treating seniors, the poor, and other ethnic groups with respect and equality.

When my wife and I decided that we would try Temple Beth El in Providence, Rhode Island, I didn't realize that this temple would further shape me as a Jewish male. Rabbi Les Gutterman is probably the most significant Jewish male influence in my life. My wife and I decided to take the course "Introduction to Judaism." I felt I needed a refresher course, and I was right. This was the first time I had ever finished a seder, thanks to Rabbi Gutterman. His sermons also greatly moved my wife and me, as well as his fantastic sense of humor.

It was here that a Brotherhood member asked me to come to a Brotherhood meeting, and within a couple of years, I became Brotherhood president. Holding this office was indeed a privilege and an honor, and it has also opened many Jewish doors as well. I tried to expose the men of my Brotherhood to a *dv'ar Torah* at the beginning of each meeting and introduced a Jewish program involving dads and sons participating in a *Havdalah* sevice. My next step was agreeing to attend a leadership weekend presented by NFTB (National Federation of Temple Brotherhoods), with no idea of what was about to happen to me. This journey that I have now taken has introduced me to more Jewish learning, and I have gotten to know and become friends with some very passionate Jewish men.

Among the many scholars I was introduced to were Rabbi Jake Jackofsky and Rabbi Richard Address, who facilitated Torah study, where Jewish learning and humor became an experience I would never forget. One time I took my thirteen-year-old son to a Torah study at an NFTB meeting. As we entered the room, I was wondering what everyone might have been thinking, including my son. I have always regarded the Torah study as a special time when I can expand my Jewish knowledge far beyond what I presently know. I consider these sessions a highlight at NFTB meetings. When Ben, my son, and I were walking back to our room, I asked him what he thought. He said he loved it. "Ben Bag Bag teaches: 'Turn the Torah, and turn it again, for everything you want to know is found within it'" (*Pirkei Avot* 5:22). As I have grown older, my thirst for Jewish learning has also grown. When I was younger, I only had a taste of Jewish learning. That taste lay dormant for many years, but now instead of tasting, I am hungry to become a wiser man. Torah study is that seven-course meal. My wonderful experience has shaped me into a better man and a better Jew by trying to do my part to make the world a better place to live.

During my second year as president, my eleven-year-old daughter was diagnosed with leukemia. She has now finished treatment after almost three years and is cancer free. That experience has strengthened our family. We were supported with the help of our Jewish community and prayer, as well as many phone calls from Rabbi Gutterman. My daughter bonded with Rabbi Sarah Mack, and I believe prayer helped my family deal with my daughter's illness, but also helped others who were affected by her illness as well.

While growing up, I learned from my father how to treat people. I was able to observe him for many years while he ran his supermarket. He was indeed a mensch. I know this to be true, because even now, twenty-five years after his passing, I meet people who remember him and his family supermarket. Other than making sure that we attended High Holy Day services, had a seder, lit Chanukah candles, and that I became a bar mitzvah, my father and I never discussed Torah or being a Jewish male. At least I had those experiences with him and those memories of him.

Although my father and I never had those discussions, I feel the need to have them now. Men need to sit and talk to other men about themselves, their feelings, their health, and their spirituality. I say this as men are leaving congregations. Perhaps each one of us can play a small part in slowing down this exodus or even bringing men back. The issue is, what can we do to keep men involved? I have asked some of my friends if they were interested in a "men's only study," and to my surprise, more men said yes than no. Of course time is always an issue in our fast-paced society, but we need to make that time. I am optimistic that we will. For as Rabbi Allan Tuff's writes, "For too long Jewish men have been absent from the spiritual life of our people. To thrive, Judaism and the Jewish people need the spiritual energy that is unique to the masculine soul. As Jewish men, we reaffirm our commitment to the renewal and evolution of our sacred heritage. As biological or adoptive fathers and as teachers in our community, we fulfill the ancient commandment . . . you shall teach them to your children. We teach future generations of Jews through our words and deeds." If men are involved and engaged, then we can do our part to ensure the future of Judaism.

PROFESSIONAL JEW BY ACCIDENT

Doug Barden

I write this as someone who has spent nearly twenty-five of my thirty-three working years as a "Jewish professional," having spent ten years as a district and national director for Women's American ORT, and going on nearly thirteen years now as the executive director of the Men of Reform Judaism (MRJ, formerly the North American Federation of Temple Brotherhoods). I write this as someone who is an anomaly: I never spent a summer at a Jewish sleepaway camp; I was not active in any Jewish high school youth groups. My college years were spent as an antiwar activist and peace-education organizer. My only connection to Judaism was that my randomly assigned college roommate kept kosher. College did provide my first exposure to the Jewish philosopher who has had the most profound influence on me, Martin Buber, but this was through a philosophy of education class, not a Jewish studies course. My senior year focused on avoiding my impending change in draft status from 2-S to 1-A by applying for conscientious objector status (but not by claiming I was a Jewish pacifist). The Valley Stream draft board eventually rejected my claim, but a high draft lottery number made the whole issue moot.

Whereas most of my professional colleagues deliberately chose to work in the Jewish communal field early in their careers and have rabbinic degrees, Jewish education degrees, or M.S.W. degrees in Jewish communal service, my education background is in social anthropology (M.A.) and organizational development (M.B.A.). My initial decision to work as a Jewish professional was very much an accident and, for the next thirty years, a source of disappointment to both my parents. My mother hoped I would become a dentist, because people would always need dentists and you could make a good living, and my father hoped I would become a labor negotiator. The fact that the latter was not something in which I ever expressed an interest did not deter my father from believing it would be a fascinating career and one he could experience vicariously through me.

Like many of my friends, I attended Hebrew school at the only neighborhood temple (Conservative), but it was only for two years; my mother had kept me out until I was eleven. Most of my mother's decisions on the directions my life's journey should take were not ones I agreed with, then or now, but this one I have to give her full credit for, because my Hebrew school experiences worked out amazing well. I *loved* Hebrew school (how many people can really say that?!), as I was fortunate enough to have a rabbi/teacher who saw my potential. Rather than make me feel embarrassed by being surrounded by kids a lot younger, he had me teach the younger kids in the class. Within two years, by the time I became bar mitzvah, most of my thirteen-year-old contemporaries who had endured Hebrew school for five years were still Jewishly illiterate, dreading their performance on the bimah, and hoping that by memorizing their haftarah records it would sink in in time. I, on the other hand, was upset when I discovered my bar mitzvah date gave me the *shortest* haftarah, Isaiah, "beat your swords into plowshares." The rabbi subsequently suggested to my mother that I consider becoming a rabbi, to which my mother replied, "We didn't raise our son to be a schnorrer."

It would be fifteen years before I would walk back into a temple, to be married to my wife Rivka, and another eight years before we formally joined a temple when my oldest child Ben was ready for Hebrew school. We chose a Reform synagogue, because it was easier to understand the liturgy and what was going on.

Before that, I had dropped out of the doctorate anthropology program to pursue being an "activist" in New York City. After a series of job interviews where the first question asked was "How fast can you type?" I eventually met up with Harry Gold, an employee of "FEGS," the (Jewish) Federation Employment Guidance Service, who was determined to help me find work. Six months later there was an opening for a district director with Women's American ORT, and I soon found myself, at the age of twenty-five, as the only Jewish male professional working with approximately seventy-five Jewish women volunteers many years my senior, doing membership, fundraising, educational programming, community outreach, and yes, schnorring (i.e., fund-raising) on behalf of the Jewish people around the world. Five years later I took over WAORT's national organization department and focused on membership and leadership development. After an eight-year hiatus outside the Jewish communal field, I returned to the fold—this time, *by choice*, and still without my parents' blessing, to assume my current position with MRJ/NFTB.

With the exception of the rabbi from my childhood, it might appear that there were no religiously Jewish role models in my early years. That's not exactly true. There was my beloved *zayde*, Grandpa Benny. But he came with "baggage."

My father's father, Grandpa Benny Budinitsky, was born in the 1880s in a small town outside of Russia; he fled the pogroms in 1905 and came with his wife Gittel/Gussie and son Samuel to the Lower East Side of New York. My father was born a decade later in 1914. Grandpa Benny brought with him his Orthodoxy and also, apparently, no useful skills to earn a living. I grew up being told that it was my grandmother who put all the food and most of the money on the table by providing catering services in the neighborhood. My grandfather did work, "in the courthouse." Not as a lawyer, not as a judge, but as the elevator operator. I always had this image of my grandfather multitasking: sitting on a stool, reading his siddur, mumbling his prayers, and at the same time, using one of his hands to open and close the gates and door of the elevator, up and down, up and down, all day.

I can't say I ever really saw my grandfather performing this task. He had been retired for many years by the time I came along. I was the youngest of six grandchildren, and the Grandpa Benny I knew was a mythical Jewish figure, a small, stubbly gray-bearded man, cowering before his still all-powerful wife, and someone who tried to connect with his grandson in Yiddish, which the grandson had not been taught to speak or understand.

Grandpa Benny died when I was fourteen, a year after I became bar mitzvah. However, Grandpa Benny not only attended my bar mitzvah, but participated in an extraordinary way. I didn't think much of it at the time, but later in life I realized how unusual and special a gift I had been given. In the middle of my bar mitzvah service, the rabbi was called away, as a congregant had been in a terrible accident. Who would continue the service in the temple? There was no other rabbi or cantor. My father was certainly not going to do it. No problem. Grandpa Benny just got up from his seat, went to the bimah, and without skipping a beat, continued to lead the service.

As I grew up, the tension between my father and my grandfather Benny became more and more apparent. My father, I came to realize, never forgave *his* father for being unable to provide for his family. My father, as was true of many first-generation American Jews, subsequently rejected his father's religion as well—in this case, not only Orthodoxy but the whole religious shebang. For my father, attending services and just going through the motions bordered on total hypocrisy. What mattered was how you led your life during the week, how you treated others, and my father did not see the Torah as the source of these positive and, in his mind, universal, ethical values. Instead he turned to what was then popular leftist-oriented political philosophy. Ironically, my father spent his entire professional life as a safety engineer with top security clearance for the U.S. government. Growing up as I did in the McCarthy era of the 1950s, let's just say that my father's earlier political affiliations and voting record in the 1930s were not open to public discussion.

In retrospect, my father probably would have felt comfortable in a Reform shul. But it wasn't an option; one didn't exist in his Lower East Side neighborhood growing up, one didn't exist in our town on Long Island, and coming from a Russian background, his association of "Reform" with "snotty German Jews" was still very strong. My father truly lived a life symbolizing the highest ideals expressed in Judaism, trying to make the world a better and "safer" place, and I would like to think my social activist inclinations came from him, but publicly his Jewishness and Jewish roots were anathema to him almost to his dying days.

We skip ahead fifty years to 2001. At this point my dad had been in a nursing home for nearly five years suffering from severe dementia, and he would not make it to 9/11. Early on, the short-term memory wires went: there was no solid connection between his trying to listen and his ability to understand. Moments with my dad took on a surreal aspect of déjà vu—didn't we do this already? My dad would ask, "So, what's new?" and as you answered him, he would appear to hang on every word you said, but then you stopped and saw his face, the blank look would reappear, and the conversation would start afresh again with the question, "So, what's new?"

Patients with Alzheimer's or severe dementia may lose their short-term memories, but often their long-term memories remain intact. Not only was this true in my father's case, but I began to hear stories I had never heard before, and these from a man who had spent most of his adult life engaging in his one and only hobby: talking to other people. It was thus when I was fifty, and my father eighty-five, that I was told an amazing Barden family story.

Yes, Grandpa Benny was a lowly courthouse elevator operator. That story I had heard over and over again. But that was only half the story. Whether or not it's true doesn't matter—it is now part of Barden folklore and will be passed down from generation to generation: my Grandpa Benny was the first *Jewish* courthouse elevator operator! Before that, there were only Irish or Italian courthouse elevator operators in New York City. My grandfather was the first Jewish one, and when my father, deep in dementia, told this story, his eyes lit up, and he looked so very, very proud of his father. It was a pride I had never seen before.

As a Jewish professional, I work with many men who are at the stage in their life and careers when they are often filled with misgivings and lots of "I should have done this," "I should have done that." I do not suffer that malaise. I have always gotten a lot of psychic income from working as a Jewish professional. I am proud of my accomplishments. Did I, in the end, become more Jewish than my father? I'm not sure that's even the right question. I made a decision a long time ago that if asked why I work in the Jewish communal field, I would give this answer: I am not sure, day to day, what I do or don't believe with regard to belief in God. I lean toward Buber and Heschel and continue to be a lifelong questioner and learner. But I spend my days in an effort to ensure that my children and my children's children will have the opportunity to explore for themselves what it means to be Jewish. I just want to make sure they have a chance to choose.

On a personal level, I remain a mixture of both my grandfather and my father. I spend a lot of my time giving talks from the bimah on Friday nights. And often, before I speak, I see my Grandpa Benny looking over my shoulder and smiling. In a sense he won his fight with his own son. We skipped a generation, but he ended up with at least one grandson who came back to some form of religious Judaism. But I also know that somewhere in the audience my father is also kvelling, proud that his son is still trying to make the world a better place.

MY SON'S EYES

John A. Linder

I recall from a very young age having an active conversation and relationship with God. I felt angry and confused over the great inequities and injustices I witnessed from afar. Unfortunately, I didn't know where to go with any of this. Judaism, God, and politics were not part of our dinner table conversations.

I was born in 1957, a second-generation American Jew, my grandparents from Russia and the Ukraine. As was characteristic of many children of immigrants, my parents strove to assimilate into the fabric of American society.

I remember my father, every now and then, talking about his Jewish experience growing up. Mostly, it centered around his Jewish neighborhood, growing up in north Buffalo's Hertel Avenue section. My dad's family belonged to a traditional shul, though they were not regulars to be sure. He went to the rabbi's house to prepare for his bar mitzvah. He talked about the *shvitz*, sports, and hanging with the Jewish guys in the neighborhood. These men, like my dad, were long on street smarts. Real life experience was their university. His dad owned a couple of saloons on Buffalo's east side. After a year and a half of college, my father enlisted to serve in World War II. When he returned stateside, at the end of the war, he got busy starting a business and a family.

My father's identity was largely connected to being a provider for his family. His street smarts served him well in the scrap business. He was a guy's guy—playing poker with the boys, taking junkets to Vegas, a competitive athlete. My mother's identity revolved around the home and family. That was her domain. My father's persona took a backseat when he stepped into our home, onto my mom's turf. The guy's guy outside of the home was very passive in the home. Our dinner table was the primary stage for lessons in avoiding conflict. My father rarely took a stand, rather choosing to take the road of least resistance. Like our dishes, everything stayed on the surface.

My identity as a boy and young man was formed around sports and high achievement (neither of which were supported as wholeheartedly for my sisters). I took pride in being one of a few Jewish kids who played contact sports. Growing up in a mostly non-Jewish environment, my Jewish identity was formed more out of the gentiles' view of me as a Jew than through Jewish learning and ritual. Although I "had" a bar mitzvah and begrudgingly attended religious school through confirmation, God talk and our obligation to act in the world were not a part of the temple's curriculum as I remember it.

During college, sports continued to play a major role. At the same time, I began to form a smaller community of male friends who were searching for a more expansive way to identify as men. We reflected upon our feelings and experiences more through the lens of Joseph Campbell (*The Hero with a Thousand Faces*) and Robert Bly (*Iron John*) than through any of our respective faith traditions. Of the six in our men's group, four were Jewish. As much as I could see the value in men being able to open up and discuss suffering in a safe public space, and understood the power of drumming circles in nature, I knew there was something missing for me. I just couldn't put my finger on it. There was nothing in my Jewish reservoir from which to draw.

During summer break, I traveled to Israel to live on a kibbutz with my dear college friend, Paul Vogel. We were two of many young, impressionable, American Jewish men walking around Jerusalem's Old City on Friday afternoon, and a couple *yeshivah bochers* invited us to the rebbe's house for a *Shabbes* meal. Delighted to have a home-cooked meal off the kibbutz, we didn't hesitate to accept the invitation. Of course, after the meal, the singing, and the schnapps, we were invited to come to their yeshivah on Sunday morning. It seemed like a small price to show our appreciation for a delicious meal and a joyful (though foreign) Shabbat experience. Paul and I, out of curiosity and obligation, agreed to come.

After a fascinating class with the rebbe, he seemed to hone in on me, recognizing that I was searching for something. As he shook my hand, he looked me directly in the eyes and asked, "Do you believe that God gave Moses the Ten Commandments on Mount Sinai?" As ill-equipped as I was to give an answer (I didn't appreciate until years later just how loaded the question was), all I could do was mumble some pathetic excuse why I was not prepared to accept his invitation to leave my cloistered, liberal arts college in New England to study at his yeshivah in Jerusalem. I knew that what I experienced in that classroom was getting closer but was still not it.

After college, I listened to that voice that had been there since child-hood, calling me to get a job as a community and labor organizer. This was a tangible way for me to be engaged in making a difference in the world. As passionate as I was about my work, I could not sustain my drive in the same way as my fellow organizers—based on machismo and ideol-ogy alone. Something was still missing, I just didn't know what. I married during those years, and my wife, Nancy Levy, and I moved back to Buf-falo, where I went to work in my family's scrap metal recycling business. My energies moved away from my passion to being a successful provider. In my heart, I knew these were not mutually exclusive. I just didn't know how to bring them together.

In my midthirties, my wife and I were blessed with a beautiful boy, David Joel. Nancy and I knew that we wanted our son to grow up in a home where Judaism was more central than we had experienced it. My son's eyes became the most powerful mirror reflecting my own life. I knew that the greatest test of my manhood, and the greatest gift I could give my son, was to be open, authentic, and true to myself. And in that moment, Judaism and God were there as my partner.

Through our son, we reconnected as a family to the synagogue. In those first few Saturday mornings, studying Torah with Rabbi Steve

Mason, it was one aha moment after another. "So that's where that voice comes from!" Our biblical story spoke directly to me. I could see myself in the text. There was Abraham, the first patriarch of the Jewish people. What courage and faith he had to go forth, *lech l'cha* (Genesis 12:1), leaving his comfort zone and all that was familiar, for deeper meaning in his life. Although not exclusive to men, I knew Abraham provided a powerful role model for men. Our patriarch was not only a spiritual seeker, establishing a personal relationship with God; he was pursuer of justice. God makes it clear that Abraham's mission, the reason he was chosen to be the first Jew, was to teach his children and the generations to come by "doing what is right and just" (Genesis 18:19). Abraham's intimate relationship with God does not compromise his integrity to confront God. With the fate of Sodom and Gomorrah on the line, Abraham speaks truth to power, challenging God, "Must not the Judge of all the earth do justly?" (Genesis 18:25).

Torah was the missing fuel I needed to sustain me intellectually, spiritually, and in deeds. The vulnerability and uncertainty I felt as a new father and my deep desire to be a role model for my son opened me to receive our sacred text. Torah helped me love my father for who he was and what he gave to me, while being comfortable in creating a different home for my family. A *sh'lom bayit*, a peaceful home, could embrace both intimacy and confrontation. I now better understood the rebbe's question at the yeshivah in Jerusalem and how to answer it. I didn't have to abrogate my intellect, or relinquish questioning Jewish tradition, to be enriched by it. On the contrary, at its essence, "Judaism is both faith and reason; two beacons each shedding its own light, but both fusing ultimately into one bright beam."[1] I now better understood what was missing for me as a community and labor organizer. Torah gave me permission to let go of machismo and feel secure in my vulnerability as a man. Our biblical story was so much more real than any ideology—the experience of a flawed people striving for a connection with the Divine and a desire to make a difference in the world. I now better understood that it was possible to integrate my passion, my personal life, and my work life. I could see Torah as the hub connecting the spokes of each part of my life.

In hindsight, and now in my experience as a rabbi in the community, I can see the power that Torah can have in grounding men and boys at different stages in life. Our sons yearn to nurture their relationship with God, to connect to the divine spark in their souls. Expert and accomplished in other areas of life, men are looking for a way to access the basics of Judaism. Men want role models—not those who are perfect—but those who stumble, who struggle, who cry, who make mistakes and change.

As a rabbi, as a husband, as a father, as a son, as a friend, as one of those role models, and as a Jew, I strive to engage in that struggle: to have the courage to cry, make mistakes, and change. In that way I hope to teach my students, my peers, my friends, and most of all my son that to be a Jewish man is to defy the stereotypes of machismo and invulnerability. That is the Torah as I try to teach it.

NOTES

1. Adapted from Abraham Geiger, *Abraham Geiger & Liberal Judaism, The Challenge of the Nineteenth Century* (Cincinnati: Hebrew Union College Press, 1981), p. 263.

PART OF A COMMUNITY

Alan Neuhauser

"Oatmeal or chocolate chip?!" It's one in the morning, and my counselor's shout has just woken me up from a deep sleep. I am groggy and unfocused, and there's a cookie being held an inch from my nose. Guess correctly, and I win the cookie; guess wrong, and I get tossed into a cold shower. This was Camp Harlam at its best: unexpected, fun, personal, interactive, and led with enthusiasm by my counselors. From my first welcoming high five from "Beer Mug"—a.k.a. David Weinglass—as a shy new twelve-year-old camper, through my summer in Chavurah (the separate campus for high school seniors), these young men created the defining moments of my camping experience. They were why it was just so much fun, why I returned summer after summer, and why as a college student and Camp Harlam alum, I decided to become a counselor myself. Although as a camper, I did not think of my counselors in the context of religion and gender, with hindsight I realize that they helped me define my identity as a Jewish male. They created the place and space for my bunkmates and me to step out of the stereotype, step out of the minority, and step into a comfortable, welcoming fraternity.

The boys (and girls) in my Sunday school and Hebrew school classes tended to show up sullen and tired. None of us wanted to wake up early

Sunday morning or go to temple on Tuesday afternoons to spend more time in school. My classmates were friendly enough, but going to temple was just one more scheduled activity in our school-year schedule. The adults at my synagogue were also just part of the background. The men chatted with my parents, sat at services—sometimes sleeping through the rabbi's sermon—but they were not an active part of my Jewish experience. For three seasons of the year, being a Jewish male seemed mainly about preparing for bar mitzvah and about showing up—to Sunday school, to services, or to seder. It differentiated me from most of my school friends but did not contribute significantly to my identity as a Jewish man.

By contrast, at Camp Harlam, being a Jewish male was all about being active and about being part of a cohesive community. My counselors were upbeat, athletic, artistic, adventurous, and always seemed happy to be with us at camp. They demonstrated a level of strength, vitality, and vivacity that created an inviting place to be Jewish.

Over the years when I have told my friends from home and school about Camp Harlam, they have often asked what exactly about the camp makes it a Jewish camp, besides the obvious fact that all the campers and staff are Jewish. For many years, I responded by describing our weekly Shabbat services at the outdoor Chapel on the Hill and Chapel in the Woods, the daily period dedicated to Torah study (called *shiur*), and the camp's kosher-style meals. Since becoming a staff member, however, I have come to reconsider my answer. Although religion-centric activities provide a strong foundation for Camp Harlam's existence as a Jewish institution, I have come to realize that it is the people, more than the details of the program, who make the "magic" that I experienced almost daily at Camp Harlam. The embracing Jewishness of Camp Harlam was people-centric.

The environment that my counselors created helped me transform from a shy, reserved, and largely insecure boy into an outgoing and confident Jewish young man. True, Shabbat services and *shiur* did introduce us campers to foundational Jewish ethos, such as the importance of respect, trust, and dedication, but it was during the rest of the day's activities that these values were taught and applied. It was in shaking hands after an epic game of capture the flag, in relying on a counselor to belay me as I climbed the fifty-foot alpine tower, and in diving to block a shot during a soccer game to save a goal for my team. It was while playing goofy card games with my bunkmates, jockeying for hot water during shower hour, and being silly during bedtime Flashlight Time that we made summer and lifelong friends and became comfortable in our Jewishness.

Camp did not change the fact that I wear glasses, stink at soccer, and never travel without a book or two. But it is where I emerged from my shell. It's where I learned to make new friends and to deal with those who would never be part of my circle. Over the years, most of us were repeat campers, and it was always with great anticipation that I looked forward to seeing my camp friends. The first day of the season was full of laughing, hello hugs, and quickly reestablished connections. Although we were far from clones and had diverse backgrounds and personalities, our Jewishness was an important part of what connected us, and through camp, we became comfortable expressing our Judaism. Sure, camp was always about having fun, but the complete Camp Harlam experience was also about feeling *right*. Through our everyday interactions with my counselors, we campers bonded not just because we were in camp together, but also because we shared a bond as Jews.

To this day, I clearly remember and seek to emulate "Beer Mug." I started camp as a twelve-year-old, a bit later than most, and was assigned to Arava Boys 1, a bunk that consisted almost entirely of returning campers. I felt a little out of place and withdrawn, but that first night, as my bunkmates were brushing their teeth and getting ready for bed, Beer Mug discreetly came over to chat. He made sure that I was not homesick and that I had had a good first day. Through the rest of the summer, Beer Mug introduced us to such bands as Phish and Guster, and he and other counselors entertained us with antics in the bunk and dining hall. Beer Mug and my other counselors demonstrated to me that Jewish men could be warm, funny, and most of all, cool, and they showed me that I could be all those things, too—while still being myself. By practicing the Jewish value of welcoming the stranger, they not only helped me to immerse and integrate myself into the Camp Harlam community, they helped me grow as a person. Today, I count among my best friends the boys—now young men—whom I met at camp.

After six years as a camper, I decided to be a bunk counselor. As campers, we all sought to emulate our favorite counselors, who lived up to Camp Harlam's namesakes, Betty and Joseph Harlam, by being "living" Jews. The counselors set the example and the tone. They created the magic, and after so many great years at camp, I wanted to be a part of creating that for others. And to be honest, I wanted more summers with my friends, many of whom shared my desire both to "give back" and to be together. We were not ready to give up the magic.

In my two years as a counselor, I came to appreciate the huge amount of work and dedication it takes to create the extraordinary camp experience that I enjoyed and to become an effective counselor. The days are full: keeping campers safe and to their schedules, working through homesickness and tending actual sickness, and above all making sure campers are having fun. Added to this, day in and day out, counselors teach campers important life lessons, both through instruction and through example. Sometimes it's direct—talking to campers about good sportsmanship; other times it's subtler—shouting encouragement to both teams during a game. This may not sound difficult, but maintaining both endless patience and limitless energy takes its toll. It can become easy to get hung up on maintaining good behavior and enforcing the rules—to lose the forest for the trees. But, then it comes back to the campers for inspiration—remembering why I am here at camp, and why so many of my friends and I chose to return to Camp Harlam as counselors. This was not a job that we took for the money.

As a counselor, I found that although my role and responsibilities significantly changed, my overall camp experience did not. In making the switch from simply living the camp magic to creating it, I have come to appreciate the effort and planning that goes into creating such a wonderful environment. More important, I have experienced another kind of magic—that created by our campers. I have enjoyed the exhilaration of a shy camper who has mastered the climbing tower, the spontaneous hugs, and the bringing together of individual boys who come from diverse backgrounds and experiences into our community—where it is comfortable and cool to be Jewish—and where you can make best friends for life.

Who you are at camp is, I think, truly who you are. When you leave, you become more *yourself*. You're back to your school self, and back to your neighborhood-friend self, but you carry with you the "confident Jewish man self." And as a counselor, the job is not just trying to impart the magic to the youngsters who come after you, and it's not just being a role model for the kids (although that of course is important), it's that you become a role model for every community of which you are a part.

THE BLESSING OF BROTHERS

Jennifer Jaech

"Here, Rabbi, let me fix a plate for you." From the moment I stepped into the building that Sunday morning, I knew the "Brothers" were in the building. The smell of coffee, scrambled eggs, and lox filled the synagogue. I couldn't resist walking down into the kitchen to greet the men cooking breakfast. They laughed and talked as they worked getting ready to feed the hundred people expected to attend their program. The head cook, Neal, an affable man clothed in an apron, greeted me with the offer of breakfast. I couldn't linger too long before I had to dash off to my religious school duties.

The men cooking in this kitchen seemed comfortable as they sliced bagels and arranged the lox and capers on decorative plates. They clearly felt at home. And I felt at home with them, despite my being the only female in the room. This is no surprise, because we see a lot of each other. Members of the Brotherhood are often in our building, perhaps more than any other group of volunteers in our temple community.

Brotherhood members support our synagogue in a variety of ways. Several times a year, I find them working with teenagers as they sort clothing and make sandwiches for Midnight Run (a program that brings food, clothing, and conversation to homeless people in New York City).

As autumn approaches, Brotherhood members undertake the massive job of coordinating parking and ushering for our High Holy Day services. Even in the pouring rain, every Rosh HaShanah and Yom Kippur, Brotherhood members stand outside directing traffic, figuring out how to park hundreds of cars on our limited property. In the cold and dark month of January, our Brotherhood brings stand-up comedians to our synagogue for a Saturday evening "Comedy Night." Brotherhood members also help with our Purim and Chanukah carnivals, serving as carnival emcees and purveyors of kosher hot dogs. And while many volunteers avoid the necessary but difficult task of raising funds to support the congregation's operating budget, the Brotherhood has consistently done just that.

Brotherhood's commitment extends beyond our congregation as well. In the summer of 2006, members responded to the crisis in northern Israel by phoning all the congregation's members and asking them to pledge money for humanitarian relief through Israel's Magen David Adom. In just a few days, our Brotherhood raised thousands of dollars. And in recent months, our Brotherhood has made contact with a fledgling Jewish community in Poland. They sent a *Kiddush* cup to a newly-wed Jewish couple there as a token of their warm wishes and support.

The men in the Brotherhood do a lot for our congregation and for our larger community, but their activities extend beyond their service. In recent years, I have noticed greater attention focused on their members' growth, both in Jewish learning and in spiritual expression. The Brotherhood has an annual retreat for the men of our congregation, during which they have the opportunity to focus on their spiritual development. Brotherhood members have also organized a series of adult education classes. When I had the chance to teach one of these classes, I found our discussion to be among the liveliest and most stimulating ones I've experienced in my years at our synagogue. And every year, Brotherhood members ascend the bimah to lead the congregation in Shabbat worship, complete with a Brotherhood choir.

It is remarkable that our synagogue's Brotherhood is so active and vital at this time that our Reform Movement expresses concern about the decreasing participation by males in our synagogues. Even more interesting, since 1991, our congregation has been led by a female senior rabbi. Helene Ferris led the congregation for fifteen years; I succeeded her in

2006. It is possible that the female spiritual leadership from the bimah served as an impetus for our congregation's men to create their own camaraderie. But I also wonder if there is something deeper at play.

When I greeted the members of Brotherhood cooking in our kitchen on the morning of their breakfast, I felt as if I were greeting my brothers. I'm used to being surrounded by brothers, having grown up with five of them. Growing up, my playmates were mostly my brothers and their male friends. We often played games that boys preferred. (I am still grateful to my brothers for teaching me how to avoid throwing a baseball "like a girl.") When I had the chance to play with girls in the neighborhood, I adapted easily to their company as well. As a result, I never developed the sense that baseball was superior to Barbie, or vice versa.

I also had the advantage of growing up during a time when, thanks to the feminist movement, we were rethinking traditional roles for men and for women. Two or three times during my elementary school years, I remember our teachers showing us the film *Free to Be You and Me*. In the film, we learned that it is okay for boys to cry (Rosie Greer told us so), and it is okay for girls to play with trucks. When I became vocal about my career ambition to become a racehorse jockey, no one ever told me that I couldn't do it because I was a girl. The world seemed wide open to me.

Thankfully, my son also benefited from the new freedom in gender roles. Never once in his childhood was he discouraged from playing with dolls or freely showing his emotions. Since he was a baby, we have belonged to two different congregations, both led by a female rabbi. He never thought it strange to have a woman lead the congregation, nor did he ever express to me that he noticed the lack of male role models on the bimah or among the teachers in religious school.

This freedom brings with it its own challenges. In the traditional Jewish world, men are the ones obligated to perform the mitzvot (commandments) essential to our communal life: prayer, Torah study, and so on. In the liberal Jewish world, the obligation extends to women—and, of course, the notion of being "commanded" at all is called into question. This new freedom can alienate us by giving us too much choice and not enough certainty, or we can embrace it and redefine how we wish to function in the community. This is what women have done in the synagogue, and this may be the secret of our Brotherhood's success as well.

The members of our Brotherhood are no longer locked into a given set of assumptions about who they are and what they should do as Jewish men. They are free to redefine their role in our congregation, and they have done so with great success. Brotherhood can take on traditionally male responsibilities (directing traffic, building carnival booths) and can also explore territory previously occupied almost exclusively by women (cooking breakfast for the congregation, going on spiritual retreats).

The men of our Brotherhood are all busy with careers, family, and other commitments. But they keep coming back to our synagogue because the time they spend here enriches them. They have found a community within a community. They enjoy each other's company. They listen to each other, support each other, and together they accomplish a lot. As their rabbi, I want to do whatever I can to ensure that their vitality continues and their ranks grow. As their sister, I feel blessed by their presence in my life.

"Sure, Neal, I'll take what you're cooking," I responded that morning in the kitchen. Neal smiled and handed me a plate of delicious food.

MY MANY SONS

Daniel S. Robison

This past December, my oldest son, Max, came home from kindergarten and asked if we could get a Christmas tree. After a somewhat cold reception from me, he came back a little later and asked if we could get a Chanukah bush. How do I respond?

We are a Reform Jewish family living literally and figuratively in the shadow of the National Cathedral, the sixth-largest cathedral in the world and home to the Episcopalian bishop of Washington, D.C. I say figuratively because I teach at St. Albans School, an all-boys school located on the grounds of the cathedral. My sons are very connected to both St. Albans and its community. Max attends our local public elementary school, where he is one of two Jewish children in a class of twenty-one. Our middle son, Harry, attends preschool at a Conservative synagogue, as our Reform synagogue does not have a preschool program. Leo is less than a month old as of the writing of this essay but will likely follow in his brothers' footsteps. While we are lucky to be a part of so many different environments, Chanukah and Christmas are a source of confusion to our children. Not a day goes by during December that either a student, one of the children's friends, or a neighbor asks whether we celebrate Chanukah and how. Ultimately, they want to know what it means to be Jewish. Our children feel that they must identify with one holiday or the other, and that confusion for them perfectly illustrates the issues that my wife and I are slowly working through at home. How does Judaism fit into our world, and how do we in turn respond to our children, who want to understand where we stand with regard to religion?

This discussion starts with the families in which my wife and I were raised. I was brought up Unitarian but have Jewish ancestry traced back to the Vilna Gaon (Elijah ben Solomon), a prominent eighteenth-century rabbi, Talmud scholar, and kabbalist. At a young age, I felt more Jewish and related more to Judaism than to any other religion. My father is fond of telling the story about a long car ride home from a family vacation from Florida. For most of Georgia, I asked him to teach me the Four Questions in Hebrew and English. For hours, I practiced and practiced, driving everyone in the car crazy. Early on I started to read various Jewish books to create my own path to Judaism, starting with Chaim Potok to Elie Weisel to Martin Buber. Each provided a new perspective into Judaism and manhood.

My own father was brought up Jewish (my grandfather was president of his synagogue for years) but left Judaism after a rabbi would not perform the marriage ceremony for my parents (my mother is not Jewish). My father was and still is a wonderful role mode in many ways, especially for being a father, but not necessarily for being a Jewish father. His main focus was and still is today his family, even at the cost of his career at times. He also instilled a sense of curiosity and learning that I carry with me today. Judaism I have had to learn on my own. My wife's family's sense of religion is also complicated. Her mother's family was Jewish. However, her grandparents turned away from Judaism in order to be better integrated into Detroit, Michigan, society in the 1940s and 1950s. This never settled well with my wife's mother, and as a result, she was steadfast in telling her own four daughters that they were Jewish. Religion in my wife's home was defined by a strong sense of family and the importance of supporting each other.

Now my wife and I are trying to determine the path that best suits our family. Our rabbi's words are our guide. He has told us to make our home a synagogue. We try to do that. We want to instill a sense of Judaism. At the same time, we want our children to understand and respect the religious preferences of others. Additionally, we let our children and their daily experiences guide us. We discuss religion with our children and incorporate what they are learning in their respective settings into our household. While neither my wife nor I celebrated Shabbat growing up, we have incorporated it into our family, as our children have learned about it at school and bring home challah on Fridays. Friday nights are now a highlight each week for the whole family. We also try to stay in tune with the Jewish calendar to give us a sense of time passing throughout the year and to create a connection to a rich and ancient heritage. The big question that we face in the future is whether our boys will participate in a formal Jewish education leading to their becoming bar mitzvah.

Raising my own children is a big part of my life. The rest of my hours go to teaching thirteen- and fourteen-year-old boys in an Episcopalian school that attracts many more Christian than Jewish boys. On top of the regular challenges of teaching this age group, I am constantly challenged by the sense of what is to be a man, a Jewish man, and hope to serve as a role model to my students. I want them to see me not only as their teacher, advisor, and coach, but also as a father, a community member, and a Jewish man. I want them to know that I am comfortable in all those roles when I sit with them in chapel three days a week and that I am in earnest in pushing them to be themselves and explore all matters academic, physical, and spiritual (or as we say at St. Albans, mind/body/ spirit). A question often asked at school is, "What does it mean to be a male?" Some offer an answer that is very traditional. A man is one who does not lie, steal, or cheat, or he is one who takes the hard right over the easy wrong. Others try to define a male by the framework of the Christian story, literally the life history of Christ. Through these parables, many lessons of manhood are taught. I urge the boys, both Jewish and Christian, to recognize themselves as young men of a larger community, one that incorporates many religious orientations. Being a man means avoiding and breaking down stereotypes and prejudices that can be so divisive at that age, as young teenagers are desperate to belong to a group or identity. How does one do this? Many of my students look to me for the answers.

I wish I had the answers for them. As at home, I try to be a role model of a good citizen first and encourage discussion between students to create better understanding. From my perspective, it is a process rather than a set path. These boys, like my own (and like myself), will have to make decisions based on the best information they have and then on faith and intuition.

EPILOGUE

When King David falls in love with Bathsheba and then assassinates her husband, the prophet Nathan has a difficult problem. In an ancient world devoid of parliaments, congresses, supreme courts, and most other checks and balances, I imagine that rebuking a sitting king was not done lightly. So Nathan chooses to tell the story of a wealthy farmer who wishes to serve dinner to some guests, and instead of slaughtering one of his many fine animals, he steals the lone, treasured lamb of his poor neighbor. Hearing the story, David flies into a rage and dictates that the wealthy man must be punished "four times over." Nathan then springs his trap and declares, *Atah ha-ish*, "You are the man." David immediately understands, recognizes his error, and repents (II Samuel 11–12).

That is the power of a story. It reveals truth. In the complexity of life, stories often can be more instructive than explication. The method of this book is to tap into the power of story and to heed the truths contained within. Some of those truths are expressed overtly, while others remain buried deeper. Nevertheless, in the voices of these authors, certain themes emerge that instruct us in the nature of Jewish manhood today. If we are serious about nurturing Jewish men's souls, then these truths will help guide our priorities, improve our programs, and

strengthen our communities. By understanding them, we give professionals more effective tools with which to reach and inspire men, and we
give men more options for self-expression and exploration.

Using the Narrative

These individual stories and the truths they contain fit into a larger narrative arc that I have described through the metaphor of yet another story,
the Elijah legend. This narrative defines the three primary dimensions of
a Jewish man's life today: the axis between embracing traditional masculinity and rejecting it, the axis between spiritual confusion and discovery, and the axis between men's alienation from and their connection to
other men. Every Jewish man can locate himself within this three-dimen-
sional schema: defining his masculinity, his spiritual experience, and his
male relationships. Other important dimensions exist as well—Jewish
men's relationships with women (Jewish or otherwise) could be a volume
by itself—but those axes remain beyond the scope of this book.

On all three axes—those of masculinity, spirituality, and relationship—men struggle to find a location that comfortably defines selfhood.
The stories in this book give us clues as to how the Jewish community
can aid in that search. Those clues point to our weaknesses in serving
men, but they also give us opportunities.

RE-CREATING MASCULINITY

For much of Ashkenazi Jewish history, the defining experience of
masculinity has been one of denial and adaptation. Ever since Greek
athletics required an uncircumcised penis, Western rulers have denied
Jewish men access to the most esteemed forms of masculinity—for
example, sporting competition, military leadership, large landholdings,
and political office. Jewish men responded to these restrictions by
adapting Jewish activities to include the masculine norms denied by
society—competitive, aggressive yeshivah study, for example. But as
Jewish men moved away from the male-dominated bounds of Orthodoxy, they entered a limbo in which masculine roles were undefined
by both secular society and the Jewish community. Feminism further
intensified this disorientation.

The authors of many of the essays enter this gray zone and propose the re-creation of Jewish masculinity in new and unexpected ways. Even as the writers use typical masculine imagery, speaking of things like "zeal, sweat, enthusiasm, and, perhaps, testosterone," they apply this language to surprising ends. In the quotation above, Matthew Stern describes Jewish *song leading*! Benjamin David speaks of athletics for the sake of *tikkun olam*. Mark Criden describes synagogue fund-raising in the language of hunting. Douglas Sagal sees a championship boxing belt as a ritual object like a tallit. These men grasp a need for masculine methods, emotion, and experience but seek to transform it. Our challenge is to follow their lead and think beyond the old dynamic of secular exclusion from and Orthodox alternatives to masculinity.

One area of Jewish masculinity in particular needs significant updating: the way that Zionism functions in the American (and Israeli) Jewish imagination. For a long time the Israeli man epitomized the American Jewish fantasy of access to all of that secular power denied throughout the ages. Israeli men were tough, tanned, strong, carried guns, worked with their hands, and built a country. As Jeffrey Salkin describes in his essay, this was the product of an intentional Zionist project of creating a new man who stood in direct opposition to the Diaspora experience. When Israel conquered threatening enemies in only six days of June 1967, this image reached its apex. But as Marc Rosenstein argues, the constant state of war, occupation, and stalemate over the last forty years has taken the bloom off the rose of Zionist masculinity. In light of the failure of toughness to produce peace and normalcy, Israeli men and their American brothers now have more complex attitudes about masculinity. While many American Jewish men still admire and advocate for Israel, Rosenstein argues that the power of the Israeli masculine myth has diminished greatly. This message was driven home to me as I realized that none of the authors solicited for this book mention Israeli masculinity even once.

As we strive to create new Jewish masculine forms, we often lack a frank language of gender. For many authors, writing for this book was their first experience speaking about gender, and they felt the difficulty of language. As Neil Hirsch explains, "I was jealous that the women of my class were worried about their gender and had the opportunity to explore what being female means." The academic study of gender offers a solution. Michael Kimmel shows how studying the social constructs of gender helped him to reconcile Judaism's message of *tikkun olam* with the remnants of misogyny and patriarchy found within our own religion. Jonathon Crane found a similar experience and explains how, at every stage of his life, conversations explicitly about gender became catalysts in the formation of communities of meaning. And David Segal longs to integrate a male form of gender studies into his experience as a rabbinic student, and he challenges feminists to engage men more fully in the feminist project. All of these men have used academic lessons of gender studies to create practical tools for a new self-understanding of masculinity.

We can also find a new language of gender by listening to the men who have been forced to find it. I speak of gay Jewish men who recognize their place outside the bounds of a traditional masculinity that places high value on the wooing of women. As Philip Saperia explains in his essay, "The growing opportunities and unstated social pressures for male-female interaction were difficult to avoid. Since I couldn't summon the appropriate feelings and attractions, I felt uncomfortable as a man— more accurately as I imagined men should feel." Already by adolescence, gay men feel the discomfort that emanates from a tension between selfhood and social norms of masculinity. This tension drives them to seek answers and that leads them to redefine not only their sexuality but also their masculinity. Hearing the voices of our gay brothers can be instrumental in leading the rest of us to discover new options of male selfhood.

This redefinition of masculinity takes on an urgent tone because of the centrality of social action to the liberal Jewish community. Because early Reformers decided that they need not base behavior on Jewish law, embraced a modern rationalism that deemphasizes spirituality, and aspired to assimilate—which, consequently, left Jews without the educational confidence to participate in Torah study—ethics was all that remained. The problem is that the crucial rules for contemporary male success (strength, toughness, emotional withdrawal, unswerving loyalty, swagger) often contain the roots of unethical behavior (domestic abuse, date rape, sexism, closed mindedness, even perhaps presidential machismo). In criticizing the latter, liberal Judaism often implicates the former. This leaves some Jewish men choosing between a masculinity they find socially necessary and a Judaism based almost solely on ethics. Since they do not want to stop being men, should we be surprised when a great number of men stop acting Jewish?

The solution is to marry the social action impulse to the project of creating a new masculine ethics. Rick Recht articulates this position well: "It was the concept of *tikkun olam* that would lead me to draw the connection between my personal aspirations to improve the world and the importance of acknowledging the power, privilege, and impact I have as a Jewish male engaging in these efforts to make a difference." Multiple authors follow this example. Whereas Greeks and Romans once rejected Jews from masculine forms of power, now Jews seem to be rejecting masculinity's abuse of power.

On a practical level, these lessons—the need for a new language of masculinity, the power of gender studies, the insight of our gay brothers, and the Jewish ethical impulse to create alternative masculinities— translate into a curriculum for Jewish male innovation. Jewish women of the past generation have exemplified this spirit, and the tools of feminist ritual, text, community, and behavior can be translated into a male context.

Karen Perolman demonstrates this creativity as she presents the idea of a "glass floor" holding men back from participation in Jewish community (a highly original and helpful concept that deserves much fuller explication than this book allows). The normative notions of masculinity place such an emphasis on achievement and success that day-to-day communal concerns, like general participation, become devalued. Like women who can see advancement through glass ceilings but cannot reach it, men can see participation through glass floors but feel blocked from what we see "below." Maybe we discriminate against ourselves or against other men, psychologically labeling general participation without a specific leadership role as "beneath us." Perolman's innovative idea springs from her feminist thinking and illustrates how that creativity can assist men in our process of re-creating masculinity.

INVITING SELFHOOD

Just as men must travel an axis of masculinity, so too do men locate their souls on a spectrum of confusion and understanding. This search is highly personal and operates with even less social guidance than the quest for masculine self-definition. In the liberal Jewish context of low religious expectations and personal choice, men are frequently left to find a way frequently on their own. This can be very difficult for a group who stereotypically does not like to stop and ask for directions and whose alpha tendencies are to always appear confident, competent, and in control.

How do we understand the search for spiritual understanding? Avram Mandell uses the language of Maslow's hierarchy to call this kind of spiritual search "self-actualization." As Maslow points out, this kind of experience is predicated on the security that lower needs in the hierarchy have been fulfilled. Most importantly, men need to feel confident, enjoy community respect, and develop a healthy self-esteem. Jewish men have no problem in these areas in their secular lives, but the Jewish context often undermines these prerequisites. I will not be the first author to note the contrast between many Jews' secular educational success and Jewish educational failure. Mandell describes exactly this dynamic as the difference between "Successful Businessmen and Lawyers (SBLs)" and "Learned Jewish Males (LJMs)." How are "SBLs," men who base so much of public life on success, power, mastery, and competence, supposed to feel secure in an environment that emphasizes all of their educational gaps?

Instead, we need to empower men to see their form of Jewish identity as authentic and valued. That would require a broadening of the definition of Jewish learnedness and spirituality. A number of essays describe Jewish identity and spirituality in unexpected ways. Wilson Baer focuses his Judaism on *menschlichkeit*, how he carries himself and treats others. Irwin Ayes's essay centers around the value of reaching out and helping other people. Alan Moskoff identifies the essence of his Jewish identity as "to help my customers as best as I can and with understanding, treating seniors, the poor, and other ethnic groups with respect and equality." Luminaries no less than David Ellenson, the president of the Hebrew Union College–Jewish Institute of Religion, and Eugene Borowitz, the foremost Reform theologian of our day, describe major aspects of their Jewish identity by illustrating a wide variety of role models who operated outside of the synagogue altogether.

If Jewish men find meaning and purpose (indeed, Jewish purpose) through the development of upright character and altruistic behavior, then perhaps those traits should be counted and promoted as legitimate expressions of Jewishness. Yet our communities emphasize study and prayer, while acts of loving-kindness are often limited to formal synagogue programs. The only time we uphold and honor someone's character is in their eulogy. Men should not have to wait until they die to be honored for what they see as their fundamental Jewishness. Altruism, giving, service to others, ethics, and the courage to stand up to peers are all elements of the soul and should be included in the spiritual mission of our congregations.

While some men find Jewishness in the concrete quality of behavior and character, other men discover a place within Judaism through an embrace of the unknown. Lary Bloom, Meir Feldman, and David Gottlieb all struggled with Judaism until they realized that part of the journey was a comfort with the as-yet unresolved elements of life and faith. This openness to the unknown requires tremendous confidence and can be crushed in an environment where it seems like everyone else "knows" what is going on or "knows" what they believe. In order to validate and reassure a seeker, especially a man with a lifetime of baggage pressing him to always show competence, leaders need to show vulnerability and lack of certainty. Feldman, for example, describes the importance of Rabbi David Wolpe sharing his doubts in the development of his own Jewish confidence.

To return to Maslow, all of these issues—the problem of uneven Jewish education, the need to broaden definitions of spirituality, and the embrace of the unknown—require that we follow the example of Daniel Zemel, who aims to create "a welcoming place where people can relax and feel free, confident, and themselves as opposed to judged and intimidated." For Zemel, his baseball jersey was less a statement about masculinity and sports than it was a signal that his Temple Micah is a place where people can be themselves. Too often our synagogues come laden with expectations—a strong Torah education, an obvious spirituality, or a sureness in areas of belief—that prevent men from feeling comfortable enough to engage in self-actualization.

If we do not alter the way we communicate spiritual security, then men will privatize their spiritual searching and Jewish identity. Richard Gartner describes how he always had a sense of different "Jewish men dancing inside me" but that he rarely expressed his Judaism. Only in psychoanalysis did he find enough security to allow the analyst's Judaism to penetrate his private domain. Many men never find that kind of security.

This issue of inviting men to find selfhood in Judaism is huge in the Jewish world today. As I write this epilogue, Ron Wolfson's book *The Spirituality of Welcoming* is currently inspiring all types of synagogues to reconsider how they invite people to participate. As boards, committees, and clergy reconsider welcoming, they would do well to include the powerful implications of gender on the subject. Men and women need different kinds of welcoming.

Honoring Male Relationships

Joseph Soloveitchik's masterwork *The Lonely Man of Faith* compares the two versions of the creation of humanity found in Genesis 1 and 2. The first Adam was created in God's image, to rule over the creatures, and he "constructs his own world and succeeds in controlling his environment through manipulating his own mathematical constructs and creations."[1] The second Adam, by contrast, was formed from dust, unable to breathe without God's help, existentially lonely and seeking relationship. When I utilize this text with men's groups, the men invariably associate the first Adam with men, and the second with women. Then I present Soloveitchik:

> Adam the first, majestic man of dominion and success, and Adam the second, the lonely man of faith, obedience, and defeat, are not two different people locked in an external confrontation... but **one person** who is involved in self-confrontation. In every one of us abide two *personae*—the creative majestic Adam the first, and the submissive, humble Adam the second.[2]

The men start with the idea that they ought to be independent beings whose sole purpose is work. Soloveitchik reminds them of the part of the self that needs love, family, friendship, children, loyalty, and community. Men know the need for relationship is there, but they do not wear it on their sleeves.

As Soloveitchik points out, this tension between independence and intimacy, goes back to the beginnings of Judaism, if not the beginnings of humanity. The sage Hillel picked up on this when he said, "If I am not for myself, who will be for me? And if I am for myself alone, then what am I? If not now, then when?" (*Pirkei Avot* 1:14). In fact, in his book *A New Psychology of Men,* psychologist William Pollack chooses this quotation as his epigraph to the chapter on relationships. Pollack connects male stress in relationships to the early formative years in which a young boy separates from his mother while struggling through an Oedipal competition with his father.[3] Whatever the reason, we can safely say that Genesis, Hillel, Soloveitchik, and Pollack are onto something.

Unfortunately, the essays in this book suggest that the need for male relationships is not obvious to the men. Like Elijah who had to be instructed to find a disciple, men often ignore or neglect their male relationships. Instead, they often seem to form deep connections without intention. They usually do not go out and say, "I need to share my emotions with other men," but they will find an activity, pretense, or environment that enables just that kind of connection. For Benjamin David and Stephen Wise, that is sports. For Michael Freedman, it is freemasonry. For Stephen Breslauer and Charlie Niederman, it is Brotherhood. While these men do not usually speak about relationships explicitly (Freedman does talk about his father's involvement as a Mason as well), the subject lurks in the background.

The authors who do explicitly mention the need for male bonding were either in crisis (like Stuart Debowsky or Dan Moskovitz) or operated with a heightened gender awareness (like Neil Hirsch). For these men, either the urgency of the crisis or their postfeminist education broke through the more typical male obtuseness surrounding the need for relationships. What we can learn from this is that other men who are not explicit about their need for male community still might yearn for its presence—even if they do not know it.

Because of changing cultural norms and the ethical imperative of egalitarianism, many of the all-male communities of the past—the *schvitz*, the minyan, the shabbes afternoon Torah study—no longer exist. While their memories provide many men, like Norman Cohen and Philip Saperia, with a comforting foundation for male identity, their present absence leaves many men wanting. Some writers describe the few remaining Jewish all-male communities—Alan Neuhauser describes the male bunk life at camp, while Charlie Niederman and Stephen Breslauer illustrate the importance of their Brotherhood experiences—but many men hardly experience these forms.

This means that male communities need to be created. (When we follow the ethical imperatives outlined in the introduction to this book, male communities do not portend an atavistic approach to Judaism.) For some reason, not having women in the room allows men more freedom to ask themselves big questions. Perhaps it is the absence of perceived women's expectations, or the need to uphold a certain image in front of women. Whatever the reason, James Prosnit's and Dan Moskovitz's essays demonstrate how easy men's groups are to form and how effective they can be. Even for men who do not participate, an imagined community, like the one that Victor Appel describes in his essay, can widen a man's outlook and provide a potential option for personal discovery, even if it is not utilized.

A second method of deepening male relationships is through the use of ritual. David Bergman articulates the power that ritual has to bring men together, and even though he has found a ritual to connect with peers, he longs for other rituals to help him connect with his father. Men have begun to create new rituals, most notably the *Kiddush L'vanah*, a product of the Jewish Renewal Movement described in Owen Gottlieb's essay. While this ritual, reminiscent of Iron John style male gatherings, might work for some, it might be too alternative for others. What about rituals within the current framework of the synagogue?

Can we think creatively about the existing areas of male interest and activity in the synagogue—Brotherhood bagel breakfasts, leadership experiences, High Holy Day ushering, the building committee—and add an additional frame of spirituality to those experiences? Can we move beyond Brotherhood Shabbat to find *g'milut Chasadim*, acts of loving-kindness, that speak to particular male life moments? Are there particular things we should be doing for men who go through divorce, men who lose their jobs, men whose sons are in the midst of rebellion, or men who have just seen their favorite team win the World Series (see Daniel Zemel's essay)? All of these rituals could be meaningful in themselves, but they also serve as pretense to bring men together and to foster relationships.

One particular male relationship deserves mention here: that between fathers and sons. Father-son relationships have always had their share of strife, rebellions, and tensions, and essays in this book point to a need for opportunities that give men and their sons reasons to come together. (Maybe our rituals need to serve that need as well.) Dana Jennings's letter to his sons demonstrates how powerful a Jewish conversation can be between the generations. But most essays about dads and sons contain a sense of unspoken conversations. Most men want something different out of their fathers. Either because they are dealing with real pain and rejection, like Simeon Maslin, or because of a desire to connect across differences, like Paul Schoenfeld and David Bergman, many men feel estranged from this key relationship. Doug Barden finds some solace by synthesizing his father's and grandfather's values into a form of validation that his father alone could not (or would not) give him.

On the opposite side, a number of men found the fatherhood experience extraordinarily valuable in the formation of Jewish identity. For Yigal Rechtman, an Israeli, it was fatherhood, not army service, not growing up in a Jewish state, not speaking Hebrew, that raised fundamental questions about what it means to be a Jew. John Linder asked similar questions when his son was born, and these questions led him eventually to rabbinical school. So from the perspective of both sons and fathers, a need and opportunity exist for religious conversation, ritual, support, and celebration.

Catalyst

As I worked on gathering essays for this book, I discovered a powerful lesson about the nature of Jewish masculinity today. Even though many of the men were confused or stumped by the initial request to consider the intersection of masculinity and Judaism, they found the task highly rewarding. The community formed between me, the soliciting editor, and them, the writers, was enough to initiate a journey toward meaning, and almost every one of them thanked me profusely for presenting the idea.

The lesson from this experience is that while the conversation is relatively new and the language, structures, and communities largely unformed, the desire and ability is there, in men, waiting. All we have to do is ask.

The problem is that we are not asking. We need leaders, and in particular rabbis, who will initiate new male Jewish conversations. Unfortunately, very few rabbis engage in this kind of work with their congregations, and rabbinic training does not yet contain enough emphasis on exploring masculinity, manhood, or male community. (I had more educational sessions in rabbinic school on transgenderism—not that there's anything wrong with that—than I did on men!) While the vast majority of rabbis are ordained with a significant knowledge and understanding of the importance of feminism and its implications, few possess an equal understanding of particulars of men and Judaism. Without such awareness and without rabbinic time and energy, a serious embrace and encouragement of a new men's Judaism will not get off the ground.

We should note that the gender of the rabbi does not matter. Jennifer Jaech's essay shows how a synagogue that has had a female senior rabbi for over a generation—Rabbi Helene Ferris served the congregation before Rabbi Jaech—can also have a thriving male community. The female rabbi simply needs an awareness of the changing nature of masculinity, men's spirituality, and the different ways that men form relationships. Jaech clearly demonstrates this awareness. So naysayers who complain about female clergy pushing men out stand on very shaky ground.

My aspiration is that this book can function as a form of mentorship, relationship, ritual, community, authenticity, security, and language, in short, an example of how to construct a new men's Judaism. The ideas presented in this epilogue all stem from the essays themselves. Leaders, groups, and individuals can use this text as a catalyst for a new and more creative approach to men in our community.

The great lesson of these stories and the narrative they form is the journey from *expectation* to *self-definition*. Whether the *expectation* is a tired stereotype about manhood or an estranged connection to God, it is based outside the self, and it forms within the individual disillusionment and alienation. These emotions are likely the root of emotional discontent and stress and could even lead to unhealthy antisocial behavior. *Self-definition*, on the other hand, is something sought by the individual, emerging out of the path from confusion and often appearing unexpectedly. The unpredictable nature of this redemptive experience—like the "still, small voice," that is surprisingly more divine than the obvious natural demonstrations—leaves space for the individual to define his own path and to share that path with others. I pray that this book helps initiate men on the route from expectation to self-definition and in doing so will help our community form healthier, stronger, and more constructive forms of Jewish masculinity.

NOTES

1. Joseph Soloveitchik. *The Lonely Man of Faith*, New York: Three Leaves Press, Doubleday, 1965. pp. 18.
2. Ibid., pp. 80–81.
3. William S. Pollack, "No Man is an Island," in *A New Psychology of Men* ed. Ronald F. Levant and William S. Pollack (New York: Basic Books, 1995).

APPENDIX

Men's Voices Project

What does it mean to be a man? Fifty years ago the answer was obvious, and the question ridiculous. Terms like manly, manhood, and masculine did not need explanation. But today, when women assume so many of the roles formerly reserved for men, and when men take on many of the traits usually associated with women, and vice versa, do we really know how to answer this question?

And what does it mean to be a Jewish man? As long as we have been in the Diaspora, Jewish men have had to define themselves separately from, and sometimes in contradistinction to, the surrounding culture. So the stereotype became the bookish, indoor, intellectual accountant, as opposed to the athletic, strong, outdoorsy quarterback. But as the relationship between "us" and "them" warms and cools, the options for Jewish men changes as well.

Just as women's inclusion forces questions about gender roles, so too does greater assimilation force questions about Jewish distinctiveness. So all of the old assumptions are up for grabs. While none of us want to go backwards—re-excluding women or separating from American society—we also do not quite know what it means to move forward.

Simultaneously with all of this, the traditional models of Jewish manhood have disappeared. The cultural fixtures of Eastern-European immigrant Orthodox Judaism—the *schvitz*, the Shabbes afternoon study session, and the early gathering hashkama minyan—used to be the places where a boy would learn how to be a Jewish man. Today, who teaches our young men how to be Jewish? Even if he lives in the same town with his family, his father largely does not show up, the male communities of the past do not exist, and the leadership of the community may in fact be female. Where are the male role models?

Not only do individual men live in an age of gender role confusion, but as a community we see decreasing rates of male participation across the board. Girls outnumber boys in all youth programming. Women show up for services without their husbands. According to one landmark study, "the 'action' where Jewish activity among the moderately affiliated is concerned now rests with women." If Jewish men question how to define their identities, few seem to turn to our tradition or communities for answers.

We need a national conversation on how our communities can better serve men, and how men can better define themselves. The purpose of this book is to start that conversation. I hope to record the myriad ways that Jewish men experience life and reflect upon their own manhood. The book includes men who consider themselves religious and those who do not. It includes men who epitomize traditional forms of masculinity—athletes, soldiers, business leaders—and the average Joe among us. It includes the perspectives of those who spend time in the few remaining male spaces—the camp counselor, the fraternity president, the Orthodox Jew—and those who watch the reactions of men in mixed spaces. The reflections included herein represent individual voices responding to a communal change. Through this project I hope to give the Jewish community a snapshot to consider how men's lives and their souls are evolving in the present moment.

URJ Men's Voices Project
Rabbi Michael Holzman

Thank you for agreeing to participate in the Men's Voices Project. We hope to gather a large number of short essays that capture the perspectives of Jewish men today. Please consider the following guidelines in your writing.

- Pieces should be 1000-1500 words long.
- All essays are due by December 31, 2006 (of course earlier submissions are always helpful).
- Essays should reflect personal experience and observation.
- If you know of someone who might have offer valuable input to this project, please feel free to contact me to suggest a new writer.
- Contact me with any questions or your final submission. All submissions should be electronic in Microsoft Word. Please e-mail me (rabbiholzman@hotmail.com)
- While we hope to print as many submissions as possible, the publisher reserves the right to limit the number of essays, and I cannot guarantee that your work will make it into the final book.
- Selected works will be edited and the editor may request additional drafts.
- All submissions become the property and copyright of the URJ Press and we will not be able to return any essays to the author.
- Authors of published essays will receive two copies of the book as a small token of appreciation.
- Text excerpts or quotes used in the essays should include full citations, including title, author, publisher, year, page number (or if from a journal, volume number and page number). Please do not write, "The Torah says," or "The Sages teach," but rather give the full citation (i.e. Babylonian Talmud Kid. 31a.).

Please include with your submission:
1. A 2-3 line brief bio.
2. Your address, e-mail address and telephone information.

When writing, your essay should represent your own opinion, perspective and observations. Think about yourself, your personal identity as a Jew and as a man in America. Also think about the way in which you instruct or influence other Jewish men, and consider the men who have influenced you. Also consider the path of manhood and Judaism that you have defined for yourself.

Men's Voices Project
Leading Questions

The purpose of this book is to hear your voice and perspective on Jewish manhood today. You probably fall into one of three categories:

1. If you are a Jewish man, this is about the way your live your life, how Judaism fits into that life, and how being a man might affect the way you see the world and our religion.

2. If you work with Jewish men (and are a woman), then I am curious to hear about your observations, perspectives as a Jewish woman. I am curious to hear about what you think of Jewish manhood today and how you feel about the way that today's masculinity affects your life.

3. If you are a both a man and you work with Jewish men, then you can reflect on both what you experience and what you observe. You can also reflect on how your version of Jewish masculinity serves as a model to other Jewish men.

For group 1, consider the following:

- How does being a man influence the ways you think, the options you allow yourself, the expectations you have?
- How does being a Jewish man affect you?
- In what ways do you teach other men in your lives (your sons, brothers, colleagues, students, friends) about Judaism and masculinity?
- Who taught you about Judaism and manhood and what did they teach?
- How do you think the experience of being a Jewish man has changed since your father's generation, or your grandfather's generation?
- What would you like to change about the way that Jewish manhood functions both within the Jewish community and the larger world?

For group 2, consider the following:

- What do you observe about the way that Jewish men interact with their Judaism and their awareness of their gender?
- How do the expectations placed upon Jewish men today affect your life as a woman, and as a woman who works with men?

- What would you like to change about the way that Jewish manhood functions both within the Jewish community and the larger world?
- Do you think that Jewish men are generally healthy spiritually?

For group 3, consider the questions above and the following:

- What elements of masculinity and Judaism to you project to other Jewish men? Do you do this consciously?
- How does your work with other Jewish men change the way you think about your own Judaism or your masculinity?

AUTHOR BIOGRAPHIES

RABBI MICHAEL GARRET HOLZMAN is associate rabbi and the director of the Youth Learning Program at Congregation Rodeph Shalom in Philadelphia, Pennsylvania. He is a graduate of Washington University in St. Louis, and the Hebrew Union College–Jewish Institute of Religion in New York. Holzman lives outside Philadelphia with his wife, Nicole, and their children, Avi and Talia.

RABBI VICTOR S. APPELL, a native New Yorker, grew up in the Reform Movement. In high school, he served as a regional NFTY president and spent three summers on the staff of URJ Joseph Eisner Camp in Great Barrington, Massachusetts. After a decade-long career in sales and marketing, Appell decided to pursue a lifelong dream of becoming a rabbi and was ordained from Hebrew Union College–Jewish Institute of Religion in 1999. For four years he served as assistant and then associate rabbi of Temple Jeremiah in Northfield, Illinois. For two years Appell served Temple Emanu-El in Edison, New Jersey. In July of 2005 he joined the staff of the Union for Reform Judaism as the Small Congregations Specialist in the Department of Synagogue Management. Appell, his partner, and their two children live in Metuchen, New Jersey.

IRWIN AYES is a native Floridian who attended Emory University in Atlanta and medical school in San Francisco. He is a retired podiatric physician and surgeon. He and his wife, Hannah, live in Largo, Florida. They are members of Congregation Bnai Israel in St Petersburg, Florida.

WILSON BAER is an eleventh grade student at Lenox Memorial Middle and High School in Lenox, Massachusetts, where he serves as a peer mentor for middle school students and participates in the band, chorus, and theater programs. A member of the confirmation class and youth group at Hevreh of Southern Berkshire in Great Barrington, Baer also participates in regional and national NFTY events and is an alumnus of URJ Joseph Eisner Camp. In 2003, Baer wrote a prize-winning essay published on Interfaithfamily.com, and he is a contributor to the "Young Judaism" column for the *Berkshire Jewish Voice.*

DOUG BARDEN assumed the position of executive director of the Men of Reform Judaism (formerly the North American Federation of Temple Brotherhoods) in February 1994. In early 2006 he authored *Wrestling with Jacob and Esau: Fighting the Flight of Men, A Modern Day Crisis for the Reform Movement.*

DAVID BERGMAN is senior manager at Health Dialog, a disease management company. He has served in a variety of professional and lay capacities in Jewish communities in Oregon, San Francisco, Chicago, New York, and Jerusalem. He currently serves as the president of the Noyes Street Shul (Congregation Shaarey Tphiloh), the oldest Orthodox synagogue in Portland, Maine, where he lives with his wife, Anne, and their children, Jacob and Elisheva. Bergman was a proud member of WeSTY (Western States Temple Youth) and served as the youth group president for Congregation Beth Israel in Portland, Oregon from 1990 to 1991.

LARY BLOOM is a columnist for the *New York Times* and *Connecticut* magazine. His latest book is *Letters From Nuremberg*, a collaboration with Senator Christopher J. Dodd. Others include *The Writer Within, Lary Bloom's Connecticut Notebook*, and *When the Game Is on the Line* (with

Rick Horrow). Bloom teaches memoir, writes plays and lyrics, and lives in Chester, Connecticut. His Web site is www.larybloom.net.

RABBI EUGENE BOROWITZ, PH.D., is Distinguished University Professor and Sigmund L. Falk Distinguished Professor of Education and Jewish Religious Thought at Hebrew Union College–Jewish Institute of Religion, New York. In 1996 the National Foundation of Jewish Culture presented him with its medal for Lifetime Achievement in Scholarship, Jewish Religious Thought. In 2005 the Union for Reform Judaism bestowed its Maurice N. Eisendrath Bearer of Light Award to him for his contribution to Reform Judaism. His most recent book is *A Touch of the Sacred: A Theologian's Informal Guide to Jewish Belief.*

STEVE BRESLAUER is a husband and father, a scientist, a national and international Reform Jewish leader, and an ardent Zionist. He has held several positions of leadership in the Jewish community, including the Houston Jewish Federation, United Jewish Appeal, and World Union for Progressive Judaism. His roots are midwestern, he lives in the South, and his perspective is worldwide.

ELLEN BRESNER is a public school special educator of thirty-two years. She lives in Marblehead, Massachusetts, with her husband Mark. Their young adult sons Bobby, Ethan, and Alex have begun independent paths beyond home. Bresner participates weekly in Shabbat services and Torah study at Temple Emanu-El with Rabbis David Meyer and Debra Kassoff.

RABBI JONATHAN K. CRANE is a Ph.D. candidate at the University of Toronto. A former Wexner Graduate Fellow, he has published on Judaism and war, Jewish law and ethics, Jewish burial of gentiles, human rights, Gandhian philosophy, and modern Jewish thought. He is currently writing his dissertation on the rhetoric of modern Jewish ethics. He lives with his wife, Lindy Miller, in Chennai, India.

MARK CRIDEN has been the executive director of Temple Beth Zion in Buffalo, New York, one of America's largest and oldest Reform synagogues, for eleven years, following careers as a merger and acquisition lawyer and investment banker. He and his wife, the psychotherapist Nicole Urdang, have two children, Madelaine, a graduate of Hamilton College, and Maxwell, a sophomore at Hampshire College. Criden keeps his spear as sharp as possible.

RABBI BENJAMIN DAVID has been the assistant rabbi at Temple Sinai in Roslyn Heights, New York, since 2005. He is an avid writer and runner and is cofounder of the nonprofit initiative RunningRabbis.com. David and his wife Lisa met as campers at the URJ Camp Harlam in the Poconos. They currently live in Forest Hills, New York.

STUART DEBOWSKY is an architectural project manager, specializing in multifamily residential development in South Florida. He holds a professional undergraduate degree with honors from the University of Miami and a master's degree in construction management from Florida International University. An award-winning designer, Debowsky currently resides in Coral Gables, Florida, with his new bride, Shari, and their Jack Russell terrier, Lucy. In addition to being an avid traveler and supporter of the arts, Debowsky serves on numerous service committees at Miami's Temple Beth Am, advocates for the Reform Jewish youth movement, NFTY, and supports his lifelong summer camp alma mater, URJ Camp Coleman.

(JOEL) JOE EGLASH is a recognized authority in the field of Jewish music, developing and marketing musical artists and products with his firm, Eglash Creative Group. In 2006, Joe launched oySongs.com, the first Web site with exclusively Jewish music downloads. Formerly managing director of Transcontinental Music Publications, music publishing division of the Union for Reform Judaism, he has hundreds of publications to his credit. Eglash is active as a guitarist, arranger, and composer in Tulsa, Oklahoma, where he resides with his wife, Cantor Kari Siegel-Eglash, and daughter Arielle.

RABBI DAVID ELLENSON, PH.D., president of Hebrew Union College–Jewish Institute of Religion (HUC-JIR) and I. H. and Anna

Grancell Professor of Jewish Religious Thought, is a distinguished rabbi, scholar, and leader of the Reform Movement. He is internationally recognized for his publications and research in the areas of Jewish religious thought, ethics, and modern Jewish history. He received his Ph.D. from Columbia University in 1981 and was ordained by HUC-JIR in 1977. He is a fellow at the Shalom Hartman Institute of Jerusalem and a fellow and lecturer at the Institute of Advanced Studies at Hebrew University in Jerusalem. Ellenson's extensive publications include *Tradition in Transition: Orthodoxy, Halakhah and the Boundaries of Modern Jewish History* (1989), *Rabbi Esriel Hildesheimer and the Creation of a Modern Jewish Orthodoxy* (1990; nominated for the National Jewish Book Council's award for Outstanding Book in Jewish History, 1990), and *Between Tradition and Culture: The Dialectics of Jewish Religion and Identity in the Modern World* (1994). His latest book, *After Emancipation: Jewish Religious Responses to Modernity*, a compilation of essays on Jewish values and identity, the challenge of emancipation, denominational responses, modern responsa, and contemporary works of legal and liturgical creativity, was published by Hebrew Union College Press in 2004.

RABBI MEIR FELDMAN is most proud of being husband to Rabbi Tara Feldman and father to Gabriel (Gavi), age five, and Adina, age 2. Along with Tara, he is presently associate rabbi at Temple Israel in Memphis, Tennessee, and before that served as a Marshall T. Meyer Rabbinic Fellow at New York's B'nai Jeshurun. Prior to Meir's Jewish journey, he was an attorney for seven years, first as a litigator at a Wall Street law firm and then as a federal prosecutor in Los Angeles. Beyond his family, Meir's passions include scuba diving, skiing, Jewish texts, Israel, and the melodies of Shlomo Carlebach.

JASON FREEDMAN recently served as regional director of youth for the URJ's Southeast Council and assistant director at URJ Camp Coleman. He is currently enrolled at Dartmouth's Tuck School of Business, studying ways organizations can better address the needs of the world.

MICHAEL FREEDMAN, ED.D., is a retired high school science teacher and department head formerly with the School District of

Philadelphia, and a retired assistant professor of science education formerly with Fordham University Graduate School of Education. He is a past master of his Masonic Lodge and currently serves as its treasurer.

DR. RICHARD GARTNER is a psychologist and psychoanalyst practicing in New York City; a training and supervising analyst at the William Alanson White Institute (and founding director of its Sexual Abuse Program); author of *Beyond Betrayal: Taking Charge of Your Life after Boyhood Sexual Abuse* and *Betrayed as Boys: Psychodynamic Treatment of Sexually Abused Men*; and a past president of MaleSurvivor: The National Organization against Male Sexual Victimization.

DAVID GOTTLIEB is executive director and cofounder of Full Circle Communities, Inc., a developer and manager of affordable housing. He is one of twenty Chicago-area participants in the 2006 cohort of the Wexner Heritage Program. He is coauthor of *Letters to a Buddhist Jew* (2004) and frequently writes on Jewish issues in his blog, *True Ancestor* (http://trueancestor.typepad.com). Gottlieb, his wife, and three children live in Northbrook, Illinois.

OWEN GOTTLIEB is currently a third-year rabbinic student at Hebrew Union College–Jewish Institute of Religion in New York City. Gottlieb has taught Hebrew at Central Synagogue in Manhattan and hip-hop and modern dance in Arad, Israel, and he has written film and television scripts for Paramount and Universal Studios in Los Angeles. His passions include teaching Torah through popular culture, Judaism in nature, dance and movement liturgy, and meditation. He holds an A.B. from Dartmouth College and an M.A. from University of Southern California, School of Cinema-Television, and is a member of the Writers Guild of America, West.

RABBI GARY GREENEBAUM is the U.S. Director of Interreligious Affairs of the American Jewish Committee. During his career he has also served as a congregational rabbi and a Hillel director.

NEIL HIRSCH is a rabbinic student at the Hebrew Union College–Jewish Institute of Religion's New York campus. He is originally from Houston, Texas, and attended Tufts University, where he studied art history and classics. Neil began studying gender issues from a Jewish perspective while in college.

RABBI JENNIFER JAECH serves as senior rabbi of Temple Israel of Northern Westchester in Croton-on-Hudson, New York. Jaech received ordination from Hebrew Union College–Jewish Institute of Religion in 2003 and earned an M.A. in Hebrew literature from HUC-JIR in 2002 and a B.A. from the Evergreen State College in 1985. Prior to pursuing the rabbinate, Jaech lived in Washington State and worked in higher education administration, government relations, and politics. She lives with her husband, S. David Sperling, and her son, Isaac Meyer, in Peekskill, New York.

DANA JENNINGS is an editor for the *New York Times* and the author of the forthcoming *Sing Me Back Home: Love, Death and Country Music*. He is a member of Temple Ner Tamid in Bloomfield, New Jersey.

BETH KANDER is a freelance writer and actress, but she does have a day job as director of programming at the Goldring/Woldenberg Institute in Jackson, Mississippi. She earned her master of social work degree from the University of Michigan and spent her undergraduate years at Brandeis University. A perpetual wanderer, she'll always slow down for good sushi, good conversation, or bad jokes; she shares weekly observations at www.bethweek.blogspot.com.

MICHAEL KIMMEL is a professor of sociology at SUNY Stony Brook and the author or editor of more than twenty volumes on men and masculinities. His most recent books include *Manhood in America, the Gendered Society* and the forthcoming *Guyland: The Inner Lives of Young Men, 18–26*. He is national spokesperson for the National Organization for Men Against Sexism (NOMAS) and lectures all over the world supporting gender equality.

RABBI STEVEN Z. LEDER is the senior rabbi of Wilshire Boulevard Temple in Los Angeles. His is the author of numerous articles and essays as well as The Extraordinary Nature of Ordinary Things and More

Money Than God: Living a Rich Life Without Losing Your Soul. Best of all, he is Aaron and Hannah's dad and Betsy's husband.

RABBI JOHN A. LINDER grew up in Buffalo, New York, one of five siblings, and received his B.A. degree from Amherst College, graduating cum laude in American studies. John spent his first career as a community organizer for Massachusetts Fair Share and a labor organizer for the Hospital and Health Care Employees Union, 1199/AFL-CIO in Columbus, Ohio. Linder went on to work in his family's recycling business, establishing himself as a leader in the industry before making the decision to enter seminary at Hebrew Union College–Jewish Institute of Religion in Jerusalem and Cincinnati. He received a master's in Hebrew letters in 2002 and was ordained in 2003. Linder serves as a rabbi at Congregation B'nai Jehoshua Beth Elohim in Glenview, Illinois, and counts his blessings for his wife, Nancy Levy Linder, and their son, David.

AVRAM MANDELL holds a master's in Jewish education from HUC-JIR Rhea School of Education and a B.S. in marketing from Miami University. He is currently the director of education at Leo Baeck Temple in Los Angeles, where he has been since 2004. He is a purebred of the Reform Movement, having grown up at Baltimore Hebrew Congregation, participating in NFTY and working at URJ summer camps. His hobbies include stand-up comedy and percussion.

RABBI SIMEON J. MASLIN is a past president of the Central Conference of American Rabbis and of the Chicago and Philadelphia Boards of Rabbis. He is rabbi emeritus of Reform Congregation Keneseth Israel of Elkins Park, Pennsylvania, and previously served historic congregations in Curacao and Chicago. He is the author of numerous articles and of a forthcoming volume of biblical essays.

ALAN MOSKOFF is a registered pharmacist. He and his wife, Maria, have two children, Ben and Micah, and live in Somerset, Massachusetts. He is a member of Temple Beth-El in Providence, Rhode Island, where he is a past brotherhood president. His interests include reading and spending time with his family. Currently, he is a national officer of Men of Reform Judaism (formerly the North American Federation of Temple Brotherhoods).

RABBI DAN MOSKOVITZ was ordained at Hebrew Union College–Jewish Institute of Religion in 2000 and also holds a master's degree in Jewish education from HUC-JIR. He is a rabbi at Temple Judea in Tarzana, California, where as part of his rabbinate he continues to lead a monthly men's discussion group and a variety of men's programming. Moskovitz is also the coauthor of the forthcoming *The Man Seder: A Passover Seder Experience for Jewish Men* (MRJ, 2008). He is married to Sharon Mishler, and they are the proud parents of Judah.

ALAN NEUHAUSER spent six great summers as a camper at URJ Camp Harlam in Pennsylvania and then "completed the cycle" by returning as a counselor for two years. He attends Vassar College, where he is majoring in history and is a member of the varsity swim team and contributing writer and photographer for the Vassar student newspaper.

CHARLIE NIEDERMAN is the chancellor of the Jewish Chautauqua Society, the interfaith arm of the Men of Reform Judaism, and also serves as the president of Temple Beth David, Westminster, California. He is also the Orange County coordinator of the Walking Together interfaith program for Christian, Muslim, and Jewish fourth to sixth grade students and their parents. He is a retired Coast Guard captain and had a later career as an executive in the Orange County government. He and his wife Cathy have four daughters and two grandchildren. Their third daughter, Deborah, is a Jewish educator.

KAREN PEROLMAN grew up on the East Coast and is a graduate of the University of Maryland, where she pursued Jewish and women's studies programs. She currently lives in New York, where she is a third-year rabbinic student at the Hebrew Union College–Jewish Institute of Religion.

RABBI JAMES PROSNIT was ordained in 1981 and has been senior rabbi at Congregation B'nai Israel in Bridgeport, Connecticut, since 1990. Prior to serving in this position, he was associate rabbi at Holy

Blossom Temple in Toronto and Congregation Rodeph Sholom in New York City. He is a lecturer at Fairfield University in the Department of Religious Studies. Prosnit has served on a variety of URJ and CCAR commissions and committees, including the Commission on Social Action and the Commission on Interreligious Affairs.

MIKE RANKIN is a retired navy medical officer and is a professor of psychiatry and behavioral sciences at George Washington University School of Medicine. He is a member of the URJ Board of Trustees, vice chair of the Commission on Religious Living, Synagogue Music, and Worship, and a member of the Commission on Reform Jewish Outreach. Additionally, Rankin is a member of both Temple Rodef Shalom, Falls Church, Virginia, and Anshe Chesed Congregation, Vicksburg, Mississippi.

RICK RECHT is the top touring musician in Jewish music, playing over 150 dates each year in the United States and abroad. Recht has revolutionized and elevated the genre of Jewish rock music as a powerful tool for developing Jewish pride and identity. Recht has played at over seventy URJ, Ramah, JCC, and private camps around the country. He has also been featured in concert at the NFTY, BBYO, and USY international conventions, CAJE, URJ Biennial, and major Jewish festivals throughout the country.

YIGAL RECHTMAN grew up on Kibbutz Tzora, near Jerusalem. He served in the Israeli Defense Force's Communication Corps. He then relocated to New York, where he first earned a computer science degree from New York University and later his M.S. in accounting from Pace University, New York. Following his graduation, he continued to work as a computer specialist and an auditor. He is now a certified public accountant with specializations in forensic accounting, internal controls, and fraud detection. Rechtman lives in Brooklyn, New York, with his wife and two children.

DANIEL S. ROBISON lives and works in Washington, D.C., with his wife, Hadley, and their three boys. In addition to teaching, he has worked as a beekeeper, a mountain guide, and an environmental economist; he is currently a portfolio manager.

Rabbi Marc J. Rosenstein grew up in Highland Park, Illinois, at North Shore Congregation Israel and first visited Israel in the Eisendrath International Exchange (EIE) program. He was ordained at Hebrew Union College–Jewish Institute of Religion in 1975 and later received a Ph.D. from the Hebrew University. He served as assistant rabbi in Port Washington, New York, and as a day high school principal in Chicago and Philadelphia. In 1990, Rosenstein made *aliyah*, moving with his family to Moshav Shorashim in the central Galilee. He is the director of the the Galilee Foundation for Value Education, which engages in programming that fosters pluralism and coexistence.

Rabbi Douglas B. Sagal is a native of New Jersey. He has served as rabbi of Congregation Beth Shalom-Rodef Zedek in Chester, Connecticut, and KAM Isaiah Israel in Chicago, and he is currently the senior rabbi of Temple Emanu-El in Westfield, New Jersey. He continues his career as an amateur boxer.

Scott Sager was born and raised in Chicago and now resides in Brooklyn, New York. A former social worker and teacher, he is well ensconced in his second career as an at-home parent, neighborhood mensch, and freelance writer.

Rabbi Jeffrey K. Salkin is the founding rabbi and executive director of Kol Echad: Making Judaism Matter, a trans-denominational learning community in Atlanta, Georgia. A well-known teacher and writer, his books on Jewish spirituality have been published by Jewish Lights Publishing. His most recent book is *A Dream of Zion: American Jews Reflect on Why Israel Matters to Them* (Jewish Lights).

Jeremy Sandler grew up a committed Canadian Reform Jew in Toronto and lived in Kingston, Ontario, Ottawa, and Vancouver before returning home. A graduate of Queen's University, he attended Carleton University's School of Journalism and now works as a sports reporter with Canada's *National Post* newspaper. A travel enthusiast who loves being outside, his favorite activities are playing with his eight nieces and nephews and spending time with the light of his life, his wife, Barbara, a teacher in Toronto.

PHILLIP A. SAPERIA is executive director of the Coalition of Behavioral Health Agencies in New York City. His liberation from a career as a Jewish communal service professional has allowed him to focus and reflect upon personal Jewish and related matters—through his shul in Brooklyn and local politics. He lives happily with his life-partner of thirty-three years in Brooklyn and Stockton, New Jersey.

PAUL SCHOENFELD, PH.D., is a clinical psychologist who lives in Seattle and is the director of behavioral health at the Everett Clinic. He is a member of Temple Beth Am in Seattle. His wife, Diane, and his two young adult children, Maya and Naomi, help him remember the importance of love and relationships in his life.

DAVID SEGAL was born in Houston, Texas, in 1980. He attended Princeton University, where he concentrated in classics and Jewish studies. After graduation, he worked in Washington, D.C., at the Religious Action Center of Reform Judaism as a legislative assistant on issues such as civil rights, civil liberties, and criminal justice reform. In addition, he supported the Reform Movement's interfaith activities as an assistant to the Commission on Interreligious Affairs of Reform Judaism. He now attends the rabbinic studies program at Hebrew Union College–Jewish Institute of Religion in the class of 2010.

RABBI JOEL SOFFIN served for twenty-seven years as the rabbi of Temple Shalom in Succasunna, New Jersey, where he is now rabbi emeritus. In retirement, he is the Social Action Rabbinical Scholar-in-Residence at the Barnert Temple in Franklin Lakes, New Jersey. His worldwide social action projects continue through the URJ Adult Mitzvah Corps and the Jewish Helping Hands Foundation.

MATTHEW STERN is in the graduating class of 2008 at Brandeis University, studying in the Near Eastern and Judaic Studies and Music Departments. During high school, Stern was heavily involved in NFTY, and he has spent two summers working as a song leader at URJ Camp Harlam in Pennsylvania. He teaches religious school during the year, when he isn't busy musically directing a theater production at Brandeis or doing schoolwork. In the future, Stern hopes to become a conductor and, of course, to stay involved in the Jewish community.

RABBI STEPHEN WISE is the incoming rabbi of Shaarei-Beth El Congregation in Oakville, Ontario. Before joining SBE, Wise spent two years as the assistant rabbi at Temple Beth El in Boca Raton, Florida. He was ordained from the Hebrew Union College–Jewish Institute of Religion in May of 2005. Wise was born in Toronto, Ontario, and grew up at Holy Blossom Temple, spending his summers at the Young Judea–sponsored Camp Shalom. He majored in history at the University of Toronto and received a master's in Jewish communal service with a focus in Jewish education from the Hornstein Program at Brandeis University. Wise has focused much of his rabbinate in striving passionately to connect Jews of all ages to their Judaism. Recently he has planned and participated in youth group workshops at URJ camps and NFTY conventions geared toward teenage males to increase the amount of programming specifically for this demographic.

RABBI DANIEL G. ZEMEL is the rabbi of Temple Micah in Washington, D.C. He has served in this position since 1983. Zemel pursued his undergraduate education at Brown University and his rabbinic education at the Hebrew Union College–Jewish Institute of Religion in Jerusalem and New York. A native of Chicago, he received his earliest Jewish and secular education at the Anshe Emet Day School. He is married to Louise Sherman Zemel. They have three children, Shira Michal, Adam Solomon, and Ronit Elana. Finally, and for him most significant, Zemel is a passionate fan of the Chicago White Sox and has not been the same since they won the 2005 World Series.